Hawai'i - Stolen Paradise

Hawai'i – Stolen Paradise
A Travelogue

Stephanie C. Fox

QueenBeeBooks

Bloomfield, Connecticut, U.S.A.

Copyright April 2013 © by Stephanie Carole Fox

All rights reserved. Published in the United States by QueenBeeBooks, Connecticut.

Library of Congress Cataloging-in-Publication Data
Name: Fox, Stephanie C., author.
Title: Hawai'i – Stolen Paradise: A Travelogue / Stephanie C. Fox.
Description: Connecticut: QueenBeeBooks, [2013].
Identifiers: ISBN: 978-0-9996395-9-7 (paperback)
Subjects: 1. United States – State & Local – General—History. 2. Hospitality, Travel & Tourism – Industries—Business & Economics. 3. General—Travel.

www.queenbeeedit.com

Cover design by Stephanie C. Fox
Cover photographs by Stephanie C. Fox
Printed in the United States of America

This travelogue is dedicated to
the people of Hawai'i
and to my parents.

Also by Stephanie C. Fox

The Book of Thieves

The Bear Guarding the Beehive

Elephant's Kitchen
– An Aspergirl's Study in Difference

Almost a Meal
– A True Tale of Horror

An American Woman in Kuwait

Scheherazade Cat:
The Story of a War Hero

Nae-Née
Birth Control: Infallible, with
Nanites and Convenience for All

Vaccine: The Cull
Nae-Née Wasn't Enough

New World Order Underwater
The Nae-Née Inventors Strike Back

What the Small Gray Visitor Said

Intrigue On a Longship Cruise

Hawai'i – Stolen Paradise:
A Brief History

Table of Contents

Planning the Trip...and Studying For It 1
A Brief History of Hawai'i 8
The Flight Out 35
A Side Trip to San Francisco 40
A Flight and an Agricultural Declaration Form 62
Aloha and a Lei 66
The Ko Olina Beach Villas 70
The Ko Olina Resort 95
Daddy's Fantasy – Avoiding H-1's Heavy Traffic 122
Ala Moana Center and Na Hoku 124
Visiting the Dead at the USS *Arizona* Memorial 130
Exploring O'ahu by Car 159
An Electric Submarine Ride Off Waikiki 173
'Iolani Palace 195
The Royal Hawaiian Band 229
Washington Place – Lili'uokalani's Home 234
Foster Botanical Garden 238
A Hokey Lu'au 257
Princess Ka'iulani and Her Pet Peacock 270
Na Kahili and a Petition: 276
The Bernice Pauahi Bishop Museum 276
Honolulu International Airport 296
Aloha to Kona 302
A Ride Between 2 Volcanoes but Not Over Another 314
A Ride Back via Kohala 329
Downtown Kailua-Kona on Ali'i Drive 337
Kona Mountain Thunder Coffee Plantation 349
New Landscapes – Volcanoes National Park 361
A Lu'au at Historic Kamakahonu 398

Petroglyphs	427
Hawaii Tropical Botanical Garden	441
Huggo's on the Rocks…and Other Eateries	465
Hulihe'e Palace	475
Kona International Airport	484
The Return Trip…an Unwanted Adventure	488
Glossary of Hawaiian Words	497
Bibliography of San Francisco Research	500
Bibliography of Hawai'i Research	504
Acknowledgements	510
About the Author	511

Planning the Trip…and Studying For It

By the time I was finished reading the college course's worth of books that I had assigned myself, I knew that we would be visiting both the 50th state and a stolen nation.

It all started over a year and a half before we actually went on what became a trip first to San Francisco for a day and two nights, and then a week on O'ahu followed by five days on the Big Island of Hawai'i. After that, we intended to fly straight home.

My mother suddenly said, "We're not doing anything – let's go somewhere!"

My father and I looked up at her as we ate dinner.

My father is retired.

I write e-books which I hope will also become printed ones, and edit and tutor when I'm not doing that. I'll edit anything. That's the fun of it, and it exposes me to other fields than my own, which are women's studies, history/herstory, and law.

I do edits of my husband's scientific journal articles, and my work is acknowledged at the end of many of them. His name is David D. Haines, Ph.D. (he had to work, so he would not be coming with us on this trip). I also edit the political writings of Fatemeh Haghighatjoo, an expatriate Iranian politician.

But back to our big moment at the kitchen table.

"What do you have in mind?" I asked, wondering what was up.

"Let's travel!" My mother said.

Travel…okay, but what was she thinking of? A road trip? That's not that expensive.

"You decide," my mother continued. "Paris or Hawai'i, or somewhere else exciting like that," she summed up.

Oh. Expensive, I thought. "Hawai'i – definitely Hawai'i," I said. "Paris means a lot of walking, and we've all been there," I added. Plus, I doubted that my father could walk fast enough to make the experience worthwhile, and Paris is a walking city where having a car would be a nuisance, paying for cabs would cost my mother way too much, and jumping in and out of buses and the Métro would not work out well.

My mother seemed really into it, though. She said, "Great! Plan it, Stephanie."

It turned out that her motivation was partly health issues – hers and my father's. What was the point of waiting to enjoy life until it was too late for the endeavor to be enjoyable? That was logical.

Dazed, I delved into the process that night, up in my room at the computer, researching Hawai'i on the Internet. How hard could this be? A travel agent would be involved at some point, my mother had added.

I thought about what I already knew about Hawai'i:

1. There are 8 islands.
2. It was either the 49th or 50th state – probably the 50th.
3. It had hurricanes for part of the year, so I needed to know when and plan to go during the other part.
4. It was the southernmost of the United States.
5. It was a tropical paradise with its own, unique culture and history.
6. The attack on U.S. Navy ships at Pearl Harbor on December 7, 1941 had precipitated our entry into World War II.
7. That same attack had led to an embarrassing prejudice against American citizens of Japanese descent, which in turn had led to our government dispossessing them of their property and livelihoods for the duration of that war and imprisoning them in ramshackle camps in the deserts of the western United States (mainland). Some had died from the harsh conditions there, homesick and unhappy, without amenities like heat, hot water, and electricity that made for a happy and healthier quality of life elsewhere.
8. Poi was from Hawai'i, and it was made of a plant called taro, which was ground to a paste.

9. People from Hawaiʻi said "Aloha" whenever they meant "Hello" or Good-bye" – and they gave each newcomer a beautiful lei to wear, made out of flowers that grew on the Islands.
10. The United States had stolen the place from the native population.

For now, that would have to suffice as I made the most basic of decisions: what time of year to go, which islands to visit, how many, and how long the entire trip ought to be.

Another important consideration that came immediately to mind was the fact that our starting point would be Connecticut. That meant that if we went directly and nonstop to Hawaiʻi, we would be too exhausted when we got off the plane in Honolulu to really enjoy that magical moment when someone put a lei over our heads and said "Aloha!" to us.

Accordingly, I should think it all through so as to achieve maximum enjoyment.

The first thing I did was to look up Hawaiʻi's climate on the website for NOAA – the National Oceanic and Atmospheric Administration. I wanted to start with the hurricane question. Here is the website: http://www.prh.noaa.gov/hnl/cphc/ It revealed that they tend to hit in August or September, so those months were out.

But there was more: the rainy season starts in November, and it is over a hundred degrees Fahrenheit in the spring and summer. October looked like the best time to visit. I didn't want to spend the trip dealing with heat exhaustion, but not going during the sunny season just seemed like a waste of money. We ought to visit the place when the weather is nice, I reasoned.

Okay, what would be a good length of time to spend there? My mother said two weeks.

That meant two islands, then. Which two islands?

Definitely Oʻahu – how else would we see the USS *Arizona* Memorial, and many other cool things that were on that island? That one was not to be missed.

And one more island. I looked them up on Wikipedia, well aware that it should not be used as a source in a published academic paper. All I wanted was enough of an overview to make an intelligent decision that would point me in the direction of more research. Here is what I learned:

Oʻahu – The Gathering Place: it has the capital city, lots of great beaches, and the royal family was based there when Hawaiʻi was still under their jurisdiction. That meant that Oʻahu would have their residences and other historic sites of interest to me. I love history.

Mauʻi – The Valley Isle: it is two sections, with a small northwest one connected by a valley to larger southeast one. What do people do on this one? They hike and enjoy the beach, for the most part.

Kauaʻi – The Garden Isle: it is round, also mostly about nature and beaches, and many Hollywood movies were made there in the mid-twentieth century.

Molokaʻi – The Friendly Isle: an ironic name, considering that the quarantine leper colony was on it, but there it is. Father Damian lived on that island, helping the lepers, until he foolishly stuck his finger in a common dish of poi and contracted the dreaded disease himself. It's another beach and hiking island.

Lanaʻi – The Pineapple Island: it has pineapple plantations, and 5-star golfing resort hotels.

Kahoʻolawe – The Target Island: the U.S. Navy used it for target practice, made a terrible mess of it, and no one lives there.

Niʻihau – The Forbidden Isle: a native population of Hawaiians live on it, it is privately owned by a family named Robinson, and visits are by invitation only, and only after a health inspection. The point of that is to ensure that the residents, whose immune systems are not primed against the Earth's pathogens due to their insulated existence, do not catch some lethal plaque from a visitor. The visitor could be immune to that pathogen, but a carrier. Also, the one Japanese pilot from the 2 waves that attacked Pearl Harbor to crash on the islands crashed on this one, and terrorized the residents for a couple of days until one of them killed him.

Hawai‘i – The Big Island: the nation/state gets its name from this island...obviously...and it has active volcanoes on it.

The web page also contained the information that the Islands had been formed by two things working together: a tectonic plate that is continually (even now) moving northwestward while a plume of lava pushes up through the Earth's crust. That plume stays more or less constant, while the land masses move diagonally away from it. This process takes eons – millions upon millions of years. Then there is land recession, which means that some land falls back into the ocean under sea level.

Added to that data was the information that each island has its windward and leeward side, with the result that the weather on the leeward side tended to be lovely, warm, sunny, and minimally rainy. The windward side of an island tends, not surprisingly, to be cloudy, overcast, rainy, and otherwise disappointing to tourists. I looked it up on Google, and found a website with more detail on the subject: http://www.bestplaceshawaii.com/tips/hints/windward_leeward.html

The case file was coming along nicely.

What about that second island? Why? Easy: my parents weren't going hiking. We wouldn't just lie around on a beach, and none of us surf. We aren't an athletic family. I am unhappy if I am not learning something new regularly. That ruled out Mau‘i, Kaua‘i, and Moloka‘i. Lana‘i looked unaffordable, and not sufficiently enticing. Kaho‘olawe and Ni‘ihau were off limits.

That left the Big Island of Hawai‘i, which had extinct and active volcanoes, tropical gardens (all of the islands had those, and six of one is half a dozen of another when you don't have forever and unlimited funds to see absolutely all of them), and a striking landscape.

I went to Barnes & Noble and found a National Geographic book and a Frommer's guide on Hawai‘i, and brought them home to show my father. We flipped through them, showed them to my mother, and waited to see what she would announce next.

My father was the one variable I couldn't plan for.

I Don't Wanna Go Do Fill-in-the-Blank

My father was cranky and cantankerous as I delved into the planning process.

He put it down to arthritis. I put it down to his personality in general. He would look serious, sound serious, and act as though nothing could make him happy. It drove me crazy and still does.

I began to figure out the trip, and chatted at dinner about my findings.

But my father didn't want to think about it just yet.

My mother said that he had to think about it at least enough to book things.

With reluctance, he listened to a few of my ideas: a submarine ride, a helicopter ride, museums, gardens, a lu‘au on each island, restaurants, and so on. He expressed enthusiasm for a couple of things, and then we moved on to discussing other things – not the trip.

That is, we moved on until we were all out in the car and my mother encouraged me to chat about the plans some more. As my father sped down the highway, he was a silent, captive audience.

A pattern emerged, and repeated with at least three ideas: the USS *Arizona* Memorial, ‘Iolani Palace, and the observatory atop Mauna Kea. These were things that I could not forgive myself for not doing if I went to Hawai‘i, I had decided after checking into them all.

Here is how it played out: I would bring up the idea and say what it was, why it was special, and add that I really wanted to include that in the trip. My father would wonder why it was of interest, so I would go over all of the details. My mother would enthusiastically agree that we would definitely do that.

And then, after a few days – or even after just a few hours – my father would do an about-face on that idea and say, "Forget the *Arizona* Memorial/'Iolani Palace/Mauna Kea's observatory."

To which I would respond with outrage, saying why were we even going if not to do anything…and my mother would roll her eyes at my father and say that we would go without him and just leave him at the hotel.

Well! My father has always insisted upon hanging around with us, chauffeuring us to everything and silently participating, even if it is as dull and mundane as going to a shopping mall. Granted, I don't like to shop much, so he goes with just my mother most of the time, but the effect is the same – if we're doing something, he wants to be in on it.

Whenever my mother suggested leaving him behind, it worked like a magic spell. My father would instantly say that we would all do everything together.

The third or fourth time that he pulled this, I waited until I was standing at the kitchen sink filling up the tea kettle. My father stood over by the desk in the kitchen, leaning against it as he took out his evening pills.

Then I turned around and said, "You should hear yourself." He looked at me. I affected a gruff voice, mimicking his – and why not?! – he can be a terrible tease when he gets going: "I don't wanna go see the USS *Arizona* Memorial. I don't wanna go to 'Iolani Palace. I don't wanna look at the stars and nebulae atop Mauna Kea. I don't wanna go do fill-in-the-blank."

He stood there listening, and suddenly starting shaking with silent laughter.

Got him! He didn't do it again.

When I told his sister, my Aunt Joan Fox, about that, and asked her if this was typical, she said, "I don't know. I've never planned a trip with him." She was amused, though.

It just seemed extremely and inexcusably rude to go all the way to Honolulu and not visit the sailors who were buried aboard the USS *Arizona*. In any case, I Don't Wanna was coming with us to do these things.

The Plan and Study Resumes

I had a Nook e-reader, and I loaded it with 10 history books. I started with the autobiography of Queen Lili'uokalani, Hawai'i's last reigning monarch before the theft of the nation. I had wanted to read that for years, but now I had a reason to do so. Legislative session reports were free (most people could care less about those, but I wanted to flip through them rapidly just to see what lawmakers had talked about in the nineteenth century and early twentieth there). I topped the small collection off with some fiction by Jack London and Robert Louis Stevenson, a language guide, and a brief travelogue by a retired man from Australia.

Next, I went online to Amazon and Barnes & Noble to get printed books because some of the things I wanted weren't digitized: Mark Twain's articles from his 1860s trip to the Islands, and a book about Shigenori Nishikaichi's reign of terror on Ni'ihau.

It was a good start. I figured that when I saw a book that could only be found on the Islands, I would have to either buy it on the trip and read it later.

With that, I read more, and more, and more. I spent roughly four months before we left reading and reading about Hawai'i. I realize that most people don't do this. They are content to laze around in the sunshine there, surf, hike, snorkel, and check out the nightlife in Waikiki or wherever they are staying.

Not us – the first thing my father said was that he didn't want to stay at Waikiki.

Good. Neither did I. Too crowded, too much noise, too much ambient light.

My mother discovered that there was a great travel agent at AAA in Avon who knew exactly how to handle the planning. I printed up the research that I had compiled thus far – it was short file, only 15 pages of widely spaced copy-pastes from the Internet interspersed with my notes on what we hoped to see and do in Hawai'i.

The travel agent proved to be a lovely and very experienced woman, and she had spent some time on O'ahu. I explained that we didn't want to stay at Waikiki Beach, and why. She knew just where to send us for our hotel stay. She said it was called Ko Olina. Okay – she must know what was good and what was not.

We thanked her and left, trusting the logistics to her.

Planning in Earnest

Our itinerary was set by midsummer in 2012. We were going in October, and we would be gone for two weeks and two days. My uncle would come over to feed our cat, the Phantom Menace. We hoped he wouldn't be too upset. Cats hate the slightest change in their lives.

My father showed little indication of looking forward to the trip, despite my efforts to elicit a response from him. His right hip was worse. He told us to be patient with him. We said we would, and I kept reassuring him that the plan had been made with that in mind.

He could swim in the hotel pools, sit in the hot tub, and drive the rental car all over each island, exploring them with us. He loves to drive and tour around. He just doesn't want to stop.

My mother had suggested hopping on and off of buses and not renting a car at all when this started, until we met the AAA travel agent. I was skeptical from the start, and looked forward to discussing it with the agent, as there seemed to be no such thing as public transportation on the Big Island, and none that went from anywhere on O'ahu except for inside the city of Honolulu.

Sure enough, rental cars would be required if we expected to do anything.

We would leave on Saturday, October 13, 2012, by plane, and travel by way of Chicago O'Hare Airport to San Francisco International Airport. From there, we would stay in a hotel close to the airport, the Hampton Inns, for two nights. That would give us all of the 14th to see the city and eat a couple of nice meals there.

On Monday, the 15th, we would fly to O'ahu and arrive at Honolulu International Airport in the evening, not too tired to enjoy it when we each got a lei and smelled the tropical air. We would pick up a rental car and drive across the southern part of the island to the Ko Olina Beach Villas, which was where we would be staying for the next week.

We would be going on an underwater tour off Waikiki in a submarine.

My father had responded with enthusiasm when I suggested it, so that was settled.

We would also go to a lu'au on O'ahu at a place called Paradise Cove.

On Monday the 22nd, we would fly to Kona International Airport on the Big Island, get another rental car, and drive to our hotel, where would stay for five days and nights. For both flights to the Islands, we would leave in the afternoon and arrive in time for dinner.

A helicopter ride over the world's only continuously active volcano, Kilauea, was scheduled for the day after our arrival on the Big Island.

On the way back, we would go up the access road to the visitor center on Mauna Kea to look up at whatever we could see through the telescope(s): planets, stars, nebulae, pulsars, you name it. I thought it would be the coolest thing to end the day with, and when would we ever get to do anything like that again?

The W.M. Keck Observatory, even farther up atop Mauna Kea, is off limits to the public; it's for the Ph.D. astronomers. But this would be the next best thing, open until 10 o'clock each night. It was as close as I was going to get to experiencing what I had seen the character Rajesh Koothrappali doing on *The Big Bang Theory*. To think that we could see some of what the professionals enjoy seeing was fun just to think about!

Another luʻau was also on the agenda, this one by the Island Breeze Productions company, which I had researched in some detail. I was hoping for a history and culture lesson in it, and it promised to fit the bill.

My mother reminded us that even the best-laid plans could go wrong, and not to get upset if they did. My father and I looked at her, saying nothing much. Who knew what could happen on this adventure? As long as our luggage wasn't lost and we didn't crash, as long as we didn't get robbed at any time, how badly could things go wrong?

Well, travel is an adventure.

Going home looked like an exercise in exhaustion, though, and my mother wisely took the day after our scheduled arrival at home off. We were to check out of our hotel on the Big Island on Saturday, the 27th, and take a flight to San Francisco in the evening. The next morning, we would spend five hours in the airport and go on to Chicago, then go on to Bradley International Airport in Windsor Locks, Connecticut, arriving at almost 10 o'clock at night.

I kept working, and prepared an e-book just for the three of us. It had the information on every museum and garden that we hoped to see, plus confirmation codes for every booked hotel, rental car, flight, activity, and dinner reservation. I also printed three copies, one for each of us.

The e-book was a skeleton of what I intended to expand into this travelogue. It had a bibliography at the end, a cover that showed travel guides, and copy-pastes throughout of various business logo. My mother was impressed; she took her copy out in the car on a ride through New England with my father and flipped through it, narrating an overview to him as they drove.

This is the cover that I made for our personalized travel guide. It's still on my Nook reader.

I sent it via Skype to my husband, who was happy for me that I was going on this trip. David is an immunologist and veteran of the Gulf War. I wanted the option of talking to him, too, so I sent this to him, complete with the hotel phone numbers. Receiving calls on a cell phone from Skype is expensive, and not included in the monthly minutes.

Just before we left on the trip, I bought a book on San Francisco with thick, fold-out maps of the city and details on points of interest. I had not made much of an effort to research it compared with my in-depth study of Hawaiʻi.

The travel agent supplied us with a fold-out map of Hawaiʻi. My mother bought small bags that would fit in the overhead storage bins of the airplanes. She even came home with AAA luggage tags, which I filled out and attached to the bags.

For months, my mother had insisted that we would check no bags. That had me worried; TSA agents would take away my tweezers, my contact lens solution, my cosmetics, my you-name-it in the name of airport security. There was that and the fact that people shop when they travel. How could we expect to bring the stuff home without a checked bag?! There were so many rules and weight limits that I was quite nervous about it all.

At last, my mother realized that it would never work. We would take small checked bags. What a relief; some items had to be checked, and this would make it possible to bring stuff home. Also, with small checked bags, we ran no danger of exceeding the per-bag weight limit.

She had gone online and printed up the TSA rules for carry-on luggage and checked bags: Put all toiletries in clear, plastic bags to save the agents time. Have all liquids in 3.4-ounce or less containers. No scissors in the carry-ons.

I would not be bringing my laptop on this trip. I didn't want to carry it – it's heavy! And I didn't want to have to worry about losing it in a hotel or anywhere else. And…I didn't want to do work. This was supposed to be a vacation.

I would, however, be bringing my Nook Color e-reader. To prepare as well as possible, I used it to look up each and every website that we might need to check during the trip, and then saved them all to Favorites on it: United Airlines, the hotels, the rental car company, and so on.

That left only the cat to feel sorry for. He would be very lonely; we're roommates.

A Brief History of Hawai'i

I don't write travelogues merely to revive pleasant memories.

I write them to share what I learn, and I love to learn things.

Not only that, but I care about the point of view that I take. In college, I minored in women's studies, so taking the position that Hawai'i was stolen from the Hawaiian people rather than belonging to a judgmental, invading, white malestreamed population comes naturally to me. Doing otherwise feels wrong and selfish.

The United States is a stolen nation. Granted, we aren't going to move. Things have gone on too long and too far for that. But we should acknowledge the truth in our histories.

As this history will explain, Hawai'i was stolen without the slightest excuse. The Puritans could at least claim religious persecution when they left for North America and landed at what came to be known as Plymouth, Massachusetts. Not so for the missionaries who came to Hawai'i to convert the people who lived there, and their sons who built economic empires for themselves.

The Visits of Captain Cook

My research on Hawai'i began with the intriguing discovery that it was on the Big Island that Captain James Cook had died of what turned out to be stupidity. That was my assessment, concluded after a quick study of the tale.

Captain Cook had gone more than once to the Islands in the late eighteenth century.

He was mapping and exploring the islands of the Pacific, and had stopped in Mau'i as he headed south. His benefactor was the Earl of Sandwich, so he named the place the Sandwich Islands, even though the people living there had already named it.

Eight weeks later, after visiting Samoa, Tahiti, and various other places, he came to the Big Island of Hawai'i. As he traveled, he kept giving all of these places new names in English, regardless of the fact that the people who were already living there had already chosen their own names for their own native islands.

Now he was back, but on another one of the Islands – the Big Island of Hawai'i. He arrived in Kealakekua Bay in late 1778. When his ship, the *H.M.S. Resolution*, was sighted by the residents, they thought that it carried the god Lono because its sails resembled Lono's standards. Lono was the god of fertility and agriculture, so he was important. As a result, when Captain Cook disembarked and went ashore, he was greeted as a god.

At first, his forays into the culture had gone well for him, and for his crew. He was treated like a god due his status as the leader of his group and to the fact that his skin tone differed from that of the native population. The women entertained (had sex with) his crewmembers. This intrigued the English; the native women were obviously not prostitutes, but their culture did not inhibit them from rowing out to the ship, boarding it with lei for the crew, and then spending the night. Added to all this was the fact that it was still the growing and hunting and fishing season during Cook's first visit.

But when he and his crew shoved off into the Pacific Ocean in early 1779, one of the masts of their ship broke, forcing them to turn back. When they arrived, it was during the four-month period of rest when the Hawaiians traditionally played games and lived off the supplies they had amassed during the rest of the year. And since it was a small island society, resources were finite.

Cook and his crew were greeted with a somewhat cooler reception this time.

A visiting foreign ship, regardless of whether or not it harbored a god, was full of people who would use up a large amount of resources. The annoyed Hawaiians decided that as long as Cook's crew was there to chop down a huge koa tree and make a new mast out of it, they might as well take a canoe ride, and shoved off in one from the *Resolution*.

Cook was worried – would he get it back? How would he and his crew manage without that canoe? That was when he made a colossally and lethally stupid decision: he grabbed a hostage, and chose the chief, Kalaniʻopuʻu.

Well, what happens whenever one physically threatens the leader of any society?

That leader is typically surrounded by a group of individuals whose duty it is to handle his or her personal security. It's just not wise to bother that individual.

One of the security force, an aliʻi – that's Hawaiʻi's chiefly caste, the one with warriors and governors – stabbed Cook.

He bled.

Wow….blood! That meant that he wasn't a god – he was just a different human, which made sense, since he wasn't from Hawaiʻi! They stabbed him some more, and he fell face down in the shallow waters off the coast of southwestern Hawaiʻi, at Kealakekua Bay. He drowned quickly.

Cook's men didn't just stand around gaping as this happened; four of them rushed to his aid and got killed, and two more were wounded.

The Hawaiians, once it was over, felt bad about the whole thing. Cook had been a pleasant enough guest on the previous visit, and this was clearly just a terrible misunderstanding. They took his body and gave it a decent funeral…according to their own culture, which was all that they knew. They reduced his corpse to its bones, and interred them high in the mountains.

Cook's remaining crew was allowed to finish fixing the mast (reasonable – how else did the Hawaiians expect them to be able to leave?), and then they found out about the funeral.

With difficulty, they managed to communicate that they had to bring what remained of Cook home to his wife, er, widow, Elizabeth, and could they please have it all back?

The Hawaiians wrapped it all up and gave it back.

What a mess.

Captain Cook had not been the first visitor from Europe to come to the Islands. A Spanish ship had been there two and a half centuries earlier, and at least two sailors had elected to stay permanently. There isn't much documentation about that, in part because Hawaiians kept track of their history through memory and oral recounting rather than writing it down.

At the time of Cook's "visit", there were roughly 300,000 Hawaiians living on the Islands.

The Ancient Polynesians Arrive

The first people to live on the Islands arrived, according to most recent estimates, around 300 C.E. They rowed themselves there from the southwest, originating from the area of Tahiti, Samoa, Aotearoa (that's what the Maori people call New Zealand), and other nearby islands. They did so in long pairs of connected canoes with a covered area in the middle, and with a large sail over that. The travelers knew astronomy to guide them.

They carved petroglyphs in rocks, and created songs that were unique to each individual so honored. The fact that oral rather than written history was the normal way of remembering the past was not a mark of anything other than the Hawaiian people's difference from the Europeans. They used what they had, not because they were primitive but because they had nothing else and because they understood that it was finite and so could not be wasted.

The travelers had brought pigs and chickens with them, and skills. They knew how to grow crops, how to fish, and how to make canoes, which they called *na waʻa*. (In Hawaiian, the word *na* is used to make a noun plural, while the noun is left as is. The word *waʻa* means canoe.)

The Hawaiians made clothing out of tree bark by pounding it into soft cloth with a *kapa*, making short loincloths for men called *na malo* and long sarongs for women called *na pa'u*. The aristocrats were advised by *na kahuna* of various kinds. There were priests, political advisors, and others. A kahuna is an expert of whatever field that the kahuna has studied in depth.

The Hawaiian Culture

For over a millennium, the Hawaiian people lived on the eight islands, developing their own dialect of the Polynesian language, which became their own branch of it after that much time in isolation. Their religious beliefs went on undisturbed and, not surprisingly, the volcano goddess Pele figured prominently in their thoughts.

There were wars, there was peace, and the chiefs became known as ali'i, which meant the ruling class. They tended to be very, very tall people who spent their childhoods developing their athletic skills and learning how to govern the common people with the advice of the kahunas around them. The high chief was called the ali'i nui.

The closer that a member of the ali'i could prove her or his lineage to the ancient gods and goddesses, the more mana, or spiritual power, she or he had. This was all oral history, so the people's memories were very strong, well-versed, and devoted to rote memorization for accuracy. Nothing was written down, and there was a lot to remember: history, lineage, lore, songs, skills, crafts, social mores, and so on and on.

The people spent their time fishing, growing crops, making canoes, building a one-room hale for each family out of koa wood and long strands of dried leaves, beating tree bark into cloth and dying it or drawing patterns on it. The ali'i, the chiefly caste of aristocrats, took part of what the people produced as taxes, and traveled around with the king and his household touring each island to check on the welfare of the people.

Both common people and rulers enjoyed a variety of entertainments in their spare time. These entertainments included games, sports, hula dance, singing, song creation (done from memory, not by writing), and chants.

For four months of each year, the people rested, living on their efforts of the other months. It was a kapu time, both sacred and taboo to interfere with. An ancient kapu system was in place during Kamehameha I's time, and he would not think of relaxing or abolishing it. One of the customs associated with it was that common people would drop close to the ground if the king or a member of the ali'i passed, so as not to let their shadow fall on that individual.

A good chief would visit the common people at their croplands and fishing villages without staying in their homes, camping nearby with the ali'i who traveled with him. A bad chief would stay in some random hale, turning out the farmer or fisher, and not reining in his ali'i companions, instead leaving them to sleep with the women of the family at night. A bad chief could get himself killed and replaced by operating that way.

Wars were fought from time to time over territory, until Kamehameha the Great finally united all eight of the Islands under his rule in the late eighteenth century. After that, there was peace among the Hawaiians, and just in time, as a new threat had discovered the existence of the tropical paradise: haoles, or foreigners.

The Kamehameha Dynasty

Kamehameha I became known as Kamehameha the Great. He had spent most of his reign in battle, fighting for control of island after island until he had united them under his rule. After that, peace ensued among the Hawaiian people, who had a friendly culture in such conditions.

Kamehameha was seven feet tall, and Ka'ahumanu was not his only wife. She herself was six feet seven inches tall. An ali'i is typically a towering, tall individual, someone who is charged with the people's safety and security. In a non-industrialized, natural society, the biggest, strongest, tallest individuals are the most imposing, intimidating, and capable of defending the people. No one would consider messing with or fail to respect someone like that.

Kamehameha the Great, as the first of five kings to bear that name, was responsible for uniting the eight islands, so he became Hawai'i's first reigning monarch in the late eighteenth century, when he was a young man. He lived to be sixtysomething...the exact year of his birth is not known.

He was born circa 1750, though other estimates have suggested 1735. Before he could conquer them all, a prophesy warned him, Kamehameha would have to build a massive temple – called a heiau – to his war god. He had this done in 1790. It worked. By 1795, he had conquered all of the Islands but Kaua'i. The chief of that island surrendered to him rather than have his people suffer a battle such as those on O'ahu had suffered, being pushed over the cliffs to their deaths. Ni'ihau, the westernmost islands, was part of that deal.

Conquering and uniting the islands had been a common goal among the warring ali'i chiefs, but Kamehameha I accomplished it in part because of the presence of European ships. Another reason was the stupidity of one of the ships' commanders: British captain Simon Metcalf visited Kona, invited a lesser ali'i aboard his ship, and then humiliated him – by yelling at him and having his bosun beat him – for some incomprehensible (to the guest) breach of the ship's rules.

Kamehameha swore revenge when he found out about it, and as luck would have it, the next ship to appear was commanded by Metcalf's son Thomas. It was the *Fair American*, and soon it was under new ownership. Payback was swift; the Hawaiian warriors boarded it as if to trade, then tossed the haoles overboard and beat them in the water until they drowned. One haole escaped, Isaac Davis. He was allowed to live, but had to adapt to life in a strange, new culture. When Simon came back, looking for his son's ship, a search party came ashore. One man, John Young, got separated from the group, and Kamehameha kept him.

Now Kamehameha had two haoles. They could not go home. The Hawaiian king was clever; he had no intention of killing either one of them, nor of making their lives miserable. He intended to learn all that he could about the haoles, since it was obvious that, likely sooner rather than later, so many more of them would arrive that an attack would not get rid of them. The king found both Young and Davis ali'i wives, and made them his advisors. They joined the kahunas of the court, and showed Kamehameha how to use the weapons aboard the captured ship.

Once he had united the Islands, Kamehameha did what became a tradition with the ali'i nui: he made a home base for himself, but left frequently to make the rounds of each island, visiting the people there, checking in with the ali'i who was governor of it, and then returning home. He had his own transportation for that, a royal wa'a (canoe).

Ka'ahumanu was a strong-willed and intelligent woman. She was also her husband's favorite wife. He had another whom he had married earlier, and who was queen alongside her but that other wife was chosen merely because her lineage was "purer" than Ka'ahumanu's. There were also other wives. But it was Ka'ahumanu who Kamehameha loved. He was very jealous and possessive of her, and he demanded that she not take any other husbands.

When I read that, I was fascinated. So Hawaiians had practiced not only polygamy, but polyandry also! Of course, that ceased when the Christians taught them about Calvinism, and insisted that their religion was better than that of the Hawaiians. Still, equal time...

The common people and the ali'i each wore similar clothing – a short malo wrapped around the waists of each kane (man) and a long pa'u wrapped around the waist of each wahine (woman) – but the ali'i had some additional accoutrements that set them apart.

An ali'i woman (or man) would wear a necklace called a lei niho palaoa made of braided human hair with a carved ivory or whale tooth dangling in front. A woman would also have a feather lei around her hair, and another one, called a lei hulu manu, around her neck. She also wore tortoise shell and/or bone bracelets. An ali'i man would wear a fitted mahiole (helmet) and cape or long cloak made of fine netting crafted from olona wood with human hair used to fasten feathers to the mesh.

In this painting by Herb Kane (in the lobby of the Courtyard Marriott King Kamehameha's Kona Beach Hotel), an aging Kamehameha is on the right, greeting a visitor, while his favorite wife, Ka'ahumanu sits at the left.

The feathers came from birds with red and yellow plumage: the 'i'iwi bird was the source of the red feathers, which grow all over its body, so the Hawaiians would eat it. The yellow feathers came from the mamo and 'o'o birds. The 'o'o bird's feathers were mostly black, with yellow ones only near the wings and on its tail. The Hawaiians would catch them, pluck the feathers, and release them. Unfortunately, the 'o'o bird went extinct anyway…after the haoles arrived.

The yellow feathers showed higher rank than the red. The ali'i nui – high chief or king – could wear all yellow, while the governor chiefs had capes and helmets with lots of red feathers. The best way to explain the value of these feathers as work materials and the capes as completed products is to express it in terms of money.

In the mid-nineteenth century, the long, all-yellow, feather cloak that Kamehameha the Great wore was valued at approximately a million dollars. Haoles had their gold and gemstones, and Hawaiians had their feathers. Each one was impressive, special, and of great value.

Beautiful feather kahili were made for each member of the royal family, in pairs. These were tall poles with cylindrical arrangements of feathers at the top. Ancient kahili included the bones of vanquished enemies. The kahili pair was carried by attendants throughout the life of the ali'i wherever she or he went, and when the ali'i sat down to eat or rest, they would be waved above, for fanning and cooling.

Kamakahonu – Kauhale of Kamehameha the Great

A kauhale is a compound of household buildings for the ali'i nui, including a men's eating house, a women's eating house, a house to sleep in, a cooking shed, another shed for a canoe, and whatever else a family of aristocrats might want or need. A hale is just one building, and the ali'i nui is the high chief/king. When that living arrangement was standard for Hawaiian leaders, this was what Kamehameha the Great had.

He chose to make his home base on the Big Island of Hawai'i, at Kailua Beach in Kona, on the leeward side of the island. He was born at Kohala, north of Kona, but he chose this spot after conquering several islands and uniting the remaining ones under his rule via diplomacy. Like many other kauhale compounds, this one had a fishing pool for the chief's exclusive use, with shrimp in it. Kamehameha called his home Kamakahonu, and kept the kapu system in place, convinced that prophesies about his success in uniting the islands were connected to that system.

In the late 20th century, a group of Hawaiian historic preservationists decided to reconstruct and forever maintain a part of Kamakahonu. They did a beautiful job of it – at least, to a haole like myself, it looked amazing. They didn't recreate the entire kauhale; only one hale, with ki'i placed all around it. A ki'i is a tall, thin, wooden, carved image of a Hawaiian deity. In pre-haole times, groups of these images were placed all around the ali'i nui's kauhale and at any heiau. There is a native species of wood that grows on the Hawaiian Islands called koa, and this was used for the ki'i carvings.

After the missionaries established themselves and their beliefs on the Islands, they demanded that each heiau be broken down, and all ki'i images destroyed. Fortunately for history, posterity, archaeology, and the preservation of the Hawaiian cultural identity, some Hawaiian people did not comply with this demand. Instead, they hid many ki'i images. When Kamakahonu was being recreated, many of them were brought out and placed around it.

Clearly, the Hawaiians were adept at hiding things so well that they could not be found.

When Kamehameha the Great died, long wooden spears were crossed in front of his doorway. His son left until the kapu was lifted by the kahuna priests.

Kapu means taboo. A taboo is put on anything that is deemed sacred, but that is not all that there is to it. Sometimes a thing is simply considered a bad act, and thus is deemed kapu. Under the kapu system, Hawaiian women did not have any control of the common food supply. They were forbidden to eat fish, pork, coconut, or bananas. They also had to eat separately from men.

A typical funeral for an ali'i lasted for weeks, and the songs that had been composed at his or her birth would be sung. The kahili set would be held or placed around the body. The common people would wail, keen, and mourn with tremendous energy. Some would even smash out their own front teeth in their grief. This practice was discouraged by the missionaries.

To this day, no one – well, no haole – knows where Kamehameha the Great was buried.

I did say that the Hawaiian people were adept at hiding things.

The Missionaries Arrive

Things changed when the missionaries from New England arrived in the early nineteenth century. They were Calvinists who believed that work brought one closer to heaven, and that sex, music, dance, and enjoyment were sins. This was the exact opposite of what the Hawaiians believed.

Nevertheless, the Hawaiians did not get angry and tell them to pack up and go.

Why not?

The best answer I can glean from all that reading is that the king, Kamehameha II, and his kuhina nui (regent), Queen Ka'ahumanu, realized that the Calvinists came from a technologically developed society, and that there were many, many more of them who would follow. It was clear to these aliʻi that the only way they could hope to cope with that and thus protect their people would be to learn all about them and adapt to as many of their ways as they found feasible.

Having had the advantage of interacting with John Young and Isaac Davies, and thus learning about the technological capabilities of the haoles, Kamehameha II and Kaʻahumanu felt forced into accepting the Calvinists. They arrived shortly after Kamehameha I had died and Kaʻahumanu was installed as regent, but he had anticipated this. After all, that was why Kamehameha the Great had captured and assimilated John Young and Isaac Davis. This foresight proves that people from less technologically advanced civilizations are as intelligent as those who have developed technology.

A recurring theme was about to play out, as it had in the past. Whenever Europeans traveled, they would force religious and cultural conversions on whatever society they met, insisting that their ways were the best…until people around the planet began to speak up and tell them otherwise. That ethnocentric and xenophobic attitude persisted until much damage was done to many cultures, and because of it, Hawaiians have lost the practice of speaking their own language to such an extent that few of them now know how to do it.

It seems that the desirable "gifts" to the Hawaiians from foreigners have been few: written literacy, convenient cotton for clothing, and the right of women to eat any food they wish. Kaʻahumanu put a stop to the ancient kapu system as a widow when, along with Queen Keopuolani, she broke the eating kapu.

Keopuolani was even happier to do this than Kaʻahumanu was, because her manu was so high that she had been living in near isolation. This was because, under the kapu system, if a commoner so much as saw her, he or she would most likely be put to death. Kamehameha himself was always careful never to let his shadow fall on her. Keopuolani was happy to stop living under such terms. Also, after long and careful consideration, Kaʻahumanu chose to convert to Christianity.

The unwanted gifts to the Hawaiian people have been many and damaging: leprosy, syphilis, gonorrhea, loss of their language, their livelihoods, near-loss of their beloved hula dance, the introduction of many non-native species (including the mongoose and rats that have caused more problems than anything else), and finally, the loss of their nation's sovereignty.

This was accomplished by a slow and hostile takeover, first of their culture by the missionaries, and next by economics, perpetrated by both the missionaries' sons as they grew up to be big businessmen, as well as by some other haole arrivals. Finally, those same men, in their late middle age, along with their sons, dissatisfied by the concessions granted to them by the royal family, resorted to force.

The missionaries disapproved of hula dancing, and did their utmost to persuade the Hawaiians that it was shameful to dance, male or female, while wearing only grass skirts and shaking one's body to show it off. They disapproved of dancing and singing most evenings and on into the night rather than spending that time in quiet prayer and study. The list went on, and the missionaries devoted themselves to finding willing converts to their way of thinking.

That was not an easy task, self-appointed though it was.

Imagine how the Hawaiians must have felt as total strangers, men and women, showed up on their shores wearing many more layers of cloth than could be practical or comfortable in a tropical climate, then started crying and turning their heads away as they looked at the people who lived there! The Hawaiians must have sensed that resistance would ultimately be futile, yet felt insulted, invaded, and imposed upon. I would have.

Among their converts was David Malo, a Hawaiian who learned to read and write in Hawaiian. He wrote a book entitled *Hawaiian Antiquities*. It describes Hawaiian life and culture as it was before the missionaries arrived, detailing fishing and farming practices, including sophisticated methods of aquaculture, the making of clothing out of tree bark, games and other amusements, and the interaction of the common people with the aliʻi.

Oddly, there was one Hawaiian custom that the missionaries did not devote huge amounts of energy to changing: hanai. Hanai is adoption. It could be done for orphans or non-orphans; there were more reasons for it than just to make sure that every child had a home with parents. A significant reason for hanai was to share children with childless couples who were upset about not having their own children. Another was to forge emotional alliances by sending one's children to live with another aliʻi couple. The purpose behind that was to prevent wars from ever starting. If the hanai children grew up with two sets of parents, they would grow up to love both, and to want peace with both.

Kamehameha II

Liholiho took over when his father died, having grown up in a time of peace, never having known military conflict. He was the eldest child of his father and Queen Keopuolani, with two younger siblings, a brother named Kauikeaouli and a sister, Nahiʻenaʻena. His brother would rule after he did. The boy was only five years old when his older brother became the new king.

Nahiʻenaʻena was the first wahine aliʻi to have a feathered cloak made for her, and it is on display today in the Hawaiian artifacts room of the Bernice Pauahi Bishop Museum. She did not live a happy life; the missionaries put her at war with her cultural upbringing. Half grown up, she had been destined to marry Kauikeaouli, who was just a year older than she was.

This was considered a sacred right in pre-missionary haole culture, a normal way of preserving the aliʻi status and mana of the children that the couple would have. The missionaries, however, shamed her terribly, telling her that the match would be a mortal sin. It is unfortunate that scientists were not there instead to teach her about the genetic damage that such unions can inflict upon offspring.

Nahiʻenaʻena suffered emotionally because of the missionaries, married the governor of Mauʻi, and died at a young age of a broken heart. It was 1836; she was either 20 or 21 years old. Her treatment by the missionaries was somewhat ironic as Liholiho already had at least two wives, and his favorite was Queen Kamamalu, his half-sister by one of his father's other wives, Kalakua.

But during Nahiʻenaʻena's eldest brother's 5-year reign, she was witness to a less stressful change: the demise of the kapu system. Kaʻahumanu wanted it gone, and had for a long time. With her husband dead, she took two other husbands and pressured Liholiho relentlessly to break kapu publicly by eating at the women's table.

At last, Liholiho did so, silently getting up from the men's table, sitting down at the women's table, and eating. The people watched in amazement, then paused to consider that nothing else happened. Life just continued. The kapu system was over. Their religious belief that the ancient gods would be disturbed had been successfully challenged, and the missionaries struck, stepping in to fill the void in Hawaiian society with their own religion.

Meanwhile, Liholiho had some other issues to deal with, particularly economic ones.

He had begun to dress as a European king, in a red military uniform with gold feather trim (Hawaiian colors, at least), and his wives dressed as European queens, in the fashions of the haoles. The haoles demanded the right to own land in Hawaiʻi, including trading and commercial rights. To hang on to his realm, Liholiho decided that he would need to make a steady show of adopting Western habits. To finance them, he would have to make money, a thing that no Hawaiian aliʻi had needed to do before.

Things were changing throughout his reign. The young king had to face overwhelming upheavals the whole time as the life that he had been trained for in childhood when his father was alive ceased to exist, abruptly replaced with a foreign culture that had taken over his home.

How was he going to make money? By selling the sandalwood that grew on the Islands.

The result of this decision, an inevitable one, was that the Hawaiian people were forced to divert their activities from necessary tasks such as farming and fishing and aquaculture to felling sandalwood trees.

As if that weren't enough trouble for Hawaii, savvy foreigners fooled the naïve Hawaiian people and their king about the true value of sandalwood, grossly underpaying them for their precious – and finite – natural resource.

Soon the king had run up horrendous debts to pay for Western trappings, while the diseases of whalers and traders who stopped in Honolulu and Lahaina decimated the native population. Less than half of the Hawaiians who were alive when Liholiho came to power were alive when his reign ended.

It ended because he and Kamamalu took a trip to London, England.

The purpose of the trip had been to follow through on his father's intention of asking the British to make Hawai'i a protectorate, but they both came down with measles before the Hawaiian king could meet with the British king, George IV. Hawaiians, whether ali'i or commoners, who lack prior exposure to the pathogens that the humans on the rest of the planet had been able to build up immunities to, were equally helpless when infected by unfamiliar diseases.

Kamamalu died first. When Liholiho heard about it, he was so upset that he went into a coma and died after six more days. The bodies were brought home by their Hawaiian traveling companions, Boki and Liliha, the governor of O'ahu and his wife. Traditional Hawaiian death rituals were not observed as they had not planned on dying when they went traveling (who does?!), and so had not brought priests on the trip.

Kamehameha III

Kauikeaouli was only eleven years old when he became king. He needed a regent even more than his adult but inexperienced older brother had. He had Queen Ka'ahumanu, and a warrior chief from his father's reign, and others. But Ka'ahumanu died in 1832, when he was seventeen years old – still not ready to rule on his own. His older half-sister, Kina'u, took over the role of regent. His wife was Queen Kalama, an intelligent woman who was talented in business and finance. When she died in 1870, she was an independently wealthy woman.

Kina'u lived five more years. She was a Christian convert who attended services at the new Kawaiaha'o Church in Honolulu. There is a stone successor to that church still standing today; the Hawaiian royal family used it for major life events such as marriage and funerals until their rule ended.

Kauikeaouli resisted Christianity while the missionaries promoted it relentlessly, claiming its superiority and citing the technology and strong immune systems of the haoles as proof. The missionaries worked steadily at creating a written form of the Hawaiian language, and after four years of steady effort, succeeded in 1826, less than two years into his reign.

The advent of a written language, along with the schools established by the missionaries, transformed Hawaiian culture. Literacy became universal. Queen Ka'ahumanu set an example for her people by learning to read and write while decreeing that all Hawaiian must do so as well. Soon Hawai'i had the highest literacy rate in the world.

Added to the missionaries' efforts for literacy were the schools that they established on each of the Islands where they gained a foothold. Their motive was to spread their own religion and culture among the Hawaiians, but the end result was nonetheless beneficial: literacy, and knowledge of how the haoles thought about the world.

The haoles were both a benefit and a deficit to the young king.

The benefit was that they became useful political advisors to him, including one Dr. Gerrit P. Judd, whose descendant would later become a governor of Hawai'i in the early twentieth century, when it was a U.S. territory. Gerrit P. Judd took over when the princess Kina'u died in 1839. The king never joined a Christian church, but he made good use of the missionaries.

The deficits were many. So many ships arrived that Hawaiians left with them in droves to try whaling, trading, and whatever else appealed to them, until the king outlawed it, fearful that there would soon be too few Hawaiians living in Hawaii. Not only that, but haole diseases continued to decimate the native population his reign.

The haoles pressured him for the right to establish businesses in Hawaii, to own land for them, and to hire Hawaiians to work in them. This meant stores, ranches, and plantations. The first plantation was on rented land, established in 1835.

One of the missionaries to arrive in Honolulu in 1840 was Daniel Dole, the father of Sanford B. Dole. He went to work at the Punahou School, which was the first one to teach in English.

The king made the most of the benefit of his haole political advisors by getting his realm out of debt and promulgating a constitution in 1840, and then another one in 1852. A legislature was established with a House of Nobles for the ali'i, Hawaiian males, and select resident haoles were given the right to vote.

A brief crisis developed in 1843 when a British navy commander by the name of George Paulet arrived and forced the king to surrender Hawaiian sovereignty to British control. Five months went by as the British Union Jack flag flew over Hawaiian buildings and lands, until French and American protests brought about a reversal. Rear Admiral Richard Thomas sailed to Hawai'i when he found out what Paulet had done, met with the king, got his assurances that British interests in Hawai'i would be protected, and that was that...for the time being.

However, ali'i women had positions on the king's Privy Council, and his father's great-granddaughter, Princess Ruth Ke'elikolani, was appointed as an advisor on it in 1847, when she was 21 years old. Ruth valued traditional Hawaiian culture above haole ways, though she had been taught all about both, and balanced them by wearing Victorian clothing and coiffures while living in a native Hawaiian hale. She later became the governor of the Big Island of Hawai'i.

At last in 1848, the king caved to pressure from Dr. Judd and other haoles to divide up feudal lands so that it could all be subject to sale and individual ownership, as it was in other nations. There was the land owned by the king, land owned by the konohiki – the ali'i who were landlords under the king. They wanted a large share of Hawaiian lands for themselves.

The king went first, of course, taking a million acres as his personal property, leaving three million more to divide up. Of those three million, he decreed that half were to become government lands. That left the rest to the konohiki. The royal mahele (division) was the first authority, followed by a confusing new Final Land Commission.

In 1850, kuleana, small land grants of two to three acres, were allowed to Hawaiian commoners who intended to be farmers, but most Hawaiian commoners did not understand land ownership, and lost their grants. These reverted to the crown, which ended up owning half of all Hawaiian land.

Next came the haole businessmen, who found the attitude of common Hawaiians toward land ownership to be odd. Because the haoles were raised to acquire land and make money, they could not understand why Hawaiian people wouldn't be determined to do the same thing. And because the Hawaiians had been raised with a completely different expectation, they did just the opposite of what the haoles did.

A bad thing appeared in Hawai'i in the 1840s, something that caused separations: leprosy.

Leprosy, also known as Hansen's disease, attacks skin, nerves, and bones, causing bones to shrink and nerves to atrophy, leaving no sensation in the affected areas…which, perhaps, is just as well, because over time, the patient's extremities can die and fall off. It starts with skin lesions that don't hurt or show any discharge, and gets worse as time goes on.

Another looming problem that haunted Kamehameha III's administration was the threat of annexation by the United States. The U.S. was in the midst of expanding its territory, having acquired enough of it to stretch from the Atlantic to the Pacific Ocean, and still it wanted more territory. In 1851, there were rumors of adding the nation of Hawai'i.

A distraction from this issue came in 1853, in the form of a smallpox epidemic, which reduced the total number of native Hawaiians from 150,000 to 70,000.

During this anxious time, in 1852, another constitution was promulgated that limited the king's powers: it required him to share rule with a legislature made up of ali'i and haoles, and to swear an oath to uphold it.

King Kamehameha III and Queen Kalama had had two sons, but both died as infants. This was a common fate among Hawaiians; not only were their numbers being reduced by foreign diseases, but many were unable to have any children at all, or else the ones that they did have were unable to grow to adulthood, reproduce, and raise their own.

The king and queen responded to this personal and political crisis by adopting as hanai children the sons of Queen Kina'u, Alexander Liholiho and Lot Kamehameha. Lot was older, and he was quiet, so it was erroneously assumed that he would be less capable than his brother, who was named as the king's immediate successor.

The king died in 1854 after 30 years of rule, and Alexander Liholiho took his place.

Princess Victoria Kamamalu

The younger sister of Alexander Liholiho and Lot Kamehameha was Hawai'i's first queen.

She was beautiful and, like many of her family, a talented musician.

She was queen for a day – just one day, and then her brother took office as Kamehameha IV.

It was never the plan for her to stay in office. She simply found herself there for that much time as kuhina nui (queen regent) presiding over the king's Privy Council, as she had been before her uncle's death. Her brother discontinued the position, and with that, she was out of office.

But that wasn't all that there was to her; Victoria Kamamalu led a very interesting life.

History has overlooked her, but herstory won't.

The princess grew up as close friends and foster sibling to Lili'uokalani, who became queen of Hawaii in 1891. They shared everything together. Her father ended up raising Victoria Kamamalu by himself after her mother, Kina'u, died when she was a year old.

Princess Victoria Kamamalu was betrothed to a distant cousin, William Charles Lunalilo, and she wanted to marry him. The Hawaiian people also approved of the match.

But her brothers were absolutely opposed to it. They didn't want nieces and nephews to be born who would outrank them in mana.

Lunalilo was a closer relative of Kamehameha the Great than they were, and they allowed their jealousy to trump their sister's happiness. Kamehameha IV also persuaded his cousin Lili'uokalani not to marry Lunalilo for the same reason. She ended up marrying the American John Owen Dominis.

Princess Victoria allegedly had an affair with a married Englishman who was a frequent dinner guest of her family, but that ended when her brothers found out and banished him from the Islands.

Princess Victoria Kamamalu thus never married or enjoyed any further professional successes, and died at age 27, single and childless.

Kamehameha IV

Alexander Liholiho did what his predecessors did, and took the official name Kamehameha.

The new king wasted no time in discontinuing all negotiations with the United States about annexation, making it clear that he intended to maintain his nation's sovereignty, not surrender it.

His claim to the throne came from both his lineage and his hanai adoption, and on top of that, he had been formally named heir to the throne by his predecessor. There was thus no difficulty in taking charge at the age of 20. The new king was very handsome, and he had an outgoing demeanor, which made him popular with the people.

Just five years earlier, he and his brother had gone on a trip to the United States, visiting San Francisco and New York, and to Panama and Jamaica, and Europe, to see London and Paris. Dr. Judd had been their chaperone. The trip had two purposes: to show the young princes the outside world, and to negotiate with the French government over a trading dispute. The French refused to meet with Dr. Judd, and the dispute went unresolved until 1853. Meanwhile, he brought the princes home in September of 1850, just two days less than a year since they had left.

Alexander Liholiho had a good time in London. He was particularly enamored of British royalty and its trappings of prestige. However, he did not have as a good a time in the U.S., where he had an unpleasant experience with racial prejudice.

Regardless, the trip left him with more of a Western bent than that of his predecessors, neither of whom had been raised with such a background. For Kamehameha IV, things Western were part of his background and experience, which shaped his view of the world, and affected his attitudes and decisions.

When he returned home, he was given a place on his uncle the king's Privy Council, which he held until his brother's death three years later. As a result, he had some valuable political experience under his belt when he became king.

The new king discontinued the position of queen regent and relied on his haole advisors, all of whom had been required to swear oaths of loyalty to the Hawaiian king and to Hawai'i long ago in order to serve in government there. He appointed Prince Lot as general in command of Hawai'i's military.

The first piece of advice that the new king received was that he ought to get married so that he could produce an heir, thus providing continuity and stability to the Kamehameha dynasty. Accordingly, he asked his childhood sweetheart, whom he had known since his days at the Chiefs' Children's School in Honolulu.

Emma Naea Rooke was the granddaughter of John Young, the scout whom Kamehameha the Great had kidnapped and co-opted as one of his two haole advisors. She was also a distant cousin and a princess, someone whom the missionaries could not object to. Like her fiancé, she too had been adopted as a hanai child. The two were married on June 19, 1856. He was 22, she was 21, and they were very happy together.

The king attempted to replace the constitution of 1852, but was unsuccessful.

The whaling industry took off during Kamehameha IV's reign, and gas lighting came to Honolulu in 1859. In 1860, a steamship called the *Kilauea* went into service as an inter-island transport, considerably shortening the time it took to travel between the Islands.

King Kamehameha IV and Queen Emma founded an Episcopalian chapel in Hawaiʻi, in contrast to his predecessor, who had had no interest in foreign religion. The Hawaiian people were not delighted about this.

After nearly two years, a prince was born to the couple, and he was named Albert Edward Kauikeaouli Leiopapa. Queen Victoria and her husband Prince Albert agreed to be his absent godparents. He was to be his parents' only child.

Unfortunately, he didn't live to grow up and have children himself. When he was four years old, in 1862, he died after a brief illness. The illness was likely brought on by a seizure that was not recognized as such, but instead treated as an out-of-control tantrum, then aggravated by his father dousing the boy with ice-cold water. That left the king with a lasting sense of guilt.

Just over two years earlier, Alexander Liholiho had mistakenly believed that his personal secretary, an American named Henry Neilson, was having an affair with Queen Emma. Before the king realized that it wasn't true, he shot his friend in the stomach. The king rushed to get medical help. Neilson lived in discomfort for two and a half more years, and then he died.

The king had already been feeling guilty over the death of his friend, which was quite obviously his fault, and now he was convinced that he was the cause of the death of his only child. His friend and his son died one right after the other, in 1861 and 1862.

The king's health deteriorated rapidly, and he became more and more religious. He had chronic asthma, lost the will to live, and died at the age of twenty-nine, after nine years of rule.

Queen Emma was devastated. She never remarried.

Kamehameha V

Lot Kapuaiwa became king when his brother died with no heir, and died without leaving one.

He had hoped to marry the princess Bernice Pauahi, but she chose to marry a haole man named Charles Reed Bishop in 1850. Princess Bernice was happy with Bishop, an American who became a naturalized Hawaiian citizen and a banker. They had no children. She was determined to learn as much as she could about haole culture by immersing herself in it. Marrying into it and living as one of them seemed like an effective method of doing that.

Lot didn't get over it, nor did he make up his mind to marry someone else and leave an heir.

He did name his younger sister, the princess Victoria Kamamalu, as his heir, but she died.

With that plan nixed by fate, Lot still needed to settle upon a willing fiancée.

Instead, he found himself in love with his sister-in-law, Queen Emma. That was a futile emotion as well; she was devoted to her husband's memory and not interested in him.

Unlike his younger brother, Lot was not handsome or charismatic. He was a very calm and quiet man, and he took office without complaint, inspiring confidence with his demeanor, measured reasoning, and self-assurance.

Lot also had no great love for foreign ways, preferring traditional Hawaiian customs and beliefs. He did dress in a European-style military outfit, and he did not attempt to undo each and every foreign change that had come to Hawaii, but he was not interested in adding to them.

Lot ended up ruling for as many years as his brother had – nine.

When he took office, he was asked to swear an oath to the 1852 constitution. He refused.

The haole Cabinet thought that amendments would be made to that document, and that it would continue in service, but Lot had other ideas.

In July of 1864, he called a constitutional convention to discuss the details of a new document, focusing on a provision concerning voting rights. It limited the vote to residents who could pass a literacy test (no one objected to that) and to those males who either owned property or earned a certain level of income.

The agreement broke down as the delegates looped into a series of debates, so Lot dismissed the meeting and said he would give them a constitution. He did exactly that on August 20, 1864, signed it into law, and that was that. The Hawaiian king now had many of the original powers of office back, with those of the Privy Council scaled back, and those of the king and Cabinet in a dominant role. Lot toured the Islands to meet the people and spread the news of the new constitution, which was well-received.

During Lot's reign, two significant historical events took place: one was the sale of the island of Ni'ihau, and the other was the escalation of the isolation of Hawaiians suffering from leprosy.

In 1864, he allowed the sale of the entire island of Ni'ihau to Elizabeth Sinclair for the sum of $10,000 in gold. Her daughter, Helen, had married one Charles B. Robinson, and they inherited the island from her. The Robinson family was based on Kauai, but frequently traveled the short distance of just a few hours by sail or rowboat to Ni'ihau. The people of Ni'ihau thought of the widow Sinclair as their chiefess.

To the present day, the island of Ni'ihau is known as the Forbidden Island, and visits are by invitation only. Each visitor is checked for indications of pathogens that could attack the immune systems of the residents, who speak only their own dialect of the Hawaiian language. They have had no contact with the pathogens that outsiders have built natural immunities to.

The Robinson family still owns the island. They pay astronomical sums in taxes to the United States government each year to keep things as they are. But…there are only two childless cousins left. Hopefully, the people of Ni'ihau will be left alone.

To prevent contagion, a leper colony was established in 1865 on the northern side of the island of Moloka'i. At first, patients could be visited by their relatives, but eight years later the colony was put into total quarantine, isolated from anyone and everyone who was not infected. Scientists have since determined that 95 percent of humans are immune to leprosy.

It made no difference who showed the early signs of the disease – there were no exceptions, no exemptions, and no redemptions. A commoner or a musical celebrity or an ali'i could all be sent there for life, with only a brief glimpse of their relatives waving good-bye to them at the pier as they boarded the boat. A member of the Privy Council was found to be infected; he was banished for life to Moloka'i. In just 3 years, 8,000 Hawaiians were sent there. Being sent there must have felt like the end of the world, with no contact with one's family allowed ever again.

Meanwhile, the sons of the missionaries had grown up. They had no interest in a religious life. They wanted to make money, and they were very busy doing so, dominating many aspects of economic, social, and political life in Hawai'i.

Sugar plantations (over 30 of them), pineapple plantations, inter-island transportation companies, utility companies that offered gas lighting and electricity, and shipping companies that ferried goods to and from the Islands flourished. Haoles from America, England, France, and Germany became wealthy, and they wanted more, and more, and more.

As a result, the haoles were bringing in more and more outside help to labor cheaply on their plantations or in their other businesses, from China, then from Japan, and later from Portugal. Soon there were many more foreigners living on the Islands than there were Hawaiians. The total number of native Hawaiians during Lot's reign was estimated to be around 60,000.

Whaling was a waning industry thanks to the discovery of petroleum oil in Pennsylvania.

In 1866, Mark Twain visited the Islands, touring O'ahu, Mau'i, and the Big Island of Hawai'i. He was a journalist then, not a famous author yet, with no published books out. He came to write articles for a Sacramento newspaper, the *Union*, and he managed to stretch his visit out to far longer than the time agreed upon by his employer. He paid the newspaper back with plenty of letters for publication. He saw Kilauea, smelled coconut oil on native women, and observed that Hawai'i "had more missionaries…than would take to convert hell itself."

A hotel was built in 1872, the first of many. It was a huge, rambling, Victorian building, painted pink, called the Royal Hawaiian Hotel, and it had the approval of the king. It was the first of many.

As for King Lot Kamehameha, he had the palace that his brother had ordered built, Ali'iolani Hale, designated an administrative building instead of a royal residence due to fiscal concerns. Today it houses the judicial branch of Hawai'i's state government, and faces 'Iolani Palace.

However, he also had a royal barracks built, a quarantine house for immigrants, a prison, an insane asylum, and the Royal Mausoleum.

When he died (of morbid obesity) in December of 1872, he left a nation heavily in debt.

His efforts to name a successor had not produced a new monarch, either.

He had attempted to name Princess Bernice Pauahi Bishop as his heir, but she said no.

A crisis over the end of the Kamehameha dynasty ensued as a replacement was sought.

Lunalilo Rules for Over a Year

With the death of the last Kamehameha, Hawai'i had to look to another branch of the ali'i families for a new king or queen, and one who was as closely related to Kamehameha the Great as possible was desired.

The 1864 constitution decreed that the king could name his successor, and that the House of Nobles would have to confirm that individual. But Lot hadn't been able to follow through on that, so the legislature had to decide. The Cabinet scheduled a January 1873 meeting.

The choices were: 1. Prince William Charles Lunalilo, who was most closely related; 2. Princess Ruth Ke'elikolani, the dead king's half-sister, a great-granddaughter of Kamehameha the Great, and experienced governess of the Big Island of Hawai'i, who kept to traditional Hawaiian ways, choosing to speak the Hawaiian language even though she understood English; 3. David Kalakaua, a lawyer who was descended from the ali'i warriors of Kona on the Big Island who had supported Kamehameha the Great; and 4. Princess Bernice Pauahi Bishop, a great-granddaughter of Kamehameha the Great.

Bernice didn't want the job – so she was out of the running.

Ruth Ke'elikolani was considered too traditional for it – out also.

That brought it down to the two men.

They campaigned for the post for the remainder of December 1872, and Lunalilo won.

Kalakaua accepted his defeat gracefully. Lunalilo appointed a Cabinet of one Scot and the rest Americans, which included Princess Bernice's husband, the banker Charles Reed Bishop, and an attorney named A. Francis Judd. He was the son of Dr. Gerrit P. Judd.

Lunalilo had strong American preferences, democratic beliefs, and he enjoyed drinking. The Hawaiian people liked him, and he walked barefoot to Kawaiahaʻo Church to take his oath of office. Thousands of Hawaiians cheered him on.

During Lunalilo's reign, there were some further developments concerning leprosy.

A Belgian priest by the name of Father Damien arrival in Honolulu in 1864. He was soon assigned to the Big Island of Hawaiʻi, where he remained until his bishop asked for volunteers to go to the leper colony. The year was 1873. The bishop didn't want to order anyone to go, because he was certain that they would catch leprosy and die horribly. But four priests volunteered, and Father Damien was the first one, which is why history remembers him so well.

A year later, Father Damien noticed the early signs of the disease.

He is believed to contracted leprosy by sharing poi with others at mealtimes, perhaps to make the patients feel less emotional isolation. Poi, a paste made of pulverized and cooked taro, a starch vegetable, is served in dishes and eaten by dipping one's finger in, then licking the poi off. With multiple eaters sharing the same dish of poi in this way, anyone not infected but also among the unfortunate five percent who are not genetically immune will contract leprosy.

Father Damien died of the dreaded disease after ten years, in 1884. He accepted his fate calmly, and allowed himself to be photographed while suffering from leprosy but still able to work, and again on his deathbed. He was forty-nine years old when he died.

Aside from this, two issues figured most prominently in his reign – two related issues.

Both concerned the United States. One issue was that of sugar: the Hawaiian government wanted a reciprocity treaty, so that sugar could enter the U.S. duty-free. The other had to do with Pearl Harbor: the U.S. wanted to use it as a port for its naval vessels.

This set the stage for a quid pro quo deal…until the Hawaiian people protested and the issue was left unresolved for the time being.

A harsh Hungarian commander, Joseph Jajczay, had been hired to direct the Royal Household Troops, and they mutinied, fed up with him. They wanted him removed, along with Charles H. Judd, the adjutant general.

This crisis was only resolved when the king, suffering from tuberculosis after a lifetime of drinking, pleaded with them to stop. He ended up disbanding them, leaving only the Royal Hawaiian Band.

Lunalilo did not marry or produce an heir.

The woman he had wanted, the sister of his predecessor, had died.

He had been insulted by his would-be brothers-in-law as they jealously guarded their own positions as top mana-wielders, and he was still angry about that.

As a result, when he died at the age of 39 of pneumonia and tuberculosis in early February of 1874, he left instructions that he was not to be interred in the Royal Mausoleum with them.

His father had a small mausoleum built just for him next to Kawaiahaʻo Church.

A Hotly Contested Election

This time, the candidates were David Kalakaua, Queen Emma, and Bernice Pauahi Bishop.

Once again, Princess Bernice Pauahi made it clear that she did not want to be queen.

That was an unfortunate decision for a couple of reasons. One was that when Princess Ruth Keʻelikolani died, she left all of her property to Bernice, which made her the wealthiest person in Hawaiʻi, in possession of one-ninth of Hawaiian lands. The other was her lineage. As a great-granddaughter of Kamehameha the Great, she would have been ideal for the job, having the highest mana in the nation.

A portrait of Princess Bernice Pauahi Bishop by Jennie S. Loop that hangs in her museum.

But no, she didn't want to be queen, even though she got along well with haoles and Hawaiians alike, and was well-respected by all. She understood both Hawaiian and Anglo-American culture completely, so this was a disappointment.

Princess Bernice Pauahi lived until 1884, and Charles R. Bishop opened the museum in her honor in 1891. It houses the largest collection of Polynesian artifacts in the Pacific.

Queen Emma, the widow of Kamehameha IV, ran against Kalakaua, but lost. She never spoke to him again, or his wife, despite having to attend many events that aliʻi were expected to appear at. Kalakaua and Kapiʻolani, however, behaved politely to her.

When she lost the election, a huge riot by her Hawaiian supporters ensued, prompting Kalakaua to allow the troops on board 3 military ships anchored in Pearl Harbor, 2 American and 1 British, to put it down. This set a disturbing precedent for his reign, not that he had much choice when faced with such a disturbance. One man was thrown out of an upper-story window. He later died from his injuries.

Queen Emma kept track of politics in Hawaiʻi for the rest of her life, deeply concerned by the possibility that it might someday become a part of the United States. She died at the age of 49, in 1885, having founded a hospital for her people, whose numbers continued to dwindle.

The Political Disarming of the Merrie Monarch

King Kalakaua's reign is memorable for both a spectacular success and a disastrous failure.

His success was in reviving Hawaiian culture, and he immediately went to work doing that after his election to the throne in 1874. Kalakaua became known as the Merrie Monarch, because he restored the practice of hula dancing to Hawaiian culture. He had it performed at his coronation ceremony. That was held in 1883, after a new ʻIolani Palace was completed in 1879, to replace the older, much smaller hale (house) that had been infested with termites.

Kalakaua revived surfing and lua, the martial art of Hawaiʻi. He and his sisters and brother were great songwriters; they wrote music and lyrics, and his *Hawaiʻi Ponoʻi* is now the state song of Hawaiʻi. He also commissioned the statue of Kamehameha the Great in his traditional attire and feather helmet, which stands across the street from the Palace, in front of what is now a judicial building.

He traveled extensively to establish Hawai'i as a nation in the minds of other reigning monarchs and heads of state, visiting Japan, Siam, and other countries in Asia and Southeast Asia. King Kalakaua was the first reigning monarch of any country to travel the world, and to visit the United States.

Kalakaua hosted Robert Louis Stevenson on his boathouse in Pearl Harbor, and showed himself to be an amiable host to each visitor to the Islands. He was determined to show the outside world through pomp and circumstance that Hawai'i was as advanced and current with world events and practices as any other country.

His failure was political and financial.

He spent a lot of money doing this, and put his country $2 million in debt to a wealthy man from California by the name of Claus Spreckels by 1886, but later paid him off by borrowing from others.

Kalakaua left his sister, Lili'uokalani, in charge when he was away. While he was traveling in 1881, a ship arrived at Pearl Harbor with goods from China…and smallpox. Lili'uokalani responded by promptly closing the port, because smallpox typically decimated the native Hawaiian population.

That did not sit well with the sons of the missionaries, who by now were wealthy from sugar and pineapple plantations, and from shipping and transportation. They ultimately became known to history as the Big Five – representing five wealthy and powerful corporate interests in Hawai'i. They protested that they needed (!) to make money without the slightest interruption; they did not care about the native people, only their wallets. Lili'uokalani replied that her first duty was to her people; she didn't care right back.

Things reached a breaking point over the nation's finances and the king's efforts to promote Hawaiian security for Hawaiians, both present and future. Although the haole ministers whom each king appointed had long been required to swear an oath of loyalty to Hawaii and to the king or queen, a secret coup was being planned.

A secret political organization called the Hawaiian League was formed. It was made up of non-native citizens of Hawaii and haoles, and led by a group of men who called themselves the Committee of Thirteen. This group allied itself with three companies of the Honolulu Rifles. The individuals in those groups were all non-native volunteers.

This statue of Kamehameha the Great in his traditional warrior attire as a strong, active, young warrior was cast by the artist Thomas Ridgeway Gould in 1880 and installed in 1883, the year of Kalakaua's coronation. It stands in front of Ali'iolani Hale, Hawai'i's judicial and legislative building, and it faces 'Iolani Palace.

In 1887, at bayonet-point, the Big Five forced King David Kalakaua to accept a new constitution that practically eviscerated his own political powers. It also required that one own property in order to vote, which disenfranchised native Hawai'ians, as it was only the ali'i who actually held title to any. Haoles had been allowed to buy property for quite some time, and they had used it to amass wealth and to gain footholds as advisors to the royal family, with the consequence that many white men held prominent positions in the national legislature and the king's Cabinet.

That was the same year that the king sent his wife and sister to represent Hawaii in London at Queen Victoria's Golden Jubilee celebration. They weren't home for the events of the Bayonet Constitution. Instead, they traveled by boat to San Francisco, then across the United States to Washington, D.C., up to New York City, and by boat again to London, England.

Queen Kapi'olani had her gown made up in Manhattan. It was fabulous, with beautiful peacock feathers sewn into it. Princess Lili'uokalani had something spectacular to wear, too: a butterfly pin made of diamonds to wear in her hair. The wings were separate pieces with springs behind them, so that the butterfly appeared to flutter as she walked. The two ali'i women were treated with as much respect as any visiting royalty in London, and Queen Victoria gave them a private meeting.

Kalakaua and his wife, Queen Kapi'olani had no children, so his sister, Lili'uokalani, was next in line to the throne. But his sister and her husband, John Owen Dominis, who had emigrated to Hawaii from Boston, Massachusetts, had not had any children either. So, next in line came their niece, the daughter of their dead sister, Princess Likelike, and her Scottish husband, Archibald Scott Cleghorn. Her name was Princess Victoria Ka'iulani Cleghorn, and her aunt named her as heir to the throne when she became Queen of Hawai'i.

Princess Ka'iulani

It's funny how movies often sacrifice historical accuracy for drama. A case in point is that of *Princess Ka'iulani*. In it, when the bayonets came out in 1887, the widowed Cleghorn grabbed his teenage daughter and took her away to attend boarding school in Britain for several years. She was very upset to leave her home, which she loved and was the only place she knew, but her aunt and uncle could hardly have wished her to stay for that. She came back an educated, eloquent young woman, but to the devastating news that her country had been lost.

The movie evoked great sympathy for the princess and, for me, interest.

What actually happened was a bit more drawn out. Ka'iulani didn't go away to school until a couple of years after her uncle was bullied into accepting that constitution. When she did go, it was well-planned and publicized, and her father went with her as far as San Francisco. There was no hurry or anxiety to it, only a fond farewell with lei and ceremony to it. She went the rest of the way to school with a chaperone. Of course, a movie showing her dad grabbing a kicking, crying, objecting teenager and carrying her away from gunfire is much more exciting to watch...

The princess did come back when she was in her early twenties, several years later.

Princess Ka'iulani had gone to see President Grover Cleveland and the First Lady, Frances Folsom Cleveland, on her way home to Hawai'i, and begged for his help. But when Ka'iulani met Cleveland, it was 1897. Cleveland was on his way out of office after his second and final term, and he had been out of office for one term – 4 years – while his political rival, a Republican named Benjamin Harrison, was president.

The annexation talks had resumed during that time. Now, as he was leaving again and another Republican, William McKinley, was taking his place, the annexation talks had resumed. He could do little more than greet Ka'iulani pleasantly, promise her nothing more than good wishes, and say good-bye.

It was 1897 when Ka'iulani finally headed home. Her education was complete, and she realized that there was no reason to delay, or to wait to be summoned home. Her absence was pointless. She had stayed away at first for the sake of her education, then to avoid causing distraction when the attention was meant to be on her aunt, and still longer when she attempted to help by traveling in the United States and being seen as a dignified, poised lady who would either rule capably or get along with others, depending on the situation.

Princess Ka'iulani went home to her father, retired to her estate and pet peacocks in Waikiki, visited with her aunt the queen, and lapsed into a depression as she failed to readjust to the tropical climate in the land that she loved and had missed so much. She died in 1899, after catching a terrible cold while riding a horse in the misty mountains of the Big Island. She was 23 years old.

But back to the king, whom the princess called Papa Moi. She called the queen Mama Moi.

Kalakaua Returns One Last Time

Kalakaua's health had been deteriorating under the stresses that he was under from the haoles, from the ever-increasing financial pressures on his government, and from the attacks on his sovereignty. He decided to travel in the United States again, but had died while doing so in 1891, and his sister had ascended to the throne.

The Hawaiian people had been preparing celebrations to welcome him home, and the colorful decorations that they had put up were hastily covered with black as the ship carrying Kalakaua appeared on the horizon, also draped in black.

Queen Lili'uokalani

Lili'uokalani was a talented songwriter, just as her brothers and sister had been. She was a tall, large woman with a pretty face and regal bearing, and she had no problem assuming political authority when it befell her.

Lili'uokalani still lived across the street from 'Iolani Palace, in Washington Place, where she had moved upon her marriage to John Owen Dominis. The house is still there. It is a white painted structure with a porte-cochère, a yard with a garden around the house and the walled perimeter, and lots of palm trees with a curved driveway sweeping across the front of it. Today, it is a National Historic Landmark, protected from use and shown by appointment only. The governor's mansion is right behind it.

She preferred to live there, across from the back yard of 'Iolani Palace. That was where she had lived since marrying her childhood friend, John Owen Dominis in 1862. She had moved in with her husband...and his racist mother-in-law. Gradually, the two woman adjusted to one another. Meanwhile, her husband became her friend and political advisor. That made losing him in September of1891 doubly hard for Lili'uokalani. He had been the governor of O'ahu from 1868 until his death. She appointed Princess Ka'iulani's father, Archibald Cleghorn, to the post.

Even though she was upset by this loss, Lili'uokalani forged on, determined to work on behalf of her people and to get back the political rights that her brother had lost during his reign. She wanted a Cabinet that would vote favorably on measures that she intended to pass, and she wanted a legal system that would not require her to get approval from the cabinet on every act that she chose to sign into law.

To get that, she had to dismiss a few Cabinets before she had one that she was satisfied would be sufficiently loyal to her, and cooperate with her agenda. That took two years. Meanwhile, the queen learned the administrative basics of running the country from Honolulu, then spent her first spring and summer in office doing the traditional royal tour of the Islands to greet her people, only to come home to find her husband dying.

Added to those problems was the fact that of the total human population residing on the Islands, only slightly less than 40,000 of them were native Hawaiians. The queen faced serious difficulties in maintaining the legitimacy of Hawaiian political control as different groups organized themselves against her: the Patriotic League, which consisted of anti-royalists, and Lorrin Thurston's Annexation Club. No need to explain its purpose…and his club organized another group of thirteen men called the Committee of Safety, armed and threatening.

Lili'uokalani was not a weak queen. She had never been happy about the Bayonet Constitution. She was determined to replace it with one that restored the Hawaiian monarchy's powers, enabling her to properly care for and ensure the well-being of Hawaiians. But she didn't have an army to enforce her will, and she knew it. The last thing she was about to do was ask her people to lose their lives in a pointless battle that would end up with the loss of Hawai'i even if they fought bravely.

The Theft is Accomplished

The Big Five bullies knew what she was like, and made sure that her Cabinet would not support her. When the effort fell through, at least Queen Lili'uokalani knew that she had done her duty and tried, doomed to failure as it was. She surrendered in 1893, just 12 days short of two years on her throne, and was escorted from her palace.

American Minister John Stevens had assisted in the theft, despite the lack of express authority from the President to do so. He had provided the usurpers with American troops from U.S. Navy ships that were docked in Pearl Harbor. The queen, lacking even the semblance of an equal force, decided to live to fight another day.

By that time, President Cleveland, a Democrat, had sent an investigator by the name of James H. Blount to Hawai'i in 1893 to see what had happened. The president accepted Blount's analysis that the nation had been stolen. He refused to recommend that the U.S. Congress discuss annexing Hawai'i.

But it wasn't enough to restore the queen to her throne.

Her opponents from the United States, who did not live in Hawai'i but who wanted possession of it, sent someone else. He was Albert S. Willis, and he was officially there to apologize for the actions of Minister Stevens. Unofficially, he was to find out what the queen intended to do about the usurpers if she were to be reinstated. He came away from the meeting with a rather convenient misunderstanding, which was that she would have them beheaded. She had no such intention, but the damage was done.

The Republic of Hawai'i was established on July 4, 1894, with pineapple baron Sanford B. Dole installed as its President. The irony and hypocrisy of doing this on the date of Independence Day for the United States was not lost on the Hawaiians. Before long, a campaign to have Hawaii annexed as a territory to the United States was underway.

In 1895, the queen was formally deposed, despite her hopes that the United States would rescind the actions of the usurpers. When they deposed her, they presented the queen with a document saying that she ceded away her political powers. She asked them how they wanted her to sign it. "Lili'uokalani Dominis," came the reply.

She looked at them, wondering whether or not they were serious; queens do not take their husbands' surnames, after all, so that was never her legal name. The signature would be a bogus one. She asked them if they were sure about that, and they said yes, caught up in the fun of humiliating her. She did it, not being inclined to enlighten them.

The Queen Fights Back – With an Anti-Annexation Petition

But Lili'uokalani wasn't going to just give up, and neither were her people.

There was a plan to restore the monarchy. One of its leaders was a man named Robert William Kalanikiapo Wilcox, who had received military training in Europe during Kalakaua's reign. He was Hawaiian on his mother's side, and ali'i, too. But he was caught, along with the rest of the queen's supporters. She did not realize what was going on, because they had not told her about any of it.

The Big Five managed to uncover (or perhaps plant) some weapons in her gardens.

Wilcox and Prince Kuhio ended up in prison together. Kuhio's fiancée visited him and wrote to him daily. He was free after a year, which was the entire prison term. Wilcox got 3 years.

The usurpers arrested the queen and locked her in the palace for eight months, in an upstairs room, to be visited only by one of their wives during the day, and forbidden to walk on the lanai (veranda/balcony) outside her room until after dark. She sewed a quilt with nine sections during her captivity, deprived of most news but determined to record her plight in the decorative stitching on the quilt, plus her family tree.

At last she was allowed out, having been insulted during her imprisonment at the palace on the ludicrous charge of treason. She refused to break during her sham of a slanted trial, sitting stoically throughout the entire insulting experience.

The charge of treason was changed to "misprision of treason", which meant that she was accused of knowing all about the overthrow and doing nothing to stop it. What else was a deposed queen supposed to do?! She certainly wasn't going to act like the usurpers had any right to her realm. Fighting the situation was the honorable course of action, not behaving as if she had sworn allegiance to her usurpers.

They knew what they were; they told her that she was to be confined to Washington Place for five more months, then to the island of O'ahu for eight months after that, and then they gave her a passport and said she could travel. It was 1897.

Off she went, glad to feel free, with two loyal Hawaiians as traveling companions.

Her itinerary was not announced, as she didn't want to be prevented from going.

As she left, a rainbow was seen by her Hawaiian subjects, a sign that an ali'i is traveling.

She was armed with a petition against the annexation of Hawai'i.

It had been signed by approximately 38,000 of the 40,000 native people of her stolen nation, with separate sections for men and women at the queen's instructions. Hawaiians don't discriminate against women as other cultures do, but Lili'uokalani was taking no chances. She wanted something to present to the U.S. President and Congress that they couldn't dismiss.

She went to Washington, D.C., and attended many events so that influential people in government and society there could see that she was an educated, cultured head of state, not some barbarian. They saw her.

She went to Boston, Massachusetts to see her in-laws and friends. She and her husband had gone there together years before. They all welcomed her back with great affection, sympathy, and outrage over what had happened to her and to Hawai'i.

But they couldn't fix it.

The queen wrote and published her autobiography, telling not only the story of her life but also her side of the story of her country's loss, while in the United States, where Dole, Thurston, and the others could not get to her. It is both in print and available as an e-book: *Hawai'i's Story by Hawai'i's Queen*.

While in Boston, the queen made a doll to show how Hawaiian women looked and dressed at the time. She named it for her niece, Ka'iulani. Princess Ka'iulani heard about it while she was in England, waiting to be told that she could return home.

Annexed Anyway

The annexation happened anyway, in 1898.

President Cleveland had made only lame efforts to assist the Hawaiians, despite his gracious behavior toward the ali'i. He did not sign off on the annexation, instead leaving it to the Republican administration of President William McKinley, which took office in 1897. Ignoring the petition against annexation, he and the U.S. Congress went ahead and annexed Hawai'i.

The temptation was too great to pass on having full ownership and control of Hawai'i so that, 1. The naval base at Pearl Harbor could be permanently at the disposal of the United States, and 2. The tropical paradise could be a territory of the United States. The Spanish-American War was underway, and the Americans wanted a conveniently located port in the Pacific Ocean. Hawai'i, less than but almost halfway across to the Philippines, was the ideal stopover.

There was a ceremony, and Queen Lili'uokalani, her niece Princess Ka'iulani, and other ali'i were invited, but they all stayed away. Ka'iulani had put on a brave face at social event after social event, attending them with haole thieves with a polite smile and never discussing the deteriorating political situation, but the idea of attending this event was too much. She spent the day with her aunt, quietly, mourning the loss of her country.

During the last few years of the nineteenth century, many native Hawaiian people visited the princess and the deposed queen, behaving as their tradition dictated, bringing small gifts such as chickens, or just coming to show that they were glad to still have an ali'i nui to visit.

The princess and the queen could not fail to notice that most of them were living in poverty, with a standard far below that of the haoles who had stolen the Islands. The ali'i could do very little about it at that point, as the thieves had abolished the posts of governor of each Island, something that the Hawaiians had maintained since the reign of Kamehameha the Great.

These were the same people who were able to boast of having the highest literacy rate on the planet, the result of Queen Ka'ahumanu's decision to require that every Hawaiian learn to read and write. They had lost their country...but they were ready and able to vote intelligently, keeping informed of political events.

Now all that the ali'i had left to offer their people were hospitals and schools that had been established using their own personal wealth for the exclusive benefit of native Hawaiian people. These institutions are still functioning today, and they have helped many Hawaiians, but there is also a significant number of homeless native Hawaiians. They are not easy to spot, because the state government of Hawai'i has done its best to force them out of the potential sight of tourists, who are a lucrative source of income and thus treated as more valuable than native Hawaiians.

Queen Lili'uokalani retired to Washington Place, occasionally spending time at her beach residence in Waikiki, and died at the age of 79 in 1917.

Not As the Big Five Planned It

The thieves had planned the theft of Hawai'i rather differently than the way it turned out. They had planned to require voters to own property, a thing that was alien to Hawaiian culture. But literacy became the requirement instead, and the Big Five had to accept the fact that Hawaiian men could vote. Not only that, but Prince Kuhio and Robert Wilcox each went to Washington, D.C., where they found places in the U.S. Congress to represent Hawaiian interests.

Prince Kawananakoa became active in politics as well, participating in a national presidential convention on Hawai'i's behalf. If they couldn't have an independent nation, these ali'i were determined to do whatever they could to look after Hawai'i's interests via other avenues.

This theft had not gone off without a hitch after all. The Big Five fumed. There was nothing they could do about it, other than to keep making money and abusing the press by intimidating the Hawaiian-language newspapers as much as they could for their opposing point of view about plantation management, labor relations, and promulgating other repressive policies.

The Big Five men had gotten away with the most insular of representation in all facets of Hawai'ian life as long as it was a territory of the United States, with a handful of the same men holding multiple board positions on education, labor, utilities, and transportation boards, and in governmental posts.

How the Big Five Ruined Hawai'i for Hawaiians

The Big Five built luxury hotels, starting with that huge, rambling pink one called the Royal Hawaiian Hotel in Waikiki, completed and opened in 1872, and have continued until there is nothing now but developed, heavily built-up land everywhere one looks in the area.

In 1921, they had an area in Waikiki, a wetlands that stretched back into Manoa and had been cultivated for crops by Hawaiians for centuries, filled in. Construction began on a canal, called the Ala Wai. Its purpose was to drain the wetlands and associated streams and then serve as a northern border for the Waikiki district, which became a tourist destination. It was finished in 1928. It is a fetid, unsanitary place that had untreated sewage dumped into it after severe storms in 2006. One person fell in, contracted cholera, and died.

Queen Lili'uokalani had a summer place in that area once.

The Hawaiian people had fed themselves there with their own labor, as their own bosses.

No more.

If they needed an income, there were always the plantations, said the Big Five barons. The plantations had overseers who wielded whips, spoke harshly to the workers, and paid a pittance. The Hawaiians had never lived like that, and they weren't about to start.

The Big Five imported more foreign labor; the precedent had already been set in the nineteenth century by inviting Chinese and Japanese laborers, who then sent for mail-order brides and stayed. Portuguese workers followed; they invented the ukulele.

Hawaiians, dispossessed, ended up in menial jobs, in Hell's Half Acre, a slum area of Honolulu, jammed into unsanitary, ramshackle tenements with few toilets or sinks, with shared kitchen facilities, to scratch out a living. The ali'i were still around, but for the most part only on call in a dire emergency. The princesses had money, but they couldn't solve everything.

The Racist Haole Woman Who Lied

These abuses did not change even when they were exposed by the Massie case in 1930-1932. A haole woman by the name of Thalia Massie, aged 19, a relative of Teddy Roosevelt by way of an illegitimate cousin, was living with her husband in the Manoa neighborhood of Honolulu while her husband, Tommie, was serving in the U.S. Navy.

Thalia was an unfaithful wife who loved to party. She suffered from undiagnosed and untreated Graves' Disease, which made her almost blind and gave her an odd gait. Tommie had a terrible temper, and in later years was diagnosed as a schizophrenic.

One night in the fall of 1930, Thalia, who hated living on the remote Islands, which would not be connected to the mainland of the United States by underwater communications cable until the next year, got into a fight with a boyfriend, and he hit her in the face.

Tommie had taken off earlier with other friends after insisting that she go out with him.

Walking back in the dark, Thalia got a ride from some passing American haoles, whom she could not see very well. She had leaned into their car window to ask if they were white, which had amazed them, as it was not that dim out.

When she and Tommie were both home, she concocted a rape story to explain her face.

He called the police. The Honolulu police consisted of both native Hawai'ian and white men – no women – and some others, including a man upon whose career the character Charlie Chan was based, Chang Apana. The highest-ranking officers were white.

A doctor and nurse at the local hospital examined her and found no evidence of rape.

Regardless, five men were chosen as likely suspects, trotted out in front of Thalia, who calmly put her glasses on, and accused them of being the perpetrators. They were Hawaiian, Chinese, Japanese, and various combinations of those ancestries. Their names were: Ben Ahakuelo, Henry Chang, Horace Ida, Joe Kahahawai, and David Takai.

The police proceeded to build a case against them, and the U.S. Navy was squarely behind it, with frequent and irate visits by the commanding admiral to the governor on behalf of the lying haole accuser.

The car that the men had used while out together the night before was found – it belonged to the sister of one of them – Horace Ida – and driven to the alleged crime scene. The officer heading the investigation deliberately made tracks there with its tires.

When the white officer who functioned as the C.S.I. investigator was asked to photograph the tracks, he packed up his camera and got back into the car to wait for the return ride to the police station. He refused to aid and abet in the fabrication of evidence.

A brilliant defense attorney represented one of the falsely accused men, a mixed white-Hawai'ian named William Heen. Heen was contacted after the mother of Ben Ahakuelo called Princess Abigail, the widow of Prince David Kawananakoa, desperate for help.

Princess Abigail was entertaining the visiting king and queen of Siam when that call came, but saw her first duty as being to her people if they needed her. She didn't go back to her guests until she had called William Heen and asked him to help. He told Abigail that he would meet the accused, and that if he thought the man was innocent, he would take his case.

Heen took the case. He ably defended the lot of them along with the other attorneys for the defense, while the prosecutor proceeded to dig himself into a hole of lies that he couldn't climb back out of.

The men were acquitted.

The Dishonor Killing

Thalia's self-entitled mother, Grace Fortescue, found this outcome unacceptable. She rounded up Tommie and two rough sailors to kidnap one of the falsely accused, Joe Kahahawai. They murdered him at her rented house, and attempted to drive to a cliff with a strong current swooshing into an underwater cavern to dispose of his body, but were caught.

Clarence Darrow, the hero of the Scopes Trial on evolution, broke due to the Crash of 1929, agreed to come out of retirement to defend the criminals. He tried the case as an honor killing, while the women of the Big Five put up posters everywhere they could find space that depicted Hawai'ian men as lecherous raping monsters peering out from behind palm leaves.

This, despite the fact that Hawai'ian men had earned themselves just the opposite reputation by being respectful of women. They were good people living in a stolen land being judged and subjected to the cultural prejudices of the thieves.

No one bought any of the defense's claims, least of all the jury, which was a mix of white men and those of other resident races. No, the guilt of this group was obvious. It didn't matter that lynching was a common and widely accepted practice in the South on the mainland. It was murder, and this wasn't the South. Clarence Darrow annoyed the jurors by talking to them as if they were back-country ignoramuses, too.

The jurors who almost ruled for acquittal could not go through with it; the prosecution was being handled by a competent, experienced attorney, and this time the evidence – a dead body, a sheet from the house, blood, a weapon, and so on and on – backed up the charge.

The group was convicted of the crime, and a sentence was handed down: 10 years hard labor. But...Governor Judd was persuaded to commute it to time served aboard the navy ship that had housed Mrs. Fortescue during the investigation and trial, plus one hour in his office for the lot of them. Grinning smugly for the press, the group posed outside the capitol building for photographs.

Governor Judd later hired the Pinkerton National Detective Agency of New York City to investigate the entire matter, which was paid for by the Territory of Hawai'i. The agency's conclusion, which he kept private, was that no rape had ever occurred – only rampant racism – but that a horrible murder had. Judd kept the finding quiet because the uproar over it had only just died down; no one in government there wanted to revisit it.

Things went back to the way they had been.

World War II Deposes the Big Five

When the Japanese attacked Pearl Harbor, things changed.

The U.S. Navy militarized the Islands, seizing all resources and governmental control, instituting martial law, and breaking the Big Five's stranglehold. The Matson shipping company felt the change keenly when their luxury ocean liners, which had made supply and passenger runs between the Islands and San Francisco, Los Angeles, Oregon, and Washington, were seized and painted gray.

Blackout rules applied to all windows and street lights in case the Japanese decided to come back...even though they preferred to attack on weekends, holidays, and daylight. Of course, the Navy couldn't know that they weren't coming back.

Supplies ran low, and goods often rotted on the docks as the Navy considered the Big Five exports to be a low priority next to the war effort.

Hawaiian residents of Japanese descent watched as their sons demanded a role in the war effort, offering to go fight and die in the European theater, where their presence would not raise concerns of loyalty to Emperor Hirohito's expanding empire. They served with distinction, winning medals, and some came home to a hero's welcome. They were established as citizens rather than foreigners on the Islands.

Hawai'i Becomes Five-O in 1959

The Hawaiian Islands became the 50th state on August 21, 1959.

That's why the television show about cops in Honolulu is called *Hawaii Five-O* – it signifies that Hawai'i is the 50th state in the Union. The show gives the impression that the police station is in Ali'iolani Hale, the legislative palace across the street from 'Iolani

Palace. Alex O'Loughlin's character, Commander McGarrett, went into the Ala Wai Canal in a recent episode, and all I could think of was that he would get a lethal plague. Instead, he dragged out the suspect, and then injected himself with a vaccine once he was back at the police station.

In November of 1993, President Clinton apologized formally to the Hawaiian people for the theft of their country, by signing a document issued by the U.S. Congress. There are Hawaiians who would like their nation's sovereignty returned, and their lands back, but they lack the numbers and political clout to achieve that. The U.S. Supreme Court has been unhelpful, siding with the State of Hawaii in a 1999 case, construing that apology as strictly symbolic.

Today, Hawai'i has universities, with some native people on their boards and faculties, and not all of them are ali'i. It also has hospitals, museums, and lush gardens, some set up by foreigners who moved in, and some by ali'i. There are few speakers of the Hawaiian language, but hula dance is in full swing all over the Island along with Hawaiian music. It's about more than merely providing a pleasant atmosphere for tourists. One can major in hula dance in Hawaiian college programs. There are even Hawaiian history and culture courses at other universities in other states, including, I found out at home, in Connecticut.

The Hawaiians lost their country for many reasons, but one of them is that their Islands are so beautiful in every way: beautiful for the flora and fauna, beautiful for the music and dance, and beautiful most of all for the friendliness of the people themselves.

For that, haoles want to visit them and their Islands again and again.

The Flight Out

We got up at 3 o'clock in the morning on Saturday the 13th of October. I hadn't had much sleep the night before, having pretty much given up on turning my internal clock around just by going to bed earlier. I resolved to get really tired and sleep in our hotel once we got to San Francisco.

Everything had been packed the night before.

All I had to do was get up, get dressed, pack my makeup and toothbrush, eat something, and bring my stuff downstairs.

My parents seemed to be planning to defer eating altogether, but traveling takes a lot of energy. We would be walking, pulling and lugging bags, waiting in lines, stressing about logistics and flights being on time, lifting and heaving bags, taking off and putting on shoes, empting and refilling pockets, and so on.

We wore fall clothing and jackets. My mother wore winter boots. I wondered what we were going to do with all this extra stuff for the 2 weeks in between. Then I forced myself not to think about it.

It felt weird leaving the house – and the poor cat – at 4 a.m., but off we went into the chilly darkness, with my father driving my car. It had been decided that we would park my car at the airport for what we expected would be a two-and-a-half-week absence.

Bradley International Airport

We got to Bradley International Airport in Windsor Locks, Connecticut with plenty of time to spare. My father let me and my mother out with all of the bags minus his brown carry-on and the camera bag. Then he drove into the parking garage to stash the car and walk to meet us at his glacial pace.

My mother and I went in and checked in…or attempted to do so.

The check-in system is set up in such a way that passengers are expected to go up to a kiosk with a touch computer screen and enter their check-in data – flight number, etc. That sounds great until one actually tries to do so, and the system promptly breaks down.

The numbers had been changed between the time that the flights were all booked, which was the previous summer, and the time of departure. Great.

Actually, I was glad, because I really wanted a human being to check us in. How can a machine, which is a moron, be trusted to check us in without problems?!

Fortunately, there were people working in the middle of the night at the airport terminal, checking everyone in for their flights. A tall blond woman with short, curly hair and a calm demeanor took the paperwork I handed her plus our passports (we had my father's with us) and looked everything up. Yes, the flight numbers had changed, but no problem, she punched up the new data and out spewed our boarding passes. She took our 2 checked bags just as my father caught up with us.

Around the corner to the left were the rest rooms and the passenger check-in lines.

We availed ourselves of the former and headed for the latter.

First we showed our passports and boarding passes to an official who sat or stood at a little podium, then walked on past that to a more elaborate setup: conveyor belts with gray plastic boxes awaited us, as did full-body scanners. What fun…

Off came our shoes, which meant unlacing mine, ripping the velcro loose on my father's orthopedic black sneakers, and yanking off boots by my mother. They went into the gray boxes. Handbags and camera bag went into others. Little round gray boxes were produced for the contents of our pockets. Pocket watch, keys, and folded Kleenex came out of mine and went into one of those. The small carry-on roller-bags went onto the conveyor belt with all of this.

We walked through the scanner, and my hair-clip caught the attention of the TSA agents.

A TSA woman looked at the shape, then at the bun it held in place on the back of my head, and waved me through. She did not ask me to take my hairstyle apart and show her the clip. That was easier than I had expected it to be.

The hard part was reassembling ourselves at the other end of the belt.

The object of the game was to go fast enough so as not to hold up the people who kept coming behind us while also getting out of the way of the TSA agents who were watching the whole process at the back.

There were some long metal benches to sit on for such maneuvers. Once that was over and done with, we suddenly realized that we had time on our hands. That felt strange…so this was part of the feeling of being on vacation! Time to do whatever we felt like doing, unplanned and unhurried.

We found ourselves looking at a back hallway with tall black lanterns to light the way. They looked like old-fashioned street lanterns. To our right were some poufy chairs and a sofa, and after that, a small newsstand-bookstore.

My father sat down on the sofa to wait while my mother and I shopped in that store, facing the hall that led to our departure gate. Our flight wasn't until 7 a.m., so he looked relaxed…tired, but unconcerned about our schedule.

My mother found a Michael Crichton novel, and I got a Sudoku book.

We came out of there, sat down with my father, and leafed through them until he said we ought to go to our gate.

We found our gate, announced ourselves, and then sat there to watch the sunrise until boarding time. We were flying with United Airlines to Chicago O'Hare International Airport, then on to San Francisco International Airport.

We were seated in a row together each time, fortunately on the left side. We had to check our boarding passes for our boarding group. Passengers have to wait and enter the plane in groups. I had actually forgotten all this during the eight years since I had been on a plane. The planes were both the type that offered seating with one aisle between rows of three seats on either side in economy class.

I say fortunately because this meant that my father could sit with his right side facing the aisle, and thus stick his foot out into the aisle as long as the drink cart wasn't in use. And I got the window seat! I love to look out the window. My mother was happy to let me sit there and peer out for hours; she had traveled west many times to attend nursing conferences.

We stowed our bags in the overhead compartment, all together. We were lucky not to be in the last boarding group, so that was easy. We sat down and settled in.

As we waited for take-off, I asked her if she thought that our flight-path would take us over cropland like what we saw in the George Clooney movie *Up In the Air*, with huge circles set in rows of squares. She said yes, that she had seen those before. I hadn't, and was curious. It is one thing to see them on Google Maps and in the movies, but quite another to see them in reality.

My mother and I stared out the window now that the sun was up, trying to spot and identify aircraft from other airlines. We didn't see anything that unusual, which was no surprise. Why would we? We were in rural Connecticut, not at JFK or Newark Airports.

At last it was takeoff time. I love flying! Turbulence is fun, too. I know it's just air pockets, and not an imminent threat of the plane breaking apart, so it doesn't scare me.

Soon we were up in the air, climbing above…clouds. Damn. We wouldn't see much that way. A few miles or so after the plane leveled off, though, and land was visible. We were traveling across upstate New York, Ohio, Lake Erie, Indiana, Michigan, Lake Michigan, and finally to Chicago. It was like looking at the satellite view of Google Maps upside down.

My mother had packed everything for this trip, and bought every travel remedy she could find, including ginger gum. This gum is meant for people with motion sickness, among other problems. On this particular flight, and on this entire trip, I got an unpleasant surprise: I needed that gum.

    This came as a surprise to me because I have flown many times before: when I was 7 years old and we flew to Florida; when I was 15 years old I went to France with my French class; that same year when my great-aunt took me to England and Spain; the next year at age 16 when I went to Toulouse, France to return the visit of a French boy who was with us the previous summer; when I was 19 and went to London for the fall of my junior year in college; when I was 26 and my parents brought me to Florida; when I was 32 and my husband and I went to Colonial Williamsburg for our honeymoon; and when I was 34 and 35 (6-month stay) and I took our cat to Kuwait. So why now, when was I was 42, did I need help with motion sickness on a plane?!

    Lamenting the need was pointless. I asked my mother for the gum.

    It was delicious! It was like chewing on a gingersnap cookie that never lost its taste.

    And it worked fast! A nauseating migraine headache was stopped in its tracks – abruptly.

    The flight was 2 hours and 24 minutes long. I saw mountains, farmland, wetlands, shorelines that looked both synthetic and natural, and finally Chicago. As we approached the city, I stared carefully, looking for the remains of the 1893 Chicago World's Fair grounds, which were designed by Frederick Law Olmstead (who also designed New York City's Central Park). My mother and I had both read about that in Erik Larson's *The Devil in the White City*, so I knew the basic design…but I could not find it. Too bad.

    Drinks were served, but the days of meals being included in the cost of a plane ticket are long gone. Either that, or the flight was just not long enough for a meal to be included. The drinks were sodas, juices, and coffee with milk and sugar. My parents got sodas; I got what claimed to be cranberry-apple juice, but was really sickly-sweet corn syrup with red concentrate in it.

    The plane taxied to the gate and we debarked.

Chicago O'Hare International Airport

    This was the first time I had been to O'Hare Airport, so I stared, interested in everything.

    Looking up at the high ceilings, I saw light coming in from the upper windows and metal trusses that criss-crossed overhead. We were in a long hallway that was lined with duty-free shops and small eateries.

    We found the restrooms, then decided to move in the direction of our connecting flight's gate. Once we were oriented and walking that way, we began to think of breakfast. My oatmeal had worn off a while ago and my parents hadn't had anything yet.

    There wasn't much choice: Starbucks or Starbucks.

    We chose a Starbucks that was on the way to our gate.

My father and I ate scones, and we all got coffee. But I got something that was new: blond roast. For three extra minutes of waiting time, I could have that, they informed me. Since I hate the burnt, dark, bitter-tasting roasts that Starbucks offers, I was happy to try it. My mother glanced at me but said nothing. She and my father don't notice burnt bitterness like I do. We had over an hour and twenty minutes to wait, and the blond roast coffee tasted like...good coffee.

Starbucks seemed to have a monopoly on every major airport that we visited.

Our next flight was much like the first, with us in the three seats to the left, my father's right leg able to stick out, our bags stowed over our seats, another piece of ginger gum, another can of sickly-sweet cranapple juice, and me staring out the window. It was four hours and forty-four minutes long.

But now I was seeing everything that I had been hoping to see in the months leading up to our departure: circle-shaped croplands, windfarms made up of tall, white, three-propeller turbines, suburbs, and lots of mountains. My mother leaned over and looked whenever I got excited over some new and interesting sight. We saw the Rocky Mountains, and then the Sierra Nevadas. My father identified those.

San Francisco International Airport

Final approach into San Francisco International Airport brought us low over the Bay and onto the runway. I could not see the Golden Gate Bridge, but I knew that the airport was well south of the city, and that the bridge was northwest of the airport.

We deplaned and went to retrieve our bags.

There were just the 2 of them, my pink one and my mother's blue one with a fluorescent pink belt around it. We got a cart and I walked up to the conveyor belt in baggage claim to wait and watch for them.

Soon our bags made their appearance, and their colors had the effect that I had counted upon: they gave us no time to obsess that they had gotten lost just by standing out. I grabbed them off one by one, noticing that the pink fluorescent belt was gone.

There was a shuttle that would take us to our hotel, which was one of many that surrounded the airport. We found out where to meet it, which meant going outside and waiting on an island in the middle of two ramps that stretched around the terminal.

A little Chinese man who spoke enough English to help his passengers pulled up and loaded the bags in the back of the vehicle. Next, he hopped into his seat by going up the steps into the bus with us and then climbed through a small hole to get to his seat. We could see through that hole and out the windshield, plus out the windows on either side.

The shuttle was driven around and around hotel entrance after hotel entrance, but we could tell that we were hugging the airport the whole time. The third time this happened, it was for our hotel, the Hampton Inns.

We got our things out, thanked the driver, my mother gave him a tip, and my father availed himself of a hotel luggage cart. He was quite pleased with himself for this, as there weren't very many of these. We piled our bags onto it – all 5 of them, plus the camera bag and the extra Vera Bradley handbag I was carrying. It was full of travel guides and cords for my camera, cell phone, and Nook Color reader. My mother said it was too heavy, but I could handle it.

The front desk was on the right, just after a little shop with candy bars and nuts. A set of two sofas and a fireplace were to the left, which was amusing since palm trees were growing just outside. Behind one of the sofas was a breakfast area.

We went up in the elevator, found our room, and my father parked the luggage cart next to the bureau with the television. He had no intention of relinquishing it until we left the hotel, as his hip was bothering him. We left him to handle it as he saw fit.

When we checked in, I made sure to ask for the hotel's wi-fi code so that I could log onto the Internet with my Nook. My mother discovered that the TSA agents had not lost or thrown out her fluorescent pink belt; they had packed it in her blue suitcase. I was amused, but refrained from commenting. She put it back on the outside of the bag for our flight to Hawai'i on Monday.

It was mid-afternoon now. We had landed at half past noon, and it was almost two hours later. Dinner was to be in the city. We got comfortable, washed up, and I put the little Knopf guide to San Francisco in my handbag.

Time to try out the public transportation system.

A Side Trip to San Francisco

So why have a chapter about a side trip to San Francisco in a travelogue about Hawai'i?

It turns out that San Francisco was visited by Hawaiian monarchs – several of them. It thus made perfect sense to stop here on our way to Hawai'i.

In addition, stopping in San Francisco would allow us to arrive in Honolulu feeling a lot better rested than if we had attempted to go straight from Connecticut to Hawai'i in one day.

It was a fun evening and a fun day after that, and I spent the time looking at the city with Hawaiian history in mind, having done the bulk of my studying for the trip before leaving home. Would I see any Matson shipping containers? Would I see any of that company's ships in the Bay? Would I see anything that hinted of Hawaiian history?

Of course, I realized that the entire city of San Francisco had been leveled by an earthquake in 1906, after Hawai'i had been annexed to the United States, so I doubted that I would see any of the things that the Hawaiian travelers of the pre-annexation days saw there.

Accordingly, I expected to simply enjoy seeing the twentieth-century version of the city.

Yes, I know that this is the early twenty-first century, but most of what we saw was from the previous century, as it will likely be until the next huge earthquake. What a cheerful thought...

The B.A.R.T.

San Francisco has a subway train called the Bay Area Regional Transit system, or the BART.

We decided to try it.

This meant taking the shuttle back to the airport, which is where one arm of the BART stops last. We had to wait for it, so we decided to call my grandmother and uncle to say that we were off the plane, safe, and ready to explore San Francisco. We did that, and found out that the cat had not appeared when they went to feed him. What a shock.

When the shuttle arrived, we got back on and stared out the windows to the right. My mother immediately spotted some condominiums on a hill that overlooked a lovely view of...the airport. It was so odd that she asked me to take some photographs of this.

We got out at the front doors of the terminal that we had just left, and looked around for signs that led to the BART. They were to the left.

We headed that way. My father, with his bad hip, hobbled along as best he could.

The sun was shining brightly, the weather was lovely, and I put my sunglasses on.

We entered the sliding doors and found one person in a booth who took questions, and the ticket-vending machines to the left. The BART trains were unfamiliar, so it was annoying to realize that the one we wanted was just leaving as we figured out that we wanted it and would have to wait half an hour for the next one.

The tickets cost almost eleven dollars apiece, and that was just one-way.

Once we had them, we went through the turnstile to a round seat and sat down to wait.

I took out my cell phone and called my aunt Joan to say that we had arrived. She had been worrying about our flight.

Eventually, the next BART train showed up and we got on. That wasn't difficult.

Getting off was another story.

We had to climb up some stairs to the street level after riding an escalator.

Then we had to get to Fisherman's Wharf. We had gotten off at a stop that was as far north as we could go, which was called Embarcadero, but it still wasn't close enough.

So, with difficulty, we managed to hail a taxi. My father had trouble getting in, but was soon settled into the front seat of a Toyota Prius.

Once there, we figured that the fun would start, and my father and I were armed with our cameras, ready to record it.

Dinner at Fisherman's Wharf

My father wanted to eat dinner at Fisherman's Wharf.

Fisherman's Wharf is no longer something that stands out as a place populated by fishers. It is populated by restaurateurs who offer menus that feature, showcase, and emphasize fish. Its history is as a trading point for the efforts of fishermen, but now they are hardly in evidence.

And what of the fisherwomen, I asked myself? It is always my habit to ask about the women.

I did get an answer to that question after dinner, before we left the restaurant.

In the personal e-book that I had made for our trip, there were a couple of famous fish restaurants at Fisherman's Wharf. I did not know what to expect beyond a brief online glance at their menus. Both seemed equally impressive, but only an in-person look at them would settle the question of where we would end up that evening. Such is the adventure of travel.

We settled on Alioto's Italian Seafood on San Francisco's Fisherman's Wharf. That really is the entire name of the place. Its address is #8 Fisherman's Wharf, e-mail Info@Aliotos.com with a website of www.aliotos.com. It is open daily from 11 a.m. to 11 p..m. Reservations may be made by calling (415) 673-0183. We had no reservation, but after a minute or so, they seated us at a lovely table overlooking a marina with the Golden Gate Bridge in the distance.

The place has two dining areas, one informal at street level with outdoor as well as indoor seating, and a formal dining room upstairs with a lovely view of the marina out back. We chose to eat up there. We would have done so under any circumstances as we love gourmet food, quiet, and a chance to get out of heavily traversed areas. We lucked out, because we ended up being seated at a table with a direct view west.

Fisherman's Wharf is on the north side of the city, to the east. Fort Mason, which no longer has a military function, is directly west, and beyond that is the Golden Gate Bridge. I looked out the picture window and south at the city, and saw a large sign on a metal skeleton of a stand: Ghirardelli. We later learned that this was Ghirardelli Square, where an upscale condominium and shopping area was being built.

Our dinners were as delectable and pleasantly filling as we had hoped after a long day of air travel and scant food at convenience eateries. We had fried oysters with cayenne chili and garlic aioli sauce and fried calamari with spicy tomato sauce for appetizers, followed by fish entrées. My mother had a fish dipped in egg batter. My father and I got the wild barramundi with crimini mushrooms and pearl onions on a bed of mashed potatoes with a hint of truffle oil. We were traveling, so we wanted something different. My father got a beer that the waiter recommended. Dessert was an assortment of tiramisu, cannoli, and fruit.

The dining room was carpeted with a ramp that sloped to the upper seating areas. I went around that to get to the staircase, which we had not used to get to our table. The elevator had taken us past various split levels, which I now discovered as I walked down to the women's room. I was getting tired enough to feel dizzy at that point, but it wasn't all that late – only six o'clock in the evening (which meant nine o'clock back in Connecticut, where we had started!).

The rest room was nice – clean, floral, and as expected.

But it was the history of the place that I was interested in, so I sneaked down the hall to the stairwell, hoping that my excursion wouldn't delay dinner too long. Large, framed black-and-white photographs with little plaques with captions under them lined the walls of the hall and stairwell. Pay dirt!

The Alioto family had come to San Francisco when fishermen – men, not women – made a living by trading their wares on the wharf to restaurateurs and fishmongers. Rose Alioto was the wife of one of these men, but she found herself widowed with several children to feed and raise before that task was completed.

And she found herself with a problem that has been faced by many women: she had learned all of the skills that she needed to succeed in the fish and restaurant business from her late husband, but the other men at the wharf did not wish to trade with a woman. How unreasonable; why should she be expected to just give up and work for a miserable, back-breaking pittance with no respect in some factory or cannery?!

Fortunately, a male family friend traded the fish for her, and she continued in business. The tale of Rose and her children's development of their beautiful restaurant was chronicled in framed photograph after framed photograph.

After I got the gist of this family history – which felt strange, cursory, and even a little sloppy – I went back to our table. When I study history, I feel a responsibility to do a more in-depth job than this! But…I suppose that a taste of the sort of quick study that most people do was enough for here.

We were in San Francisco more for fun than for study, after all.

Outside, I paused for some photographs of the sidewalk and the iconic crab signpost.

There was a plaque set into the sidewalk right outside of Alioto's Restaurant, and it stated that the place was founded in 1925. I didn't see any indication as to when the plaque was laid in the concrete, however.

The crab signpost stood just across the street, but my parents wanted to find a cab and leave for the hotel. My father could not stand on concrete for long. I hurriedly shot the photograph and followed them; I was tired too, and expected our quest for a cab to be a huge chore.

I glanced at the viewscreen on the digital camera to see that I had gotten a good shot before catching up to them. There they were, walking away, in the lower right of the image. When I caught up, I told them so and added that they were definitely going to be in this travelogue. It was David's turn when we were in Kuwait, and now it was their turn for San Francisco and Hawai'i. "You're going to be famous," I said with a grin.

My father had no particular reaction to that; he seemed resigned to it. My mother grinned.

The street was full of tourists. We were looking east at the Embarcadero again, a long street which runs along the eastern edge of the city, curving around to finish up at Fisherman's Wharf, joining up with Jefferson Street. We stood on Jefferson Street, looking up and down at the busy traffic (both foot and vehicular), and pondered the situation.

The Berber Taxi Driver

After the expense and hassle of riding the BART, my parents were disenchanted with it. Henceforth, we would ride in cabs. Fine. But how were we supposed to get one? Obviously, we were supposed to hail one in the street, but that proved to be difficult.

At last, after watching my father stand by the side of the road while my mother and I tried and tried to get a cab for almost an hour, we had one. It was sheer luck. Calling for one had produced nothing, despite being prepared with a phone number. Apparently, cab drivers were only too happy to drop people off at Fisherman's Wharf, but every cab that disgorged passengers either filled up on the spot or else took off in answer to a phone call. We were relieved to finally get away.

Why had we decided to stay outside the city, we asked ourselves?

Why indeed – we didn't know the city, and thought it would be more convenient to be closer to the airport.

Why hadn't we rented a car?

Well, then my father would have had to park far from our destination and walk – too hard.

So here we were.

The next morning, we swore to take a cab and get some phone numbers so that we wouldn't have this problem again.

Falling asleep on cue was not difficult. I was getting a headache from staying up too long after too little sleep, so I took some Tylenol PM pills and let them work.

We had breakfast in the hotel the next morning, and asked the woman at the front desk to call us a cab. Then we sat on the sofas and waited, feeling determinedly optimistic.

The cab that pulled up to take us into the city was a white sedan driven by a large man with a friendly demeanor, dark, wavy hair, and a tanned complexion. He chatted with us as he drove, gave us his business card, and listened sympathetically as we told our tale of woe about the previous evening.

He was a Berber, he told us.

My mother wondered what that meant, so I told her it meant he was from north Africa.

"Right!" he said, pleased that I knew what part of the world he came from. He had immigrated legally twenty years earlier, and now he owned some land in the Atlas Mountains. His sister and her family stayed there most of the time, while he lived in San Francisco and worked. He had a girlfriend here, who drove one of his cabs.

He had a small fleet of cabs, it turned out. He told us to call him while we were in the city today, and he would send one of his cabs to ferry us from place to place. We agreed to do this, since dragging my father down into or out of the subways again was out of the question. He dropped us at Spear and Mission Streets, a block south of the Embarcadero stop that we had gotten off at the night before.

Brunch at Yank Sing Deem Sum

Someone my mother knew from her office, a woman whose daughter has had a place in San Francisco for the past fifteen years or so, had told her about Yank Sing, which our Berber cab driver said was the best place in the country for dim sum. This office acquaintance had given my mother a lot of advice about what to see and do in San Francisco.

The dim sum advice was excellent. The other advice...well, more on that later.

Yank Sing has 2 locations. We went to the one in Rincon Center, a building that housed a former U.S. Post Office, complete with historic art deco murals inside. And that was just the entrance!

It led us through a foyer and into a large commercial complex that appeared to be more about offices than shopping, except for the restaurant. Inside was a large, round fountain set into the floor. Straight overhead was the water source, another large, round fixture.

There were tables arranged all around that fountain, and I realized that they were part of the seating for Yank Sing. There were a couple of other food vendors there, but those businesses were closed. Waitresses in beautifully colored silk dresses, Chinese dresses with embroidered birds and floral patterns, wended their way from table to table.

The front door of the restaurant was wide open, and the waitresses came from there.

For this, I had called ahead weeks ago to make a reservation. We only had a day to play in San Francisco, so I wanted to leave as little to chance as I could. There was no problem; we went inside and looked around, announced ourselves, and were soon seated.

Each table had its own complimentary glass pot of jasmine green tea, and it was delicious. We didn't need water with this tea, and the staff brought another one when we had drained it.

They also brought us the dim sum menu, a long, thin strip of paper that listed everything they offered. I had seen photographs of just about every option online at http://yanksing.com/our-cuisine/deem-sum-gallery/index.html. The categories are: steamed; specialty; deep fried; vegetarian; and dessert. I wanted to try just about all them…not the pork, though.

Carts with Peking Duck rolled past. It took me a few tries, but at last I managed to get a photograph. The wait staff was very accommodating once they knew what I wanted to do.

Everything was set up to be easy to serve. Pre-sliced duck was laid out on plates just below a whole one for maximum efficiency paired with attention-catching presentation.

My father tried the ribs, we all tried the duck, and I got some of almost every fish and vegetarian item. Most dishes were steamed or fried, and served in small, round stainless-steel containers with lids. Inside were bamboo slats and three or four of a given dim sum.

Some vegetarian dim sum, shown clockwise from the top: spinach, snow pea, and savory; Shrimp and pork dim sum.

    This was food tourism at its best. We got full – a bit too full – and didn't care. This was definitely not the time to be on a diet. There were several fish entrées that we wanted to try, including fried sea bass with a basil leaf and a sliver of sweet taro with red fruit sauce that might have been pomegranate. It was delicious.

    It didn't stop there. Yank Sing had: lobster dumplings with broccoli and roe; goldfish dumplings shaped like koi with orange eyes made of roe and filled with shrimp; fried stuffed crab claws with both shrimp and crab; and phoenix-tailed shrimp.
    For dessert, I had the sesame balls, which my parents were persuaded to try too since the plate came with four of them. Inside was a delicious sweet yellow bean paste. My father tried the mango mouse…and then we were truly full. Time to go.

An Afternoon in the Bay City

    There were several things that we hoped to accomplish in one afternoon: see the Ferry Building, visit Union Square so that we could walk around the flagship store of the Williams-Sonoma company, and then find a skyscraper with a viewing tower so that we could look out over the entire city and take some photographs. We managed to do all that, and at a decently relaxed pace.

The Ferry Building was, conveniently enough, close by. My father could not walk around or stand for long periods of time, so he intended to stay at the Rincon building and sit in the atrium until we came back for him.

We walked east and soon saw the Ferry Building, which has been converted to a beautiful food hall of gourmet shops. San Francisco is known for being the headquarters of the Ghirardelli chocolate company, but it also has the Recchiuti chocolate company, and I was counting on shopping in its store. I found a nice box of chocolate for my grandmother. I always buy her chocolate when I go somewhere.

The Ferry Building had shops with wines, cheeses, artisan soaps, fish and shellfish, honey, more chocolate, and endless other goodies. There was a book store with pretty cards in the back, and a boardwalk with seagulls perched on the railing enjoying the sunshine.

When we came out of there, we decided to head across the Embarcadero to look around before going back to meet my father. There was a craft fair set up in the grassy median, and we love to walk around tents looking at whatever is for sale, even if we don't buy much.

I also noticed that there were many homeless people sleeping on benches about a hundred feet away from the craft tents. They were of all ages, and I wondered which ones were travelers who wanted to keep their trips as inexpensive as possible, and which ones were permanently living on the streets. There was one dog, and one shopping cart, so I couldn't tell.

We walked around and found all sorts of things, including tie-dyed clothing and matted prints of photographs. That was definitely worth a careful look; for 8 dollars, I got a beautiful photograph of the Golden Gate Bridge, something that we would not be seeing up close.

The photographer himself, an elderly man named Quan Li, sold it to me and even re-matted it because I liked the black matting better than the white. After it was ready, he signed the matting in white ink.

After that, it was time to go back and get my father. We walked the two blocks and found him easily. He had stayed put with his camera. Now I brought out the cardamom chocolate truffle that I bought at the Recchiuti store, which I ripped apart. We all shared it, then called the Berber cab driver.

This is Union Square – a raised area with palm trees and stepped gardens. There is a café in there, too.

He said he wasn't in the area, and that he would send one of his cars to get us. We waited a long time, but accepted that this was a lot easier than what we had dealt with the evening before. At last, we were riding to Union Square. My father headed for the square, to sit and wait in the sunshine while we toured Williams-Sonoma and whatever other shops caught our attention.

We saw my father head across the street and into the sunshine, which peeked through the tall buildings all around Union Square. It was warmer here than back in Connecticut. We were all enjoying that, with lighter jackets and shoes.

Without further ado, we went to the north side of the square to see Williams-Sonoma.

This is the view of the store from across the street, and how the store looks when one walks in off the street, complete with La Cornue stoves on either side, baskets of tools and canned goods, a chandelier, and friendly sales associates who offer tastes of seasonal treats.

It may sound ridiculous to some people, but I don't care. Since I had worked at one of these stores in Connecticut ten years earlier, I had always wanted to see this particular store – the flagship store. Williams-Sonoma is a gourmet kitchen supply store with items imported from France as well as those made in the U.S.A. and Japan. Nothing is cheap or flimsy or in any way disappointing if it is from this store.

Our manager had described this place, and now I was seeing what was so special about it: like the Manhattan store, it had museum-quality displays of Chuck Williams' old cook's tools in glassed-in frames all over the store. It also had the usual white walls, light wood panels and flooring, white marble countertops, and five balconied stories of wares to view. At the top level, two chefs were just finishing up a recipe of butternut squash risotto, and they told me that Williams himself, still active and in his nineties, appears there twice a week.

In short, this place was everything it was cracked up to be. I was thrilled.

My mother and I wandered all over this store, taking our time to view it all. She likes great kitchen tools and equipment as much as I do, so we lost track of each other a couple of times. We were having fun, though.

When we had seen it all, we found a nice rest room on the top floor, and took the elevator down. I love to walk up stairs when I am touring, thus getting a full view of whatever there is to see, and then take the elevator down.

We went next door after that and walked through the Tiffany store, which had just two stories, then out and down the street to see whatever else looked interesting. There was a Zara store down Post Street to the east, so we went through it, but we didn't buy anything. It was a Sunday, so everything was open.

These chefs were a lot of fun to chat with, and they gave me a taste of their fresh butternut squash risotto, which was delicious.

With that behind us, we were done looking and went to find my father again.

He was fine, and in a good mood. If it weren't for the arthritis and bad hip, I wouldn't have been concerned about him. He has always insisted on coming along with us while we toured shops, and then found a place to sit and wait. It seems like a boring pastime, but he just likes to be along for the ride.

My husband does the same thing when I want to walk around a shopping area, with a twist: instead of finding a place to sit and space out, he follows me around, making amusing comments. He also gets bored partway through and says, "Can we go?" dragging his words out comically. What's really going on is that he just wants to banter with me and hang around with me, not actually stop touring shops.

Anyway…we managed to find ourselves a cab this time without calling the Berber driver.

A Celebrity Sighting

Our next stop was the Fairmont Hotel, which was uphill. Our purpose was to find a place to look out over the city. My mother's co-worker had advised us to go there for that. Accordingly, we rode a cab up and up and up, with the vehicle going level at each street that crossed the hill, just like in all of the movies and television shows that have been shot in San Francisco. It was a fun ride, though I suppose it must get old to residents.

We got to the top and found ourselves looking at a beautiful area that got plenty of sunshine. The Grace Cathedral was on our left, a replica of Notre Dame of Paris but smaller, in metal as well as stone, and Episcopal rather than Catholic. Next, moving right/east, was a large mansion of brownstone. I soon found out that it was a private men's club.

To the right of that was the Fairmont Hotel, a beautiful, colonial-style white structure with a slew of flags out front.

As we went in through the revolving front door, we glanced up at the people who were walking out. It was Tony Bennett, the singer. He was in a navy blue striped suit, looking exactly as he does on camera, chatting with whoever he was walking with. I took that in with one good glance, and walked in without changing pace. I don't approving of stopping a complete stranger to chat about what would be basically nothing important just because she or he is famous.

My mother is the same way, but she loves Tony Bennett, so I knew that she was thrilled.

"Did you see Tony Bennett?" she asked me happily.

"Yes," I said, "but I wasn't going to say anything to him."

"Neither was I," she replied.

We went in and looked around. What I had noticed about this hotel as we approached it was that it didn't seem to be tall enough to hold a viewing deck that would show us all of San Francisco. Puzzled, we walked around, looked at the lobby and shops (might as well as long as we were there – the shops had interesting wares and nice clerks).

Then we asked the people at the information desk about the viewing deck. It was dismantled in a huge renovation fifteen years ago – gone! "How old is most of J---'s information about San Francisco?" I asked my mother. "15 years," she said, "but her daughter still lives here, and she still visits her here!"

My father took in this news with a final disparaging look. "Don't tell us about any more tips from J---," he said.

Time to go elsewhere for a view! As it turned out, the hotel across the street, The Mark Hopkins, had a viewing deck, so we went there.

Finding a High Vantage Point

Across the street was a beautiful tower of a hotel. Like the Fairmont Hotel, The Mark Hopkins was built in the early twentieth century. It had recently undergone a restoration and renovation, and was decorated in an Italian style. The viewing deck was not open yet; we had to wait until 5 o'clock to go to the Top of the Mark, as it was called.

With no reason to hurry, I looked around and got out my camera.

Here is The Mark Hopkins Hotel. At the Top of the Mark, a lounge on the top floor, we enjoyed a great view.

The front of the hotel had a large parking and turnaround area, complete with the obligatory well-appointed entrance and doorman.

As I looked around, a San Francisco trolley car rolled fortuitously past.

No sooner had I gotten my one and only shot of that than I turned around and noticed that I was looking down at the familiar row houses of Nob Hill, so I shot an image of that too.

My parents were sitting in the lobby inside, calmly waiting for the Top of the Mark to open. I took my time, enjoying the sights and marble in the rest room, a little museum room with menus from eighty years ago and a model of the future Ghirardelli Square, and finally the lobby when I wanted to sit and rest.

At exactly five o'clock, my parents wanted to try to get to the Top of the Mark.

We boarded the elevator, and hit the button for the top floor. It didn't light up.

Here is a view of Grace Cathedral and that private men's club building... with a reflection of my handbag in the glass. The view is northwest, and one can see the Golden Gate Bridge between the tall buildings at the top. Looking northeast, we could see the Transamerica Pyramid.

A hotel manager, a woman in a pants suit, was in there and she told us that it was set on a timer lock. She tried riding with us and hitting the button, assuring us that it should light up any time now.

We rode up and down with her and three transgender people who looked at us as if to say, "Come ON, can't you tell what we are?" I had made eye contact with one of them, a tall, large-boned individual who wore a white dress of some filmy, gossamer-like material and wire-rimmed glasses without quite catching on. I hope I didn't disappoint her/him. Needless to say, we enjoyed our ride to the top.

I lost interest in that as we exited the elevator.

At last, my father seemed to be interested in the proceedings. Out came his professional camera for the first time as he focused and clicked at the view from windows on each side of the building.

I did the same.

For the price of one drink each, we were allowed to sit in the lounge of the Top of the Mark for about an hour. I had a glass of Merlot. My father got a beer. My mother had the Cabernet. We saw what we were after, and enjoyed it.

Dinner at Greens Restaurant

Next stop: the famous vegetarian Greens Restaurant. We did not arrive in San Francisco with reservations. In fact, although I had a cookbook from this famous place by the chef, Annie Somerville, I had completely forgotten about it until I looked at the little Knopf guide at our hotel. My parents had agreed to eat our remaining San Francisco dinner there when I explained what was special about it. We went there with a day-old reservation.

The place is in Fort Mason, which has several old barracks buildings that have been converted for commercial uses. To get there, we needed yet another cab, and decided to take our chances hailing one. Since we were just coming out of a hotel, it was easy! A hotel employee flagged one over, and in we got.

The driver was a nice Burmese guy who didn't know where anything was, but we weren't about to be picky. He usually worked on Mercedes Benz cars as a mechanic, and only did this job once or twice a month, he said, and this was only his first day on the job!

All of the Fort Mason buildings look like this on the outside. This is the entrance to the Greens Restaurant.

Not to worry – I had the Knopf guide with its fold-out maps, and he pulled over when we were almost at Fort Mason to figure out where to go.

He was nervous, so we chatted with him a bit, telling him how hard it had been to get any cab at all. He told me how to pronounce the name of Aung Sang Suu Kyi (that last part is what I needed help with: Kyi is pronounced "chee"), the famous Burmese Nobel Peace Prize winner who spent decades in seclusion under house arrest for her political activism. He said that it is just too dangerous to think about going home, even for a visit.

Soon he figured out how to get us as close as possible without being charged for entering the gate: just drive in, let us out, and then leave right away. The gatekeepers were reasonable; they didn't try to extort fees from every livery service that passed through.

We got out while it was still quite light out, despite the fact that dusk was about to fall.

We went inside, and I took out my camera again. The place was modern, with interesting paintings and views out the windows of marinas and the Golden Gate Bridge.

My parents sat down to wait while I shot photo after photo. This was going well; I was finding plenty of incidences of down-time in which to use my camera. It was still light enough out that I could see red when I looked at the Golden Gate Bridge.

Later on, I took another image of the marina. It was the light on the clouds that made the photograph memorable:

The dining room was an interesting place, and I spent some time documenting it. Though I haven't put every last image in this travelogue, it's always good to have them stored later on. We can always show them to friends.

For this segment, I will show what we ate, because each plate was presented artfully, and our table, which appears below.

When we sat down, I could tell that my father was starting to relax and enjoy this trip because of what he said. "I'll have a steak!" he announced, with a devilish grin.

"No you won't," I said, grinning back. Hah! Trapped with healthy but delectable food!

So what did we eat?

My father and I both opted for a spicy meal: Fire-Roasted Poblano Chili.

My mother had Knoll Farm Eggplant and Summer Squash Lasagne. We shared ours, eating half and then switching plates. She found my food too spicy, which came as no surprise. My father enjoyed his, and ate it all up. But…whenever I mention how good the food was, he says, "I had no choice – there was nowhere else to go." Hmmm…meat-lover. No wonder the doctor told him to eat a diet that is pretty much like mine – fruits, vegetables, grains, some fish.

There was also a cheese plate for an appetizer with herbed goat cheese and fruit.

For dessert, we had some more great recipes that felt like food adventures.

I had berry sorbets with almond biscotti, which I shared with my mother. My father had lemon cheesecake with huckleberry sauce. We tasted it – it was good.

That did it for our food tourism and other tourism in San Francisco. It was time to go back to our hotel and sleep so we could be ready to leave for Hawai'i the next afternoon.

The Berber Taxi Driver Again

The Berber taxi driver came to get us outside Fort Mason.

It was a pleasant ride that took us through the business and political areas of downtown San Francisco. We saw the courthouse, Symphony Hall, and lots of restaurants and diners. Then we were on the highway – no, the freeway as it is called on the West Coast – and looking at the lights on the water to our left as we headed south.

And at the meter. The Berber taxi driver never turned it on.

My mother nudged me when I asked – or started to ask – about that.

The taxi driver chatted merrily with us all the way back, and promised to pick us up the next morning and drive us to the airport. Really…it was just next door. We could take the shuttle for no fee, we all thought. How odd…

When we got back to the hotel, my parents said what we were all thinking: that we would take the shuttle back to the airport.

He wanted more money, perhaps didn't think that we had given him a big enough tip in the morning, so he had deliberately driven us with the meter off at night. He was keeping the whole fare for himself, that was obvious.

We didn't care how he handled that, but we were not getting back into his cab.

So, we took the shuttle to the airport the next morning.

My mother called the taxi driver and thanked him profusely for all of his help, promising to recommend him to others and to call him the next time we were in the city.

A Flight and an Agricultural Declaration Form

On Monday afternoon, we were on our way to Hawaiʻi at last – to the island of Oʻahu.

We waited in San Francisco International Airport, eating lunch at the food court nearest our departure gate. There was a Boudin Bakery there, so we had something healthy to eat that tasted good, followed by some Ghirardelli chocolate, which I had bought on the way into the terminal.

There were little shops and kiosks in every section of this airport selling bags of every flavor of that company's chocolate, in little individually wrapped squares. We were going to experience the flavors of the city of San Francisco on our way in and out of it if San Francisco had anything to say about the matter.

The flight was quiet, but disappointing. I had wanted to look out the window during the flight at the land masses as we approached…and we ended up in the middle seats. This came as a surprise to me, because the previous plane rides had been on aircraft with just one aisle between 6 seats – 3 on each side. Now we had 3 on each side, with 2 aisles and 3 seats in the middle.

All that excitement memorizing Hawaiʻi's land masses – the shapes and sizes and names of the Islands – and I couldn't see anything! I did ask the people at the ticket counter about changing this, but they said I would have to ask someone to switch seats with me.

Forget that.

So we boarded the plane, got settled into our seats, and I did my best to focus on whatever else, aside from having an unimpeded view out a window, that might be a plus.

That didn't work immediately. There were individual movie screens on the backs of every seat, and we soon figured out how to synchronize the earphones with the channels…but the *Spiderman* movie starring Andrew Garfield and Emma Stone just did not play smoothly. It was a movie that I had not yet seen, but wanted to see very much. The other choices did not interest me at all – I checked them out.

I was getting pretty disgusted at this point. Flights cost more and more, and passengers get less and less. No food is part of the deal anymore; everything is extra. Only the entertainment was part of the deal, and the airline couldn't be bothered to keep its equipment in peak condition.

Granted, there were other movies to watch that worked just fine, but I didn't want them. What I was after was an experience that would sedate me by making me completely forget my surroundings. I knew that if I could find one, I wouldn't feel motion sickness and the anxiety I was feeling would disappear. I had to make this work. I have Asperger's, so I can get fixated on what I want, and am anxious when traveling. Finding the right distraction, in this case, the *Spiderman* movie, helps.

I called the next stewardess over and told her that the movie did not work properly. She fiddled around with it, then informed me that the other movies worked. I looked at her, deadpan, and said, "But they won't be *Spiderman*. I feel like the airline stole something from me by offering it but not keeping everything working perfectly."

She looked at me for a split second, then said she would see what she could do.

"Thanks," I said, and gave her a polite smile. At least, I hoped that my face looked pleasant.

Regardless, the stewardess was successful; she reset the DVD player and the movie worked properly. I was delighted. I kept chewing ginger gum and watched the movie, and it worked. Soon, I was perfectly calm, and I stayed that way.

After the movie was over, I got up to use the rest room, and saw the stewardesses – a group of them – near the back of the plane. The blond one who had reset the DVD player was among them, and I saw that they were each wearing aprons with beautiful tropical flower patterns.

The blond stewardess asked me if I had enjoyed the movie, adding that she had "jumped through a lot of hoops" to make it work. I said yes, that I had loved it, and that I really appreciated what she had done. I would have added that her effort distracted me enough that I had felt absolutely no motion sickness, but she had more work to do, so I went into the restroom.

More sickly-sweet cans of cranberry-apple juice were brought out, and I looked at the label. High-fructose corn syrup! No wonder so many Americans are overweight and have diabetes.

When we were about an hour away from Honolulu International Airport, the stewardesses started handing out forms to fill out. Their specific instructions were that one person from each party had to fill them out, so I volunteered.

I knew what they would be about thanks to all of the reading I did before we left. When a volcanologist went to stay in on the Big Island of Hawai'i for 3 years (1969-1972), he and his wife had a minor complication: they wanted to bring their cat.

That was how I learned about the environmental laws of Hawai'i.

There were other sources that tipped me off to the fact that there are restrictions about what life forms might be brought to the Islands illegally. Most of them were little details here and there in the history books I had gathered. If you read enough stories about how haoles brought in rats or mongoose or parrots or whatever else, it becomes obvious that rules were eventually put in place to protect the environment there.

That couple I read about had to send their poor cat on ahead in a crate, then leave him in quarantine for four months. That's a long time in a cat's life – it seems to me that cats don't live long enough to justify taking them away from their humans for such a length of time. And why aren't vaccinations enough to satisfy Hawai'i?! Of course, Britain is even worse – a year!

Well, we weren't bringing any pets, so I concentrated on filling the form out.

The form wanted to know what we might possibly be knowingly bringing to Hawai'i down to the last microbe, from pets (cat, dog, bird, reptile, other) to plants (fruit/vegetable, flowers, potted plants, bulbs or seeds, soil or sand, live seafood, bacteria/fungi, insects, amphibians, and so on and on). Odd…didn't people fantasize about sneaking black sand OUT of Hawai'i, rather than bringing stuff like that in?

Well…Hawai'i can't risk having any unauthorized science experiments smuggled in. I have read and watched enough Michael Crichton stories to appreciate that.

Not only that, but I was actually excited to fill out this form, to read every word of it, and see confirmation that Hawai'i was being careful of its environment. I was seeing firsthand some useful evidence of what I had spent time studying!

My parents showed a surprising lack of interest in it. Why didn't anyone else get a kick out of this? Oh well. Being the only one to feel such a thrill over something new was a very familiar experience. I started filling the form out.

It was only Side One of the form that was concerned with the environment; Side Two was all about demographical surveying. That side wanted to know how long we would be staying, how many of us were coming, how old we all were (just age ranges, but we didn't care if strangers found that out about us), why we were visiting '(it isn't always about fun when people fill these things out), and so on.

As I worked on it, a stewardess came by and noticed that the dozing guy in front of me wasn't working on his form. She spoke to him about it, and he said that he was just stopping over in Honolulu, not staying. She patiently explained that it was the law that everyone fill it out, regardless of their plans, and offered to find him a pen.

He stirred in his seat, fully awake now, and I offered him a pen. He accepted, and I told him how Hawai'i had suffered some environmental problems thanks to plantation owners importing mongoose to get rid of rats that had stowed away on ships, only to have these creatures prey on indigenous species instead. That was why these forms were such a big deal to the Hawaiians.

The guy nodded and seemed quite willing to cooperate at that point, so I left him to it.

When I was done, I got up to hand it in, heading for the back of the plane, where once again the stewardesses had gathered to chat until there was something else to do. They wore United Airlines uniforms with a Hawaiian twist here and there. Most of the twists were aprons and scarves with tropical floral patterns. The blond one was among them. She was pretty, with long, slightly waved hair and a nice-looking face, and tall – about five feet nine inches.

When they noticed me there, I smiled, turned in my form, and asked if it would okay if I took another, blank one, to keep, and explained that I was writing a travelogue about the this trip.

They all perked up and smiled, said it was fine, and gave me one. Then they asked me about the book project, so I said that it was my second one, that the first had been about a trip to Kuwait with my husband, and that this would be an e-book. They seemed rather pleased, and actually a bit interested. They even asked me a few questions about my other published books.

I thanked them and went back to my seat with the form.

It was definitely going in the travelogue.

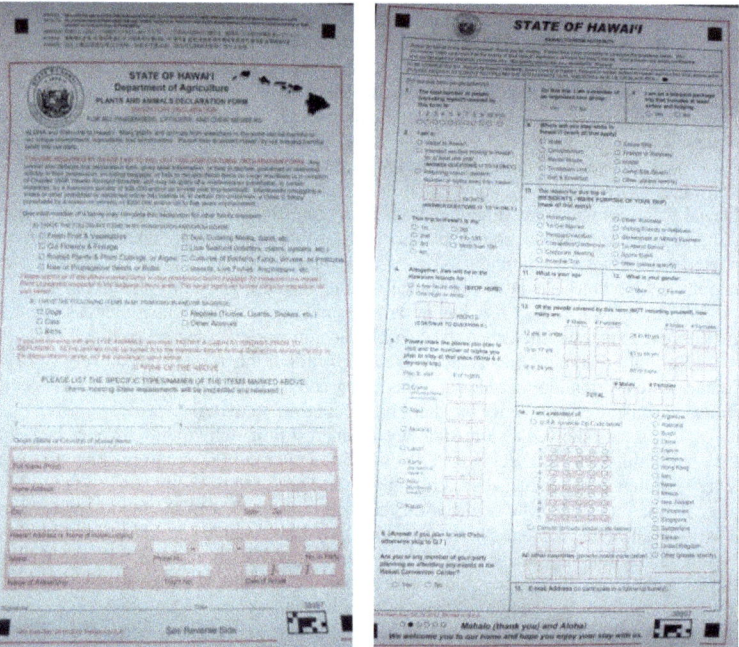

Side One of the State of Hawai'i – Department of Agriculture – Plants and Animals Declaration Form. Notice the words in red just below all that, in block capitals: "MANDATORY DECLARATION." Side Two of the form: State of Hawai'i – Hawai'i Tourism Authority. It said "thank you" over and over again – in Hawai'ian – "Mahalo!" for filling it out, even though it was not optional. And it made it quite clear that everyone had to do it, regardless of how many times they had ever been to Hawai'i for whatever reason, and how many times they might ever come back.

As the plane began its descent, a blond woman to my left began to wake up. She opened her shade. I struck up a conversation with her, and did my best to see out her window. It was still late afternoon, so the sun was still out.

We could see land masses – which ones, though?

Either Mauʻi or Molokaʻi, we thought, though we couldn't see enough to be sure.

The couple was from New Zealand, though the wife had grown up on Oʻahu, because her father was a professor there. It was obvious that the wife missed it.

Why not live there now, I couldn't resist asking?

"He likes living in New Zealand," she said, looking cheerfully resigned to it.

Interesting. David recently assured me that he would not try to settle anywhere that didn't please us both, and that he would arrange things so accordingly as soon as he could. So…we won't be moving to Afghanistan, Iraqi Kurdistan, Iran, or Saudi Arabia. Good.

The former resident of Hawaiʻi and I chatted some more until we landed. I told her that there was a funny loop of her hair sticking up in the back when it became clear that her husband saw it but did not tell her about it.

She thanked me and redid her ponytail, saying that he never points these things out, and she wished he would!

He looked like someone had just woken him up when she said that, but he smiled gamely.

By then it was early evening. No more sunlight…and the lights of Honolulu showed in the windows on both sides of the plane. Pearl Harbor was on the left, where I had been facing the whole time.

We all stared out at it, and prepared to deplane while staying seated.

The plane hit the ground and taxied into the gate.

Aloha and a Lei

The experience of landing at Honolulu International Airport and then walking outside had been hyped to us for as long as we could remember as the balmiest, most delightfully scented breath of fresh air one could ever hope to inhale.

It certainly was the best landing and deplaning I had yet experienced.

We got off the plane and headed for the baggage claim area having completely forgotten about any greeting of "Aloha!" or a lei, but we didn't get very far before we got just that.

A middle-aged man with dark hair and glasses was standing just outside the gate with a sign that said "FOX" and 3 orchid lei. True to form, he said "Aloha" and presented them to us, explaining that he was from the travel agency that AAA had booked our trip through, Pleasant Holidays. That done, he told us which direction the baggage claim area was and went on his way.

We thanked him and headed that way, down one level.

As we rounded the corner to the staircase and elevator, we saw a great sign and paused for some photographs. It was now almost 7 o'clock Hawai'i time. My father looked really tired. We were all eager to find the bags, get the rental car, go to the place we were to stay at, get that over with quickly and have dinner.

Regardless of that agenda, we were happy to have the lei, even though orchids have no scent. They were just new and exciting to us, and we admired how the fishing line was strung carefully through the blossoms with little plastic separators between them.

Even so, my parents gamely paused and posed for a couple of photographs before we went down the escalator to get the luggage, and then my mother shot one of me as well.

I put the camera back into its bag and we went downstairs. The crowd was almost done forming around the baggage claim turntable, and I quickly moved right up to the conveyor belt to watch the stuff emerge from the depths below, up through its center.

My parents caught up and took up a position by a pillar off to my left.

My mother always smiles perfectly for photographs. My father just wanted to get the bags and rental car already!

Here I am, ready to see Hawai'i…as soon as we get settled.

It got a bit monotonous this time because it took a while for our bags to appear, so I began to look around and chat with strangers. Before leaving on this trip, I had supplied myself with a little pile of business cards that had my e-books in small print on the back. This was a good time to see if I could hand any out.

Soon I had met a nice couple who had just returned from the Democratic National Convention, a retired military man and a social worker, not yet retired. She wanted my card! Great – I handed one over.

Funny…our parents raise us not to talk to strangers, but when we grow up, we find that we do a lot of that. How else would we learn anything about anyone else? We just have to be careful how much we tell others about ourselves.

Eventually, our bags appeared and I grabbed them. The fluorescent pink belt was not on my mother's hard, bright blue suitcase again; the TSA agents had put it inside again. I didn't care as long as the bag was there, not lost, and nothing was missing inside it. It was fine.

I noticed a woman in a red Hawaiian dress with a hibiscus pattern on it and commented about how beautiful it was. She was leaning against a pillar a bit away from the baggage area, holding a sign carelessly in her right hand, as if she didn't see any reason to hold it up yet. She heard me and smiled. Something about her smile puzzled me, but I was busy figuring out our next move.

We found someone at a desk near the baggage area and asked her where to go to pick up our rental car. She told us to go outside, in front of the airport, then walk across the main driveway to the parking area and keep going until we found the office, because the rental car counters of the airport closed after 6 o'clock. Great...so this was going to be a bit of a production.

This woman had a pretty Hawaiian blouse on, in purple, also with a hibiscus pattern. When I complimented her, she told me that it was a uniform. Really? So that woman in the red dress... Yes, that was a uniform too. I glanced back at her. She had heard it all before, and she had just heard this exchange. I was the gazillionth tourist to admire a uniform that was actually attractive.

Well what was I supposed to do?! Where I live, uniforms aren't attractive!

We did not rent an airport cart. We just put our smaller carry-on bags on top of the colored ones and took off, outside to the left, and into the balmy Pacific air.

Now we smelled the wonderful warm, fresh breeze that we had heard so much about.

But I should add that I did not smell anything floral. Honolulu International Airport is close to the water and surrounded by the city of Honolulu. Unless a flowering tree of the kind that includes pollen (not all flowers have pollen – orchids don't) is close by, one will just smell air.

Still, the air smelled like the promise of consistently warm and comfortable weather.

That was what we were after.

Connecticut was about to get a lot colder, but we were not going to have to deal with it until we got back. It felt deliciously sneaky.

As we walked off to the left, which would take us to the front entrance of the airport, the man who had given us the lei reappeared. He was just walking that way too. He told us that we were going the right way, don't worry, just keep walking. Everyone else was walking that way too, so we kept going.

Now it was dark, and a sprinkle of steady but light rain had started.

Terrific. We would wander around a strange place and get slightly wet.

Oh well. I left parents in the light and took off across the front driveway into the darkness, looking for the Hertz stand. There it was, back slightly to the right, pitch dark and deserted. Was this what the woman inside the airport had meant? It was outside of the airport, not in!

All around me were parking spaces filled with cars. They were rental cars, with signs indicating what row was what, what section, and so on. There was a wider aisle down the middle of many rows.

Across that was a longer stand, and this one had lights on and a man and a woman working behind the desk. I rolled my stuff over there. More pretty Hawaiian shirts for uniforms – royal blue with bird-of-paradise blooms this time. These people told me that the Hertz place was closed. I would have to go to the Hertz office building. It was beyond all these rows of cars, they explained, one of several similar buildings, and near the middle of the row.

I thanked them and went toward the front driveway to call my parents over at that point. No sense walking too far through the darkness, and they had been able to see me walking around the whole time thus far.

They came across, dragging the rest of the stuff.

It was getting a bit better anyway; already we had seen the airport, and we would be coming back to it in a week. My parents caught up with me (I had come to a complete stop) and we ventured into the darkness, looking for the Hertz building.

Sure enough, it was straight back there. More Hawaiian shirt uniforms…but ugly! Brown and yellow, like the corporation's colors, and the floral pattern looked like nothing that is found in nature. Who cared at that point; the employees were very friendly, and we were soon signing in.

I took out the little folding dark blue canvas thing that held all of our travel papers: tickets, vouchers, you name it. One of the things I had decided to print up before leaving was a piece of paper for each rental car, one for each island, with the reservation bar code and confirmation code on it.

My parents were up at the desk, asking the employees to look us up in the computer, and I came up behind them with the Oʻahu car rental paper. My father looked annoyed by the interruption, but after a few words he caught on and happily took the piece of paper. That sped the process up considerably. The Hertz guy scanned the bar code and had our keys in another minute. I felt pleased with myself.

The car was, alas, back where we had come from, almost all the way back to the deserted booth in the darkness. My father limped after me as I headed back to that area, armed with the parking space number and row number of our car. My mother walked with him.

I found it quickly – a gold-hued Toyota Corolla – and stood next to it, watching my parents walk closer and closer.

We loaded the trunk and happily got in, with me in the front and my mother in the back. I was to navigate until we got where we were going.

My father familiarized himself with the Toyota, started up the windshield wipers, and pulled out of the space. Soon he was driving down the aisle, out to the left, and then right, to H-1. I brought out the sheet of paper with the directions to the hotel, which was on the southwest coast of Oʻahu. We would be driving down the highway until it became a main road.

As we got onto the highway, I took out the small black flashlight that I carry in my handbag and shined it onto the directions. When I began to read them off, my father didn't want that! He thought it would be a while before he needed all that data. Fine, I thought. We are about to take some wrong turns, but let him find that out…

Sure enough, as we neared the resort area, and I saw the first of two signs that read "Ko Olina," he showed no indication that this meant anything to him. Hadn't had reviewed the directions at all?!

"There's a sign for Ko Olina," I said, as we passed it.

"Why would I want to go there?!" my father said, sounding annoyed. He was tired already!

"Because that's our destination!" I replied, exasperated. "You'll have to find a turnoff so that you can double back."

Annoyed with himself now, my father drove another couple of miles before we saw a place to do that. As we neared the signs again, he slowed down and made the exit this time.

It was no ordinary exit.

It was a beautifully landscaped, with a wall of reddish volcanic rock that had been carved out on the right, sloping sharply upward. Bright green grass lined the edges, and colorful flowers in many tropical hues hugged the volcanic rock.

The off-ramp curved around to the left, and we found ourselves at the main gate of the Ko Olina Resort on Oʻahu.

The Ko Olina Beach Villas

We rounded the curve of the Ko Olina exit ramp and found ourselves at the entrance to the resort. There was no map of it, so we didn't know what to expect, how big or small it was, or what part to go to. It was now half past eight at night, and our thoughts were on dinner as well as on finding where to go, getting checked in, and ditching our bags.

A guardhouse was in the median of the entrance, but my father went right on by. I didn't see whether or not anyone was in it. We passed a lot of grass and greenery as I read off the last of the Google Maps instructions, which told us to find Waialiʻi Place. Unfortunately, the sign for that street was a typical small green one with white lettering that I could not see until we were right on top of it, and then too fast to really read it before the car had passed it.

The upshot of this was that we soon found ourselves at the very end of the long main drag of the resort, which I later found out was called Aliʻi Nui Drive. Down High Chief Drive we went until the road simply ended in a curved turnaround. That couldn't be right.

I was concerned that we were losing time now. How were we supposed to get settled and into one of the resort's restaurants before they all closed?! We had passed a couple of huge hotels on the right, so my father turned the car around and pulled in there. I got out and brought the paperwork with me, confident that the staff would be able to tell where we belonged.

As it turned out, we were at the last of the resort hotels in the line, the Marriott's Ko Olina Beach Club on Waipahe Place. Well, both streets did start with "Wai"...but we needed to hurry up and find out where to check in. It wasn't here.

The hotel staff that we saw consisted of only a couple of people in a huge, brightly lit hall with sandy-hued walls and floors, plus an enormous, beautiful, varnished to a high shine outrigger canoe in the front hall. It was a reproduction of a traditional Hawaiian waʻa on display as art. There were also several kahili in glass cases behind the desk.

Looking left as I walked in, flustered and confused, I realized that this was one of at least two buildings, and that I was in an open lobby that looked directly out at the greenery and night to the left, and the front desk to the right. Past a pretty woven carpet and a long, carved wooden table was a wrought iron balcony that overlooked...something.

I didn't really care what it was. I just wanted to be able to go back to the car and say that I knew where we should go next. At the same time, I was sorry not to be able to photograph this gorgeous hall. But, if we weren't going to stay here, I couldn't pause to do that.

A girl in yet another beautiful uniform, a dress with a tropical floral pattern on it that matched the male employee's shirt, looked at my paperwork, and then got out a map of the whole resort. Why hadn't the AAA agent been able to give us one of these?! Oh well...the girl also got out a pen and drew a line to show me where to go to get to the Ko Olina Beach Villas.

The most important thing to know was to take the SECOND left, not the first. The first one would just take us around to the service area of the place we were already at. Great! I thanked her and went back to the car.

My parents were tired, but resigned to the fiasco of figuring out where to go.

Whatever...I got back into the car and we drove down Alii Nui Drive, pausing at the first turn, then going in at the second one. At last – the correct buildings! It was now completely dark, and we were definitely hungry.

We pulled into a circular driveway, and I realized that we were on level ground in this driveway, unlike in the previous one, that the lights were a little bit brighter (or perhaps there were fewer tall trees), and that the place seemed a bit deserted.

The circular driveway during daylight.

My mother got out with me this time to do the check-in.

Inside, we found a very nice clerk who assured us that we still had time for dinner and that we could get settled calmly. My mother went over the paperwork with him and found out that we could leave the bags with him and go to dinner right away. He would be there when we returned.

This clerk, whose name was J----, promised to wheel a cart with all of our things up to our unit for us while we had dinner. He also said that we could go over the rest of the details – keys, room cards, parking space, etc. – when we got back, because he would still be there.

Wow – someone to help us late at night, just when we needed him. Excellent!

But...we had to go to dinner right away, he said. There was only one place that was open until 10 o'clock at this resort, Chuck's Steak & Seafood. He told us not to wait any more, or to worry about the check-in process, plus he gave us sympathy for our confusing night tour.

Soon we were driving off into the darkness again, back where we had just come from.

Dinner...at Chuck's Steakhouse

So...the Lagoon level of Marriott's Ko Olina Beach Club had (of all things that we could have found at home!) a Chuck's Steak & Seafood restaurant in it. It was down a huge staircase at the end of that fabulous but sparsely decorated lobby, then back across the length of the place again, to an area just below the front hall with the huge canoe.

When we pulled up to the porte-cochère again, I got out, approached the outdoor podium (this place had every convenience, it seemed!), and asked about valet parking. No problem, my father could just get out and leave the car for them to deal with, the hotel people said.

He did it, taking his camera bag out of the trunk first.

Our awkwardly out-of-sync paces resumed as I walked on ahead to figure out how far my father would have to walk while my mother walked in between us, calling back to my father what I relayed to her as he complained that I was going too fast for him.

There was an elevator, but my father went down the stairs, annoyed and wanting to just get to the restaurant before it closed while the elevator moved between floors. The situation wasn't that urgent, but I didn't point that out.

We were the only customers in the restaurant, which was dimly lit and partially outdoors, under a very tall lanai. That is, the roof that overhung the patio we sat on was two stories up, and the back of the resort really was open to the elements – no glass.

Here we were, I thought, having flown all the way to Hawai'i only to find the sort of restaurant that we tended to avoid at home. I hate steak, and this wasn't a food adventure by reputation.

But...I refused to just assume that this would be so in Hawai'i.

Perhaps a quick perusal of the menu and a recitation of the specials by the waitperson would reveal otherwise. We only had a week on O'ahu and five days on the Big Island, so I was determined to not to eat the way that I did in Connecticut in any restaurant. That just seemed silly; I was here for new culinary experiences, among other things.

The host told us we could sit anywhere we wanted since we were the only customers, so we chose a table right next to the edge of the patio. It overlooked the koi pool, which was a beautiful, winding, curve-bordered one that wrapped around the back of the building.

Several large koi in hues of bright orange, yellow, and white were swimming off to the back right. Beautiful tropical plants, the names of which I had yet to learn, grew around the manicured lawn that bordered the other side.

We sat down. I chose a spot by the water so I could watch the fish.

The waiter came over to us and handed out the menus, and gestured to the salad bar, which was in a dimly lit room through a doorway to my right. Oh yay...ranch dressing and iceberg lettuce, I thought, but said nothing.

We looked through the menus and he came back to rattle off the specials.

Good news – there was something called ono, an indigenous Hawaiian fish whose name means delicious, with baked purple sweet potatoes. I could have had that with huge steak fries, ordinary mashed potatoes, or rice pilaf, but all that sounded like a pronounced turnoff.

I ordered the ono and purple potato dinner, and we all got the salad bar. My mother chose some fish dish that she could have had in Connecticut, and my father ordered a steak...probably to compensate for the vegetarian entrapment of the evening before, I guessed.

My mother looked at me as I perked up at the promise of a Hawaiian meal, and I looked at her, wondering why she didn't want one, but we just got up and headed for the salad bar. That was just like some mundane array at home, but I filled up a plate with fresh, raw vegetables, and found some baby spinach, thus avoiding the big bowl of iceberg junk (90% water, 10% nutrition, 0% taste).

That Hawaiian dinner was delicious. The fish was cooked in a butter sauce, and the potatoes tasted different and great. They were soft, too.

We didn't care about dessert after that. It was time to get into our unit and see it.

Back to the Beach Villas

Back at the Beach Villas, J--- was waiting for us, smiling and welcoming. Yes, our bags were in the unit on a cart, which the staff could get the next day. Here was the wi-fi code, here was a map of the parking garage, and here were our keys. The keys were not really keys. They were cards to be kept because they identified our unit as being in the building closest to the beach (there were 2 of them), and the cards were on a key chain with a small gray object.

The gray object was a little plastic thing, perhaps two inches long, with a tiny light bulb on the tip, which curved and tapered to a thin edge. This was the most important part of the "key" because we had to hold it up to everything – doors, elevator controls, pool gates, and the parking garage box – to enter. A lost one would cost us $100. We didn't lose them.

We got back into the car – I was still in the front seat, since there was one more thing to navigate – and showed my father the map of the parking garage. We had an assigned space! It was down on the second level, under our building. So that was why the place looked so picture perfect and idyllic – no parking garage above ground, and no parking lot – just buildings, pools, and flawlessly manicured grounds.

My father held the gray key up to the parking gate. The bulb on the gate flashed red. "No, the other way," I said, "so that the light bulb is in front of the gate's light bulb." He tried again and the bulb turned bright green, and the gate's arm went up.

Down the concrete ramp we went, into the garage itself and to the end, then around the corner, down the other side of the aisle, and then we saw another ramp that curved sharply downward. My father went down it, and came out on an identical level. Our assigned space was towards the back on the right. He pulled into it.

My father's facial expressions don't change much unless he is surprised, furious, or amused. Without a doubt, he was relieved to be finished driving with the thought of bed and sleep imminent, but he made no comment. I knew all this, so I made no comment either.

Across the level was a glass door with wood-paneled walls and carpeting behind it.

Next to our rental car were two luxury vehicles that appeared to have been parked there long-term. The one farther away was a Porche, and it was utterly filthy. Several times during our stay, I thought of writing "WASH ME" or "Also available in gray" in the sheen of filth, but I would then have had to go upstairs with a dirty finger, trying not to get any in my pocket or on my cloth handbag. The one closer to us had a specially fitted cover and was plugged into a charger that stretched from an outlet on the wall. It was a Mercedes coupe with a convertible top.

Late in the week, the Mercedes coupe was revived by its owner, who also owned one of the Beach Villa units. He was a very friendly guy who told us that he hadn't been on the Islands for over a year, which explained why his attempt to jump-start the car with a battery that he hooked up failed. You can't leave a car just sitting that long and expect it to work. We saw him later that day and he said he had it towed to the dealer.

After we were alone again, my father told us that the entire computer system would probably have to be reset, and that it would be expensive. Before that, he and the guy talked a little about Mercedes. My father has always driven Mercedes cars, but they have always been the practical, C-Class or other least expensive models, and always sedans. Sedans have 4 doors, which is more useful as a family car.

But back to the night of our arrival.

We trudged across the parking garage, figured out that the gray key had to be held up to everything – door to the elevators, the elevator controls both inside and out, and finally our unit door, and did so.

The décor of the halls was attractive every which way we looked, with wall-to-wall carpeting, wood panels on the lower halves, wooden trunks, and handmade oars or carved wooden rectangles that depicted plant life on the walls.

Our Unit

We got out and quickly found our unit, because it was the first one on the left as we came out of the elevator, on the sixth floor (our building had eight floors). A tall, dark wooden door with a brass handle worked after my mother held the key chain up to it.

Wow...

The place had been expertly laid out by a high-end designer. The kitchen was outfitted per the instructions of Master Chef Roy Yamaguchi. I didn't know anything about him, but I know that there are usually only 50 master chefs on the entire planet at one time. They qualify for that title after taking a four-day, $11,000 test that consists of preparing full-course gourmet meals for a panel of judges. It probably costs a lot more than that now though, because that figure dates from the mid-1990s, when I toured the Culinary Institute of America.

Our luggage was on a large hotel cart, as promised, so we relaxed. I grabbed the bags and started putting them in the rooms, something that the hotel employees would have had to guess at in order to choose the correct rooms. Then I took out my camera and immediately photographed the entire unit before we could unpack or move anything. I wanted to be able to show it as the staff had prepared it for us later.

My mother seemed to notice what I was up to, and she didn't shut herself up in the bathroom while I did this. My father, however, got ready for bed as I was finishing up by simply stripping down to his undershorts and shirt, so tired that he wasn't paying attention to what room was his. Just as I was coming out to photograph the kitchen and living room, he emerged from my bathroom, and I laughed and said he belonged on the other side of the unit. Off he went, bemused, and flopped on his bed to sleepily watch my mother unpack a few items.

I was getting tired – it was eleven o'clock – but I wasn't exhausted. My mother talked about breakfast the next morning, and I wanted to go with them. There was nothing to eat here; we had to go grocery shopping. That happened late the next afternoon.

But back to the images I gathered of our unit.

This is the dining area, seen from a spot in the living room, just behind the tall chairs at the kitchen island. The lanai was behind me.

The living room, as we found it that night, with the television on. We could not figure out how to operate the entertainment system right away, nor could we do much with the ones in the bedrooms, either.

The next day, we got the hang of using the television. Hawaiian election ads were on, and they were mostly for the race for a Senate seat between Linda Lingle the Republican vs. Mazie Hirono the Democrat, a thing that we would never had learned had we not heard it ad nauseum ad infinitum during our stay here. Hirono won.

The kitchen was fun to use when we started to do that the next evening. The fixtures really were ideal, all stainless steel, with a microwave oven that pulled out like a drawer from the counter near the sliding glass doors. I had never seen one like that before. The dishwasher had two levels, which ran independently. One held more stuff than the other – it was probably a water-and-energy saving design.

A quick tour of tools and bowls and pans revealed equipment that might have been bought at a Williams-Sonoma. The place lacked for nothing; cooking here was going to be easy! There was salt and pepper and olive oil already; we could get whatever else we needed tomorrow. The oven and stove were easy enough to figure out, with a black glass stovetop, just like ours at home. The fridge had long double doors, and there was bottled water inside. We put our lei in a shelf in the refrigerator door.

Fridge, toaster, stove with tea kettle over the oven, coffee maker, and drawer-style microwave oven.

The island in the kitchen had three chairs and a sink, and a view out the sliding glass doors.

    The clerk had told us that there was a grocery store nearby, a Foodland, but we ended up shopping at a Shaw's one highway exit away from the resort. I had fun choosing fresh fish such as moonfish, salmon, and scallops over the course of the week. There were also more purple potatoes for sale, and ice creams in tropical flavors that were hard to find at home. And…we found Kona coffee there! The first bag we chose wasn't spectacular; I explained to my mother that it was cheaper than the others. We tried another that was a bit higher up the price scale – good enough.

    The bedrooms were a lot like the online photo gallery I had previewed before coming here, as were the bathrooms, but seeing it in person felt different. Now I saw how it all fit together, and I admired the deep bathtubs. Maybe my father could soak his hip in one! No…a moment later, I realized that he could get in, but getting out would be a problem. But, the place had a hot tub and a swimming pool, to be seen later on.

Paddles over my parents' bed. The curtains hid another sliding glass door, but they just used the one in the living room and kitchen area. The lanai was just a narrow balcony area here.

Note the wooden slatted "window" to the right: the bathtub is behind it. The doorway goes through my parents' suite to the closet and shower stall at the end, with the bathroom to the right, behind this wall.
Here it is, the bathtub behind the wooden slats, just as advertised online.

My parents' bathroom. I'm in the photo, taking the picture in the mirror.

This is the shower stall in my parents' suite. Every day, the maid came into our unit and folded the smaller towels in an elaborate fan shape, and then tucked them into a washcloth.

My room. I slept by the window, and covered the glowing clock numbers with a book.

The television in my room was tuned in to the same tale of Ko Olina as the others. A Hawaiian woman was being interviewed in part of a continuously repeating show, saying that her aunt had always wanted a resort hotel to be here. Interesting... so a Hawaiian owner had allowed the land to be developed of her own free will, it claimed.

My bathroom sink area. Every day, the maid brought more papaya-scented shampoo, conditioner, bath gel, and lotion, plus a small bar of papaya face soap, and a larger bar of mango honey bath soap. It smelled wonderful.

This thick, luxurious terry robe was hanging just like this when we arrived. It was so warm that I never took it off the hanger. I just put on my nightgown after each bath and admired it. It felt too thick for comfort, in my opinion. The laundry closet was just outside my bathroom. I saw it whenever I exited my room. To its right was the living and dining area.

My work done for the night, I took my bath and shower, then went into my room to settle in. Plug in the Nook reader, the phone, the camera battery (couldn't risk being stopped from photography by a lack of energy!), set up the clothes, get the travel guides ready, lay out the maps...and whatever else came to mind.

That, and set the alarm clock I had brought (I prefer my own, familiar, tiny folding battery-powered one) for eight o'clock. Breakfast was one of my favorite meals. Dinner was the other. Lunch...well, I wouldn't miss sandwiches if I never saw another one. And here I was on one of what Captain Cook had tried to name the Sandwich Islands...hah!

I inspected the windows in my room. They were halfway up the high walls, with beautiful wooden borders, and they opened by falling toward me, still attached at the bottom. The curtains stopped them. Perhaps I would have figured out more ways to manipulate these huge, heavy panes if the curtains hadn't been so thick and heavy, but I was glad to have the help in propping the panes. It would keep the sunlight out until I wanted to let it in.

But with that window open, I could enjoy the warm breezes. The air smelled different here. It smelled like...tropics, ocean, warmth, and perhaps flowers.

I went to sleep smelling it.

Swimming in the Honu Lagoon

On Thursday afternoon, after touring the underwater curiosities off Waikiki Beach, lunching there, and then driving around Honolulu and a few suburbs, we wanted to goof off and quit driving around for a while.

It was the perfect time to try out that fabulous human-made lagoon next to the Beach Villas.

Each lagoon was constructed with the same design, and can be seen on Google Maps from above. A near-perfect circle is surrounded by beach sands on most of its circumference. The remaining portion, which is bordered by the Pacific Ocean, has a barrier made of black pumice – volcanic rock. The pumice stones are boulders, piled high in four sections so that three openings allow the ocean to wash in and out, keeping the lagoons clean.

The view of the lagoon from our unit, with the footpath to it.

We could see the Honu Lagoon out our lanai by just walking onto it and looking left.

We had admired it each day, and it would have been ridiculous not to put on our bathing suits and go out to it. There was no lifeguard, and we are not athletes, but what could possibly go wrong? Well, something, but nothing that we couldn't cope with.

Out we went, ready to enjoy a tropical resort beach in the Pacific Ocean.

This was the stuff of movies, travel guides, travel articles in newspapers, television shows, and whatever other medium came to mind. We brought towels and my camera, and set off.

The manicured lawn and gardens below, and the footpath to the lagoon. Gardeners were out there every morning at daybreak, using fairly low-decibel trimmers on the lawn and edges of the gardens.

This view shows the four reefs of black pumice boulders.

The beach was exactly as we could have dreamed, complete with straw umbrellas and not crowded at all. There were families and couples walking and swimming, but mostly not swimming. We put our stuff down under the nearest umbrella, I shot several photographs, and then hid the camera under my mother's wrap. Time to test the waters.

This was the lovely scene that greeted us when we walked out onto the lagoon's beach.

My mother had walked in up to her knees, lost interest in swimming, and headed for the umbrella. This came as no surprise; she likes to sit and gaze at the beach far more than swim. My father and I went farther than that, however. He flopped down into the water, sitting down up to his waist. He looked like he was enjoying the water, as he had many times before, so I left him to it, and walked off to the left.

It was difficult to move!

That was the unexpected part of the experience. I thought, "Wow, this is serious exercise. But I need the exercise, what with my sedentary career, so I will stick with it." I sloshed in a straight line across to the last bit of sand by the leftmost pumice barrier, going in up to my hips.

When I got there, I looked back. My parents were both out of the water, sitting under the umbrella. I turned back to the pumice rocks and carefully climbed to the top to look out at the ocean. The rocks were porous, which came as no surprise (I had a geoscience course in college), black with some vague tones of dark purple or bronze, and the pores felt sharp. That's why I moved carefully. I didn't want to skid on these rocks and get cut up.

A young couple was up on the top of the rocks, staring out at the ocean. If they could get up there, so could I. I didn't talk to them. Usually, I talk to strangers and ask them questions, but I was determined to keep my balance. I made it to the top, keeping low to the stones, almost in a crouch, and looked over. The sun was going to set in an hour, it seemed. I climbed back down.

Now I decided that I might as well swim across to the other side of the lagoon.

Without much thought as to how that would feel to an out-of-shape woman in a place where just slosh-walking across had felt, I walked into the water up to my neck. It wasn't cold, but it wasn't warm. I started swimming immediately to warm up, and it only took a minute to do that.

Next came the surprise. I got a quarter of the way across and had to tread water for a rest, and then kick on my back to keep going. I wanted to go to one of the openings in the pumice barriers and look out, but now I was suspicious of my ability to actually stay inside the lagoon, so kept to the right side of the right-most opening.

This was where I swam. It was beautiful, and worth it, but one should not underestimate the strength of water currents.

Time to swim back; I started across to the point where I had started. My parents were there, watching me move. It didn't seem that far. I chatted with some people who had been at the rightmost stones after swimming a quarter of the way back, needing to pause and tread water again. They did not know that it was illegal to possess a piece of pumice and take it home, out of Hawaii. They were tourists, here for fun, like the rest of the guests.

Disgusted with myself for being so out of shape, I began to think about rejoining the health club near my home in Connecticut when I got back. David and I had belonged to it during our engagement and for the first six months of our marriage, until we had left the area. I missed it, and now I was convinced that it was the only solution for weight loss. It's not like I ate huge quantities of food, or a lot of junk.

I continued to swim toward my parents, determined to get this over with and not to forget how this felt – the exercise, the difficulty, and the annoyance at myself for the difficulty. Two more pauses to tread water were necessary.

The undertow of the current was at work, and I could feel the water coursing in and out through the pumice boulders, but it didn't have to be this difficult. I could get stronger. But later...after I was home. It was too late to devote my time to this here. I had to see more of the museums and gardens of O'ahu!

At last I was across, and my feet touched the bottom. I walked out of the water, up the sand, and over to my parents. My mother had picked up our towels.

She told me that my father had been unable to get up out of the water due to the undertow and his bad hip. But some guy we didn't know had walked up to them as she tugged at my father, trying to get him up, and proudly said, "I just completed my EMT training!" He and my mother both pulled my father up.

By the time I was out of the water, the EMT was long gone.

We looked around a bit more at the beach, since there was no desperate hurry to leave.

We walked up to the benches along the stone wall above the beach and my mother and I paused there to talk to some strangers. They were from Tennessee, and enjoying their stay. My father had immediately started walking back to our unit, since he moved so slowly.

When we left, the sun was still shining, but we had dinner reservations for Roy's Hawaiian Fusion restaurant at the golf club, and we wanted to dress up. We all made it back in plenty of time to take showers and do that, and my father looked terrific in his Hawaiian shirt. I had bought in online for his birthday, from the Paradise Clothing Company. He liked it; it was dark blue with red-and-blue and blue-and-yellow macaws, and palm fronds.

A Walk Around the Beach Villas

My parents have a knack for finding out about the real estate costs involved in just about any piece of property. They find it interesting, and my father had spent part of his career in real estate, combining it with his planning and zoning expertise.

They soon informed me that the Ko Olina Beach Villas were built in the late 1990s and early 2000s, and that each unit had cost around $800,000 when it was new. But due to the all-important consideration of location, buying one now, used or not, cost even more. This place was prime real estate, and my research into Hawaiian history backed that up.

Just for fun, while writing this, I looked up the resort on Wikipedia. It's there. I don't want to quote anything from an encyclopedia site, but the entry has some interesting facts, and an aerial photograph of three of the lagoons. Suffice it to say that the resort now enables its paying guests to enjoy the beach and property on a level that Kamehameha the Great and Queen Kaʻahumanu were able to whenever they stayed there.

No wonder this place was so expensive.

This is what we saw when we walked out of our building and toward the front lobby. The curving driveway is visible here, too.

On Saturday, I walked all around the Beach Villas with my camera, and then left to explore other areas of the resort (separate chapter for that). I had an ulterior motive for doing this: I wanted to be free of the camera on Sunday, when my mother and I would go swimming in something that she called an infinity pool. The next day, she explained what that meant: the slate border of the pool slants downward into the water, so that the water continually laps like waves at the edge. It's pretty.

The point of going all around the Beach Villas with my camera was to document a walking tour of the place. It was fun, and I got to meet a local girl who was working at the front desk and ask her about her life. She lived not very far from the resort, in some of the inexpensive homes that we had seen off the highway just one exit away. She had two cats, a brother, and a father. I had been wondering where all the people who were employed at the resort lived, and how far their commute was, and this provided some insight about that.

She was working in the pavilion, the central structure of the Beach Villas. It had potted silk orchids, beautiful wooden carvings in the wall panels, and water coolers with fresh-cut fruit in them. There was a seating area with little statues of Hawaiian women, and rest rooms were around the corner to the right, on the path to the back gardens and koi pond...and the curving swimming pool.

The Beach Villas included two large buildings, and the one that faced Aliʻi Nui Drive was taller than the one closer to the Honu Lagoon. That made sense; the people in the upper floors might be able to see the beach from their windows. I wondered whether or not the real estate agents had had a tougher time marketing the units in that taller building.

This plumeria tree was in full bloom. The taller of the Beach Villas towers over the back yard.

The infinity pool was behind the taller building, with lounge chairs and a hot tub, and a room full of exercise equipment was visible through the blinds of the ground floor windows. The koi pond, was a long, winding, curving place that meandered all over the back yard between the swimming pools, and it had a natural, dirt floor, so it wasn't a pool. Flowering trees and shrubs grew all around it, and water lilies sprouted right out of the water.

There were little footbridges over the koi pond, and I followed it to the infinity pool, which was fenced off. I took out the little gray key to let myself in, walked through the area snapping photographs, and back out of there. Everything around me was a thing of beauty, and flawlessly maintained.

These koi were bigger than our cat, I couldn't help thinking, and he's a large cat. The koi pond was more like a winding canal around the back.

After I had seen it, I was even more enthusiastic about going for a swim in the infinity pool.

Water lilies and lily pads; the blossoms grew straight up out of the water.

The most interesting aspect of this swimming pool was not the water lapping lightly at the edges. It was the fact that on either side, one could sit in lounge chairs that were actually inside the pool. I had never seen a pool with this design. People were sunbathing in those chairs, and I imagined how that must be: slather oneself with sunscreen, lie down for a while, get overheated, roll off and splash in the water without really swimming, and then get back in the chair. Nice.

The gate to the infinity pool had a beautiful bronze circle on it, plus a sign demanding quiet inside. No screaming, shrieking children allowed – which sounded great to me. I love it quiet. And this is the hot tub – not an infinity design, but great to sit in.

This is what I saw just inside that gate. The windows with the exercise equipment are at the back. Note the part of the pool that is to the distant left; it is a very shallow area for partially submerged lounge chairs.

After seeing the infinity pool, I went back through the koi area, over the bridges and through the paths, and into the gate with the other swimming pool. This one was behind our building. It had a cookout grill next to it, more areas with partially submerged lounge chairs, and a kiddie area with gray gravel.

The next day, when my mother and I went in this pool, we noticed that the water was warmer in this one than in the infinity pool, and that the gravel kept getting washed into it. It was fun to swim (actually, we walked through the still water) all around the pool. The hot tub for this pool was taped off, out of order.

The winding swimming pool.

Outdoor grilling was an option for guests.

The lounge chairs were shaped like leaves, and made of dark, woven wicker.

Out beyond the winding swimming pool was a small, rough (if anything here deserved to be called that) pavilion. It looked like a place to eat a self-cooked barbeque dinner with a private party of any size. A guy was reading a book in a lounge chair next to it.

This part of the path goes between the lagoon beach and the back of the Beach Villas, where the winding, curving swimming pool is. Our building is up to the left. The pavilion where at the edge of the winding pool is at left.

With my self-guided walking tour of the Beach Villas complete, it was time to leave for the other areas of the resort that I wanted to see. I went back through the koi pond to the lobby, and out the main driveway, where I found more to photograph.

There were flowers everywhere I looked, and I wanted to get close to them all: spider lilies, bird-of-paradise, plumeria, hibiscus, all in full bloom. Some of them smelled amazing, and others lacked pollen and so had no scent. I paused by the door to our building at a plumeria tree and pulled a branch down for whiff. It was wonderful! Maybe I could find some plumeria perfume.

This is a white spider lily, though I hadn't memorized this fact when I shot the image.

The plumeria tree that I paused to sniff was off to the left. This is the view as I walked out of the Beach Villas, with the Disney Aulani resort hotel across the vacant lot. A bird-of-paradise in bloom along the wall outside the Beach Villas on Waiali'i Place.

That was great, but there were more things I wanted to do with my independent day to explore, so I walked up the street to the main drive, and off to see the next place on my list, and the next, and to use my camera. I took so many photographs that I had to use the spare battery.

Swimming in the Infinity Pool

Sunday morning at the infinity pool was a relaxing experience, despite the fact that I was preoccupied with wondering how I would manage to persuade my father to take me to the Bernice Pauahi Bishop Museum in Honolulu, plus have enough time to go through it.

We met people in the hot tub, which was where everyone slowed down enough to chat. They were from western Canada, from Toronto to Vancouver, and from the western contiguous United States. It was interesting to observe that people from the western half of North America plan their beach vacations with a view westward, while on the East Coast and a ways inland, we do just the opposite, thinking of Florida, Georgia, and South Carolina, or the Caribbean Islands.

The family from Canada included little kids and a grandmother as well as the parents. We briefly spoke with some other people to find out where they were from, with my mother and me doing all of that. My father had arrived ahead of us, and was on his own, basking alternately in the hot tub and the infinity pool and back again. He had found a great way to relax and feel good.

My mother and I went back and forth once, enjoying both the hot tub and the infinity pool, and then left my father to enjoy the place. We wanted to know what it was like to swim in both pools, so we headed for the winding swimming pool. The people in it were reading and swimming, and some little kids were shoveling in the gray gravel kiddie pool. No one was grilling anything, even though lunchtime wasn't far off. The place was quiet, even with people in every curve.

It was the best swim ever!

Lanai Views and Fabulous Sunsets

My father used his camera a lot without even going anywhere.

He loves to photograph sunsets and beautiful skies, and all he had to do to get those images was go out onto our lanai each evening. Since we ate dinner in the unit most evenings, he had ample opportunities to do this.

As for myself, I wanted to show my friends and others what we saw from that lanai.

I shot photographs of the views straight down on the right and off the front, then more of the views straight into the distance, which showed two of the other hotels in the resort, and the lagoon.

Here is my father, sitting at the dining table, calling out photograph advice to me. This brightly lit image gives a good view of the room, and of the counter seating area, where we ate breakfast every day.

This was the view straight down from the right side of our lanai. The concrete ramp that went down into the underground garage is in the lower left.

My father took advantage of the fact that I was constantly within earshot and using my camera to call out advice on how best to use the camera, the memory card of which was running out of space. But no problem – I had another one! My mother had packed hers, but had no interest in shooting pictures. Why bother when my father and I had it covered?

This is the lanai facing the lagoon...

...and facing the Waiʻanae Mountains.

It was nice out there on the lanai, and the weather was absolutely perfect and beautiful every single day. I had done it – planned our visit to Hawaii outside of the hurricane season. My parents were very pleased with this place, though the credit must go to our AAA travel agent. She had visited this place personally on a business trip, just to scope it out, so she knew where she was sending us.

My father shot this image at dawn. It shows Aulani at right and the J.W. Marriott Ilihani Resort & Spa at left.

This view shows the building and parking lot between the Beach Villas and Aulani. My mother heard that it was for private events, including weddings.

My parents like this image of the sun setting over the Honu Lagoon, and my mother adopted it as her desktop computer wallpaper when we got home. It's one of my father's photographs.

My father shot this image too, and it's my favorite sunset photograph at Ko Olina.

Ko Olina was the perfect place to stay. It was quiet, not crowded, not polluted by smog or ambient light, it was full of friendly people, and everywhere we looked was more beauty. With all of its modern amenities, it provides the illusion of being Hawaiian royalty…even though the aliʻi of the past did not have running water, electricity, air conditioning, or fast access to anywhere else on Oʻahu that they wished to visit. We had all that and more.

The Ko Olina Resort

We could not have asked for a better place to stay than the Ko Olina Resort on O'ahu.

After we had settled in, I found out that Ko Olina means "to be filled with happiness," which seemed an ideal name for such a pleasant place. It was absolutely perfect – beautiful every which way we looked, comfortable, new, imaginatively decorated in a way that celebrated Hawaiian history and culture – and we enjoyed every day that we spent there.

It was mostly complete, with four hotels built, each next to its own lagoon: 1. The northernmost one, and to the right on the map below, was the J.W. Marriott Ilihani Ko Olina Resort & Spa. 2. The next one was the most interesting; it was Aulani, a Disney Resort & Spa. Both of these places included access to Lagoon 1, Kohola, which means humpback whale. 3. After that was the place where we stayed, the Ko Olina Beach Villas, at Lagoon 2, Honu, which means sea turtle. 4. Marriott's Ko Olina Beach Club was last, with access to Lagoon 3, Nai'a, which means dolphin, and Lagoon 4, Ulua, which is a Hawaiian fish that was used in ancient ceremonies.

The Ko Olina Marina is just around the southwestern tip of O'ahu, a short walk across from Ulua. In addition to all that is the Ko Olina Golf Club and three condominium developments, all upscale and beautiful.

We did not go into each and every restaurant, or even every hotel or spa, but we saw and tried a lot of it. We had great gourmet food at two of the restaurants, and I took lots of photographs.

I shall describe each part of the place in the order that we experienced it.

The 'Ama'Ama Restaurant

The morning after we arrived at Ko Olina, we had no groceries, which was understandable. We would take care of that in the late afternoon. Eating out was inevitable upon arrival and for breakfast the next morning, and we had accepted that, but any more breakfasts out just seemed like a disgrace. Accordingly, we decided to make the most of this one!

We got up and out of the Beach Villa by nine-thirty, and drove over to the hotel next door, a Disney resort called Aulani. That hotel had 2 restaurants. One was a buffet, called Makahiki, but it wasn't open for breakfast that day, a Tuesday. The 'Olelo Room was a bar and lounge, and Off the Hook was a poolside bar and grill, so those were out. We were going to eat at 'Ama'Ama, which is a mullet fish mentioned in many Hawaiian songs.

When we got to the top of the Aulani driveway, we found ourselves under a huge porte-cochère with valets who were eager to park the car for us. When my father realized how far away the garage was, he accepted the offer and we all got out.

When we stepped out of the car, we found ourselves facing the front door of Aulani. To either side of us were places to wait for valet service, complete with fruit-filled water coolers (orange and pineapple, to name some). Straight ahead was the front hall and lobby.

In we went, curious to see what promised to be a beautiful, upscale, imaginatively decorated resort. We were not disappointed. I couldn't stare around and photograph enough of it, but since my father was limping behind us, I decided to come back another day with my camera.

My mother and I crossed to the back terrace while he caught up to us, then doubled back to the left hallway when he did. Down that hallway was a gift shop, rest rooms, and a staircase that led to Makahiki and outside. We went that way, and followed a curving walkway to the left.

At the very end of it, we saw the entrance to 'Ama'Ama.

We continued on inside, and saw a pretty bouquet of what I would learn – later in the week – was anthuriums. I had seen these before in pictures, but now that I was in Hawai'i, they were everywhere I looked.

Part of the appeal of this place was the opportunity to just look around, and my parents didn't mind the photography. This was part of my agenda, and my mother started pointing out all sorts of things that she thought I should get a shot of. The first thing that caught our attention was the koi pool that faced the lagoon. The pool itself was a modern, rectangular one with a large half-shell on the edge near the desk that Venus would have looked good in, except that it was upright.

The koi themselves were very interesting because I had only ever seen white and orange ones before. These koi were blue, turquoise, and those familiar colors. As for my father, he laughed when he was the upper pool of water, just above that pool, because after all of the money spent on upscale, modern décor, it had a rough-looking water faucet. It looked like something that one would attach a garden hose to on a house.

We were led to our table after the photography, just to the right of this koi pond. It was all outdoor seating under a long lanai. The waitress uniforms were beautiful periwinkle blue dresses, which was fun to see. More attractive uniforms to distract me, I mused. We settled into our seats and ordered breakfast.

This is what we saw on the other side of the dining lanai, across the koi pool. Notice the beautiful waitress uniform.

Here are my parents seated in the other area, a large square-shaped section.

This is what we saw when we looked up – fishing nets. The place had a fish theme due to the fact that it was named was a Hawaiian mullet.

This lace-collared pigeon walked around the ledge next to our table for quite a while. Part of what I hoped to see in Hawai'i was the flora and fauna, and I was getting my wish on our first morning there. The menu.

Kona coffee in a French press, with milk and sugar. It was delicious, and cost $9.50, so when my mother ordered a second pot, I was surprised. We could have had cheaper coffee, but drinking Kona coffee was part of our collective agenda. Why go all the way to Hawai'i and skip this?! Our waitress requested that I leave her face out of my travelogue, so I have cropped it out. I think that was about privacy vs. publicity, because she was beautiful.

My father ordered Crab Eggs Benedict. It looked nice. My mother ordered a rather heavy and familiar thing for breakfast: an omelet with fruit. I don't know why.

I had crèpes with granola, fresh cream, and several types of fruit, including star fruit, pineapple, banana, raspberry, blackberry, and strawberry. It was light but filling, and delicious. Champagne orange juice – my mother's idea. She and I each drank one... but I would have been just as happy with the fresh-squeezed orange juice.

My mother took this photograph of me while we were eating at 'Ama'Ama, and I like it. I'm in pink, smiling, and my hair has a few waves and curls. It's difficult to find images of ourselves that we actually like, so I might as well have this one in the travelogue.

We left 'Ama'Ama feeling gastronomically sated and thrilled, and drove off to Honolulu to explore and get the lay of the Island.

Walking Around the Resort

All week, as my father purposefully drove us out of the Beach Villas, down Ali'i Nui Drive and out of the resort to whatever activity was planned for the day, I stared around at the beauty of the place, longing to photograph and document it.

But there was no time for that until Saturday, when my parents decided to go out driving together so that my father could explore the coastal side of the Waiʻanae Mountains, which ran just north of the resort and up the western side of Oʻahu. I had been on the drive between the Waianae and Koolau Mountains, up the middle of the island, so I didn't go.

This was my big chance to go off on my own all day and do whatever I wanted on my own schedule. I was going to see at least half of the resort grounds this way. The place was just too big to visit the whole thing in one day, so I let that idea go. There were places that I really wanted to photograph, and that was all there was to that. If I missed any, so be it.

Out the door I went, pausing in the front lobby of the Beach Villas to chat with the girl who was on duty at the desk for a while, and then around to the back with the camera. From there, I headed out front and turned right, walking up Waialiʻi Place to Aliʻi Nui Drive. As I did so, I got some beautiful photographs of bird-of-paradise flowers, which I had only ever seen before in florist shops.

As I paused at the corner, I suddenly noticed something that I had not been able to scrutinize from the car: the waterfall and sign for the Beach Villas. It's amazing how much one can miss just by sitting in a moving vehicle, with one's thoughts focused on what's ahead rather than on what is behind. This was a beautiful piece of landscaping.

But enough of that; I kept moving, and crossed half of the street to the median. The median was a large, grassy area with leafy trees every fifty feet or so (don't hold me to that measurement, though – I am not one of those people who is adept at looking at a distance and rattling off how great or small it is).

When I got to the median, there was more to see – the signage. I wasn't moving past at thirty miles an hour, or whatever the posted speed was. I was walking, so now the lagoon sign for our street stood out to me. Its image resembled an ancient Hawaiian petroglyph of a sea turtle.

I paused to look around some more. The trees were beautiful, with umbrella-like spreads of branches overhead. As I stood in the shade of one of them, I plotted my course: down a ways, across the rest of Ali'i Nui Drive to see the golf club and look around, then down some more, across Ali'i Nui Drive again, and back to Aulani, where I would spend the rest of the day. I had brought my Nook reader with me, and I might sit and read for a while, or just check my e-mail.

With that decided, I followed the next sign, which was positioned between the two locations.

On Thursday evening, after swimming in the Honu Lagoon, we had eaten at Roy's Hawaiian Fusion Restaurant, which was in the golf club. But it was dark, and my photograph of the front door hadn't come out very well. I would go back for a retake, plus see the golf club.

Roy's Hawaiian Fusion Restaurant

Roy's Hawaiian Fusion is one of several upscale restaurants around the United States owned by this graduate of the Culinary Institute of American, a.k.a. the Other C.I.A. I have toured that campus, which is in Hyde Park, New York, and talked to some of its recent graduates. Part of the program, if the student desires it, is business school. Clearly, Roy had availed himself both of that aspect of the curriculum there and of substantial venture capital.

We had fun getting dressed up in our Hawaiian shirts and eating in a fancy restaurant, but my father was getting tired, and his hip bothered him a lot. My mother had persuaded him to pull up to the porte-cochère of the golf club and get out, and to let her park. I saw him walk almost all of the way to the door of Roy's, then doubled back and into the dim parking lot to get her.

The front door of the restaurant was a lot easier to photograph in broad daylight.

Here we are, dressed in our Hawaiian shirts, ready to indulge in what we hoped would be authentic Hawaiian recipes. Instead, true to its name, the Hawaiian was fused with just about every other cuisine.

Appetizer trio: Mongolian Ribs, Seared Ahi Tuna with Sesame and Wasabi Sauce, and Chicken Wontons.

Lobster Crab Bisque – my father's choice of appetizer. I gave him the Mongolian ribs from mine, and tried a spoonful of his bisque. It was delicious.

My father had the Mongolian ribs for his entrée. It came with broccoli rabe.

My mother and I both got the mahimahi with asparagus and lobster sauce over purple sweet potatoes.

My father got the Macadamia Nut Tart with Caramel Sauce for dessert. My mother and I had a bite too – delicious!

The other option was a Chocolate Lava Cake with Raspberry Coulis and Macadamia Nut Ice Cream. The only Hawaiian things about it were the lava and nut aspects, but it seemed silly to each get the same dessert.

This brief view of the place in the dark persuaded me to go back for another look.

The Ko Olina Golf Club

The Ko Olina Golf Club was worth taking a quick look at during daylight. I found a large map posted out front, which appears at the beginning of this chapter, plus I saw the place while everything was open. There was a shop that had been closed the night we ate at Roy's, and of the course the golfers had all left. Now I saw the place functioning as a business.

This is the sign out front, meant to catch the attention of passing drivers. I saw it when I walked out of there.

The porte-cochère in daylight. There is no valet parking, which makes sense at a golf club. If you can't walk, you can't use the golf course.

When I got to the top of the curving driveway, I noticed the large map of the resort, and something else: a small bronze statue of a girl golfer. She was a girl, not a woman, and she had earned herself some fame in the sport. Her name was Michelle Wie, and she was born in Hawaii, the only child of South Korean immigrants. She qualified in 1999 at age 10 for the L.P.G.A., the youngest player yet to do so. I enjoyed this story because golf is an acronym for "gentlemen-only-ladies-forbidden" and yet one of us had made a success the Scottish sport.

The plaque reads: The Legend of the Ladybug – "Legend says that if a ladybug lands on your shoulder, sweet talk her to your finger and with a gentle breath, send her off. Lady Luck will lead you to the cup." Statue inspired by Hawaii's own, Michelle Wie, LGPA Tour.

The golf shop during the day. Inside were vastly overpriced and luxurious tropical shirts and golf attire, hats, stuffed plush animals, other toys, all manner of golf paraphernalia and equipment, and golfers and retailers. This ball cost me 3 dollars, a silly extravagance, but it was fun to have a souvenir of the resort. These balls, which depict a ladybug and a hibiscus blossom, also came in royal blue and red. Or, if one were actually planning to play golf on the course, there were plain white ones, with tiny logos that had nothing to do with the resort – balls that you wouldn't mind hitting hard and fast with an iron.

Golf courses are nothing remarkable to me. I grew up right next to one. My father happened to build the house that he designed right next to a golf course, so there were always plain white balls on our property. Once, I even found one clear on the other side of the house from the golf course – propelled by a very bad golfer, my father had remarked.

I imagined that wealthy businesspeople came to this golf course to wheel and deal with hitting balls around the greens, and that wealthy other people came just for fun, with no such pressure. The whole place looked over-the-top-expensive to me, along with the rest of the resort. If I had that much disposable income (as my husband calls wealth), this would not be my first choice for its use. But so what – I was just satisfying my curiosity, and whatever I wrote about this place would be free and positive publicity for Ko Olina.

It was a lovely place to golf, but I prefer miniature golf. At least one can see each hole in its entirety up close, plus there is the fun of negotiating an obstacle course and admiring the creativity of the establishment. I'm with Mark Twain about this sport: "Golf is a good walk spoiled." I don't want to slow down and stop to hit the ball – I want to keep walking, fast!

The Aulani Disney Resort Hotel

Time for the main attraction of my walking tour: the Aulani Disney Resort Hotel. I remembered all that I had seen of it earlier in the week, and now I would spend a few hours there, enjoying the décor, the pool area, and whatever grounds I could see up close and at my own pace.

Already, I knew that this would qualify as a place to visit together in the future, for a vacation. It too looked very expensive, but it was just a fantasy at this point, and you never know – if the fantasy came true, I wouldn't want to be like a frog in a flashlight beam, wondering what to do next.

I crossed Ali'i Nui Drive and started walking up the curving driveway.

The first items of interest on the driveway were these 3 ki'i statues, obviously not authentic, but intricately carved and worthy of notice nonetheless. There was nothing to read about them, so I don't know whether or not koa wood was used to make them. Koa is an indigenous Hawaiian wood, but there are others.

Continuing on up the sloping and curving driveway, I passed a waterfall. It was nice, but the photographs I shot looked blurred when I checked later. Around the corner was a view that showed the gap between the two wings of Aulani, and then I was looking up at the porte-cochère through the trees again.

I walked all the way up to the valet area and paused for a drink of orange water from one of the coolers. The valets were all friendly smiling guys in tropical shirts (the Aulani uniform) who seemed to expect visitors from around the resort to explore the hotel. They nodded and smiled as I passed, and didn't ask me any questions.

That worked for me. I walked into the front hall and started shooting photographs, and most of them came out well. Soon I had the collection I had wanted all week, with fish pools, waterfalls, paintings, murals, carvings, museum displays, and the like.

This display of kahili was inside to the right, and there was another on the left. Unlike a museum, there was no explanation of kahili, nor did I find any at other Hawaiian artifact displays around Aulani. If I had not studied Hawaiian life and culture, I would have had no definite idea what I was seeing, which would have disappointed me.

Long murals that depicted ancient Hawaiian life and culture wrapped around the upper walls of the front hall. This area shows an aliʻi couple standing in traditional clothing (feather cape and helmet on the man, and a purple paʻu on the woman). All around them are Hawaiian people at work, building a hale, hunting a boar, harvesting taro, crafting tools and instruments out of gourds, and so on.

On either side of the front hall were more carved wooden images, but they looked like culturally inaccurate kiʻi to me. Maybe they were, maybe they weren't, but they were beautifully made, so I snapped away with the camera.

There was a lot to see and photograph everywhere I looked. The front desk was off to the right, with a collection of artwork boards in a rainbow of color on the wall behind it. Straight ahead was the terrace that overlooked the back yard and kiddie pool, a winding pirate fantasy. To the left was the shop, the rest rooms, and the way outside to that pool area. I was headed there.

No one else was stopping to stare at or photograph this beautiful place. The guests were used to the luxury, or perhaps they had already spent some time admiring all this upon arrival. Or not…I am used to being the only one to pause and spend so much time on this. There was that, and the fact that the purpose of my visit was to enhance the travelogue and then relax, not only to sit down and relax.

These carvings graced the arches of the left and right hallways: sea life, left, and flora and fauna, right.

To the right, the mural at the end of the hallway depicted Hawaiian men hard at work fishing. To the left, the mural at the end of the hallway depicted Hawaiian women in a canoe.

Before going down that hallway, I went straight through to the lanai/terrace. From there, I could see both wings of Aulani, and the winding, pirate-motif kiddie pool with the lagoon off in the distance. Looking either way out on the lanai, I saw chairs that faced the view, and more koi ponds by the doorway.

After admiring the view, I turned around and went back in, and down the left hallway. Bypassing the gift shop for now, I headed for the rest rooms. Rest rooms signs in other lands are always fun to compare, and these were no exception.

Kane means man. Wahine means woman. The words don't change when plural.

Now back to the shop – with no worries over forgetting to photograph the bathroom signs.

The Aulani shop was a work of art. The floor had a wooden inlay border of flip-flops. The rest of the shop was just attractively decorated in the style of the resort, so I won't describe it further. Tee shirts and other tropical shirts were the main offering, but there were also knick-knacks, Disney-themed framed art, mugs, travel guides (including one just like the Frommer's guide I had brought, but at least I wasn't carrying it), bathing suits, and a coffee bar.

Here is the wooden inlay of flip-flops. The coffee bar is at the back, to the right inside the shop. These two sales clerks were very friendly. When I told them that I was photographing the place for a travelogue, they wanted to pose for a picture! And they wanted it in the book, so here it is. They even took my business card, saying that they wanted to look up all of my books, which was gratifying.

While I was in there, I chatted with the two women who worked there, looked around, and then bought a tee shirt for David and a cup of coffee for myself. I was getting ready to sit down and relax. Relaxing while on vacation…what a concept. Everyone else all around me seemed to have this down pat, but not me. I kept finding work to assign myself!

But I didn't care – this work was fun, and I could relax with the books at home later.

This wall art shows Hawaiian men working with a fishing net. It was on the wall near the rest rooms, at the end of the hallway on the left. At that end, there was another hallway that stretched into the left wing of Aulani.

Around the corner from the gift shop, I paused at the top of the stairs to get a photograph of the living wall art over the wooden staircase. It was an assortment of potted orchids, white and pink ones. I wondered how the staff took care of them. Orchids thrive on water droplets that must be misted onto their leaves, and these were quite high up the wall.

There was an elevator, which we had used after eating breakfast here on Tuesday, but I wanted to admire the place, so I ignored it. If I went back out this way later, I could use it, but if not, it didn't matter.

Out I went, past Makahiki and into the pool area, to the left, following the curving walk.

Hawaiians make (yes – present tense, because they haven't stopped) drums and hula props out of gourds. I do not know what the hula dancers use the gourds for, only that they carry them as props while dancing. My guess is that since hula dance tells a story, the gourds figure into the tales.

It was a shame that the museum displays on the left side of the walkway didn't have any signs to explain what they were about, but then the staff would have had to worry about water damage. It rains frequently in Hawai'i, in short showers or sprinkles. I wondered whether or not these displays were dismantled and taken inside during the rainy season.

This display is about Hawaiian cloth making. There are kapa sticks laid out in front, for beating tree bark until it is soft and perfectly flat. The tools to the right are for the colors and designs, and the beautiful finished product hangs on a stand at the back.

This dramatic view shows the wa'a (canoe) motif of Aulani.

The kiddie pirate pool was well stocked with yellow inner tubes, and it was shallow. Lifeguards were on duty by the tunnel and waterfall.

At this point, I made up my mind to sit down and concentrate on relaxing. I turned right when I saw the path branch away to the pirate kiddie pool, found a cluster of lounge chairs with little tables and a small trash bin, and sat down.

It was absolutely perfect here, and I was on my own schedule, free to loll for a couple of hours. I sipped the Kona coffee with milk and took out my Nook reader and cell phone. Might as well clear both of all voice mails, check my e-mail, and see if I could read something that was totally recreational.

What a silly fantasy!

There was a message from Fatemeh on each device: she needed an edit!

So...she had lasted precisely one week without my help.

There was more than one way to look at this: 1. Damnit, I had to do work; and 2. She was making me feel useful and appreciated. I decided to go with the second one, and called her back. It was a letter, and it looked important.

But that's all of the information about what the edit was that I will volunteer.

She answered right away, apologized for looking for me in Hawaii, and explained why she needed my help now and not when I was back from the vacation.

No problem, I said, but remember, I just have this Nook reader, so I can't manipulate any of the text that I get on the e-mails. I even tried forwarding the message so that I could try to edit the text in it, but all I could manipulate there was the reply section.

As I got the end of the pool area, I found this Mickey-Mouse-shaped pool for adults with the J.W. Marriott Ilihani Ko Olina Resort & Spa overlooking it in the distance.

No choice: I would have to talk Fatemeh through the whole edit.

Once she understood the problem, she opened the file on her laptop and proceeded. At first, she stopped me to ask why this and why that correction, but I soon put a stop to that. "I'm in the tropics here," I explained, "and darkness comes on fast. I can either talk you through this, or teach you English, but not both, because soon my mother will expect me to go back. We might even have to stop this and resume hours after that."

Okay – she let me talk her through it and we picked up speed.

But about two-thirds of the way through, my cell phone beeped with an interruption, and I looked to see who it was. Surprise – it was my mother...and the sun was setting. Time to go.

Fatemeh and I signed off with plans to resume later, and I got up and tossed my empty cup in the trash. It was getting darker, and I watched it do so as I walked, intrigued by the rate of speed of a tropical sunset, heading for the lagoon. It just seemed easier to go back this way, plus it would enable me to see more of the place on the way out of it.

Just pausing for these photographs ate up a significant amount of daylight, to the extent that the nightlights all came on and I had to stop and check the results on the camera's viewscreen before moving on. I wanted to make sure that I wasn't wasting the effort, and there were people everywhere, so I felt perfectly safe.

Of course, it would be terrible for business if I didn't feel safe.

An upscale resort in Hawai'i needed to be able to pretty much guarantee safety as well as fun. But that thought had no effect on my mother, who called me as I proceeded out, chatting with me about how she had been there earlier in the day and seen a destination wedding party, most likely from Japan, and a chapel, when she was walking by the Aulani lagoon.

As I hurried past, I noticed that this Hawaiian man was giving a demonstration by the fire. He blew into his huge conch shell, and stood by the fire pit explaining something that tempted me to stay, but I didn't.

I passed the destination wedding party at the lagoon. It seemed to consist of a fairly small group, including the bride, the groom, the parents, and the bridal party, and perhaps a few more relatives from their extended families. Looking up to the left, I saw a small white chapel with a blue roof that wasn't visible from our unit at the Beach Villas. It was the Chapel of Joy.

Keeping to the areas with lots of people and open spaces, I walked past the destination wedding party from Japan, past the chapel, and around and up to the wide open and vacant lot that stretched between Aulani and the Beach Villas. I talked to my mother on the cell phone as I walked, telling her that she ought to be able to see me by now if she looked out from our lanai.

The side walls of Aulani up close. The art on these panels show a Hawaiian man fishing and a canoe with a sail.

She didn't see me, but continued to fret over the fact that darkness was falling and I was outside by myself. This is the woman who taught me how to move about in the world safely. She must have done it correctly, because I walked quickly and was soon back in our building, up the elevator, and through the door of our unit.

And there was plenty of time to cook a lovely dinner for my parents!

We had scallops that I cooked in a butter-lime sauce with a little bit of salt and pepper, plus leftover creamed spinach and cheddar mashed potatoes that my mother had insisted on getting, with a salad first and a selection of mango, coconut, and macadamia nut ice creams last.

Hours later – poor Fatemeh! – I was free to call her back and talk her through the rest of that edit. She had waited for me, and we finished up her letter. Now we both knew the drill for future situations such as this one. Even on vacation, with only a Nook reader, I could edit.

By design, I would not be weighed down with edits, or so I had thought.

Instead, I was figuratively but not literally weighed down!

Black Swans and White Egrets

All week, one spot in particular at Ko Olina had both entranced and eluded me. It was too far to walk there in terms of time management, but I had to get there for the photographs, so I kept asking my father to stop on the way out, while the sun was shining.

At last, on Friday morning, he agreed to pause and let me get the images.

The spot was just inside the front gate, before the guard house, and it was on the right, so I had thought that my father would see no difficulty in this. I was wrong; he chose to part in the median, where the pavement had a turnaround, so that he would not have to pull over and park in traffic. Never mind that it was 2 lanes each way…

I got out and walked across the street to the right, then looked back at the entrance to the upscale condominiums on the other side: Kai Lani. It was a gated community, and the gates were part of the reason for this stop, but the best vantage point for the photo-op was on the other side, at a distance.

All week, my mother and I had admired these honu-motif gates, and so we were happy to get this shot.

That done, I turned around to the main purpose of the stop: a pond with a waterfall and beautiful black swans that lived there. There was plenty of greenery, all manicured to the nines of course, with other birds as well. There were small white ones, egrets, perhaps, and maybe a night tern. At least, it looked like another one of the birds we had seen the night we arrived at the resort, the one that sat at the edge of the pool, hunting koi. Maybe it was staying up late.

There were many birds all over the left side of the pond, in among the small green plants there. The plants looked like flowering ones that had already grown and shed their blossoms. This was the image that I came for: a gorgeous black swan. It didn't honk at me, it didn't run at me – it just stood there and let me get the photograph. I kept telling it how beautiful I thought it was and that I wanted its photograph, because that seemed like a wise move. Whether or not it understood a word that I said is a mystery, but I got the shot!

Swans can be nasty, so I approached the area with caution, but not trepidation. No sense in being afraid without being given a reason for that, and if I allowed myself to worry too much, I didn't see how I could expect to get any good photographs. After all, how did the National Geographic photographers ever accomplish anything if they didn't go out with a positive attitude? And yet they all had what they went out for.

I stood there taking several photographs of the waterfall and swans since this was my one chance to do so. As I did so, my mother called and called to me not to get too close to the swans. When I was finished, I returned calmly to the car and pointed out the zoom function on the camera, which meant that I didn't have to get too close for comfort. And I reassured her that the swans were probably used to people, to being admired and photographed, and that I had talked to the one I was closest to, and asked it for what I wanted.

She rolled her eyes, and my father drove off toward Honolulu.

Daddy's Fantasy – Avoiding H-1's Heavy Traffic

My father is a city and regional planner who has worked with traffic engineers.

He knows every back road in the state of Connecticut, plus most back roads in the other New England states, and many in New York, Pennsylvania, and down the eastern coast of the contiguous United States.

Hence, he viewed the roads of Oʻahu as a puzzle to be memorized, navigated, and solved.

Alas, it was not so simple.

H-1, the interstate (my father emphasized that this is a classification of road, and that it applies despite the lack of amphibious transportation to another state from Hawaiʻi!) highway of Oʻahu, was not only the main road across southern Oʻahu, it was the ONLY one that went all of the way across. H-1 was thus the only option for getting from our hotel to Honolulu, so my father's usual M.O. of memorizing and utilizing every back road in the vicinity was useless.

Added to that condition was yet another problem: H-1 was made cheaply, out of concrete, rather than by being paved with asphalt. (Fortunately, the other roads we traveled on while visiting Oahu were paved with asphalt.)

My father assured me that there is a direct correlation between the use of concrete in road construction and vehicle crashes. He explained that it is a much rougher ride going at high speeds on concrete than on asphalt, and with that, he was off, lecturing about the topic until his familiar litany (I grew up hearing it and know it well) was complete.

The result is an unpleasant one for the rider. Instead of a smooth trek across the southern end of the island, the rider gets shaken steadily for the entire time. If she has been rushed out after a breakfast that includes such customary items as orange juice and coffee with milk, the stuff can be counted upon to cycle all of the way through to its painful resting place while the traffic crawls along with no rest room in sight.

Add to that the fact that, like any other place with a resident population that must commute to and from work in the mornings and evenings, Oʻahu's main highway tended to be filled to the limit with slow-moving vehicles for much of the time that we used it. It didn't matter why this was so – accidents, road work, whatever – the end result simply never varied.

I expected this, and figured that our best bet was to wait until shortly after 9 a.m. before departing for Honolulu, which was where many of the things that we intended to see were located. As for the return trip, well, there would be no pressure to get home on time, so why worry about that?

Not my father. He was absolutely determined to find the way out of what he saw as a maze of heavy traffic. He intended to find the clearest path through the whole mess and efficiently drive through it, arriving exactly on time for everything, even though we only had one set appointment all week, and I had scheduled it for late morning so as not to be in a rush.

This was a vacation, after all.

But my father saw a way to make it a high-pressure trek every day, lecturing us about the value and virtue of highway planning. Yes, he had planned part of a highway (I-95) in North Carolina during the Vietnam War, and spent his tour of duty doing so, and yes, it had been built to his specifications, complete with on-and-off-ramps that curved at the beginnings and endings and straightened out to long runways as they connected with the highway.

That's lovely, but he hadn't designed this one, and the deed was done. H-1 sucked.

It was like my father was a rat in a maze and the traffic engineer kept moving the exit or blocking it off from time to time just to see how aggravated it made him. My mother and I were captives along for the ride, but we mutinied when the car at last escaped from the maze only to enter the next one – the streets of Honolulu – and he wanted to continue on until he solved that puzzle also. Take us to a bathroom NOW, we insisted, not after you figure out how to get from the exit to the historic site or whatever it is that we are headed to.

Unhappily, not wanting to feel stupid for not having figured out the route yet, and not pleased to have to cede control over the pattern of movement and schedule, my father was forced to stop what he was doing and pull into a grocery store parking lot.

Oddly, once that was dealt with, his passengers were comfortable and willing to resume the adventure of looking for a place that none of us had visited before.

But this is the fun of travel: not knowing every bit of the route while venturing out armed with maps and directions, willing to risk one-way streets causing re-routings and missed turns causing circuitous routes to be taken.

I don't see why one ought to be upset over any of it. Getting there will happen, the event will be attended, the tour will be taken, and besides, as my husband's cousin, an advertisement writer for the Cunard cruise line said, getting there is half the fun.

evertheless, whenever I think of those traffic engineers that my father worked with later in his planning career, I have a fit of laughter over an incident he recounts now and then: At a party, a co-worker of his was asked what she did for a living. When she replied that she was a traffic engineer, the questioner exclaimed, "Oh! So you design those traffic jams!"

We drove through a traffic jam every day that we went anywhere near Honolulu.

Ala Moana Center and Na Hoku

Fantasies be damned, we had to drive around Oʻahu and get used to the place so that we wouldn't feel too lost and confused. What better way to test oneself in an unfamiliar venue than to go out driving with a map, on a routine errand?

Freshly fueled by our fabulous Aulani breakfast at the ʻAmaʻAma restaurant, we took off.

I had rummaged around my maps and travel guides and come up with a AAA map of Hawaiʻi that folded out into a huge rectangle and back again, and my father had pronounced us "in business". We were ready to explore. (Obviously, we had not bothered with a computerized GPS system, declining to pay extra for that when a map would suffice. One can just as easily miss a turn with an added expense in the rental car as without!)

The AAA map of Oʻahu was just a part of the whole thing, but there were several insets devoted to segments of Honolulu that were very helpful. One of them zoomed in on the area we were aiming for: Ala Moana Boulevard, which runs along the shore east of Pearl Harbor. Along Ala Moana Boulevard was the largest shopping mall on the Island. It was probably the largest on any of the Islands, for that matter.

It may sound a bit odd that after all that studying, book buying, outlining, and writing the beginnings of my own book about Hawaiʻi, that I wanted to go to a mall. Well, I wanted to get that out of the way. I tend to do all of the smaller parts of a job first so that I can focus on the main part of it, and tooling around a mall seemed like a small detail.

There was that, and the fact that I wanted to buy some really nice earrings there.

To save time, I had chosen them online and then called the store and reserved them.

How strange of me, I thought. My mother just found it highly amusing and said so.

Another reason for going to the mall was that my mother loves to shop, so I thought she would enjoy this. Some of the stores in this mall, which seemed to have absolutely everything one's heart could possibly desire in the way of franchise and department stores, were not the ones that she could find locally at home.

This is what we saw on the way to the third and top level of the Ala Moana Mall. Open air and plants...what did this place do when the weather wasn't nice? Although there was a canopy, there were many spaces open to the sky.

After meandering down the Ala Moana Boulevard heading east, we finally saw the mall. It was a little confusing to identify because it looked like a parking garage. That's what it was, too – a parking garage with a mall inside it.

As we got closer to it, signs for anchor stores and other famous brand names showed on the outside of the huge, sprawling building. It was surrounded by a thoroughly developed urban area, which might account for our confusion. We are suburban people who expect to see malls with wide open spaces around them, pretty landscaping, and parking lots as well as garages.

But my father the city planner caught on right away and turned left when he saw the entrance to the ground level of the parking garage. It was well lit and it went on and on. On the edges of the garage, well away from the entrance to the mall but still inside the garage and under shade, I saw people who might have been homeless.

Later in the day, when we shopped at a Shaw's grocery store, we saw a homeless couple who looked to be in their late teens outside, with a cute little kitten. And that was it; just two sightings. Hawai'i's government seemed to have succeeded in its effort to conceal it homeless from the tourists.

My mother declared that we would go to Na Hoku first, the jewelry store that I was going to buy the earrings from. It was on the second level, on one of the walkways that branched off from the mall's central balconies. My father went to sit in the food court and wait.

I had discovered Na Hoku nine years earlier, when my husband was writing grants in Washington, D.C. and I walked through the Tyson's Corner Mall in McLean, Virginia. But, the idea of buying Hawaiian earrings without having traveled to Hawai'i just seemed like an irrational extravagance. It seemed better to wait until I was actually going there, when it would mean more and make more sense.

Na Hoku means "the stars" in Hawaiian, and the company that was founded in 1924. Its products include yellow, white, and rose gold shaped in the forms of all sorts of flowers that are indigenous to Hawai'i, plus flip-flops, dolphins, turtles, and waves. I wanted some yellow gold plumeria earrings.

This is the top level of the mall, on one of the walkways that branches off from the balconies that overlook the center court.

    I don't like cheap junk that might fall apart, especially when it's earrings. I want to be secure in the knowledge that the back pieces are reliable, so that I won't lose my earrings. I'm very particular and specific, and would rather have a few really nice things than a lot of junk that I don't trust. Craft fairs are fun, but I don't want to shop in them for earrings.

This is the store we visited. My mother liked the wave designs; I liked the floral ones.

    The sales lady was very nice, with long, red hair and bangs pulled back in a barrette, and wire-rimmed glasses. She remembered me from our phone conversation the week before, when I called the shop from home. She brought out the earrings, cleaned them in alcohol, and sold them to me. As I observed her, I wondered about the Hawaiian word "haole" and its definition. Was it "white person"? Was it "foreigner"? I wasn't about to ask her then and there, but put it on my list of things to learn on this trip.

The sales associate chatted with us a bit more after the transaction, telling us that men often asked her to help them figure out what sort of earrings to buy for their wives or girlfriends. She always asks how large or small their earlobes are, and then show them pieces that would look good on the women in question. That was entertaining to hear.

After we left that store, we walked around to look at the mall. As we had walked into the mall and ridden up the escalators, we had seen several shops scattered randomly about that offered sarongs, shirts, skirts, and dresses in Hawaiian floral patterns. We found a few in the upper levels, but didn't buy anything.

This curving koi pool was in the hallway on the second level. The fish weren't as big as the ones at Ko Olina, but they were big.

Next, we looked in a Neiman Marcus anchor store on the top level of the mall, trying out some perfumes at one counter, and wandering through the overpriced purse area. The stuff was wasted on me; I just don't see the appeal of a name-brand bag that snaps shut in the top center, leaving the rest of the top open to pickpockets. And I think they're ugly...

But it was fun to walk through and smell the perfumes.

This is where were stood to look down and watch the hula performance.

We came out of there and heard loud music and singing, so we went over to the balcony and looked down. A man in a tropical shirt with a microphone was singing and emceeing a hula performance. It had several acts before it was finished.

The costumes were beautiful, of course, with one woman (another singer) in a long muumuu among the dancers in grass skirts and lei. All of the dancers wore yellow feather lei over their hair, but from this distance, it was impossible to know whether or not they were really feathers. I only know that ancient Hawaiians wore feather ones.

The photographs I took of the performance showed more than the view from the top balcony. That is, the zoom function made it easy to see a lot more detail later on. The emcee wore a beautiful lei of green leaves and white flowers, possibly plumeria. He stood in front of hula dance props: polished gourds, a conch shell, and 'uli'uli. These are gourds with feather fans in red and yellow, which were the favored colors of the ali'i, from the i'iwi and 'o'o birds.

People had crowded all around every balcony to watch the performance. But when it ended, they abruptly dispersed, and suddenly the stage was deserted. My mother and I decided to go find my father and see what he was doing.

We found him down on the ground level in the food court as expected. He had just finished a smoothie. He wasn't at all perturbed to hear that we wanted to look around some more (not a new experience for him!), and he liked my new earrings.

I was wearing what I thought was a summer shirt, but it was hot and uncomfortable. Strange…a cotton shirt, light pink, with a scoop neckline…that ought to be perfectly comfortable! But it wasn't in a hot, humid, tropical climate. The shirt was actually too thick for comfort, and I wanted to find something else to wear.

The emcee, leading and hosting the performance. A male hula dancer in bright blue shorts with a lei of orange flowers. No malo wrap for this guy, but I don't blame him. He was on a raised stage, and shorts are just more…reliable for staying put and keeping him covered.

We walked around several stores, even going into one full of Hawaiian dresses, but I couldn't find any with pockets that fit, so we left. Finally, we ended up in Sears, way down at the end of the parking garage. To get there, we had to go outside and pass several other shops, some of which we paused to look in. I found a couple of light-weight shirts there, one with pink plumeria flowers and a lavender-hued hibiscus on another.

The pink one ended up being my favorite for touring for most of the rest of the trip.

At last we had seen enough, and were ready to head back to the resort, by way of a grocery store. My father drove us through Honolulu, looking around briefly, then off down H-1 again. We stocked up on fruits, vegetables, coffee, juice, milk, cereals, and fish. My mother didn't want to cook, she said. "I will cook!" I promised, and did.

Visiting the Dead at the USS *Arizona* Memorial

A trip to Hawai'i would seem incomplete without a visit to the USS *Arizona* Memorial.

It would also seem terribly rude not to visit the people who died on it.

We went to see the Memorial and the remains of the USS *Arizona* on Wednesday, October 17, 2012, our second full day on O'ahu. It was a hot, bright, somewhat humid and beautiful day. Leaving after breakfast, we drove down H-1, then got off the highway at Exit 13/1A. Next, we headed for Route 99, also known as Kamehameha Highway... and promptly got lost.

Getting to the entrance of the Pearl Harbor Visitor Center is confusing to people who have never been there before. We did what we were supposed to do: we brought our fold-out map from AAA. We checked the website on my Nook Color reader. We went right after breakfast, as my father still lived in the hope that this would enable us to avoid the heavy H-1 traffic.

Despite being armed with our map and research, we got confused by the multiple over and underpasses that surround the Aloha Stadium, and headed west instead of east. Kamehameha Highway is a long road with heavy commercial development that runs along the East Loch of Pearl Harbor. We saw strip malls, diners, shops, mini-malls, and all of the sorts of businesses that one would expect to see in just about any other state, except for the fact that some advertised pineapple and guava and coconut flavors, and the street signs had Hawaiian names.

I spotted a Starbucks on the right and my father pulled up to it. Out I got, happy at the thought of imminent comfort, and plotting silently to ask for help. Once I had availed myself of the rest room, I went up to the man behind the back counter, who was busily handing out lattes and frappes and cappuccinos, and said, "We're lost. Can you help us?"

He was happy to help with directions. We had turned the wrong way, and he said to go back out, turn left onto Kamehameha Highway, and ignore the signs for Route 78 or the stadium or H-1, staying with Route 99 the whole time. The route would curve southeast, and soon we would see the place on our right.

Great! I thanked him and got back into the car, where I told my parents that I had asked for directions. For some reason, this came as a surprise to them, but they were glad to get the directions. We were on a slight hill, so my father turned onto the down-sloping side street to get back onto Kamehameha Highway.

My father took the task of finding everything as quickly and efficiently as possible as evidence of his intelligence and logical reasoning skills. I think he was being absurdly hard on himself. So did my mother. All we wanted of him was a ride to the place, and part of the adventure was finding it, even if it didn't go smoothly.

My parents were still adjusting to pronouncing Hawaiian names, and I had fun trying to get them to say them correctly, hoping that I was doing it right myself. KaMAYhaMAYha came a bit slowly to them. Before we had gotten off of H-1, my father had teased me by pronouncing Princess Likelike's name like the word "like" twice. BAD Daddy. He laughed, but stopped doing that. Then he got serious as he tried to find our destination.

We were aiming for Arizona Memorial Drive, which is a right turn off Kamehameha Highway going southeast. A very helpful sign came into view confirming that we had in fact found it. The sign is navy blue with white lettering, and lists all of the attractions under the heading Pearl Harbor Historic Sites: USS *Arizona* Memorial; USS *Bowfin*; Battleship *Missouri*; USS *Oklahoma* Memorial; and the Pacific Aviation Museum.

We went into that entrance, which is a tree-lined, oval driveway, then turned right onto Arizona Memorial Place, which runs perpendicular to the drive. Once on it, we were heading north, looking at parking lots on our left, with grass lawns and the visitor center buildings, and the harbor beyond all that.

Pearl Harbor Historic Sites – maintained and run by the National Park Service.

Still, he was soon scoping out the best parking spot.

The entrance to Pearl Harbor Historic Sites. Admission to the grounds is free.

He found one in the next lot over from the one up front. We noticed that there are parking spots reserved for survivors of the attack, and there were cars in them.

We all got out, and suddenly felt how hot, humid, and incredibly sunny it was there.

It was only 10 o'clock in the morning, but it compared to a hot afternoon in early August in Connecticut. I loved it. So did my mother, but she was already dreaming of shade, swimming pools, and air-conditioning. As for my father, he was walking slowly, limping behind us after getting his professional-grade camera in its bag from the trunk.

We tried to move as slowly as possible while not spending too much time in the direct, hot sunlight and while not moving fast enough to annoy my father, who couldn't go faster.

After we reached the front walk, I took out my camera and shot some photographs, taking advantage of the disparity in our speeds to get the images I wanted. There were some great placards that explained what there was to see here:

The truth of the matter is that admission is free only to the USS Arizona Memorial, and to the grounds. The other sites have admission fees, and the Pacific Aviation Museum is across a bridge on Ford Island.

After a few minutes, my father caught up, and we figured out that going in would not be a simple proposition. For security reasons, we could only bring in wallets and cameras. That left my father waiting while my mother and I got rid of our bags.

We were not comfortable leaving them in the car. As a result, we elected to pay a fee – just a few bucks – at the baggage storage area. We got in line, and adjusted our handbags enough to fit my mother's into mine, and thus pay just one fee. I put my wallet into one of the deep pockets in my linen shorts, and suddenly felt very glad to have gone shopping for a lighter-weight shirt the day before.

Back out by the entrance, we met my father and headed for the main gate.

At the main gate, we were each given a ticket to the USS *Arizona* Memorial, and told that the next tour would start at noon. Actually, we ended up starting at 11 a.m., but even with that departure schedule, we had plenty of time to look around and plan.

We went in and found ourselves among lots of other tourists, coming out from under the shaded entrance and into a cement courtyard that was so bright that my camera disappointed me. On the cement just inside was a huge, round map of the Pacific Ocean with details of the military situation there during World War II.

Immediately ahead, facing the entrance, were booths where tickets to the other memorials could be purchased, but we had just come to see the *Arizona*, and for the grounds.

One of our tickets.

To the left of the entrance, with two doors close on either side of the corner of the building, was the bookstore. I wanted to learn the history of this place – the entire history – and I do that by reading. My mother saw me take one hungry look at it and told me to wait, not to get stuck carrying a lot of heavy stuff during the tour.

A couple of minutes later she changed her mind.

A survivor of the attack and an author were both sitting at tables in front of the door at the back, giving autographs. And they were leaving in a couple of minutes, so we had to shop now, or be sorry later.

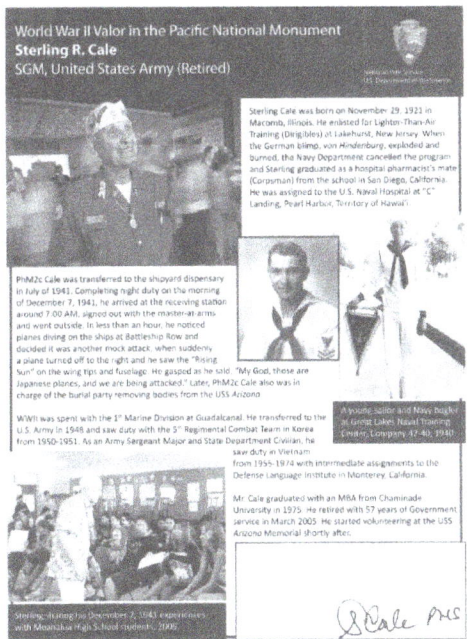

Sterling R. Cale's autographed biography sheet.

The survivor was a 90-year-old veteran of the U.S. Army, Sergeant Major Sterling R. Cale. He started volunteering at the USS *Arizona* Memorial shortly after retiring from Government service in 2005, and he was – no surprise! – tired and ready to go home for the day. The National Park Service, which handles the tours and maintains the grounds, had prepared a one-page data sheet with photographs on Cale, which he had autographed, and he gave us one.

We can't really claim to have met him. There was no time to talk to him, and we weren't willing to cause the slightest delay to an elderly, tired, friendly war veteran.

As for the author, Allan Seiden had other things on his agenda for the day, too. He has written several books about Hawai'i, and not just about Pearl Harbor, so this came as no surprise either. He told us he was about to pack up, and autographed a copy of his *Pearl Harbor – From Fishponds to Warships: An Illustrated History* for me. It wasn't something I could be certain to acquire through Barnes & Noble or Amazon, and I could forget about having it autographed if I didn't buy it then and there.

The sales lady gave me a free shopping bag with the purchase, one of those good ones with cloth handles made out of recycled materials. It had scenes of the historic site all over it in pretty shades of blue. We didn't have to pay anyone to store this, as it was bought inside the checkpoints.

Later, after dinner, I got that book out and started to read it. Just to clarify, I really do mean started – it was only half-read by the time we left O'ahu. I finished reading it at home, when I was at my leisure to organize and scrutinize all of the study materials I had acquired on the trip.

The Natural History of Pearl Harbor

There are three large bays – or lagoons – on the southern side of O'ahu that are actually a submerged river delta. When the sea level rose, the result was that a harbor with three sections, now called lochs, was formed: the West, Middle, and East Lochs. It was a maximum of forty deep in some places in its natural state, and shallower in other areas. The East Loch is the part that is known as Pearl Harbor, and it is the largest one. It has a large island in it, which is now called Ford Island.

Streams from the two volcanic mountain chains on O'ahu, the Wai'anae and the Ko'olau Mountains, still feed the former river delta. The tide from the Pacific Ocean keeps the water of Pearl Harbor and the other lochs fresh, just as it has for millennia.

The island of O'ahu formed by a combination of tectonic and volcanic activity. The tectonic plate that the Hawaiian Islands sit on moved northwest, and the volcanic plume that formed them, which is still forming more islands today, produced O'ahu by making those two mountain chains. Extinct volcanic craters – the Punch Bowl, Diamond Head, and Koko – sit east of Pearl Harbor.

Once formed, the land sat as fresh volcanic soil, ready for life to grow on it. Life blew to the Islands, bringing seeds, and birds flew over the islands, dropping more microbes in their excrement. Gradually, O'ahu became covered with vegetation of many kinds, and various species of birds took up residence on it and the other Islands.

Pearl Harbor benefited from this process, and a wetlands formed on its shores. Birds nested there, and fish and shellfish spawned and grew in it. Oysters still grow in Pearl Harbor. Coral grew on top of the lava rock in its waters, and limestone formed the shore.

Pu'uloa – Native Hawaiian Aquaculture

The Hawaiians lived on the Islands – alone – for at least a millennium. They named the lagoons first, and they chose to called this place Pu'uloa, which means Pearl Harbor. They arrived in long, double-canoes with outrigger sails and a small covered structure for shelter from the elements, called waʻa. They could fish as they sailed, so the Polynesians, as they were called until they settled the Islands, arrived skilled and ready to benefit from Puʻuloa.

Once they had arrived and settled on Oʻahu, it was not in the harbor. The Hawaiians lived inland, and used Puʻuloa as a food source only, because the place was marsh, reefs, and wetlands, with tall grasses but no solid ground to build a hale on.

Puʻuloa made a great food source, with ducks, terns, and other birds to catch, and a huge menu of both saltwater and freshwater fish, and shellfish to enjoy. The Hawaiians hunted finfish with nets and spears in their canoes, but they also grew certain species of fish in specially fashioned enclosures in the harbor.

Hawaiian aquaculture was a sophisticated endeavor. Some very basic, no-frills hale were built for the people who maintained the human-made fishponds in the harbor, while everyone else lived farther inland. The fishponds themselves were built by choosing two points of land that could be most easily connected by making a rock wall with at least one gate in the middle.

The rock wall would be mostly underwater, with part of it showing above. The gate, or makaha, was made of wooden slats lashed together. This allowed water to circulate in and out with the tide, so that the water inside the fishpond stayed clean and full of nutrients, while wastewater from the fish living inside washed out. Fish could swim in, but once they grew larger, they were trapped inside.

The fishponds were called loko iʻa. They were both inside Puʻuloa and on the coast next to it. The ones inside Puʻuloa were called loko ʻumeiki. The freshwater fishponds were inland from the coast, fed by underground water that came from the mountains. They were called loko wai. Their sizes varied with the sizes of the areas that could be enclosed. Nature formed random shapes in random sizes, so the Hawaiian aquaculturists built accordingly.

The fish in these ponds were raised for the aliʻi.

The oysters that grew in Puʻuloa were valued solely for the food inside, not the pearls. There were two varieties; one grew up to six inches across. For a long time, until Kamehameha the Great, the pearls were cast aside. The Hawaiians cared only for the oyster shells after enjoying the food in them. It was kapu – forbidden – to speak while harvesting oysters.

They made fishhooks out of the shells, and carved them into white eyes for kiʻi images, and for teeth to line the edges of wooden paddles. The shells were also useful as scraping tools. The beautiful, shimmering insides of the shells attracted the Hawaiians with artistic talents, including a great-granddaughter of Kamehameha the Great, Princess Bernice Pauahi Bishop. There is a whole oyster shell that she is thought to have painted a scene inside, on display in her museum.

Once foreigners arrived in the Hawaiian Islands, the people found out that the pearls inside oysters were valuable as well. There weren't very many pearls, and their shapes were irregular. Kamehameha the Great promptly put a kapu on pearls so that he could have a trade monopoly from the jewels. He needed a source of revenue; the foreigners all dealt in money, a thing that was a novelty to the Hawaiians. This played a role in depleting the oyster beds of Puʻuloa.

Foreigners – haole – were going to be a problem for the Hawaiians in many ways. They would have a huge impact on Puʻuloa. As the nineteenth century wore on, they made pastures for livestock that they imported and built sugar plantations on Oʻahu. Runoff from their crops polluted it with silt and mud. It deprived the waters of oxygen by filling up the harbor until it wasn't as deep as it had been in many places.

A marine biologist would explain that a healthy pond has at least three temperatures due to a sufficient depth to accommodate them. Having these temperatures is what enables algae and fish crops to grow and thrive season after season. Without that, the fish and oyster beds did not have the environment they needed to continue as abundantly as before.

Added to that was the fact that the haole traffic was affecting the fishponds and oyster beds in a dramatic way. The aquaculture system was being rapidly dismantled to accommodate first the mast ships that brought the missionaries and then the steamships that brought and carried away the goods that the haole newcomers bought and sold. Natural coral reefs were disturbed to accommodate this. Wharfs, quays, docks, and moorings were constructed as well.

By the late nineteenth century, Pu'uloa was being referred to as Pearl Harbor. Its natural appearance had been replaced in large part by a human-made, artificial one. It looked a lot more haole than Hawaiian, with haole demands for its future to match.

A Reciprocity Treaty

There was something that the haole population wanted very much by the time of King Kamehameha IV's reign: a treaty with the United States that would allow sugar and molasses from Hawaii to enter duty-free in return for the right to keep a U.S. Navy depot and dry dock in Pearl Harbor. This was referred to as a reciprocity treaty.

Twenty years of discussion ensued, during which time the Hawaiian rulers postponed the idea. Three kings later, the issue was still being pushed. Neither Kalakaua nor his sister and successor, Lili'uokalani, were in favor of it.

The ali'i siblings thought of the idea of a reciprocity treaty as a slippery slope that would lead to a loss of sovereignty over Pearl Harbor. However, after relentless pressure, Kalakaua finally agreed to have the treaty drafted. In September of 1876, the U.S. Congress approved it.

A U.S. Naval Base

The Merrie Monarch had a financially disastrous reign, so ten years later, the United States pushed for more: a naval base in Pearl Harbor for its exclusive use. King Kalakaua's foreign minister, Walter Murray Gibson, argued that this was impossible.

Undeterred, and taking advantage of the Hawaiian national debt, the U.S. Congress drew up a new reciprocity treaty in 1887 with the exclusive right to use Pearl Harbor attached in a separate convention (treaty).

Once it had that, the United States only had to wait until the time was ripe to annex all of Hawai'i. In 1900, with its naval base firmly entrenched after the 1898 Spanish-American War, the U.S. was free and clear to use the harbor as it wished.

The build-up took place gradually over the next forty years. The U.S. flag flew over Pearl Harbor, and naval technology moved in bit by bit. Shipyards and drydocks would be necessary to build and maintain the fleet. The first drydock was a failure; it collapsed in 1913 when it was almost finished. Religion was invoked – traditional Hawaiian religion – to prevent a repeat of this: a kahuna was invited to bless the next drydock project. That worked.

There were more military ships brought in year after year, though many were built elsewhere and moved to Pearl Harbor after the fact. As aviation became a part of the U.S. military machine, airstrips, fields, and hangars were built on the land surrounding the harbor and on Ford Island.

Submarines, amphibious airplanes, destroyers, battleships, tugboats, and other craft lined and littered Pearl Harbor. What was once a food source became completely militarized within the space of a century, transforming a millennium-long scene irrevocably.

To fuel all this, first coal and then oil was required. A series of oil tanks were thus installed on Hickam Field, on the southeast side of Pearl Harbor.

Battleship Row with the USS Arizona

The USS *Arizona* was ahead of its time in that it was fueled by gasoline, not coal. It was constructed in the New York Navy Yard in 1916, but never saw any action in World War I. Its entire role in that conflict was to bring home as many surviving soldiers as it could carry.

The *Arizona* was upgraded in the 1920s with more advanced weapons as technology continued to advance, and then again in 1935 to increase its crew capacity from 1,000 to 1,700. In between upgrades, in 1931, the ship was sent to the Pacific via the Panama Canal, to San Diego, California. By 1941, the *Arizona* had spent a year based in Pearl Harbor after another transfer.

The *Arizona* was one of the most heavily-armed ships in the fleet. It had plenty of company in Pearl Harbor. It was moored among several others in a lineup called Battleship Row. The white-painted, hexagonal quays of Battleship Row are still in place, even though they are now longer in use. Just look on Google Maps or Google Earth, and zoom in on Pearl Harbor to see it for yourself.

All this preparation and armament was no longer about any threat from any European power with colonies in the South Pacific. It was about Japan. Japan was busy building itself an empire in that region. Poor in natural resources, Japan was spending the decades after World War I building up its military forces and annexing whatever territory it could conquer.

Emperor Hirohito came to the Chrysanthemum Throne in 1926. Although he was fascinated by zoology and marine biology, he also wanted an empire to justify his title. Japan had been forced by U.S. Commodore Matthew Perry to open itself to foreign trade in 1854, and it viewed that as a humiliation that needed avenging. It also wanted a military force as large and as strong as those of the U.S. and European nations.

His generals were happy to oblige; among them were Japanese Imperial Army General Hideki Tojo, who went on to become prime minister, Japanese Imperial Navy Admiral Isoroku Yamamoto, who commanded his nation's navy, and Vice Admiral Chuichi Nagumo, who commanded Japan's First Air Fleet.

This is the quay for the USS Arizona, which was named BB-39 before it got its name.

Tojo was hanged after World War II. Yamamoto's plane was shot down in April of 1943. Nagumo committed suicide – by shooting himself in the head rather than by hara-kiri/seppuku – in July of 1944 when it became clear that Japan would lose the war.

A Disparity of Resources

On the United States end of the conflict, resources were split between a suspiciously calm Pacific scene and an openly hostile Atlantic that had been on full alert since 1939, when Hitler had invaded Poland, kicking off World War II.

That was the problem.

In 1940, one-third of everything that the U.S. Navy had in the Pacific had been transferred to the Atlantic to counterbalance Nazi Germany's resources. This left the U.S. exposed on its left flank, and the admirals in charge at Pearl Harbor knew it.

Nonetheless, they were in charge, so they got blamed for what followed.

They had been warned that any attack from the Japanese would come on a U.S. holiday or a weekend, just when Americans were relaxing and not focused on defense or work. Even so, without sufficient resources to mount a comparable defense, heavy damage from an attack would be the logical outcome.

Japan had 10 aircraft carriers in the Pacific, which was the latest and greatest technology of the time, making the battleship (and the *Arizona* was a battleship) only a support system. Still, battleships presented a credible and significant threat. The United States Navy had a grand total of 3 aircraft carriers in the Pacific, the *Saratoga*, the *Lexington*, and the *Enterprise*.

The scores only got worse for the U.S. from there. Battleships: Japan 12, U.S. 9. Cruisers: Japan 35, U.S. 21. Destroyers: Japan 110, U.S. 53.

It was only logical that the Japanese struck while the numbers remained thus.

Tora! Tora! But No Third Tora

So what were the Japanese planning?

Plenty: 3 air strikes, or waves, on Pearl Harbor with 5 miniature, 2-man submarines to sneak into the shallow waters of the harbor and add to the chaos with torpedoes. They planned to blow up: Battleship Row, to take out as many U.S. Navy ships as they could; Wheeler Field, a U.S. Army Air Force base; Bellows Field, its auxiliary base; Hickam Air Field, where the bomber planes were kept; 'Ewa Marine Air Station, which had 47 fighter planes; Kane'ohe Naval Air Station, in order wipe out the long-range reconnaissance fleet; and the oil tanks, so that resupplying after the attack would take as long as possible.

The planes were to fly south to Pearl Harbor from the aircraft carriers that had brought them via a circuitous route from Japan. It was not a suicide mission, even though many of the pilots rightly expected not to make it back to their ships. Still, if they could get back, that was the plan.

That seemed like a well-thought-out plan, but when plans are carried out, things go wrong.

At first, all was conducted in perfect secrecy, with the pilots told nothing until the 6 aircraft carriers, were well underway. Sake was served, and the first wave of pilots took off from the *Akagi*. Tora means "tiger" in Japanese, and although it was said three times, only two waves were ultimately sent out. Nagumo changed his mind about the third one, worried that he had lost the element of surprise.

That was a mistake – he could have destroyed the oil tanks and crippled the U.S. Navy.

The mini-subs weren't very effective either. One of them ended up beached on a reef by Kane'ohe. A key navigation instrument had been damaged, so the crew got lost. One died, and the other got captured and spent the duration of the war imprisoned on Sand Island. All 8 of the other submariners died. The 9 dead were honored for dying in the attack.

The Japanese considered capture to be a disgrace, so the tenth man wasn't mentioned. He asked permission to commit suicide in prison, which of course the

Americans denied. It was the perfect culture clash; the enemy considered suicide an honor, while the captors considered it a cop-out. That man was forced to live, and he eventually became a pacifist.

Another thing that went wrong for the Japanese was that the U.S. aircraft carriers were out on training exercises north of the Islands, so taking them out of the military equation wasn't an option. That was sheer luck on the part of the U.S. Navy.

Finally, one Japanese pilot got lost in the confusion after inflicting damage at Pearl Harbor and, with six bullet holes in his plane, headed west and crash-landed on the island of Ni'ihau.

Still, the damage done on O'ahu was considerable.

The planes on the ground were almost all destroyed, and the few that managed to take to the air in time to shoot back found little satisfaction to be had. They did have the consolation of knowing that they kept the attackers distracted from shooting at the oil tanks, at least.

The *Arizona* sank up to its upper deck in flames, with only its guns and turrets exposed. The captain of the *Nevada* tried to head out of the harbor, but once he realized that his ship was too badly damaged to make it, he deliberately ran it aground to prevent it from sinking and blocking the harbor entrance. It was later salvaged and restored to service. Other ships in Battleship Row that were hit were the *Oklahoma*, the *Maryland*, the *Tennessee*, and the *West Virginia*.

Three ships in drydock, the *Cassin*, *Downes*, and *Pennsylvania*, were set on fire. The minelayer *Oglala* and the destroyer *Shaw* were nearby, and they were struck too, as was a repair ship, the *Vestal*. Three cruisers were also hit: the *Raleigh*, the *Helena*, and the *Honolulu*.

On the far side of Ford Island by the Middle Loch, the *Curtiss* was torpedoed, but it was restored to service in 1942. The nearby *Utah* was also hit. South of Battleship Row, on the other side of Ford Island, was the *California*, in flames as well.

18 ships wrecked.

The Japanese had enjoyed a bit of luck in that the men watching the radar display at the Opana station in northern O'ahu had been told to ignore the blips that they saw. The radar blips were dismissed as a group of planes that were expected to come in from California, which gave the first wave of attackers that much longer to inflict a surprise attack.

40 civilians died from stray bullets fired from above. People came out of their homes and shops to look up – Hawaiians, Japanese-Americans, Chinese-Americans, Caucasians, and others. A significant number of the civilian dead included Japanese-Americans, and of those who lived, they remembered seeing the large red dots on the rudders of the Japanese planes and thinking of the rising sun symbol as an enemy attack, and most unwelcome.

The Ni'ihau Incident

Shigenori Nishikaichi was part of the second wave of the attack on Pearl Harbor.

He had spent his entire life preparing for his role.

Now, flying west with six bullet strikes, including one to his fuel tank, he knew he could not get back to the *Hiryu*, the aircraft carrier that he had taken off from. It soon became clear to the pilot that he would have to crash-land on Ni'ihau, known as the Forbidden Island.

Ni'ihau is 124 miles away from O'ahu, and is shaped sort of like a seal leaping up, facing northeast to Kaua'i. It is entirely inhabited by native Hawaiians, owned by the Robinson family who live on Kaua'i, and in 1941, 53-year-old Alymer Robinson was in charge.

Aylmer visited his property and checked on his wards, as he thought of the Niihauans, once a week. He got there by boat, always landing at Kii, which was the closest point from where he lived in Makaweli. He never married, and had plenty of time to concern himself with his business and the Niihauans. He kept the people under quarantine to protect them from pathogens that would compromise their immune system. The government let him do as he saw fit.

Life on the Forbidden Island was primitive, with wells, no electricity, and a dry, sunny climate. Education was provided by Aylmer through the fourth grade. After leaving school, the people tended to forget English and lapse exclusively into their own dialect of Hawaiian. They had honey, turkeys, ducks and other birds, cats and pigs that had gone feral, sheep, and horses. The men wore jeans and white shirts, and wore hunting knives in their belts. The women wore plain dresses in light colors. Firearms were banned.

Aylmer employed a Japanese couple, Yoshio and Irene Harada, as beekeepers on Niihau. They had moved there in 1938. In late 1941, Aylmer had appointed Yoshio to be paymaster also, after the previous one had died. He was to begin this duty in the new year. They lived in a house that Aylmer had provided. It had a radio, but that was for listening to the news, not for communicating with anyone else.

Yoshio's parents had been plantation workers on Kauai after immigrating from Japan. They had lived in segregation from the white plantation owners, and endured a degrading system of apartheid, into which their son was born.

Yoshio's parents returned to Japan before he was married, and although he never set foot there himself, he had grown up in a society that treated him as second-class and separate from the group that enjoyed full rights and privileges in American society.

Irene had traveled in Japan as an adult with her mother, and then returned to Hawai'i, where she met and married Yoshio. She considered her life on Ni'ihau to be a horrible banishment. If she needed to communicate with Aylmer, he had told her to signal with torches, and a boat would come. There was no quick and convenient way to leave independently, and by design.

Another Japanese person lived on Niihau, an elderly man who had married a Niihauan woman. His name was Ishimatsu Shintani, and like the Haradas, he was denied the chance at having American citizenship. His wife had lost her own citizenship when she married him.

The Japanese pilot was about to land on an island that was ripe for trouble.

But there was a bit of good luck: 29-year-old Howard Kaleohano lived on Ni'ihau. He was fluent in both written and spoken English, having been born and raised on the Big Island of Hawai'i, in Kona. He had come to Ni'ihau as an adult and married a Niihauan woman, Mabel Kahale, and became a cowboy. There are cowboys on the Big Island, called paniolos, so perhaps he had learned his trade before moving away. He lived near the Haradas, in Kiekie, on the western side of Ni'ihau, halfway down the coast.

Howard Kaleohano was the first person to encounter Nishikaichi when he stumbled out of his damaged plane, dazed and disoriented. Howard was well informed of the strained diplomatic relations between Japan and the United States to know that the presence of a Japanese fighter pilot on his island could not be a good omen.

The first thing Kaleohano did was to relieve Nishikaichi of his weapon, map, and papers.

The papers included the battle plans that the pilot had been carrying out.

After that, Kaleohano struck up a friendly conversation with the pilot while he decided on his next move. The pilot asked him if he was Japanese, which was not that odd considering the fact that the two men were of similar build, height and weight, but Kaleohano said no, he was Hawaiian. He led his "guest" toward the Robinson guest house.

Nishikaichi had difficulty communicating in English, and after asking for his papers back, he tried again on paper, but Kaleohano would not give them back. The pilot had a problem: he had to destroy his papers and plane completely so that the enemy would not be able to study them, or he would suffer permanent dishonor. It wasn't enough that he had seen that the attack had inflicted tremendous damage on Pearl Harbor.

Soon Kaleohano decided that he needed an interpreter, and curious neighbors were crowding around the house. He asked one of them to go and get Shintani, went outside to look at the downed plane, and saw the bullet holes.

Shintani arrived, spoke briefly with the pilot, turned pale, and left. He was too upset to explain what was going on, so the Haradas were sought next.

Yoshio came over, spoke with the pilot, found out all about the attack on Pearl Harbor this way, and decided not to tell the Niihauans about it just yet.

The Niihauans put on a luʻau for the pilot, played the ukulele, danced and sang, and fed him. They handed the instrument to the pilot, who played it like a Japanese samisen and sang them a song…while staying alert for any indication of a rescue submarine. It did not appear.

Then the Niihauans found out about the attack via a radio announcement; there were Hawaiian-language newspapers and radio stations on the Islands. The announcement ordered all civilians to black out their windows at night.

They confronted the pilot, and Harada translated it all this time.

The pilot was installed as the Haradas guest, with five guards, including Ben Kanahele.

Meanwhile, Aylmer was concerned about being cut off from his wards, but he did not yet know what was going on.

As for the Niihauans, it was time for Aylmer to make his weekly visit, so they went to Kii and waited for him to appear. He did not. All inter-island travel had been stopped when the U.S. Navy declared martial law for the Islands.

The pilot worked on the Haradas, talking to them about Japan and their parents, who had retired to Japan, until they agreed to help him. Soon the game was afoot as Shintani visited Howard and asked for the papers, which yielded nothing. Howard Kaleohano was no fool.

But the Haradas managed to find and acquire the pilot's weapon, Yoshio fired it at Howard as he came out of his outhouse. Howard ran, and warned the Niihauans to evacuate the village and hide. The villagers heeded this and fled.

Howard was busy meanwhile. He hid the pilot's gun in his house and the papers in his mother-in-law's home. Then he took off with a group 5 of Niihauans for Kii. On the way, they set a bonfire at Paniau at 9 p.m., south of the landing point at Kii, hoping that Aylmer might see it. He did, and was very worried, but the Navy patrols would not allow him to go to Niʻihau.

Howard and his companions had to row for hours, with only a gallon of water and no food in the boat. The trip took 10 hours, from half past midnight to 10:30 a.m. the next morning. Howard called Aylmer from the Waimea police station and told him what was going on.

Aylmer met them, took them to a Chinese restaurant, and bought them a meal.

Now it was up to the U.S. Army officers on Kauaʻi to go to Niʻihau and rescue the residents.

Not all of the Japanese people who lived in Hawaiʻi had been raised as Yoshio Harada had. One of them was an army officer, 1st Lieutenant Jack Mizuha. He had been educated in the public schools of Kauai, raised in a home with a former Japanese samurai for a father, and viewed his cultural background as a part of his identity rather than a defining element of it.

Mizuha had learned Japanese in school, but knew English as a first language, and considered himself to be an American. He had been in command of the Burns Field until the attack on Pearl Harbor, after which anti-Japanese prejudice and paranoia caused him to be demoted.

Instead of taking offense and wanting to avenge the insult, Mizuha looked for an opportunity to prove himself to be a loyal American. As a Japanese descendant who had been born on the Islands, a Nikkei, he had U.S. citizenship, and now he intended to prove that he valued it.

Here was his chance. He called his new commander, Lieutenant Colonel Eugene J. Fitzgerald, and volunteered to lead a rescue mission on Niihau. Fitzgerald accepted. Another Nikkei, Ben Kobayashi, who was fluent in Japanese, offered his services as both a member of the team and translator. Mizuha accepted, and added him to the team.

Back on Niihau, the pilot and Harada had gone back to the plane and taken the machines guns out of it.

Harada and the pilot had grabbed two Niihauan men, Niau and Kalima, and tied their hands behind their backs once they were armed. Harada had fired at some Niihauans, so he was getting in deeper and deeper, feeling that there was no way out. The pilot kept checking the radio in his downed plane, and he and Harada got a wagon for the machine guns while Harada told the Niihauans that there was enough ammunition to kill everyone on the island.

But things weren't going well. There was no information about the Japanese fleet on the pilot's radio. They sent Kalima to tell Irene that Yoshio wasn't coming back yet. Kalima walked that way until he was out of sight, then took off. He found his wife, Ella, who untied him, then met up with Ben Kanahele and told him what was happening. The group of five Niihauans wandered in the darkness, while their armed enemies did the same nearby, looking for food.

The pilot and Harada had set Howard's house on fire, which Howard had seen from the rowboat, but bravely rowed onward. Next, they went into Howard's mother-in-law's house and found her there, lame and reading. She stared them down and they left without finding the papers and map, which Howard had hidden in there.

The invader and the traitor were also getting hungry, as were the Niihauans. When they each sneaked into the village to get some food, they ran into each other, and soon Ben Kanahele and his companions were captives…again.

They told Ben to go find Howard Kaleohano, and let him walk away. Ben knew where Howard was, but played along, calling him. Ben spoke in Hawaiian to his friends, telling them that they had to get that pistol away from the pilot and Harada before anyone got shot.

Everyone was looking quite tired and worn out from the stress of it all, and Harada was unbuttoning his shirt with hara-kiri rather obviously on his mind.

Ben and Ella pounced on the gun.

Harada pulled Ella away, and the pilot fired, wounding Ben in the chest, groin, and left hip.

Ella grabbed a rock and bashed Nishikaichi over the head with it. Ben turned around and grabbed the pilot as he did one of his sheep, by the neck, pulled his knife out of his belt, and slit his throat.

Harada loaded the gun again and shot himself twice.

It was over.

Mizuha didn't know that, however, and led his rescue team over the island until they all met up. Ella grabbed the guns and ran for help, but dropped them in the dark. (They were found five years later, after a rainstorm. Ben recovered from his wounds.) At last, Mizuha and his team, guided by Howard Kaleohano with Aylmer Robinson bringing up the rear, arrived.

Mabel Kaleohano came running to meet her husband, telling him that their house had been burned down. He hugged her and said he didn't care; what mattered was that they were okay.

Mizuha spent a week compiling data for his report, which he prepared in the schoolhouse.

Irene Harada was promptly carted off to Sand Island for the duration of the war. She was allowed out after that, reunited with her two daughters and son, and lived quietly on Kauaʻi until she died in 1996 at the age of 91. She was bitter about her experience on Niʻihau, like an angry child who had chosen the wrong side and blamed the winners for the outcome. Aylmer had no use for her after the incident on Niʻihau.

Her attitude and role in it was revealed when she granted interviews in Japanese, operating on the mistaken attitude that no one would translate and thus no English speaker would find out. That this was done was something that she considered to be a personal and cultural affront.

Ben Kahalele and Howard Kaleohano were each awarded the Medal of Freedom for their efforts, the highest honor that a U.S. civilian can receive. Ella Kahalele got no medal for her bravery and the physical risk she took, which was most likely due to sexism.

Jack Mizuha went on to fight in the 100th Infantry Battalion in the U.S. Army until he was wounded in the neck, after which he graduated from the University of Michigan Law School. From there had had a distinguished legal career in Hawaiʻi. He was appointed Attorney General when Hawaiʻi was still a territory in 1958, and again a year later when it became a state. After that, in 1961, Mizuha was appointed to be an Associate Justice of Hawaiʻi's Supreme Court.

U.S. Concentration Camps

It was because of the Niihau Incident, as it came to be known, that the U.S. government disgraced itself by dispossessing as many Japanese residents that it could find on the west coast of the mainland.

It took away their homes, businesses, jobs, chances at an education, and contact with all that had become theirs and familiar to them, and interred them in concentration camps without the comforts and amenities that other Americans enjoyed – heat, warm running water, and independence.

These camps were in a cold, barren desert area of the United States.

This was not done to Americans of Italian or German descent, despite the fact that the U.S. was at war with those nations as well as Japan. No…Italian-Americans and German-Americans were treated as loyal Americans.

In 1988, President Reagan apologized on behalf of the United States government, but it felt like too little, too late to the Americans whose lives were stolen from them for three years. After that, the U.S. government disbursed over $1.6 billion in reparations to those who had been interned in those camps, and to their heirs.

Japanese-American residents of Hawaii responded to the attacks by demanding an opportunity to fight in World War II…in Europe. This group of Nikkei made up the majority of the 100th Infantry Battalion. Many of them died, and they were awarded medals such as the Medal of Honor and the Purple Heart. Those who survived also served admirably.

When they came home as veterans of World War II, they were rightfully greeted as Americans.

Cleanup and War

Cleanup at Pearl Harbor began before the attack was over, with rescue attempts.

Plenty of movies have been made about the attack, both documenting and dramatizing it. The movies describe and explain every detail of the human costs as well as the financial and military ones. I have not watched each and every one of them, and I doubt that I will. Watching the same upsetting disaster over and over again and seeing sailors drown or get burned or die however they are shown dying repeatedly seems like a desensitizing pastime for someone who wasn't there. One movie has been enough for me thus far: *Pearl Harbor* of 2001, starring Ben Affleck, Josh Hartnett, and Kate Beckinsale.

When I returned from this trip to Hawai'i and showed my research materials to my cousin, an artist who makes very convincing skin-like veneers to cover titanium prosthetics (arms and legs mostly) for war veterans and other amputees, he talked about those movies. One thing that stayed in his memory was a scene of the sailors below decks as the *Arizona* was sinking. A large, strong sailor opened a porthole and pushed his buddies out as fast as he could, then tried to follow, only to realize that he was too big and too muscular to fit through the hole. He was trapped.

Until I visited the memorial, I had guessed that the men who died on that ship had drowned, suffering terrible pain their lungs as they filled up with water, and at last blacking out.

That wasn't what happened, the National Parks Ranger told us. They burned to death.

There are no skeletons in the *Arizona*, only ashes that have washed away into the harbor.

After the attack, the U.S. Congress was suddenly amenable to funding the Pacific fleet.

This is the nice National Parks guide who told us the history of the sinking of the USS Arizona aboard the memorial, and that the sailors burned to death rather than drowned.

All of Hawai'i became militarized, and cinemas all over the nation showed newsreels before the main features that stirred up American resolve to put as much energy and resources as they could manage into the war effort. Martial law took over the entire Territory of Hawai'i, including the courts, the shipping industry, and the police. Nothing got in or out – not goods, not information, not anything – without permission from the U.S. military.

Everything that was above the water level on the *Arizona* was removed and salvaged, while everything below was left as a memorial tomb for the sailors. The upper deck is just below the water level, so it can easily be seen from above. Plumes of gasoline still bubble up from the hull. This view can be seen on the Internet without traveling to Pearl Harbor; just go to Google Maps or Google Earth, click the Satellite View option, and look. One can do a lot of armchair travel this way.

The attack on Pearl Harbor was ultimately avenged in a direct way when the U.S. Army Air Force sank all of the Japanese aircraft carriers that had brought the planes on December 7, 1941.

The plane that Shigenori Nishikaichi flew and crash-landed on Ni'ihau has been moved to the Pacific Aviation Museum on Ford Island. It can be reached via the bridge that crosses the East Loch. So much for his plan to destroy his plane, map, and papers.

Fires on board the damaged ships were put out. It took two days for the *Arizona* to stop burning. The *California*, the *West Virginia*, the *Pennsylvania*, the *Tennessee*, and the *Nevada* were salvageable. The *Shaw*, *Cassin*, and *Helm* were also repaired and returned to service. The *Oklahoma* was capsized and declared a total loss. So was the *Utah*.

Divers went underwater to see what could be salvaged. Women trained in the use of fire hoses in case of another attack. They also participated alongside men in salvage efforts above the water. This work took two years. By 1943, Pearl Harbor looked almost normal and was fully functional again, except for the sunken wreckage of the *Arizona*.

The U.S. certainly paid back Japan for Pearl Harbor many, many times over when it dropped atomic bombs on the civilian cities of Hiroshima and Nagasaki in August of 1945. Those weapons killed so many people that Emperor Hirohito went on the radio and told his people to stop fighting. They had never heard his voice before. The U.S. government had become convinced that nothing else would motivate the Japanese to stop fighting.

Surrender documents were signed aboard the USS *Missouri* on September 2, 1945. The ship was moored in Tokyo Bay for that, and a Who's Who List of Allied military commanders were in attendance, with representatives from not only the United States but also Britain, China, Australia, New Zealand, Canada, France, and the Netherlands. General Douglas MacArthur and Fleet Admiral Chester Nimitz watched as Japanese Foreign Minister Mamoru Shigemitsu signed on the required line.

The same 31-star American flag that Commodore Matthew Perry had flown on his ship in 1854 when he forced Japan to open its doors to Western trade was flown on the *Missouri*, most likely to rub the Japanese noses in their second defeat.

That was it. No tea, no nothing. Good-bye and get off our ship, Shigemitsu.

Peace and Creating a Memorial

The *Missouri* returned to service and saw duty in the Korean War, then it sat in the Pacific for 29 years until it was updated and upgraded in 1984. It saw duty in the Kuwait War, and then was decommissioned in 1992 due to budget cuts. In 1998, it became a museum ship, and has been moored close to the USS *Arizona* Memorial since that time.

After World War II, nothing more happened with the USS *Arizona* until 1950, when Admiral Arthur Radford, the Commander of the Pacific Fleet, ordered that a small platform be attached to its hull so that a flag could be flown over the wreckage.

But that wasn't good enough. In 1958, The U.S. Congress authorized funds for a better and more permanent memorial over the sunken ship. Even that wasn't enough money, however. In 1961, Elvis Presley put on a concert and donated every cent earned from it to the project.

The USS Arizona Memorial today, with the American flag flying over it.

The memorial was designed by Alfred Preis. It is 182 feet long, all in white, and it tapers in the middle, curving inwards from above and on its sides, with seven openings above showing the sky, plus seven more on either side. There is no glass; one can look straight up and out of them.

It opened on Memorial Day in 1962. A U.S. flag flies above it.

The Visitor Center grounds include the anchor of the USS *Arizona*, which has been raised, painted gray, and placed directly across the East Loch from the sunken wreckage.

The anchor of the USS Arizona.

Visiting the Dead

A tour to the USS *Arizona* Memorial starts with a brief lecture by a National Parks Ranger, followed by a 30-minute documentary movie narrated by Jamie Lee Curtis. After that, the visitors are escorted with great solemnity to a motor boat, and U.S. Marines pilot it across the East Loch of Pearl Harbor to the Memorial.

The USS Missouri and the USS Arizona Memorial, designed by architect Alfred Preis.

In the brief lecture, the Ranger explains that the *Arizona* is a tomb, not just a wrecked ship, and that visitors should keep as quiet and serious as possible. The Ranger went on at some length about this, with the upshot of it all being that we were to behave as one would at a funeral. But that is my assessment, and that phrase is mine. It is what I told myself to sum it all up, because it made more sense to me than all of the lines about respect. I like specificity, though I kept my thoughts to myself: no smiling, no laughing, no joking.

It wasn't difficult to behave with great solemnity. All I had to do was think of the poor sailors trapped in that hull, unable to swim out in time to breathe as chaos reigned and rained all around them.

Here is my father, sitting aboard the boat that took us across the Loch, with his ticket in his glass case, his sunglasses on because it was so bright even in this covered boat, and his professional camera hanging around his neck.

The movie that Jamie Lee Curtis's voice narrated showed historical footage of the attack, plus photographs and explanations of the history of Pearl Harbor's Navy facilities. Then a female Park Ranger appeared on the screen and repeated the admonition to be quiet and respectful.

At last it was time to board the boat.

As we moved out across the water, my father and I shot more photographs with our cameras. I had a small point-and-shoot camera. He had his usual elaborate one, and took the most beautiful photographs with excellent color quality. He put himself through graduate school in London, England with a camera, and has kept current with the technology all his life.

To our right, docked just off the Visitor Center, we could see a huge, long submarine, the USS *Bowfin*, which is open for tours, and a long bridge that crosses the loch to Ford Island. Beyond that is a huge white dome, which I guessed (rightly, we found at in a lunch restaurant in Aiea after leaving, when two men in military fatigues, both Army and Navy, walked in and confirmed it) to be a cover for radar equipment.

My father shot this photograph of the USS Bowfin, and shared all of the images he collected with me for this travelogue.

Here is the bridge to Ford Island, with the radar dome at left. The Arizona is to the left of it.

We saw another boat like the one that we were riding in pass us, and the Navy yards to the south, with ships that are part of the active Pacific fleet. A trip to Hawai'i, particularly to O'ahu, will bring a visitor close to a U.S. military presence almost everywhere that one looks, perhaps more so than in any other U.S. state. This is as one would expect, since the Islands are so far from every other part of the nation.

Pacific fleet ships moored in Pearl Harbor, on active duty. We were visiting a museum right next to an active military installation.

Here is another tour boat, returning from the Arizona Memorial.

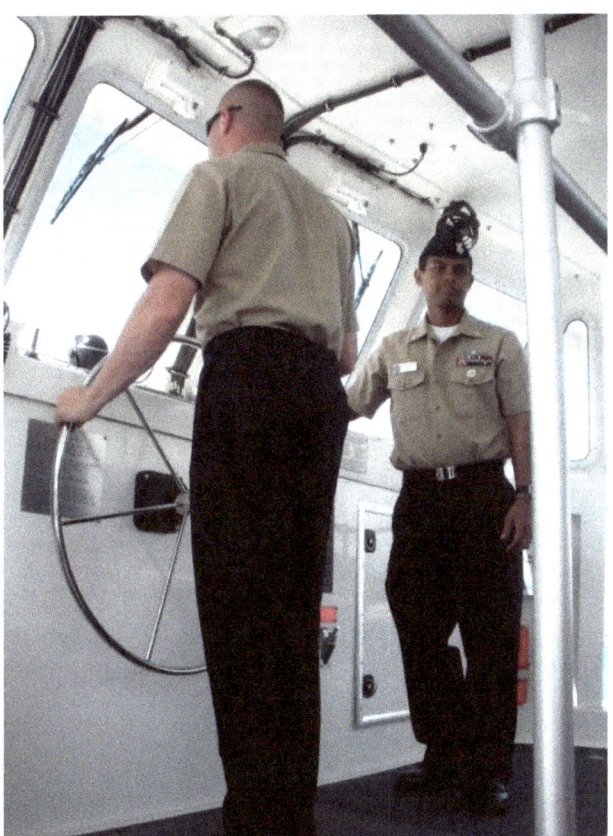
Our U.S. Marine boat pilots, taking us across to the Arizona.

At last, after so much build-up to the big moment, our boat pulled alongside the gangplanks of the USS *Arizona* Memorial, and we remembered to be quiet and solemn...again.

We were promptly urged to keep moving along and to let the previous group of visitors out so that they could board the boat and leave. We did so, seeing them only as we entered the structure. Inside were plaques that explained the history of the Memorial.

Arriving at the Arizona Memorial, we could see part of the ship still poking above the water line.

The plaques were beautifully crafted of gray metal, set into the walls on either side of the entrance. We saw them as we looked back. One of them detailed the sources of $250,000 of the funds that were allocated for the Memorial: the U.S. Congress and the State of Hawai'i. Elvis's contribution was not mentioned on it. I suppose he was one of the "thousands of individual donors" mentioned in the last paragraph. It had a picture of the Memorial on it, showing the hull of the *Arizona* below and a U.S. flag flying above it.

The other plaque was all about the dedication itself. It listed the members of the dedication commission, including the widow of the owner of the now-defunct Dillingham department store (a Big Five corporation of Hawai'i) and Duke Paoa Kahanamoku, the famous Hawaiian surfer and Olympic swimming champion who won gold and silver medals in 1912, 1920, and 1924. A litany of rear admirals of the U.S. Navy topped that.

Neither plaque mentioned Alfred Preis, the Memorial's architect. That seemed strange.

He was an Austrian who fled the Nazis in the middle of his career, in 1939. He came to Honolulu, and was detained for three months at Sand Island after the attack on Pearl Harbor.

The Memorial arches over the wreckage of the *Arizona*, and there is one hole that visitors can look down into in addition to the side views. The architect wanted to add portholes that looked straight down, but this was not approved.

Looking down into the Arizona. The shadows made it difficult to see much, but perhaps the dead sailors prefer it that way. The opening is square, with balconies all around it.

In the middle of the Memorial is a table with schematics of the wreckage of the *Arizona*. The light was so bright that getting an image of these schematics was impossible, but if I were the reader, I would wish to see what was available…so here it is.

My father found me and my mother and had us pose in front of the schematics table for a photograph. It was so bright that staring down the camera lens was a challenge, but I don't like to hide my face for photographs behind sunglasses, so I held still and made the best of it.

Here we are, my mother and I, aboard the USS Arizona Memorial in the beautiful fresh air and sunshine, while the sailors below us cannot breathe or bask in this ever again. Life is good…as long as there is peace.

After that, I wanted to look around and get as many photographs of my own as I could before the Ranger told us it was time to leave. My father may shoot beautiful photographs, but no one else can get the images that an author is looking for. I went to work, staring at everything and gathering what I needed, even if it was more than I might ultimately use. I could pick and choose later, when I was at my leisure.

This image faces north, toward Aiea. My father shot it.

This image was shot by me, also facing north, but close up on a turret tower.

Looking south at the USS Missouri, and a quay from Battleship Row. The wreckage of the Arizona is directly in front, just below the water line, but there was a lot less to see of it above the water line on this side.

Here is another one of my father's beautifully-colored images, showing the USS Missouri through the zoom lens. It is included here for the details of the close-up scene that it shows.

After looking around in the middle of the Memorial, I wanted to see what was in the back room. A triangular archway offered a peek into it from there, and a wall of names showed through. Naturally people wanted to go in there and read them. The balcony to the view down into the ship's hull was just in front of it.

Note that the Memorial is completely handicapped accessible so that no one has to miss out on a visit.

I went back there and saw that there were more windows, open with no glass, on either side. They were more like odd, randomly-shaped openings than windows – two whole panels of them on either side of a white marble plaque of names that filled the entire back wall. The names are those of each and every sailor – and marine – who died on the *Arizona*. This was the first time that I learned that there were marines on board when it sank.

The marble wall of names, with sunlight coming in from the panels on either side. The sailors fill most of the wall, and the contingent of marines who died with them is down on the right.

The area with the wall of names was raised up, with three steps that were roped off in front. To the left of the platform created by the steps was a small marble box-like structure that looked like an afterthought. It was, and it will likely be necessary to add to it soon, because there was no more room for another name. It is for survivors of the disaster who decided that when they died, they would be cremated, and then have their urns tossed by divers of the U.S. Navy into the hull of the *Arizona*, so that they could be interred with their comrades.

Lei of orchids covered the top of the box, which read "USS ARIZONA SURVIVORS INTERRED WITH THEIR SHIPMATES" and the dates of death ranged from 1982 to 2012, in three columns of 12 names. I find it hard to believe that the remaining survivors won't also want to be included in this. It's a shrine and a cemetery, and there are more survivors still living, the National Parks Ranger informed us.

The intrigue didn't stop there. I looked at the names, curious to see if any of them might be the same as my family names. The only relatives of mine whom I knew to have fought in World War II came from the east coast, and so they fought in Europe.

Both were in the U.S. Air Force – an uncle of my father, who was one of many of the men whose job it was to throw out bombs as a fighter plane flew over German cities. The other was my mother's uncle, whom I met. He was Colonel Elmer J. Rogers, Jr. at the time, and a 3-star Lieutenant General in the U.S. Air Force by the time he retired.

Hitler wanted him by name because he was a flying ace who bombed the Ploesti oil fields in Romania, which fueled the Nazi Panzer tanks.

That's nice, but I still looked with interest at the names on the white marble wall. There was a Lt. Col. D.R. Fox who commanded the unit of U.S. Marines aboard the *Arizona*. There are lots of people in the world with the same last name as mine, and my family has never mentioned him to me, so I doubt that he is a relative.

But...there was an R.W. Haines among the sailors who died on the USS *Arizona*. That is my husband's last name, so I could hardly wait to get him on the phone and ask him about it.

S1C		C. J. HAAS	MUS2C	R
3C		S. W. HADEN	COX	T
NS		F. B. HAFFNER	F1C	C
1 3C		R. W. HAINES	S2C	C
(2C		J. R. HALL	CBM	L
1 3C		W. I. HALLORAN	ENS	E
S1C				

R.W. Haines, S2c, listed on the Memorial wall with the sailors who died on the USS Arizona.

Luckily for my burning curiosity, David called the hotel that evening and I asked him about it. Yes! R.W. Haines was a relative of his who died aboard the USS *Arizona*! Tell me more about him, whatever you know, even if it's not much, I said.

Okay...my husband's relatives on his father's side were from Mount Holly, New Jersey. They were Quakers and tomato farmers who supplied the Campbell's Soup Company with their crops. Robert Wesley Haines was a cousin who left home to join the navy. He was the galley cook of the *Arizona*, or one of them.

David went on to say that from what he knew of his relative's past and personality, R.W. Haines likely had Asperger's. We Aspies (David and I are Aspies, with the benefit of knowing that we are and what that is: it's high-functioning autism) don't respond to nonverbal cues. We need directness, something that requires more words and time. Eye contact doesn't come naturally to us, either, but we can learn to make it. Military culture is as neurotypical as it gets, the polar opposite of Aspie behavior.

My husband told me that his family had known that R.W. Haines was bullied and treated with contempt aboard the *Arizona* simply for being different, and that was when Asperger's was unknown (the diagnosis has only been in psychiatry books since 1994!). This made his story all the more fascinating to me. Aspies need to carve out niches for ourselves, and fortunately, my husband and I have managed to do so. I felt sad and bad for R.W. Haines.

Back on the shore at the Visitor Center, we didn't stay long.

It was hot, humid, sunny, and my father could not walk around much with his hip bothering him, so we stopped only at the rest rooms and the bookstore. I got another Pearl Harbor bag, free mugs with purchases, magnets with images of the *Arizona* Memorial, and a reprint of a newspaper documenting the attack.

Here it is, one of my favorite parts of any museum visit: the bookstore. My parents and husband would not think of trying to drag me away from some historic site without allowing me to look around and buy some books!

The grounds were also worth a few second glances, and we shot a few more images on our way out as we followed the group back from the boat.

Looking left as we returned to the Visitor Center, we could see the USS Missouri, the Arizona Memorial, and the radar dome, plus a large, round set of benches and more plaques with names of the people who died in the attack.

A last look back at what we had come to see.

That was it. Our visit was over, and I could hardly wait to read the book on Pearl Harbor that I had bought from Allan Seiden, complete with his autograph. I started that evening, and ended up finishing it after we came home to Connecticut.

In it is a photograph of seven sailors working in the galley of the USS *Arizona*. It shows the galley as it was when the ship was sunk. After looking at it many times, I have narrowed it down to three possibilities, but I suspect that the guy with his hands in his pockets at the extreme right is R.W. Haines. His face is obscured by bright light that is streaming in from an open door at the back of the room, but his stance gives him away. Aspies don't adjust our pose in accordance with the presence of anyone else who comes near. It's not much to go on, but it's all I've got: a little knowledge of brain patterns and behavior. There is that, and the fact that he looks like David. He's tall, and his hair is dark and shaped just like my husband's hair. It's a distance shot.

It was a fun morning and early afternoon, and we were glad to have seen the Memorial.

Plus, I looked forward to learning the history behind it.

Exploring Oʻahu by Car

We spent Thursday afternoon driving first around southern Oʻahu, and then up to the north shore, a route that took us on what is thought of as a "saddle" road, between the Waiʻanae and Koʻolau Mountain ranges. I won't bother describing the harbor here because there is a whole chapter about it. Suffice it to say that it's on the southern coast, heavily militarized, and densely settled with highways and businesses close around it.

The view north from Pearl Harbor, showing the heavily developed area just west of Honolulu.

There are other gorgeous sights on the cliffs of Oʻahu, but we did not have time to see everything. I suppose that if we hadn't seen so many museums, we might have had time to do that, but I have no regrets. Besides, this gap provides motivation to make a future visit to Oʻahu and see whatever we missed this time.

It was a fascinating drive that took us the entire afternoon. We saw the extinct volcanoes on the southern shores, volcanic mountains, a military base, a pineapple-cutting demonstration, and a popular surfing spot. When the sun was starting to set, my father turned the car around and we drove back to the Ko Olina Resort.

Southern Oʻahu – Suburbs and High-Rises

Driving around southern Oahu, we saw familiar businesses, ones that we often saw at home: Starbucks coffee shops, Home Depot's big box stores, strip malls, larger shopping malls, American, German, Korean, and Japanese models of cars, and so on.

We also saw things that we would not see at home: people driving cars along H-1 who wore army and navy fatigues, volcanic rock and soil, vibrantly-hued tropical flowering trees and bushes, Matson cargo containers on tractor trailer trucks behind the Home Depot store and on the highway, and volcanic mountains and craters.

Everywhere we looked, we saw signs of a heavy military presence, which was not anything that we were used to seeing at home in Connecticut. One thing that stood out from a distance was the large white dome high up on a raised platform that housed radar equipment.

We could see that as we ate lunch at the Monterrey Bay Cannery restaurant in Aiea. Just below the restaurant were irrigated squares of crops. I wondered what they were, so I asked the waitress: sprouts. It was a nice lunch of seafood, one in which I asked questions of not one but two complete strangers. The other question was about the white dome. When two military men, one army and one navy, walked into the restaurant in their green and blue fatigues, I asked them about it.

Sprouts paddies. The paddies are grown in rotating phases, so that there are always some crops that are almost ready to harvest and sell rather than having the entire crop reaped at once.

There were crops growing all over the island. None were any that we saw at home. I loved it – even the diners looked different, offering pineapple, coconut, and guava smoothies and pies.

This is downtown Honolulu as seen from the Bernice Pauahi Bishop Museum, looking southeast. To the southwest of the museum is Honolulu International Airport, and almost directly west is Pearl Harbor.

The buildings appeared to be made of materials that we didn't see at home, either. They were mostly white, but we also saw pinks and yellows, plus natural stones on the more expensive ones. Downtown Honolulu was ugly, in my father's opinion. It reflected the building boom of the 1950s and 1960s, and the aesthetics of those decades, with many of the apartment blocks now decaying among stretches of cracked pavement. I saw fabric stores as we passed by some of these older structures, and longed to wander around inside, staring at the gorgeous, colorful tropical patterns of hibiscus and plumeria flowers, palm trees, and whatever else they sold.

The buildings appeared to be made of materials that we didn't see at home, either. They were mostly white, but we also saw pinks and yellows, plus natural stones on the more expensive ones. Downtown Honolulu was ugly, in my father's opinion. It reflected the building boom of the 1950s and 1960s, and the aesthetics of those decades, with many of the apartment blocks now decaying among stretches of cracked pavement. I saw fabric stores as we passed by some of these older structures, and longed to wander around inside, staring at the gorgeous, colorful tropical patterns of hibiscus and plumeria flowers, palm trees, and whatever else they sold.

The Extinct Volcanoes of Oʻahu

Oʻahu has at least three extinct volcanoes; fortunately none are active. The entire island was formed by volcanic activity…many eons ago. For that reason, there is no reason to worry about getting immolated in any eruptions here.

These volcanoes were the part of Oʻahu that was formed last as the plume was passed when the tectonic plate moved away from it. There has been some land recession from each of the Hawaiian Islands. Meanwhile, sea level has risen, which is how they came to have the shapes that they have today.

This satellite image shows the effects of land recession and sea levels around the Hawaiian Islands. The image is from a Google Image search, and the source is ambiguous. Many possibilities came up: geo.arizona.edu, snow.sierranevada.edu, and others. I put this image in the unpublished travel guide I prepared for my family, along with a political map showing city and island names.

The three extinct volcanoes are all along the southern coast of the island. From west to east they are: the Punchbowl Crater, Diamond Head, and Koko Head. Looking at them from a distance, one can see that grass and other vegetation has established itself all up their sides; a view of them on Google Earth or Google Maps will show more of the same.

It's quite safe inside these craters. The lava plume that formed Oʻahu is not under it anymore, because the tectonic plate that this island sits on has shifted northwest of it. And since it's okay to enjoy the space inside of them, that's exactly what humans have done.

The Punchbowl Crater has the National Memorial Cemetery of the Pacific in it. We didn't go there, but I knew that a beautiful cemetery is in it when we were driving near it. That cemetery has been shown on *Hawaii Five-O*, in a scene where McGarrett's sister went to visit their father's grave. It's a beautiful, green place with a white marble chapel overlooking the graves, and a statue of a woman who represents all grieving mothers on the chapel's side.

Hawai'i's Senator Daniel Inouye, who died on December 17, 2012, is buried there, as are people (women as well as men) who fought in the Pacific theater of World War I, World War II, the Korean War, and the Vietnam War. American POWs who were held by the Japanese during World War II are buried there, too. It is a very popular tourist stop.

This is a view of the Punchbowl Crater as seen from the Bernice Pauahi Bishop Museum, looking southeast.

Diamond Head looks like a lovely place to go hiking when seen from Google Maps, with trails winding all through it, but it is closed to the public. Inside is a U.S. Army National Guard facility called Fort Ruger. Seen from above, Diamond Head is a circle, but seen from the side, it is taller on the side that faces the ocean.

This is another view of the Punchbowl Crater, seen from an intersection of H-1.

This is the landmark that is the stuff of Hawai'i postcards, and it serves as an iconic image of tropical tourism. It also reminds me of reasons why people send home postcards that say: "The weather is here – wish you were beautiful."

Okay...that's backwards, but deliberately so. Years ago, when I was a historic interpreter at the Mark Twain House in Hartford, Connecticut, our most senior interpreter, a retired middle school English teacher, quoted a postcard that had said exactly that. I love it; anything that is simultaneously outrageous and hilarious is fun for me.

This is Diamond Head as seen off the coast of Waikiki Beach, looking northeast.

Koko Head has a lot of trees in it, and even better, it has Koko Crater Botanical Gardens inside it. That would be great fun to walk through on a future visit – with my camera, of course. I can imagine finding image after fabulous image to save and use as desktop wallpaper on my computer, or even to send to the website of *National Geographic*...but that's for a future trip.

As it is, I gathered plenty of great shots that I might send there. That site has a section devoted to photographs taken by anyone who travels with a camera and wishes to share it with others, and possibly see it online and in a printed issue of the magazine.

Between the Wai'anae and Ko'olau Mountains

We drove north after we had seen enough of southern O'ahu's busy highways, ready for an adventure in the car. My father was in his element again. I couldn't get enough photographs of everything we saw...except, of course, for the Wheeler Army Airfield and Schofield Army Barracks.

We turned north off H-1 onto H-2, which is also known as the Kamehameha Highway. Looming up above on either side were the two mountain ranges of Oahu, the Wai'anae to the west, and the Ko'olau to the east. The mountains were both a volcanic red where the soil showed through and a brilliant green where trees and other vegetation had taken hold.

We continued that way until we were in the center of O'ahu, passing the Wheeler Army Airfield. Traffic slowed to a crawl there, and military police were out directing it. We waited and waited, inching forward through what must have been rush hour traffic, both military and civilian. Traffic may have been heavy on H-1, but it was never as congested as this.

At last we were through, still going north on the same road, but not on H-2. Now it was just a road called Kamehameha Highway rather than a state highway. We were in Wahiawa, and soon we came to an intersection. The road that crossed us was called Ka'ahumanu Road, and I thought of the Hawaiian king's favorite wife again, the one who was responsible for universal Hawaiian literacy and the end of the kapu system. I really enjoyed seeing a female government official remembered and honored.

My father turned right, and I realized that Ka'ahumanu Road was just a short connector between the highway and Wilikina drive. Not long after that intersection, my mother and I needed a rest room. As we passed the Dole Plantation, we insisted that my father double back, as we had ceased to enjoy the ride. He did, and we soon realized that we were in no hurry to simply get back into the car and rush on by.

The Dole Plantation

The Dole Plantation is not really a plantation. It's a tourist stop with a maze that had made the Guinness Book of World Records for currently being the world's largest. Not surprisingly, it is made in the shape of a huge pineapple. There is a large gift shop that sells pineapple candy, tee shirts, hats, jewelry, beach towels, candy, and lots of other souvenirs, and that's just in the front. (The rest rooms, by the way, are in the back right.)

We got out and went right in, past the kiosks that were set up outside, barely noticing the maze entrance off to the right. The parking lot was shaded by lots of palm trees, set back from the road. A farmer's market stand was on the left.

The building looked quite impressive, with a huge Dole corporate logo directly over the front entrance, but I knew that the actual pineapple plantation – the one that grows the marketable crop – was on the island of Lana'i, not here. O'ahu is where sugar plantations are. Big agribusinesses ran the growing operations now, with huge machines.

The Japanese, Chinese, Philippino, and Portuguese workers who toiled for a pittance at these plantations in the late nineteenth and early twentieth centuries no longer did so. They had moved on to less exhausting work – good for them! No more of being indebted to the plantation at every payday, forced to shop in the company store for food and toiletries at far higher prices than elsewhere. No more overseers who forced their contract employees to stay bent over for hours on end in the hot sun, never standing and stretching, with a whip and an insult for those who did so.

That is how these corporations got their start. We were visiting the showcase of a Big Five corporation. The overthrow of Hawai'i's last queen, Lili'uokalani, and the forced annexation of Hawai'i had further enabled the Dole company to become a lucrative enterprise.

But nothing of that showed here. The Dole company was the one putting on this presentation, and unabashed capitalism reigned here, not the deposed queen. My mother and I decided that, as long as we were here, we might as well explore the shop and go all the way to the back, where we could watch a demonstration of how best to cut up a pineapple.

My father didn't mind. He went and sat in the car, as he always does whenever my mother and I want to look around a shop. The demonstration wasn't starting yet, so I went back to the spot between the rest rooms with my camera and took a picture of the what hung there:

Between the rest rooms was a framed aerial photograph of the Dole Pineapple Maze. It was pretty.

Next, I went outside with the camera. It didn't matter what I thought of how the Big Five had treated its non-white workers in the past; it was over, and I always want to learn whatever there is to learn, regardless of my opinions. I'm a curious person, but I won't just absorb the data like a machine, either. The human costs and elements count for a lot.

Back inside the shop, we couldn't look at enough tee shirts, because we wanted to buy some for my father and David. But…we couldn't find double extra-large in the ones we liked, which came as a surprise. I had read that Hawaiian men grew to great sizes and heights, and so that size and one larger were a lot easier to find here in almost every clothing choice. Nevertheless, we soon gave up and went to look at the candy.

There was chocolate-covered pineapple, coconut, macadamia nut, and candied pineapple.

Should we get some to take back to Nana? My mother debated it for several minutes, until she decided that carrying it back on the plane, first to the Big Island of Hawaii and then across the Pacific and across North America, would be more of a hassle than it was worth to my grandmother.

The farmers market tent, to the left of the main building.

The entrance to the Pineapple Maze, which is in the Guinness Book of World Records as the world's largest.

The pineapple cutting demonstration was starting, so we went to the back left of the store, past more souvenirs, to watch. A woman with a microphone attached to her shirt explained that pineapples grow from pollinated flowers. She talked about how to tell when one is ripe, pointing out the color and firmness of the one she held.

Next, she began to cut it open, first removing the stem, then cutting it in half, and then cutting the halves in half again, so that she had four long quarters lying on the cutting board. She removed the center portion, explaining that it contained the most fiber, and although edible, it was very difficult to chew.

She sliced each quarter, shook a reddish powder of some spice mixture that tasted okay (but I could have done without it) onto the lot, and poked a toothpick into each piece. With that, she was done, and invited us all to come up and take a piece. There must have been at least 40 people watching this, because even though I was at the front, it was difficult to get to the cutting stand. I grabbed three pieces and back off, giving one to my mother, eating another, and finally going all the way out to my father, who was sitting in the parking lot with his window open. He liked it.

Before we left to go on this trip, I read something else about pineapples that fascinated me. It was probably because I had read *The Da Vinci Code* by Dan Brown. A pineapple is formed with two interlocking helices. Eight of them go one way, and thirteen of them go the other way, just as succeeding parts of the Fibonacci sequence of numbers: 0, 1, 1, 2, 3, 5, 8, 13, 21, 34, 55, 89, 144, and so on and on and on. Each number in the sequence is the sum of the preceding two.

We took a last look around the kiosks on the porch, which were selling jewelry, then got back into the car. We had seen enough, and we were ready to go as far north as my father judged that there was time for before the it got too late in the day. He wanted to go swimming in the lagoon at the resort that evening, before we went out to dinner. He had us on a tight schedule!

The North Shore

Back into the car we got, having spent no money in the Dole building. I felt rather pleased with myself about that. Here I was, surrounded by temptations, prompted almost everywhere to surrender money, and I was saving it for books and some gifts for my husband. I was being careful with my resources.

We drove north on Kamehameha Highway, which was now a paved road with one lane going each way. It was paved with asphalt, so the ride was a lot quieter and more comfortable than on H-1. Sugar fields and tree farms were on both sides, with the two mountain ranges still close by.

A tree farm, with one different evergreen by the road. Another tree farm, with more evergreens in front, and wind turbines on the horizon.

We saw wind turbines on the right, and I kept trying to get a good shot of them.

At last I got the photograph I was after: all along the horizon, way at the back of this field, are white wind turbines.

We emerged from the saddle road of the island at last onto the north shore, and my father drove to the right, going farther north for a little while. At this point, he announced that we didn't have time to go all of the way to the northernmost point of the island, which was a mild disappointment because the Opana radar station was once up that way. That is where the first Japanese planes that hit Pearl Harbor were sighted from, but today that station is gone, and only a marker identifies the spot, so I didn't say anything.

Even though my father was budgeting our time now, he did drive up the coast enough for us to see quite a bit of the area. I found myself thinking of the Drew Barrymore and Adam Sandler movie, *50 First Dates*, which was filmed in northern Oʻahu. The area looked more or less like the scenes from the movie. I was having fun thinking of movies that were filmed around here.

We ended up going north along the coast with the Koʻolau Mountains on our right for a few miles, then doubling back and driving in the opposite direction for an even shorter stint. It is not possible to drive the other way, around the Waiʻanae Mountains and down the west coast, because there isn't a road on that tip – only a trail.

Pretty soon we were in the bright sunshine with small houses and villages all around us, and surfers. The surfers were very serious about enjoying themselves. They had a beautiful beach to rest on. There were banyan and palm trees, rocks, and plenty of sand. Spending a whole day on a beach is not something that I usually dream of doing, but this one looked really tempting.

There was a monument to the soldiers who fought in the Korean War on this beach too.

A guy next to it was packing up at the end of a lovely day spent teaching people how to surf.

After admiring the beach vistas, we headed back the other way to see the town. It was almost a historic area, with structures that dated from the early twentieth century, built when this state was still a territory. There were houses, restaurants, shops, a church or two, and even a small bus that served as a restaurant. It was painted blue, with sea creatures all over it.

The Blue Water Shrimp Café bus, with its mural of crustaceans, fish, and a sea turtle.

We continued around the bend of what turned out to be Waialua, and I took more pictures of the area. We saw pretty blue flowers growing thickly in front of one house, and that typical house colors were white and pale blue. The houses didn't appear to have basements or garages, but they looked pleasant with their lanais, lawns, and fruit trees.

This winding road curved through Waialua.

It was time to head south again. My father was persuaded not to hurry so fast that I couldn't get out and take some better photographs. Taking them from a moving vehicle really doesn't yield great results, and we weren't coming back this way.

He pulled over to the side of the road – Kamehameha Highway again – and I got out to photograph the sunlight on the Waianae Mountains. It was worth it. My father was done taking photographs for the day; he had done that at Waikiki, during the submarine ride, so it was up to me. The view was like nothing we saw elsewhere on the island, where things were so built up.

Down the highway we drove, until my mother and I wanted to stop at the Dole rest rooms again. But the doors were locked! It was after 5 o'clock, with miles and miles ahead of nothing but military areas and no other chances. The security guard took pity on us and let us back in, emphasizing that we could not buy anything. My mother almost forgot about that when we came out. I include this for the benefit of future travelers who will inevitably find themselves in this situation.

My father bore right at the intersection with Ka'ahumanu Road this time. We wanted to see what Ka'ahumanu Road was like. It was a minor deviation from the way we had come, taking us around a small waterway when we had to turn onto Wilikina Drive. Once we had done so, we found ourselves on one side of a long fence with barbed wire at the top. It was the Schofield Army Barracks, with a huge field by the road.

Families were outside playing on that field, military parents, spouses, and kids of various ages. I couldn't tell what the games were, but there were a lot of families out there. The military housing was in rows beyond them. I found myself thinking about what their lives were like. How much of Oʻahu did they get to enjoy, I wondered?

We were having a great time here, and seeing a lot. I turned my thoughts back to the beautiful mountain views until we came out of the valley and back onto H-1. It wasn't much longer before we were back at Ko Olina, ready to cook dinner and enjoy the sunset on the lanai.

An Electric Submarine Ride Off Waikiki

Our next thrill was a submarine ride with Atlantis Submarines.

That company operates electric submarines off Waikiki on Oʻahu, out of Lahaina Harbor on Mauʻi, and from Kona on the Big Island. Each submarine is a 65-foot vessel, air-conditioned, battery-powered, non-polluting vessel, certified by the Coast Guard. It emits nothing but compressed air into the water.

We set off for our submarine adventure on Thursday morning, off down H-1, through its heavy traffic, then into downtown Honolulu, looking for the right side street. Our tour was to go out at 11 o'clock in the morning from a pier on Waikiki Beach. We were required to arrive by 10:30 a.m. at the Hilton Hawaiian Village in Waikiki.

We brought our AAA map of Hawaiʻi, opened it to the section that focuses on Honolulu, and proceeded to get lost and confused. The adventure was beginning again, though not the kind that we sought.

The problem was that all we had to go on was the e-ticket from AAA and the map. The ticket gave the address simply as "Atlantis Adventures Pier, Hilton Hawaiian Village in Waikiki" and nothing more; no street name.

The map had a spot on it, just a little black square, labeled Atlantis Submarines. That seemed very helpful. A small side street labeled Paoa Place led, seemingly, directly to it. Off we went, searching for Paoa Place.

We found it, and my father turned down it.

Alas, it was a service area to the Hilton Hawaiian Village in Waikiki. It was the back, where trucks unloaded. This was not it. Where would we park? Fortunately, there were men walking around the trucks, busy unloading, so we asked where we were supposed to go. They were probably used to this. They told us to drive right to the front of the hotel, all the way around onto Kalakaua Avenue again, left and left again.

Yes, this is definitely where the Five-0 cop found a small, unobtrusive door, slipped in, and viewed recordings.

We did that, and passed a tall parking garage as we did so, glumly realizing that a parking fee was likely in our future. We always try to avoid those if possible, but sure enough, it wasn't. My father pulled up to the porte-cochère of the hotel, and agreed to valet parking when it became clear that a long walk was in store for anyone who chose to self-park.

We all got out and turned to look at the hotel lobby, which, like the one at Ko Olina Beach Villas, was partially outdoors. I wondered what the hotel did during hurricanes and other storms. Did they have ways to wall this area up? There was a huge, attractive carpet, a chandelier, and some nice lobby furniture, all open to the driveway on one side and a pool with a fountain and garden on the other side.

For now, it was idyllic.

The lobby of the Hilton Hawaiian Village in Waikiki. I'm quite sure I've seen Officer Kono Kalakaua go to view hotel security recordings at this lobby on Hawaii Five-0.

This is the pretty view we looked at from the lobby. Straight across it, beyond the pools and on the edge of the beach, is a small stand with a pale green tent top. It is visible in this image. That's the Atlantis stand.

We saw this metal elephant among the palm plants and other greenery as we walked first left and then right, around the pools, past some upscale boutique shops, and down to the beach. We looked back at the lobby and water fountain from the swimming pool here, almost to the Atlantis tent.

When I heard that there was a shop on the ship that would ferry us across to the submarine, I decided that I would look for a DVD. It would make a nice souvenir. I could study it in detail later, at home, and show it to friends and family.

Here is the Atlantis tent, but the people working under it told us that with reservations and an e-ticket, we didn't need to stop at it. We were to pass this and proceed directly to the pier, so we did.

The one that was for sale described the three places that Atlantis Submarines operated out of: Kona, on the Big Island, Lahaina Harbor, on Mau'i, and Waikiki, on O'ahu. The DVD informed us that:

> Off Kona, coral reefs grow on underwater volcanic eruptions that are 18,000 years old.
> It's an underwater garden. Yellow tangs feast on the algae that grows among the coral. Butterfly fish swim only in pairs. Raccoon butterfly fish change color. There are 2 sunken ships off Kona.

Off Mauʻi, Lahaina Harbor is where the submarine leaves from – north side of Mauʻi. Mauʻi, Molokaʻi, Lanaʻi, and Kahoʻolawe were once one island. It's another coral reef tour.

Off Waikiki, the difference was that the coral reefs were all artificially created.

But this tour was on Oʻahu. I won't bother with what the DVD said (it wouldn't play that part anyway!), as I can simply describe our own experience. We had fun!

The pier itself had a dark blue tent top, which was reached by a narrow walkway over the sands of Waikiki.

The Atlantis Pier had a ticket area, a photographer who posed each arriving party with the Diamond Head Crater in the background (purchase optional), and a long seating area with two rows arranged back-to-back, exactly as we would be seated aboard the submarine. We were each issued a ticket made of firm, flexible plastic that we would have to surrender before leaving. The company recycled the tickets by handing them out over and over again.

Here is the ticket – a boarding pass that our voucher entitled us to borrow.

We sat down and watched as the *Discovery*, the boat that would ferry us out to the submarine and back, approached. The ride would take twenty minutes each way – plenty of time to enjoy the views.

Atlantis Submarines is a very well-run, efficient operation. The staff showed us what to expect every step of the way, and we were kept comfortable at all times. We had a shaded tent to sit under while we waited, and the seating arrangement ensured that there would be no surprises.

Discovery approaches. We saw a sea turtle in the water as we waited, but the sunlight was so bright that the photograph I took didn't come out.

Discovery arrives at the Atlantis Pier.

The gangplank is put into place.

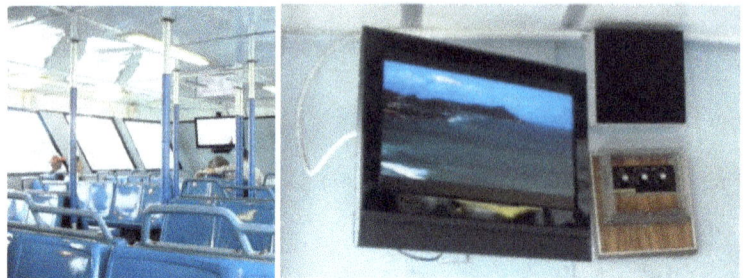

The seating area on the lower deck, inside. The DVD that was for sale played on several mounted screens around the small ship.

The gift shop was toward the back, with tee shirts, DVDs, mugs, hats, and other souvenirs.

Here it is: the submarine that we were to take a ride in: Atlantis XIV.

We boarded the *Atlantis XIV* and met Jason Q----, our guide, and were told that each ride takes 2 guides. Only one narrates, and they switch off so that their voices don't get tired. I could appreciate that; I used to do 4 tours a day at the Mark Twain House in Hartford, Connecticut.

We listened to our guide joke about everything he could think of a joke about, and when everyone was seated, he told us a little bit about himself and the crew. Some had navy experience. He himself had grown up on Oʻahu as a Native Hawaiian (and part Caucasian, judging from his name and appearance).

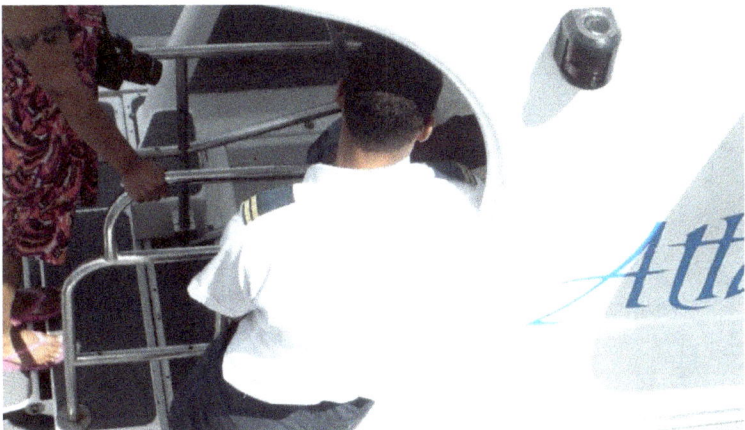

People disembarking – or boarding – the submarine. The view is the same either way. You turn to face the ladder, walk to it, then turn around to climb down, or the reverse.

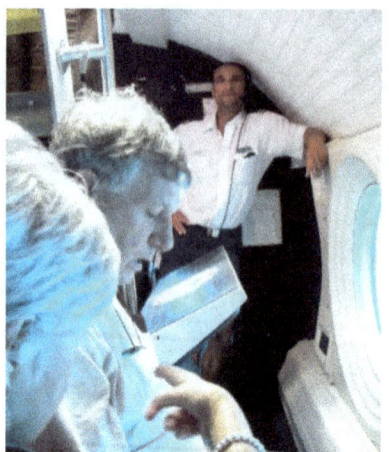

This is Jason Q----, our guide. He was cheerful and entertaining.

Jason said that his family was poor by most standards, but he had never wanted for anything because his father taught him traditional Hawaiian spear fishing. He knew all of the names of the fish we saw in Hawaiian as well as in English, and we realized that he knew and was literate in both languages. He was fun and fascinating simultaneously, an ideal quality in a guide.

The couple next to me were on their honeymoon, and Jason took a survey of the passengers: how many honeymooners? Several couples raised their hands. Retired couples, families with kids, and single women traveling in groups rounded out the tour.

This is the view down the submarine, looking to the back. We were lucky; we got the first few seats, right up close to Jason.

Our pilot didn't say anything; he just waved and smiled when Jason introduced him.

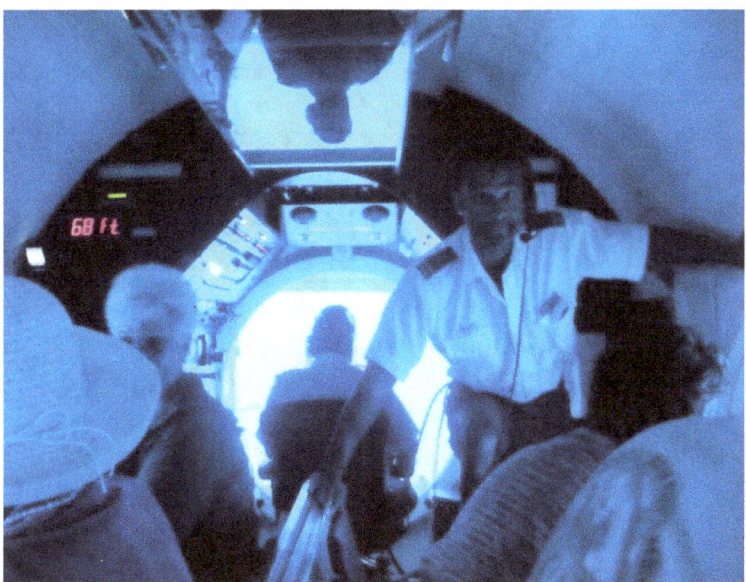

Jason, checking our reactions to his jokes.

We all got settled, and my father took out his camera. I looked forward to seeing the difference in the results that we would get with our respective devices: my inexpensive point-and-shoot versus his professional camera. He said I could have his images for this book.

It was at this point that Jason quipped, "If you're wondering which side of the submarine is better, it's the *other* side." He started to elaborate that the grass is always greener, but I chimed in with the more accurate metaphor that the water is always bluer…he liked that.

Then my father delivered the coup de grace: "No, it's the *inside* of the submarine that's better." Everyone close to the front heard this exchange, and thought it was hilarious.

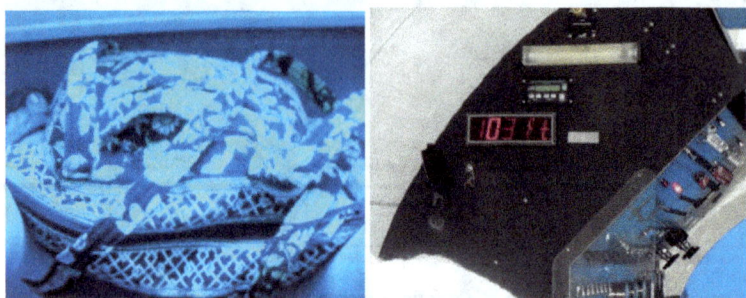

Soon everything was blue! We dropped to a depth of 103 feet. Jason did say that we were aiming for 100 feet.

As we went down into the depths of the water, Jason told us that the first color on the spectrum to drop out of our perception would be red, which would of course include any shade of pink. I looked at the pink orchid blossoms in the pattern of my handbag, and watched them turn first purple, then mauve, and then blue. I also turned to look at a woman with a red blouse and a red flower in her hair. It was fascinating to see her clothes seem black in a minute or so.

This image was shot by my father, whose professional camera produced very different images than mine, images that picked up a lot more detail.

This was one of the images that I took, so the difference was one of light blue and too much light versus the perfect amount. But, I aimed my camera at different things. This is a volcanic bubble.

As the submarine moved around under the water, I was glad that I had read about volcanic activity and how the Islands were formed. Jason pointed out a volcanic bubble on the ocean floor. This bubble was formed eons ago, and was not a threat to us, but he didn't add that.

The people on the other side of the submarine couldn't see this, but Jason announced that they would see it on the way back. I was happy to be sitting on the same side as our guide, so that I could see whatever he talked about as he did so.

With that, the submarine passed a series of layered, rectangular, sunken sculptures. Some engineering students had made them expressly for the purpose of these tours.

Sunken sculptures.

Next up: a sunken fishing/cargo boat. This boat had carried soy sauce – a lot of it.

There had been a fire on board in the early 1990s, and a new type of fire extinguisher was on board (several, actually). The foam the extinguisher was loaded with was different from the old kind. The fire was caused – somehow – by flaming soy sauce. The crew tried to put out the flames with the equipment that they had, but it just got out of control. The effect of the chemicals in the foam made the whole ship an inferno. No one got hurt in the shallow waters – they jumped overboard – but the ship was utterly ruined.

Along came Atlantis Submarines, looking for a ship to sink. They acquired this hunk of junk for the great price of one dollar, and then spent a million dollars to clean up the crud that coated its entire surface above water (the fire had been properly extinguished after professional firefighters were summoned). The ship became an artificial reef on the tour.

Sea turtles and fish swam in and out of it, but something was wrong: the divers employed by Atlantis Submarines kept finding sea turtle skeletons inside. Holes had to be cut so that the sea turtles could easily find their way back out. Sea turtles are a protected species, and this company prides itself on protecting the environment and endangered species.

Jason also informed our group that the waters off Waikiki are polluted by suntan lotion. It's not good for the coral or the fish. Tourists slather the stuff on, then go swimming, which is how it gets in the water.

The hull of the sunken ship was completely coated with coral.

Jason told us that the company has three scuba divers on duty at all times when the submarines are in operation. They are there just in case anything goes wrong; otherwise, they have a lovely time, day after day, diving and exploring the waters off Waikiki. IF something goes wrong with the submarine, such as a failure to rise to the surface, the divers swim up to the huge pontoons that weigh it down and remove them. The submarine then rises to the surface.

We felt very safe.

The ship was fun to look at. We saw the windows of the cabin, and beautiful fish swimming around it.

The crow's nest.

The next sight to see was a set of sculptures made out of a series of coils.

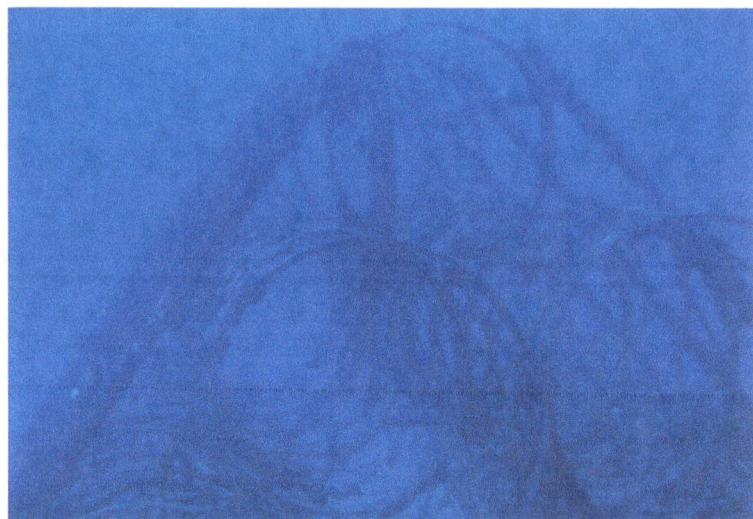

These tall sets of coils were like small triangles or pyramids.

    The last sight on the tour was the most fun of all.
    It was a sunken, crashed airplane.
    It was the same sunken, crashed airplane that appeared on the television show *Lost*. I never watched that show until the series finale, but I knew that the characters had been in a plane crash and spent years wondering what happened to them on a deserted, tropical island.
    The crash was staged – no one in real life got hurt in this plane.
    And here is the best part: in return for the use of this plane as a coral reef and tour sight ever after, the television production crew was allowed to film the series premiere right where we saw the airplane.

Here it is: the actual sunken crashed airplane from the television series Lost.

    Accordingly, many fake dead bodies were affixed to the wreckage and left in place for this.
    The television production crew worked until the daylight was all gone, and left.

They did not have time that day to remove all traces of the fictitious story they were creating, but planned to return the next day and do so.

The next day, the submarine went out BEFORE the television crew did.

As the submarine passed the fake corpses, Jason was happily into the stream of his running commentary when he heard shocked gasps from his entire audience. He turned around and did a double-take. It was hilarious! He explained the situation, and the fake corpses were soon gone.

The submarine had circled back around at the coil sculpture, so we had seen it all.

Time to resurface and get back onto the *Discovery*.

In its shop, I bought a tee shirt and a DVD, and the woman who sold them to me gave me not one but 2 Atlantis Submarines bags with those purchases. The bags were beautiful, made of recycled plastic and decorated with underwater scenes of coral and tropical fish and the corporate logo, with bright blue cloth handles. They are nearly 2 feet deep, and make great tote bags.

I wandered around the ship, out the back, past the rest rooms, which were clean, complete with soap, water, toilet paper, and towels (no roughing it for tourists!), and up the white-painted stairs hanging onto the railing.

Up on the deck, we passengers were behind the captain's section of the ship, under a white cover with plenty of seating. A flagpole flew the U.S. and Hawaiian flags. I looked down and saw the submarine pulling away, now laden with the passengers who had just debarked from this ship and onto that one.

I took this photograph through the windows of Discovery, looking at Waikiki in the distance. Then I went onto the upper deck of the Discovery.

Looking back at the submarine as we headed back to shore.

Diamond Head Crater, seen from aboard Discovery on the upper deck.

The return trip was like looking at every postcard I had ever seen of Waikiki, but in real life.

The Royal Hawaiian Hotel has been rebuilt on Waikiki Beach. It's the pink one. The original was a huge, rambling, Victorian one, also pink. I was looking for this, and there it was, easy to spot.

Lots of pleasure boats were out. We saw someone attached to a boat, wind-sailing.

Here I am in the bright sunshine, with my pink plumeria tee shirt, having a wonderful time.

Someone saw me walking around with my little point-and-shoot camera and offered to take my picture with Diamond Head Crater behind me. I accepted, of course.

Approaching the beach, we saw the area just to the right of the Hilton.

The Hilton Hawaiian Village, seen from a distance off Waikiki.

Back at the Atlantis Pier, it was announced that all of the photographs that we had posed for were developed and packaged. They were for sale, but we didn't have to buy ours if we didn't' like it. We decided to have a look at our photograph.

The photographer had them all in frames and clear plastic envelopes, plus a small magnet with each one. The magnet looked like a little picture frame, and contained miniature just like the larger one. We liked ours, and my mother bought it.

The photographer getting our photograph. Here we are, on October 18, 2012, as the date-stamp of Atlantis Submarines attests.

The walkway from the Atlantis Pier to the pool at the Hilton Hawaiian Village. The walkway over the water to Atlantis Pier.

We left the beach and explored the Hilton Hawaiian Village now that our tour was over and we were on our own. There were penguins, sea turtles, shops, and restaurants, but we were thinking of lunch. My father was thinking of sitting down to wait while my mother and I browsed, so we paused to decide that we would all meet at the restaurant by the beach.

Best of all, several sea turtles lived with the penguins, and I got a series of great images of them, swimming and sunning themselves. They looked fairly young because they were rather small; sea turtles can live for half a century or more. They need to surface to breathe. They were beautiful.

It is illegal to approach one in the water, but if one approaches a swimmer, it's okay.

These penguins looked just like the one that Adam Sandler's character bathed in the movie 50 First Dates, which was filmed on Oʻahu.

A trio of sea turtles in the sun.

This was the view from the restaurant where we ate lunch.

    My mother and I decided to finishing looking at the shops after we ate lunch so that my father wouldn't have to wait. It was time to eat now anyway. We went back to meet my father, and we found a nice table close to the stone wall and palms that bordered the restaurant. We each got the fish and chips. The chips were long, thin, perfectly cooked ones with garlic aioli sauce. I had a pineapple iced tea. It was perfect.

    With lunch over with, my mother and I went off to shop, and my father went to get the car, knowing that he would have to wait. He was prepared to do so. My mother headed directly for the kiosk that she had been drawn to when we first arrived at the hotel and inspected the sarongs. After looking through them, she bought one. It was a pretty, sheer thing in hues of magenta and orange, and she planned to wear it to the lu'au we were to attend the next evening.

After she got the sarong, we went back around toward the restaurant to look at the dresses and muumuu in the boutiques. I tried on several of them, but found nothing that fit quite right, or else the problem was a lack of pockets. I want deep, useful pockets in everything I own, so I didn't buy a dress. We went back through the main lobby to see a few more kiosks.

My mother having fun shopping for a sarong. This was the view north into a little garden area next to the kiosk with the sarongs.

Looking south in the lobby of the Hilton. The driveway is to the right, and more kiosks are ahead.

My mother started worrying that my father was being kept waiting for too long a time, so we made short work of looking through the kiosks south of the lobby. I found a gauzy white blouse with flouncy sleeves to buy that looked really comfortable and pretty for a tropical climate, but it took a while to actually buy it. Some other people were taking their time to buy several things, choosing more and more as the girl rang up the lot.

I turned and looked at the pool next to the area to pass the time. A swan with intriguing feather markings swam past. It was white with a black neck and head and a small red growth over its beak. We had never seen one like it before, and I got my camera out again.

The swan with the black neck and head lives in a nice pool with a miniature Asian temple.

At last the purchase was made and we went to look for my father. Where was he? This was not at all like him, to not be right here waiting, eager to drive us off to the next event. My mother said that we should sit down and wait for him.

Silly us; with valet parking, my father had handed over a ticket and the car had been brought back to him. After a long and confusing wait, I wandered around the poles that formed the center of a turnaround in front of the hotel lobby, and there he was. He had been told to pull up beyond the poles and wait there, but we couldn't see him from the lobby.

I went back and told my mother he was there and we got in, with me saying, "Don't laugh at us," explaining how we had missed him and waited…and waited. He didn't say anything, and off we went, to swim in the lagoon at Ko Olina Beach Villas.

'Iolani Palace

'Iolani Palace is actually the second hale (house) to stand at 364 South King Street in Honolulu. The first one, called Hale Ali'i, which meant House of the Chief, was a much smaller structure, and became infested with termites. King David Kalakaua decided to tear it down (not that he had much choice on that count) and replace it with a much grander one, a palace that would compare favorably in the minds of foreigners to those of other nations' ruling families.

He also decided, as the amenity had just been invented, to have an electricity system installed throughout the new palace, which cost as much as the rest of the building. There were also bathrooms with toilets, sinks, and tubs, but that was less of a novelty. 'Iolani Hale/Palace had electricity before the White House in Washington, D.C. It was completed in 1882, and he and Queen Kapi'olani held their coronation there in 1883.

'Iolani means "hawk of heaven" – appropriate enough for the residence of a royal family. It brings to mind the roc, the phoenix, and even dragons. Mythic birds are fascinating parts of ancient Persian, Sanskrit, European, Maori, and Hawaiian lore.

But back to the palace.

It was shown in the 2009 movie *Princess Ka'iulani*, enabling the viewer to engage in armchair tourism as the camera panned through halls with portraits of the ali'i and parquet flooring, a grand wooden staircase with electrified statues on the newel posts at its foot and a light, airy view of the upper floor at its top.

We set out after 9 o'clock on Friday, October 19, 2012, enduring H-1's heavy traffic for over an hour until we were at last sitting at the first traffic light off the exit ramp. My father had the car in the leftmost lane of a one-way, four-lane thoroughfare. It was yet another beautiful day.

One quick rest stop at the Safeway (grocery store) across the street and all the way to the right, and we were on our way to the palace. My father found it in short order, and when the car was passing it on South King Street, I asked him to let me out so I could take photographs. We were actually between 2 palaces, so riding any farther seemed like a waste of time.

He stopped the car, and my mother hopped out with me to look at everything. I shot an image that showed the 'Iolani Palace in the distance behind the gate, because it included the royal coat of arms on either side, plus lots of beautiful palm trees.

Here is how to find it:

'Iolani Palace
365 South King Street
Honolulu, O'ahu 96804-9983
Hawai'i
Phone: (808) 522-0822
E-Mail: info@iolanipalace.org
Website: http://www.iolanipalace.org/

There is a huge lawn all around the palace, which sits right in the center. A driveway goes straight up to the front of the palace, and paths go directly away from it on either side. The Coronation Bandstand is on the front left lawn. The barracks building, called 'Iolani Hale, is also on the left, beyond that left path. 'Iolani Hale holds the gift shop, rest rooms, and ticket sales area. In the back is a parking area that stretches around from part of the left to all of the right side, with a huge banyan tree providing shade for the parked vehicles. Another large tree by 'Iolani Hale spreads it leaves out like a huge fan, providing shade for the spot where the Royal Hawaiian Band performs each week.

The Hawaiian coat of arms says: "Ua mau ke ea o ka'aina i ka pono" – "**The life of the land is perpetuated in righteousness**".

After we looked at the gates of 'Iolani Palace, I turned the other way, to look at the other palace across the street, Ali'iolani Hale. King Kamehameha V had it built – or started to – for himself, but died before it was finished. It was going to be his residence until he decided that the kingdom needed an administrative building, and so it became an office building.

On the television show *Hawaii Five-O* – the new version with Alex O'Loughlin and Scott Caan – the Hawaiian police are depicted as having their headquarters in this building. The old version of the show had the police in 'Iolani Palace, which was used and abused as government offices after Queen Lili'uokalani was deposed in 1893.

It was used and abused by the Provisional Government, then by the governors of the Territory of Hawai'i, and again by the governors of the state of Hawai'i, until finally a new building was ready for them in 1969 and the restoration began. The wood floors, paneling and staircase were all refinished, and the work of reacquiring original artifacts began. It is ongoing.

The famous statue of King Kamehameha the Great is in front of Ali'iolani Hale, and I wanted to go over to it for a closer look. My mother followed me, and I shot several photographs. The statue has 2 plaques under it, one that explains the statue and another that describes the Law of the Splintered Paddle, laid down by Hawai'i's first king of all of the Islands. That statue sometimes has scores of huge lei draped over it, but it had none that day.

Thomas Ridgeway Gould made this bronze statue in 1883, commissioned by King Kalakaua. That plaque gives a brief biography of Kamehameha the Great, and details about his traditional Hawaiian attire: a *mahiole* (feathered helmet), an *'ahu'ula* (long feathered cloak), and *ka 'ei kapu o Liloa* (sacred feather sash of Liloa, worn around the waist and over one shoulder). The king carries a long, barbed spear, the *ihe laumeki*, in his left hand, and gestures in welcome with his right hand.

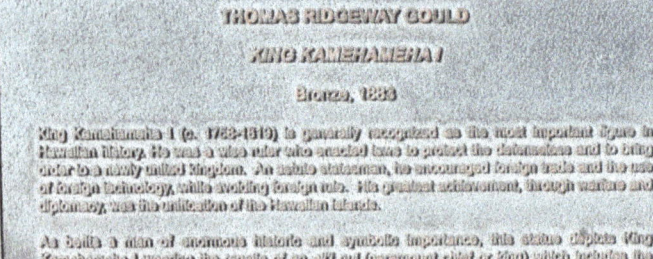

That was all very interesting, but I found plenty of books about that to buy and read. What really fascinated me was the Law of the Splintered Paddle, laid down by that same king. It promised that: *every man, woman and child would be able to travel freely and in peace, with the right "to lie down to sleep by the roadside without fear of harm."* This law was named for an incident when Kamehameha the Great was still fighting for control of the Islands. When he leaped up onto the land, someone whacked him over the head with a paddle, which splintered.

After we had seen enough, my mother and went back across the street to get tickets and tour ʻIolani Palace. There was no point in seeing Aliʻiolani Hale; it's still offices, as was intended from shortly after its construction began. We went back across South King Street, through the gate, and up the driveway.

Halfway up the driveway on the right, my mother paused by a palm tree and asked me to take some pictures. She liked it; it was tall and had a thick trunk, and we hadn't yet spent much time focusing on the tropical trees, walking up close enough to touch them and inspect them closely. Of course, that would change later in the day, when we toured a garden, but this felt new and exciting because it felt like our first chance to stop and scrutinize one.

After I took her picture with the palm tree, we continued on up the driveway to the front steps of the palace, and then turned left when we saw signs telling us where to buy tickets. We saw what I later learned was the Coronation Bandstand to the left. The Coronation Bandstand is a beautiful structure that was completed in time for King Kalakaua's 1883 coronation ceremony, and then used as a place for performances by the Royal Hawaiian Band. It has the Hawaiian flag in the shape of a shield all around its dome.

Here is the top of the palm tree that my mother liked...

...and here she is, grinning and pointing at its trunk. The Coronation Bandstand is in the background.

The Coronation Bandstand is where King Kalakaua first crowned himself, and then crowned his wife, Queen Kapi'olani. They were best friends, sorry that they had no children, and happy to spend as much of their spare time together as they could. The crowns were made of gold and red cloth in a style that looked as much as possible like those of other royal families around the world, except that the details were Hawaiian: a taro leaf motif was shown in the gold arches going up the crowns to the top.

The coronation was going off just fine, without a hitch, until Kalakaua tried to crown his wife. It wouldn't go on! The problem was her hair, which was beautiful coiffed into a bun with waves and curls piled high onto her head. The crowns had both been fitted to their heads in advance, measured carefully, but Kapiʻolani had her hair down. Princess Kaʻiulani was a little girl who watched all this, and she described how awkward the situation was as the crowd watched. The queen's ladies in waiting rushed to take out pins and smooth out the waves and curls. The king tried again – no good. A few more smoothes and tucks, and he squashed the thing onto the queen's head. Oww…oh well, at least it was over and done with!

When we turned left, we had a chance to see the details on this beautiful palace, which is the only royal palace in the United States. That's a question that has been on *Jeopardy!*, a game show that my parents and I love to watch, and I knew the answer when it came up. The bill for constructing ʻIolani Palace and the bill for installing electricity were equally expensive, and this place had electricity before the White House in Washington, D.C. did. But that's not surprising; the White House was built a long time in advance of the advent of electricity. ʻIolani Palace was built shortly after the technology was developed. It made sense to install it at the same time.

After Queen Liliʻuokalani was deposed from her throne in 1893, the haole usurpers moved into the palace and used it as office space, and this continued until a modern building was ready next door in 1969. By then, ʻIolani Palace was an abused, scratched wreck. Ten years later, it was fixed up sufficiently to open as a museum. Tours could begin, and the revenue could be used to reconstitute the lost contents. A ceremony was held, and this cornerstone laid in the left corner of the foundation.

'Iolani Palace has a unique architectural style: American Florentine. It's a fusion of styles, just as many of Kalakaua's efforts were. It was a logical strategy on his part to mix Hawaiian details with foreign ones.

As we turned left, we saw what used to be the barracks for King Kalakaua's small Royal Guard and for the Royal Hawaiian Band. Both were under the direction of the Prussian bandmaster Henry Berger. The guards hated him with his strict Prussian ways, which were the antithesis of Hawaiian ways. The band loved him, though. Music is very important to Hawaiians, and he put in the maximum effort to get it right, studying their language and writing music in Hawaiian. Understanding these things about him is the key to understanding these reactions.

We went into 'Iolani Hale, the barracks building, and got our tickets. We did not get an audio tour; that was for people who didn't understand English. We would be going on a guided tour. Inside the Hale was a small courtyard with bright sunshine. The gift shop was on the right, and the rest rooms were on the left. The tickets were sold in the foyer as we entered.

The tour would last an hour inside the palace, except for the basement, which was included and would take fifteen minutes with the guide, plus as much other time as we needed to read about all of the exhibits on display down there. And great news: photography was allowed, as long as no flash was used. I adjusted my camera accordingly. The photographs I would get would not be ideal, but they would be better than nothing. This was so different from touring the Mark Twain House in Hartford, Connecticut, which allows NO photography at all.

We were in and out of the rest rooms fast, then back outside in the sunshine heading for the back of the palace's lanai. That was where we would meet our group and our guide. Up the stairs and onto the lanai we went, to be met by a smiling older haole lady in a long dress of some sort...a dress that is a challenge to describe. It wasn't exactly a Hawaiian muumuu. It looked like it was trying to be a muumuu, but the fabric lacked a Hawaiian pattern or bright colors.

There were actually two women there, both historic interpreters, so the other woman, a much younger Hawaiian, would take the group after us. Historic interpreters are tour guides who have studied the history and literature of the building, people, and time that they describe. They are paid, and they do not necessarily have to wear period costumes, even though the ones here did.

When we got up the steps, we showed our tickets at the desk (really just a small wooden table with drawers). We were welcomed with a smile, given crime scene booties to put over our shoes (a first in museum touring for me, but cool!), and told to find seats on the benches until the tour got underway.

This was our historic interpreter. She had retired to Hawai'i from Utica, New York with her husband to get away from the cold there. They wanted constant lovely weather, which made perfect sense.

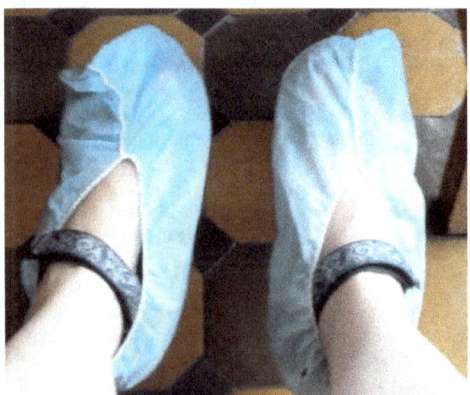

We went up the back steps onto the lanai, showed our tickets, and got crime scene booties.

At last the friendly haole guide led us inside, and around to the front door, where she paused with us at the foot of the grand staircase. Koa wood was used to make the staircase, the moldings, and the wood flooring throughout the palace, she informed us. The base of the staircase was roped off. She explained that it is closed off except for the Hawaiian aliʻi, because this palace was built by and for them.

Metal light fixtures in the forms of a woman and a man grace the newel posts at the foot of the palace's grand staircase.

Without further ado, the guide led us left, into the Blue Room. I guess many palaces – royal and presidential, depending upon the government of the nation described – have Blue Rooms. This room was a formal sitting room for receiving visitors and talking with them. There were beautiful tall, formal state portraits of King Kalakaua, Queen Liliʻuokalani, John Owen Dominis, and other royal family members hanging there.

Just inside the door of the Blue Room, King Kalakaua's portrait hangs on the left, and Princess Likelike's is on the right. Queen Liliʻuokalani's portrait is by the window in the Blue Room, on the left side of the building.

From the Blue Room, we could see the huge dining room with its red curtains.

The dining room was set for a state dinner.

The dining room was beautifully furnished. The historic preservationists had been lucky to find and retrieve most of the original furnishings, though work continued throughout the palace. Our guide brought us inside and paused to let us look. She talked for a few minutes, then asked for questions. I raised my hand and asked why the portraits on the wall were of white men. Where were the Hawaiians?

The answer was that they weren't missing at all. The custom was for visiting foreign dignitaries – diplomats and heads of state alike – to bring their portraits as gifts. Those portraits were commonly hung up in dining rooms, so that they would be seen during state dinners. The food served in here was not traditional Hawaiian food – it was haole recipes, which the Hawaiian royal family was thoroughly used to eating. However, many a luʻau with Hawaiian foods such as poi and roast pig were held outside, and at their boathouse in Pearl Harbor, and at other aliʻi homes, such as Princess Kaʻiulani's in Waikiki.

The guide showed us a small hallway that led past a small half bathroom, completely restored with beautiful wood paneling. We could see the staircase through it from the dining room.

Out in that hallway, we saw the dumb waiter that went down into the kitchen.

The dumb waiter, a wooden cupboard that could be pulled up and down like an elevator for dishes. The sink in the half bathroom by the dining room. The toilet in the half bathroom by the dining room.

After we saw the modern amenities, our guide led us out into the main hallway with the portraits, toward the back, and over to the other side, where the elevator was. As we gathered around to wait for it, my mother informed the guide that I used to do tours in Hartford, Connecticut at the Mark Twain and Harriet Beecher Stowe Houses (both on the same block). With that, the guide got quite friendly, though she was already very pleasant. We chatted for a minute or so, commiserating about the difficulty of dealing with the public, moving them along in a timely fashion while protecting historic artifacts from fingerprints and other infractions.

The guide gathered us at the front of the upper floor, facing out the windows.

We looked ahead at the front of the building, and at the top of the roped-off staircase.

The tour took us through four rooms, one on each corner of the upper floor. Each room also had a small, round room with a beautiful hanging light fixture in it, and windows all around. We could see those round rooms beyond the ropes that kept us from going very far into the four larger ones. There was also a bathroom upstairs, complete with a large bathtub. In addition to all that was a lanai all around, just as downstairs.

The four rooms we saw were: King Kalakaua's bedroom, Queen Kapiʻolani's bedroom, Queen Kapiʻolani's sitting room, and the room where Queen Liliʻuokalani was imprisoned for eight months after the 1895 coup failed to restore her to her throne. She was stuck in there day after day with no news, only a haole woman to keep her company, the wife of one of her usurpers. She sewed a quilt and embroidered it to pass the time.

This view of the wooden staircase was just as I remembered it from the Princess Kaʻiulani movie.

We started with King Kalakaua's bedroom. There wasn't much in it yet, but there was a large photograph from the time that he occupied it to show how it used to be.

This is the king's quilt, but not his bed. Here is the area of the room to the left of the bed.

This beautiful Chinese inlay table is for playing cards, which Kalakaua liked to do. This view shows Kalakaua's corner round room.

This is a photograph of the room as it looked when Kalakaua lived in it.

  The historic interpreter explained that after the haole takeover, everything was sold off to fund the provisional government that Sanford B. Dole was running. Personal items of historic interest were not valued as artifacts to be treasured for future study and cultural appreciation. Instead, as if to dispose of as much evidence of the crime as possible, things were sent off and the proceeds of the sales pocketed by the thieves. It makes no difference whether or not the haole usurpers thought of what they were doing this way; that is what happened.

  As I listened to the historic interpreter describe what happened to the contents of ʻIolani Palace after the haole takeover of Hawaiʻi, I was getting angry, but it was a very familiar anger. It was nothing that hadn't gone through my mind before when I had heard similar stories.

The whole thing reminded me of the explanation offered in *The Italian Job* by Ed Norton's character Steve: "Don't talk to me about right and wrong, because I just don't care [sic]. It was a lot of money and I wanted it." That sentiment pretty well sums up the theft of the land that became the contiguous United States and the Hawaiian Islands: it was a lot of paradise, and they wanted it, so they took it.

I'm so glad that I'm not writing as a student under the thumb of a conventional professor who holds the power of grades or a dissertation credit over me. If that were so, I would be told to keep my bias out of this, and I just don't want to. Don't talk to me about professional detachment, because I just don't want it.

We went into Queen Kapi'olani's bedroom next, which had as little in it as Kalakaua's did.

In this case, the curators have managed to recover both the queen's bed and her quilt. A close-up view of the queen's bed linens.

Here are the rest of the furnishings that have been recovered thus far, in Queen Kapi'olani's bedroom with a view of her corner round room, and a small desk.

The queen's furniture was beautifully restored – or perhaps it had just been valued by whoever had acquired it. The problem seems to have been finding things, not persuading people to either give or sell them back to the Hawaiian preservationists. Attitudes have changed dramatically since the theft of Hawai'i…at least, attitudes about historic and cultural preservation have changed. Haole possession of Hawaii is still a firmly entrenched attitude, but reconstituting and perfecting the historical record in the form of a National Historic Landmark and museum is now a respected practice.

Onward the tour went – to see the bathroom.

No surprises here – another toilet. I imagined maneuvering heavy skirts and petticoats and felt no envy. This was the dimly lit bathtub with a shower attachment over it. Did the queen have much light here? Did she sit and soak much, or read in the tub? Today's bathrooms seem like more fun to relax in than this one, polished though it is.

When we saw Queen Kapiʻolani's sitting room, we got a pleasant surprise: many of her furnishings have been recovered, restored, and set up there, complete with a lovely portrait of her. It was a beautiful room, and the collection of music on display close to the ropes showcased the musical talents of the royal family. Her husband and his three siblings all wrote music.

A view through the queen's sitting room to the round corner room. A portrait of Queen Kapiʻolani in her coronation gown overlooks her sitting room. The other side of the sitting room, with a door to the queen's bedroom.

Queen Kapiʻolani had been married before she married King David Kalakaua, but she had no children. When she married Kalakaua, again she had no children, but they were best friends. They were very happy together. Despite the grandeur of their rooms in Iolani Palace, they spent a lot of time in a large building out back, which no longer exists. It was a bungalow called Hale Akala, the Backyard Bungalow. It was two stories tall, and it had lots of plants in the landscaping all around the outside of it.

This painting of a traditional Hawaiian ship is just one of several that were on the wall to the right. Music by Lili'uokalani and Kalakaua was laid out on this conversation piece sofa.

Queen Kapi'olani is seated at right in this photograph, wearing a fabulous dress with peacock feathers on the skirt. The feathers were added in New York City, just before she and her sister-in-law, Princess Lili'uokalani, sailed for London, England, to attend Queen Victoria's Golden Jubilee celebration. The princess did the talking; the queen understood a little English, and communicated mostly in Hawaiian. Queen Victoria received them with all of the honors due to any other foreign royalty, and invited them for a private audience.

There is a whole city block behind 'Iolani Palace today, mostly lawn, but with a large, ugly, modern government building on it. This is the one that has been seen on

Hawaii Five-O. Hale Akala was in the spot where that ugly building is today. If one stands behind the palace but close to 'Iolani Hale and looks across that lawn, it is easy to see the front yard of Washington Place, the home of Queen Liliuokalani

That left the room where Queen Lili'uokalani was imprisoned to see.

Queen Lili'uokalani did not expect to be the ruling monarch when her brother became king. She had another brother, Prince Leleiohoku, who died shortly after Kalakaua became king. That was when she was named as Kalakaua's successor. She was very upset about the Bayonet Constitution, and when her brother traveled and left her in charge of the Hawaiian Islands, she was no pushover. She halted all commerce with all incoming ships until a smallpox scare was over, regardless of the outrage of the haole business interests.

This is how Queen Lili'uokalani passed the time while she was locked up with little to no human contact for months on end: she made a huge quilt, and embroidered her political history onto it, plus the lyrics to her songs. After all of the aggravation of getting only blurred, disappointing images of the queen's beautiful quilt, this image of the light fixture above it came out clear and sharp.

The queen embroidered sections of her quilt with a family tree, with the story of her imprisonment, and with lyrics to her songs. I was frustrated that I couldn't get a clearer, sharper, better image of it than this, but I could not use the flash on my camera, and the lighting was dim. Of course, a flash would have simply come out as a glare obscuring the quilt, so I guess I just couldn't win.

This is the lanai that Queen Lili'uokalani walked on during her imprisonment in 'Iolani Palace.

The deposed queen preferred her home across Beretania Street, which could be seen from the back of the building. But she couldn't see it for those eight months, as her rooms were at the front. She was only allowed to walk out on her lanai and enjoy the fresh air in the evenings, when the people would be at home and thus not see her.

After our visit to each of the upstairs rooms, it was time to go back downstairs, again via the elevator. We waited for a large group to come out and got back into the wood-paneled box. We had only seen half of the rooms on the ground floor, the historic interpreter told us. We still had to see King Kalakaua's office and the throne room.

We got out on the first floor and our guide proceeded to show us the other half of it.

The room we went into seemed to have most of its historic artifacts back, right down to the telephone. That phone likely wasn't the original, but at least it was historically accurate. It is hard to imagine this office as it was during the first half of the twentieth century and some of the second half, scuffed, full of ugly, institutional office furnishings (metal file cabinets, perhaps), with cheap blinds and invaders for occupants. But...we don't know how it looked. We only know that it didn't look this nice.

Kalakaua's office looks beautiful, and there is his photograph - upper left.

King Kalakaua's office was a fun place to visit. It had some of his original state papers, complete with his signature (maybe they were copies, but that wasn't the point), his walking stick was laid across the table, and there were photographs on the wall of him.

One showed him posing for an official picture, and another showed him on a visit to Japan, seated with three Japanese government ministers and two of his own. That was his March 1881 trip, the one in which he tried to arrange a marriage between his niece, Ka'iulani, and the Japanese crown prince. It didn't work out, but he wasn't upset...and neither was his niece.

The phone was on the wall right under the photograph from the Japan trip. People are spoiled by technological advances now, but Kalakaua must have thought that his phone was the pinnacle of innovation. An aide would likely have answered it, told the king who was calling, and then the king would have gotten up from his desk to talk to the person…unless he was "not in". People are the same everywhere; I'll bet that phone tag got underway shortly after the telephone was invented and the second one was installed!

King Kalakaua's office phone and the official photograph from his visit to Japan.

Hawai'i as it was when the Hawaiians fully owned and governed it seemed…nicer somehow. Even without the technology that we have today, it was nicer. Hawai'i had beautiful crafts, Hawaiian traditions, Hawaiian language and music everywhere, and less "development". The land was mostly still in its natural state, with a lot less human evidence. The bulk of the Waikiki area was trees, flowers, beach, and only one large hotel.

But…the plantations were full of unhappy workers in debt slavery, leprosy was still isolating and killing people, and the looming dread of and pressure to stave off haole takeover was still foremost in Hawaiians' minds.

No…life in Kalakaua's time had its detractions as well as its attractions.

The historic interpreter was very skilled at letting us get a good, long look at everything while telling us all about it yet not causing a pileup of tours coming in behind us. That's the tricky part of guiding groups of strangers through an historic building. People ask questions, they want to stay and see every detail, and the next tour might not be far behind.

My biggest problem was my camera. I have included images that show different angles of each room even when the light wasn't just right so that the reader can see what was there. With the flash banned, this was as good as it was going to get, but I am a perfectionist, so the results are frustrating even as I write this.

The historic interpreter was very nice. She could tell who was intensely interested in history and who wasn't, it seemed. She waited while I shot several photographs, using the time to tell more anecdotes. Clearly, the guides at 'Iolani Palace studied the history of the place and its people, and enjoyed telling visitors about it. It reminded me of my old job, but now I was on the other side of the situation, trying to take in as much as I could as fast as I could.

King Kalakaua's desk, walking stick, and lots of sunlight streaming in.

State papers with Kalakaua's writing on them, and his koa walking stick.

With Kalakaua's office and papers duly viewed, explained, described, and documented, we went out into the hall and around to the very front, once again facing the roped-off grand koa wood staircase. Looking to the right of it, our guide now ushered us with minor fanfare and pomp into the throne room.

The curators had made the most of all resources available to them since 1979 – photographic clues, historic records of decorative arts, and finances and connections allocated for the recovery and restoration of artifacts and furnishings – and it showed.

The carpet was historically accurate, a beautiful, brilliant red leaf pattern. The kahili were back, standing as sentinels on either side of King Kalakaua's and Queen Kapi'olani's thrones. Most of the chairs that lined either side of the room were back and restored to their original splendor. Beautiful curtains hung on the windows. The guide told us all this, and then I pointed out that there were 9 chairs on the right, but only 5 on the left. "You are very observant," she replied, and told me I would be interested to see what was on display in the basement.

Okay…I looked forward to it.

King Kalakaua and Queen Kapiʻolani's thrones and kahili.

A section of the throne room carpet, with its red leaf pattern.

That was it. Our guide took us back to the hallway, where she told us that those of us with tickets to see the kitchen and museum room in the basement could continue the tour with her. I paused to admire the huge carved vases of koa wood in the front hall.

The haole usurpers actually sold these beautiful things off! What a nuisance – and expense – to recover them. They should have given them to the aliʻi for safekeeping... but they didn't, because they wouldn't. No thief does that!

Out the back door, and down a set of stairs that led from outside and down into the basement we went, until the guide had most of our previous group in the kitchen. The walls were white with pale wooden fixtures: cabinets, moldings, doors, and a huge worktable in the center. She pointed out the dumb waiter next to the cabinets. Across from the cabinets was a huge, copper-lined, empty space. The oven and stove used to be there. The butler's pantry was just inside the door that we came through, on the right.

n the wall in between the door we walked through and the butler's pantry was a large museum sign. The sign had reproductions of a dinner menu and a program of the Royal Hawaiian Band, conducted by the great Henry Berger himself. They were beautiful, of course. Every announcement that the palace issued was presented with beautiful calligraphy and art.

Inside the butler's pantry was a workspace with a sink on the left, a table laid out with flatware and wooden serving dishes in the middle, and a storage area for all sorts of glassware – shelves – on the right. There were wine goblets from floor to ceiling on those shelves.

The kitchen: we came in through the door at the back right. The stairs that lead up and out to the back yard are just past that door. The door on the left leads to the butler's pantry.

The empty space for the oven and stove is on the left, and this view looks straight into the butler's pantry. This is the museum storyboard that we saw in the kitchen, with the menu and concert notice.

There was little evidence in this kitchen of what the work was like, as most tools had yet to be brought back. Restoring a kitchen in a museum – unless it belonged to a famous chef – seems like less of a priority and less of a problem than restoring the other rooms. The dishes and flatware might need to be there…or they could be in the dining room. But the cook's tools and equipment need only be historically accurate, so finding the exact same items that were used here is probably just a matter of time and funding. It was like that with the Mark Twain House; the kitchen and butler's pantry were last on the list.

The dumb waiter is on the right. We were directly below the dining room when I took this photograph.

The butler's pantry sink area, and the table laid out with flatware and a platter, with the wall of goblets at right.

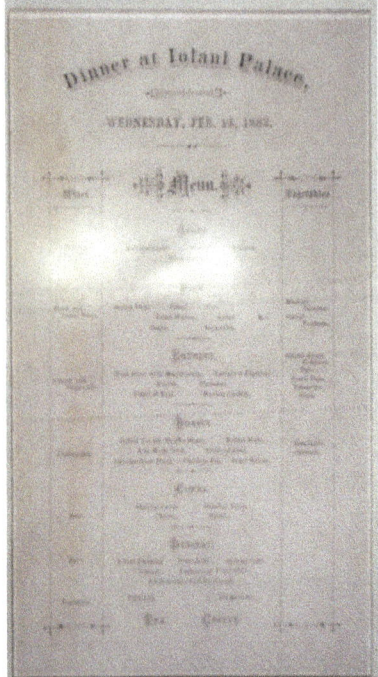 

Valentine's Day dinner, 1883: soups, fish, entrées, roasts, curry, dessert. The Royal Hawaiian coat of arms graces the 1883 Valentine's Day program for the Royal Hawaiian Band.

    The menu we saw described a typical fancy, formal dinner party of the nineteenth century. There were six courses to be consumed on February 14th, 1883, complete with wines for each course, or beer, or champagne...and finally a liqueur for dessert. How could one eat and drink all that plus coffee or tea, I wondered? One had to be careful at a meal like this, and not get full too quickly! Maybe there were small portions of everything. That would help a lot.

    Looking at the columns on this menu, I wondered who actually saw it. Was it a guide for the staff? Or was it an announcement to impress the distinguished guests? Or was it for both? This menu had a wide center column devoted to the food, with the alcoholic beverages in the left column, each lined up with its designated course, and the vegetables in the right column.

    When we had seen the kitchen, we were led out into the hallway. It ran the length of the palace, from front to back, and was well lit. A concrete walkway rimmed the basement, which allowed for large windows in every room. Sunlight streamed into each of the remaining restored rooms that we peered into. They were sealed with glass, so we couldn't go in. The rooms were for the palace chamberlain, with his safe in one, and an office for the bandmaster. That one had some musical instruments laid out in it.

    At this point in the tour, our guide had completed her duties. She led us into the museum rooms, briefly explained what was in them, and left us to peruse it all at our leisure. There was no real time pressure to take it in; she was off to her next tour, or more likely her lunch break.

The room was where musical instruments were stored by the director of the Royal Hawaiian Band. Next to it was the chamberlain's office, with a safe.

This is the other staircase that goes down to the basement. It's beautiful, unlike the outdoor, utilitarian one that we used, and roped off to protect the wood. It leads up to the back of the ground/first floor. The hall was filled with curator storyboards, which had photographs of the royal family and explanations of historic events. The anti-annexation petition was discussed, and the Hawaiian flag was shown.

The museum rooms had jewelry in four glass cases built into the walls of the first one, followed by Kalakaua's sashes and medals in the next. The windows were covered, which made it easy to see everything. It was better for security; no one could look in and see what was there.

This is the Hawaiian flag. Its design hasn't changed over time. What has changed is that it used to be the Hawaiian national flag, and now it is the state flag of Hawai'i...so it doesn't fly outside the United Nations.

Lili'uokalani's fluttering diamond butterfly hair pin is at the top of this display.

This beautiful state photograph was taken of Lili'uokalani when she was a princess.

The guide stayed with us long enough to usher us into the room after the ones with the jewels, so that she could talk about a throne room chair. There it was, up on a box inside a glass box, with its upholstery in shreds and tatters. There are plans to restore it, but for now it shows the atrocious condition that many artifacts have been returned in.

Not everything comes back looking like this chair did, however. Some people who were in possession of these stolen items – carved furniture, porcelain, silver cutlery, and other things – had been appreciating them and taking great care of them. In those cases, the problem was one of persuasion. Some items had to be bought back, while others were freely given back.

The twelfth throne room chair, not yet restored, in the palace's basement museum room.

    Our guide left us to it, and my mother and I turned back to the jewels, medals, and ribbons. The larger displays were interesting, but they didn't take very long to study. The jewelry was small, with many pieces in each section. The medals and ribbons took a quite while to look through. Most of them were gifts from foreign monarchs, some given on Kalakaua's travels, and others brought by foreign ministers.

Kalakaua's walking sticks and his ceremonial swords.

    The museum rooms and crown jewels are testaments to Kalakaua's effort to keep Hawai'i for Hawaiians, an agenda that he made a slogan of. This annoyed the haole Big

Five no end, but he had no reason to care about that. He knew what they were after; the proverbial handwriting was on the wall. He was trying to keep his country for Hawaiian people as long as possible.

Obviously, it didn't work.

But he was entitled to try for as long as he either lived or was on the Hawaiian throne, and he did. He tried acquiring all of the accoutrements of a royal family that foreigners would recognize, hoping that other nations run by monarchies would back him up. They befriended him, but they did not back him up. Hawai'i was too small and too distant geographically for any of them to come to his aid militarily. They had their own expenses to worry about, so they weren't about to pay to protect a distant chain of islands.

There was that, and the fact that the American haole community was thoroughly entrenched, digging its claws in deeper and deeper during his reign. No wonder his sister couldn't get them out of her throne room and out of the Hawaiian constitution.

Hawai'i is less than halfway from the contiguous United States to Japan. That was another consideration. Getting to the Islands got easier and easier as the nineteenth century wore on, and the haole community, the sons of the preachers who took that six-month boat trip from New England to Hawai'i, had too much money and property there to be willing to let it go. They weren't leaving under any circumstances, whether right or wrong.

The theft was inevitable; just a matter of time.

With these thoughts in mind as I walked up the stairs and out the back of the palace with my mother, I headed into the bright sunlight where the Royal Hawaiian Band was. The band was getting ready to put on its weekly noon concert on the back lawn, and we wanted to hear some of it. We were also looking for my father; he appeared right away, and I hoped that the music would interest him (he usually just wants to hear a symphony orchestra playing classical music).

Even the parking area manages to look like a paradise around 'Iolani Palace.

I looked for some shade, and noticed a huge cluster of banyan trees protecting parked cars from baking in the sunlight. But that area was too far away from the concert area. We couldn't listen from there. Apparently, one must bring a folding chair for a concert. Too bad; we usually have those in Connecticut, ready to put in the trunk of the car, but not in the rental car here!

We walked over anyway to see the beautiful hula dancer, who was smiling and chatting with the bandmaster. We admired the band, with its members dressed in white with red waistbands, the singers in red floral shirts, comfortably situated under a huge tree that spread out like an enormous parasol above them. At least they would be comfortable while they preformed.

The Royal Hawaiian Band prepares for its weekly Friday noon concert.

The Royal Hawaiian Band

When we were finished touring ʻIolani Palace, it was noon on a Friday, which meant that the Royal Hawaiian Band would be playing outside, as it does every week at this time. Admission is free. We came out of the back of the palace, and there they were: the 40 musicians, singers, hula dancers, and bandmaster employed by the Honolulu city government.

The band is its own department of the Honolulu city government, with an annual budget, salaries for each member, singer, dancer, and of course the bandmaster, and it gives approximately 300 concerts each year. These concerts are given in many venues, not just the palace grounds.

Other venues include Kapiʻolani Park, which is where the bandstand is (the fourth one to be built for the Royal Hawaiian Band, completed in 2000, and dedicated on July 4th), plus the Queen Emma Summer Palace grounds, and schools all over the Islands. The band also goes on tour to the contiguous United States, to Canada, Europe, Japan, New Zealand, and other nations.

This is the Coronation Bandstand on the grounds of ʻIolani Palace. It is on the lawn to the left of the palace, in the front yard. It was built for the 1883 coronation of King Kalakaua and his wife, Queen Kapiʻolani.

The Royal Hawaiian Band has a long history, dating back to 1836. Its first bandmaster worked for King Kamehameha III, and his name was Oliver. His full name is unknown. At that time, Hawaiian music was not written. That changed when a Prussian by the name of Henry Berger was hired by Kamehameha V, just six months before the king died. Berger was originally supposed to stay for just 4 years; he ended up returning a year after his contract expired, took Hawaiian citizenship, and spent the rest of his life with the band, remaining active with it even after his retirement in 1915. He died in 1929 at the age of 85.

Henry Berger arrived with a strong background in music, plus a Prussian military background. He quickly decided that it would be necessary to learn the Hawaiian language in order to do justice to the music, and began writing musical compositions for the band in Hawaiian. He got to know the Hawaiian monarchs, including Lunalilo, who loved music, and Kalakaua, Kapi'olani, and Lili'uokalani, who all loved music and wrote it.

The Royal Hawaiian band plays on the grounds of 'Iolani Palace each Friday at noon. Here they are with bandmaster Clark Bright, with 'Iolani Hale, the former barracks in the background. 'Iolani Hale now houses the ticket booth, gift shop, and rest rooms.

The Royal Hawaiian band keeps the sounds of Hawaiian culture alive while keeping current with new music. It incorporates Hawaiian songs with hula dancing and the instruments of a small orchestra, and it goes out marching in the streets of Honolulu. CDs of its music are offered for sale on the Internet and in the gift shop of 'Iolani Hale. While I was in that shop, I decided to get one for my aunt, who plays the flute and loves Native American music. She was pleased.

When we came out of 'Iolani Palace, we saw that the band was situated under a huge tree that offered plenty of shade for its members and the hula dancer, who stood, smiling, in front of the bandmaster. A small audience of people in folding chairs sat in the bright sunshine facing them. Still other audience members sat under a banyan tree right behind the palace, on a bench next to the parking lot.

It was a hot day, and I couldn't imagine being comfortable for the duration of the concert in a seat out in that bright sunlight, even with a hat and sunglasses. (I had sunglasses with me, but no hat.) My father would not be able to listen for long, I quickly realized. The shady bench under the tree was full, so there were no seats left. He decided to stay for a few songs, though.

Hearing that lovely music just made me want to learn more about it, so when we got home to Connecticut, I found a book on Amazon.com and read it, along with the website of the Royal Hawaiian Band: www.rhb-music.com – it is full of photographs, with brief bios of each bandmaster, plus a history of the band and its premises.

The music hadn't started yet when we went out to see the band on the lawn, so we got to watch them tuning up and getting comfortable for a few minutes. There were three men in red Hawaiian shirts off to the left who sang when the performance began. The hula dancer was a beautiful woman with a flower in her long, dark hair. She wore a long muumuu and a lei of green leaves, and she was very cheerful. The band members all wore white with leafy lei around their necks. The bandmaster was also in white. Many of the men had red sashes around their waists.

I wondered what it must be like to have plenty of time to spend in Hawaii, not on a whirlwind tour of one week, and able to slowly and carefully take in concerts by this fascinating group. It would be interesting to attend one here at the palace – in its entirety – plus another at Kapiʻolani Park or the Queen Emma Summer Palace. Maybe on another trip…

Meanwhile, I have a CD that came with the book from Amazon.com, pressed into the front cover. It has quite a collection of tunes, including one by Wolfgang Amadeus Mozart, which came as a surprise until I read the book and found out about Henry Berger.

The songs that I most looked forward to were the ones that I learned about as I read the biography of Princess Kaʻiulani: *Hawaiʻi Ponoʻi* by her uncle Kalakaua, and *Aloha ʻOe* by her aunt Liliuokalani. There are also songs by past bandmasters, not only by Henry Berger but also by Charles E. King and Mekia Kealakaʻi.

Mekia Kealakaʻi was bandmaster from 1920-1926, and again from 1930-1932. Berger himself trained him, and he was a member of the band before graduating to bandmaster. Berger plucked him from a reform school when he discovered the boy's innate musical ability, and taught him flute, piano, and trombone. Berger did that with many boys, and that was how he got most of the band's members in the early days: by taking young boys who needed guidance, and helping them to develop a skill that they loved. Kealakaʻi became such an expert flutist that the famous John Philip Sousa tried to lure him away…unsuccessfully, though.

Today, the Royal Hawaiian Band operates on a completely different basis. It seeks out members with musical training and education that rivals Henry Berger's, especially for the bandmaster. Somewhere in Hawaiʻi is a college degree program in hula dancing; a hula dance tells a story, so it can take years to properly learn the art. The bandmaster who led the Royal Hawaiian Band from 1981-2005, Aaron David Mahi, studied at the University of Hartford's Hartt School of Music in Connecticut for his bachelor's degree, and did his graduate work in conducting at Loma Linda University in California. Knowledge of Hawaiian music is required for a position in the Royal Hawaiian Band.

The Royal Hawaiian Band started as a military group, but it has expanded and added feature to its performances over time. Hula dancers gradually became a part of its act, along with a soprano vocalist and a men's glee club. A famous comedic hula dancer by the name of Hilo Hattie, for whom a retail store chain is named, toured the U.S. and Canada with the band. Meeting cruise and other ships at the pier in Honolulu was a tradition initiated by Henry Berger that was interrupted only by World War II, as were evening concerts.

The Germans gave a beautiful standard to the band, a tall ceremonial bell tree that was technically an instrument, and was carried with the band when it marched. It is called a *Schellenbaum*, and is traditionally presented to bands who are employed by royalty. It has silver bells that hang from a crescent shield, a German eagle at the top, and a flag embroidered with the Hawaiian royal coat of arms in between. Another bell hangs just below all that, with a set of three colored tassels hanging down on either side.

When the Hawaiian monarchy was overthrown in 1893, the *Schellenbaum* was destroyed, but in May of 1983, a new one was made for the band. It is a beautiful reproduction of the original, presented by Prince Michael of Prussia, handed to Queen Kapiʻolani's great-grandniece Marchesa Kapiʻolani Marignoli, passed to Henry Berger's daughter Lehua Billam-Walker, and finally given to bandmaster Aaron David Mahi.

All that pomp and ceremony seemed to heal the past injustice of the loss of the original.

This was the last of a series of images I took of the performance. I decided to show them all here, to give the reader/viewer a chance to see the sequence of the dancer's movements.

The men started to sing in Hawaiian, and I listened until my father said he had to go. The songs were enticing, beautiful chants and rhythms that I looked forward to listening to at home on the CD player, and I hoped to return someday to hear more of them live, after I understood the music better. I was determined to study the history and music of the band so that I could appreciate and enjoy it properly.

Here we were in downtown Honolulu, a place where Hawaiian history was brought to life through music and historic palace tours, with several of the original buildings, a bandstand, a statue, and a queen's house all within site of the performance. Added to all of that ambience were the beautiful trees all around us – palms, banyans, and other species – that were old enough to have been growing there when the Hawaiian kings and queens lived and worked here.

We left after hearing three songs, and drove across the street to see where Queen Lili'uokalani lived for most of her life: Washington Place. We could see it from where the Royal Hawaiian Band was performing. The band was facing her house, and it occurred to me that the queen was probably able to enjoy the sounds of its music whenever it performed on the palace grounds. Of course, the band also went to her house to give concerts just for her, so that was even better.

Washington Place – Liliʻuokalani's Home

At some point in our travels, I had hoped to visit Washington Place. When I shot this image, we were standing across the street from it, looking from the back yard of ʻIolani Palace on Beretania Street. I didn't know how we would fit any visit to it into our schedule. The place is listed as a National Historic Landmark, so I had looked it up on the National Parks Service website, but it didn't provide much insight into how to proceed with a visit.

With Friday afternoon ahead of us, we had a choice of seeing either Washington Place or the Foster Botanical Garden. Since Washington Place was across the street, it seemed like a good idea to look into the logistics of doing that first, and then decide.

We drove around to the eastern (right) side of Washington Place. There was a large parking lot there, mostly full of cars, with some tall trees providing shade here and there. It appeared to be a government lot. My parents decided to stay in the car and let me find out the details of touring the mansion, plus walk around with my camera. That way, if a tour was not possible, I could at least get the photographs.

I started off north of the mansion, looking at a long, tall wall with a gate in it. Inside the gate was a driveway that curved north and up to another, newer mansion. I didn't know what this place was. Just past the gate was a little guardhouse with a police officer in it. Time to ask questions. The guard was looking at me as I stared inside, so I waved to him.

He came over to me, and I explained that I was a lost and confused tourist, and I wanted to see Washington Place, but couldn't figure out (at least, not by looking around) how to do that. Oh. The guard was very nice. He explained that this was the governor's mansion, and that Washington Place used to be the governor's mansion until this other one was built.

As for touring Washington Place, one must first go to Aliʻiolani Hale, two blocks away (where we had just been before the tour of ʻIolani Palace!) to ask for one. Then it has to be arranged by an appointment. When I heard that, I decided to forget it. That was too complicated, and sounded like something that would require a lot more advance notice and planning.

The guard chatted with me for a couple of minutes longer, telling me that there was nothing to prevent me from going around the front of the fence and taking photographs. He also wanted my business card when I told him that I write e-books and that their titles were printed on the back of it. He thought that they sounded interesting, and might like to read some, he said.

I handed him a card, thanked him, and walked around to Beretania Street.

Washington Place is a large white mansion at 320 Beretania Street. It was built in 1844, when Captain John Dominis came to Hawaiʻi with his wife, Mary Jones Dominis and their son, John Owen Dominis. (They had two daughters whom they had left in boarding school in upstate New York, but both of them died young before ever coming to Hawaiʻi.) Captain Dominis wanted to buy nice furnishings for the house, so he kept taking off on long voyages, and was lost at sea two years later, leaving his wife and 14-year-old son alone there.

John attended a day school that was right next door to the Royal School, which was the one that the Hawaiian aliʻi children attended. He used to climb the fence and chat with them, and he soon became friends with many of them, including the Princess Liliʻu, who later became known as Liliʻuokalani. She was six years younger than her future husband.

When the princess was 24 years old and John O. Dominis was 30, they were married, and she came to live with her husband and mother-in-law at Washington Place. After that, Liliʻuokalani lived there for the rest of her life with only brief exceptions: travel to other islands, travel to the United States and Europe, brief stays at Waikiki Beach, where she had another home, and her imprisonment at ʻIolani Palace when royalists tried to restore her to the Hawaiian throne.

Her mother-in-law wasn't happy to have a non-Caucasian daughter-in-law, and the princess, like many other aliʻi, wanted children but couldn't have any. This meant that she wasn't happy living there until her mother-in-law was a lot older. By that time, the two women were used to one another and the mother-in-law had become more accepting of the princess. When I read this, I wasn't really surprised, just sorry to find out that Liliʻuokalani had had the sort of family problems that weren't her fault but also weren't unusual.

Her husband didn't spend a lot of time with her, but he was still a friend to her, and she valued and depended upon his advice while he was alive. John Owen Dominis was the governor of Oahu from 1868 until his death in 1891, several months after his wife became queen. He had a son by another woman, and the queen adopted him according to Hawaiian custom, making him her hanai in 1910. The son was born in 1883, his name was John Dominis ʻAimoku, and his mother was one of her maids. She changed his name to John ʻAimoku Dominis at that time. He lived at Washington Place with the queen until she died in 1917, then moved out with his wife and children.

That was nice; at least she had someone she liked to keep her company. The queen wrote in her autobiography that her husband had been making some changes to the house to surprise her when she returned from her tour of the Islands during the summer of 1891. It was a tradition for a new Hawaiian monarch to tour the Islands to meet the Hawaiian people and be seen by them shortly after taking the throne, so Liliuokalani had spent part of the summer doing that. What an awful homecoming, to find her husband on his deathbed when she got back!

I walked around the sidewalk to see the front yard, which was all that I would be able to see of Washington Place. It was yet another gorgeous day on Oʻahu, and the photographs were coming out great. The driveway had been paved in asphalt, a thing that had to have happened after the queen's time here. It curved all around the yard, making a semi-circle from one side of the house to the other, passing under the porte-cochère, and connected on the left with the straight part that went behind the house to the former mews – now a garage.

The house had become the governor's mansion the year after the queen died, and had remained so until 2002, when the governor was moved to the hidden residence right behind Washington Place. I wondered what I would have seen if I had gone on a tour of Washington Place. Would it have looked much the way that it did when the queen lived there? Had historic preservationists and curators had a chance to work on it? These were questions for another trip to Hawaiʻi, I thought to myself.

The trees looked old enough to have been there when the queen lived there. They were tall and they twisted gracefully upwards, providing some shade over the perfectly manicured lawn. A lanai stretched around both stories of the house, and I could picture the queen sitting on it for concerts given by the Royal Hawaiian Band, or to receive visits from the Hawaiian people, which continued after she was deposed. To them, she was still their queen, no matter what the haole thieves told the world.

Washington Place was where her supporters had hidden a significant cache of weapons in the garden: eleven pistols, thirty-four rifles, a thousand rounds of ammunition for them, five swords, twenty-one huge, homemade bombs, and sixteen smaller bombs. The cache of weapons and the small number of royalists who would have used it seemed grossly insufficient to the task of retaking their country, but it was a valiant effort.

These weapons had been buried without the queen's knowledge, and I suppose that her supporters could have managed that by working at night when the queen was asleep in another part of the house. But the queen wasn't upset that this effort had been made on her behalf and that of her people, and it seems absurd to me that the usurpers would call this treason. Her allegiance was to her own country, not some construct made by the haole thieves.

When I got to the front, I looked straight at the porte-cochère, which had the U.S. and Hawaiian flags hung over it. The queen was at home in Washington Place on August 12, 1898 on the day that the Republic of Hawaiʻi became the Territory of Hawaiʻi, no longer a rogue nation but a part of the United States. It had been just five years since it was the Kingdom of Hawaiʻi.

On that day, Queen Liliʻuokalani sat in mourning in her living room, surrounded by her niece and nephews, the Princess Kaʻiulani and the Princes David Kawananakoa and Kuhio. She had done her utmost to stop this from happening, traveling to Washington, D.C. with the anti-annexation petition and staying to attend social and diplomatic functions, all to no avail.

A Pili Nut tree grows in front of the porte-cochère.

The family stayed at Washington Place, dressed in dark clothing, unsmiling, and heard the ceremony progressing just a block away at ʻIolani Palace. They heard the Royal Hawaiian Band, which had been forced to go by a different name, the Provisional

Government Band, playing outside. The band was led by Henry Berger in a last rendition of King Kalakaua's *Hawai'i Pono'i*, and the old bandmaster cried. Then he raised his baton and led the band in playing Francis Scott Key's *The Star-Spangled Banner*. Everyone had just been given new citizenship with the stroke of a pen.

The plaque had a profile of Queen Lili'uokalani at the top, with a *maile lei* of green leaves just under it, not tied together in a loop but hanging open, as per tradition. The border was flowers, and it reminded me of a lei of 'ohai-ali'i flowers. Inside all that was the queen's song, both in musical notes at the top and in lyrics below, *Aloha 'Oe*. There was no biography, just her name, Queen Lili'uokalani, arcing above her portrait.

The queen was a highly accomplished musician and composer. She could play the organ, which she did at Kawaiaha'o Church nearby. She also played the piano, the guitar, the 'ukulele, and the zither. She was a prolific writer of music and lyrics, and she even taught music. A talent for and strong love of music was ingrained in her culture and in her family.

That was all that there was to see from this vantage point of Washington Place, so I left.

Foster Botanical Garden

Each of the Hawaiian Islands (with the exceptions of Ni'ihau and Kaho'olawe) have at least one botanical garden. What I didn't expect to find was that many of the plants in the garden were imported from tropical locations other than Hawai'i, but all of that seemed to have been done either in the 19th century or with special permission from the state environmental experts.

As usual, getting there was half the fun as we drove around a huge city block or two in order to figure out both where the entrance to Foster Botanical Garden was and how to approach it. One would think that with a map and a car, getting from one place to another ought to be stress-free, but there are always kinks in that idea. The entrance to the garden is on North Vineyard Boulevard, but cannot be approached from the left due to a large median with greenery. That means going around until one is coming up on it from the right.

The entrance itself is not obvious, because there is a small temple there, on the right as one turns into the driveway. It is called the Kuan Yin Temple. When my father saw it, he wasn't sure that we had found the garden, so he pulled up by the wide sidewalk and my parents waited while I walked in the blazing sun from there to the shady parking area inside.

Inside, I noticed a long driveway and plenty of free parking spaces, plus a few picnic tables on the right. A pair of Chinese women (they were chatting together in that language) were sitting at one with a little dog, a Shih Tzu. I went over to talk to them and ask if this was the right place to park for Foster Botanical Garden; they smiled and said yes, it was. I thanked them and went back to get my parents. After that, it was easy to enjoy the place.

Here is the address:

Honolulu Botanical Gardens
Department of Parks and Recreation
50 North Vineyard Boulevard
Honolulu, Hawai'i 96817
Phone: (808) 522-7060
E-Mail: hbg@honolulu.gov

This in the information and ticketing area, up the stairs. The two form an awning over the walkway, with the ticket booth on the right and the information area on the left.

We parked in the lovely, welcome shade (after the heat of the boulevard!) and got out.

Up to the right were two buildings, a shop at the right as we walked up the path and the information and ticket area straight ahead. Tickets were five dollars each, and I bought them. There was also a map of the garden, but we had to give it back after the tour, so I took a photograph of it.

This lady gave us the map.

A very nice older woman was running the information booth. She seemed to be enjoying her surroundings immensely. She was chatting with a man who was sitting on the bench. I imagined what it must be like to be here day after day in a shady, tropical plant-filled paradise.

This is where I bought the tickets.

This is the outside of the map, with lots of useful information on it... but I had to leave it there!

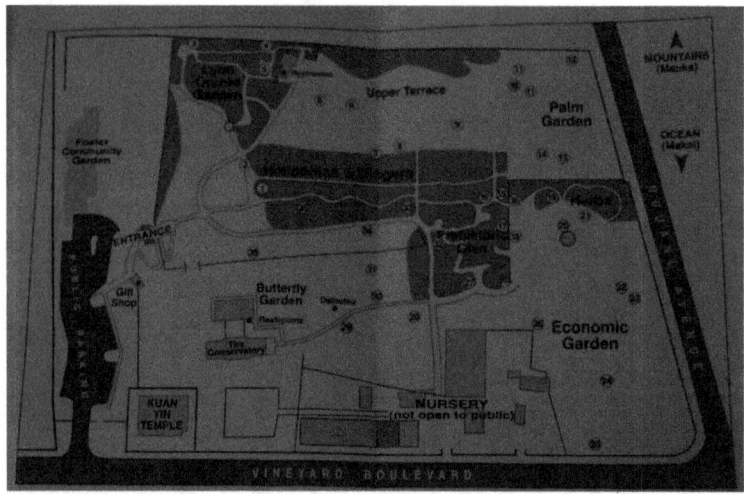

Here is the inside of the pamphlet, with the all-important map. Foster Botanical Garden occupies almost an entire city block.

We all went in, passing a little rock garden on the right.

This rock sculpture garden was on the right by the steps that led into the garden.

The first thing that my parents wanted to do was visit the rest rooms. The rest rooms are at the top of this map; look on the left where the gray shaded area is. It's by the Lyon Orchid Garden, to the right of it. When they came out, my mother said she would be walking all over the garden with me while my father sat on a bench. He swung the strap of his fabulous camera off his neck, put it over mine, and told me to take pictures of everything with it and he would see it all later.

Damn…was he having enough fun on this trip? I couldn't help worrying about that. But he wasn't coming with us no matter what I was thinking, so we left him sitting on a shady bench in beautiful surroundings and started our self-guided tour.

At the top of the steps that led into the garden was this railed walkway, which opened into what felt like another world. I could barely hear the traffic from the busy city streets that surrounded the garden while we were inside.

At the end of the walkway was this amazing view, a tropical "secret" garden. My father sat on a bench off to the right of this area, and waited for an hour while we saw the rest of it.

The garden's story begins in 1853, when Queen Kalama leased the land to a German botanist (and physician), Dr. William Hillebrand. He and his wife built themselves a lovely home on the property. He planted the trees that are now the largest and tallest of the ones that now grow in this garden. After 20 years, Hillebrand and his wife moved back to Germany, and he wrote a book about the plants he had seen in Hawai'i. It was published after his death by his son in 1888, and titled *Flora of the Hawaiian Islands*.

After that, the property was sold to "Captain" John Foster and his wife, Mary Mikahala Elizabeth Robinson Foster. They added to it; it wasn't the same size as the city block that it now occupies. They also added more plants. Foster wasn't really a captain; it was just a fun title that he acquired for founding the Interisland Steam Navigation Company, which provided transportation between the Hawaiian Islands.

Under that fairy-tale of a tree was this sign, which gave the details of the founding and set-up of the Foster Botanical Garden.

Foster had moved to Hawaii from Nova Scotia at age 22. He died when he was 54, leaving his wife an estate worth a quarter of a million dollars. Mary's father was in the shipbuilding business, which is how the couple met. Mary was descended on her mother's side from Hawaiian royalty. They were married in 1860, when Mary was 16 years old. She became interested in Buddhism and the garden. The couple had no children. The bo tree in the garden is a descendant of the one under which Siddhartha Gautama, the Buddha himself, attained enlightenment. It was given to Mary in 1913, so it is now at least a century old.

Mary lived as a widow for 41 years, until 1930, when she died and bequeathed the place to the City and County of Honolulu as "Foster Park". She had supported schools for both Hawaiian and immigrant children, donated generously to hospitals, and Buddhist temples. The garden first opened to the public on November 30, 1931, with Harold Lloyd Lyon as its first director. He served in that post for 27 years, introduced 10,000 new plants, and started the Orchid Garden with some of his own plants.

Harold Lloyd Lyon, the garden's first director, is honored with a little plaque in the ground near the history sign.

The orange leafy plants on the left are Brazilian, called aechmea blanchetiana. This is near the rest rooms and the Orchid Garden. The orchids were not in bloom. A Queen Emma Spider Lily. These are dark pink. The Spider Lily also comes in white, but that one isn't named for her – only this color.

I had hoped to look at some orchids, but the Orchid Garden was not in bloom, so I didn't take a lot of photographs there. It had some tree stumps with leafy growth all over them, which I realized was for the orchids, but few flowers, so I didn't spend much time in there. My parents came walking back from the rest rooms, so I did go over to that area, and I saw a path with some interesting plants that grew low to the ground, an open lawn with amazingly tall, thin-trunked palm trees, and a small gazebo with flowering shrubs and hanging, potted plants with flowers.

Here is the gazebo north of the bo tree and the area where my father waited. A beautiful pink hibiscus blossom by the gazebo.

An 'ohai ali'i plant in full bloom.

The palm trees were amazing here, but a rather different kind of amazing than at the resort where we were staying. What impressed me was the variety. These trees were not planted with the goal of making a manicured advertisement. They were planted to assemble a collection of as many species as possible. The plants were also arranged according to an aesthetic from an earlier time. Victorian décor and gardening was a lot busier and less spaced out than the décor and gardening of today. With only a limited amount of space in which to collect the plants, open spaces would not have been practical. Plus, plants grow and end up taking more space.

These tall palm trees were incredible. They remind me of the truffula trees in Dr. Seuss's The Lorax, except that they came in natural rather than wild fluorescent hues. They are Caribbean Royal Palm trees.

This is a cannonball tree, so named because of the small brown balls that grow on it and fall to its roots. Some split open upon impact, but not all. It was beautiful, stretching up and up, with branching stretching out every which way.

Here is a cannonball growing on a lower branch of the tree, and some flowers.

At the end of the trail with the cannonball tree was the Prehistoric Glen.

This was one of several plants that were billed as Jurassic palms.

This pine cone (or fruit – it was unclear which was correct) had fallen off of one of the plants just above this rock. The open side was worth photographing. The plaque says "Prehistoric Glen – presented to Foster Botanic Garden by the Garden Club of Honolulu 1965".

We came out of the Prehistoric Glen into the Herb area and Economic Garden.

This macadamia nut tree was growing in the Economic Garden, and white egrets were walking around the Herb area.

We turned around and started walking in the opposite direction, past the Nursery (closed to the public), toward the one large lawn in the garden and the Conservatory.

We passed this giant of a tree and I went up to it for a closer look.

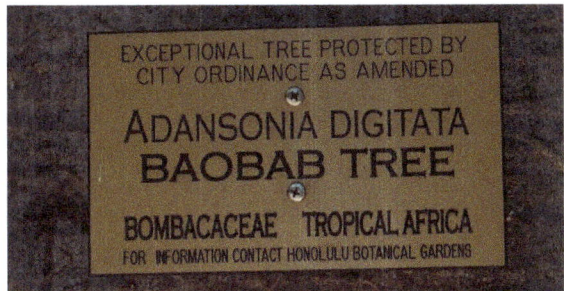

It was a baobab tree, something that I had previously only seen in photographs for the National Geographic.

Looking north as we walked, we saw this tree, catching the bright sunlight among all of the leaves and fronds.

Because I don't know much about botany, I have a hard time finding names for every plant I saw in the garden. If I knew what to look up on the Internet, that would help a lot. As I went through, I tried to get a photograph of each little green sign that identified the plant above it so that, later, I could label the images correctly on the computer.

However, some of the most amazing trees were through a lot of other low-to-the-ground plants, or just in the distance and rising up out of the others when I took pictures of them. That made my system only partially effective. Another identification method I attempted was to buy a book and look at the photographs, but that didn't answer all of my questions. The annoying result is that the previous image ended up with only this for a label: "Fascinating tall tree in the clearing." I find it most unsatisfying.

We came to the end of the path and found a wide-open space. It had a lawn with two sculptures: one of a Buddha, and another that was an abstract, modern stone shape. The Buddha was a small figure, sitting serene and cross-legged atop its round pedestal.

The Great Buddha of Kamakura.

The abstract modern stone sculpture. It was across the lawn to the left/south of the Great Buddha. A Quipo tree. Notice the thick bands of bark every couple of feet up the trunk.

We walked across the lawn to see the Buddha statue and look at it up close, but the sunlight was hot and bright, so we didn't linger there. As we continued toward the Conservatory, we noticed yet another impressive tall tree trunk in the forest to our right, through the palm fronds and other plants. Later, when I had time to research it, I managed to find out that it was a quipo tree. Every foot or so, it had a band of bark that encircled its otherwise smooth trunk.

The next tree that caught our attention was on the lawn to the right, and it had a plaque. It was a rainbow flower tree, also known as a cassia tree. It had small leaves on its tall branches, and they resembled ferns.

Next up was the Conservatory. It was full of yet more palms, some heliconias, hanging, potted plants that I had previously only seen in books, and lots of orchids. There were two rooms, and the air smelled different in there – moister than outside. We enjoyed it.

The Conservatory. The Butterfly Garden is off to the right.

I asked my mother to pause and pose in the entrance to the Conservatory. She's good at smiling for photographs.

This pitcher plant was hanging up on the right as we walked into the Conservatory. Orchids grew all around in the flower beds – many different species of orchids, in many colors and patterns.
Looking back at the entrance and the garden path.

Cattleya Orchids in a flower bed of the Conservatory. Cattleya Orchids in purple, lilac, and white with some other orchids.

Elephant ears and palms in another flower bed.

Around the side of the Conservatory is a path that leads to more rest rooms.

This beautiful flowering tree grew in front of the Conservatory and across from the Butterfly Garden.

We came out of the Conservatory and headed for the Butterfly Garden, pausing to look at a pigeon with speckles on its neck (like the one we had seen at Ko Olina on Tuesday morning). The Butterfly Garden had three signs, each with many photographs of butterflies. The butterflies came in every color of the rainbow, it seemed, and their species names were under each image. We saw a couple of butterflies fluttering around the low-growing flowered bushes there.

The Butterfly Garden.

One of the butterfly signs. They were all like this, tilted and just a few feet off the ground.

This bronze statue was donated to the garden in 2009. The butterfly bushes around it are called that because they attract butterflies, and they work.

That was it; we had seen it all. Actually, there was a heliconia and ginger trail that ran parallel to and north of the path with the cannonball tree, but my mother and I had elected to skip it because we didn't want my father to have to wait too long. He was patiently sitting in the comfortable shady spot where we had left him.

To get back to where he was, we had to retrace our steps and go back around the same path.

There was nothing left to do and see at this point but check out the gift shop, so we did that.

The gift shop. My father sat down outside and waited again.

The shop had everything one could wish for: tee shirts, umbrellas, framed prints of botanical artwork, postcards, books, and more.

My mother looked around quickly, bought nothing, and walked out. She said that my father was going to start the car. I looked around carefully, took photographs, and found a book to buy. It was Friday, and already I had a small pile of books that I would have to take home with me.

The lady who sold me the book was very nice. She chatted a bit about Hawaiian gardens, and said that there were several more on O'ahu.

As I flipped through the book later on, I realized that we had only had time for one of what are many amazing gardens. It made me want to move to Hawai'i and thus have unlimited time in which to visit them. Who knows, maybe my husband's scientific work will bring us back there.

Imperial Bromeliad Plant – just one more photograph!

A Hokey Lu'au

Okay, so it's a play on words, and the lu'au we attended on O'ahu wasn't that bad. The problem with it was that it just couldn't complete with the one we attended on the Big Island, but more on that later.

About the play on words: in 1948, the singer Jack Owens released a popular song called *The Hukilau Song*. It's a lovely, relaxing piece, one of many lu'au songs that he created.

The purpose of a lu'au is to enjoy a feast of traditional Hawaiian foods while socializing with nice people. Those people can be family, friends, or complete strangers, which is typically the case with tourists from off the Islands, so that is how we experienced our lu'au (no "s" – not when making a Hawaiian word plural!).

We got dressed in Hawaiian shirts (well, my father and I did; my mother wore the new sarong that she had found the day before in Waikiki) and drove through the resort, not quite to the gate out, turned left, and parked in the Paradise Cove lot.

Paradise Cove is a section of the Ko Olina Resort that we noticed in daylight shortly after we arrived on O'ahu. It is a large, commercial area that buses people in from the crowded hotels of Waikiki for an evening's entertainment. The buses are painted prettily with the words "Paradise Cove" and beach scenes.

This is one of the small fleet of buses that brought tourists from Waikiki to Paradise Cove for its lu'au. The ticket windows can be seen to the left.

We got out of the car and I made my parents pause for a photograph. They grinned in their sunglasses, and looked…cool. They also looked like they were ready to have fun, which was good. We had just had a long day of historic palace museum, music, almost another historic house museum, a tropical botanical garden, and a long drive each way to all of that. But, we had come back in plenty of time for showers and dressing up in our Hawaiian clothes.

We headed for the buildings up by the Paradise Cove buses. As we got closer to them, we realized that lines of people were forming at different windows. I took out the voucher that the agent from AAA had given me and asked someone which window to go up to (there were different windows depending on which package one bought: Hawaiian, Orchid, or Deluxe). Someone pointed it out to me, and when I went there, the voucher was taken and kept. That was interesting, because the people who ran the submarine rides had not kept the voucher; they had only checked it.

My parents looked great in their Hawaiian lu'au outfits! I didn't feel very dressed up, but I was happy in my Hawaiian shirt. What a double standard fashion sets up for women – here I was in a Hawaiian shirt that was a lot like my father's, as comfortable as he was, and I looked casual rather than festive. I had two, and had just worn the dressier one the previous evening, so I wore this one.

Without further ado, we were ushered into the Paradise Cove grounds. We walked through the gate and into a lovely garden with a long koi pond, the surface of which was covered with lily pads and water lilies. Halfway down on the left was a little platform of rock with a straw umbrella and a ki'i statue. A man sat under it playing the guitar and singing.

It certainly gave the impression of a paradise, but this one looked human made, not natural.

Another gate; this was where we were directed to have our photograph taken with lu'au staff who wore traditional Hawaiian malo and muumuu outfits.

We didn't know what to expect, but that was part of the fun. We had come in as a small group, without a busload of people surrounding us, so we had walked slowly up the path, admiring the waterfalls and lily pads and water lilies, listening to the musician as he strummed his guitar and sang.

Next, we found ourselves with cups of fruit punch being herded into position, flanked by a male and a female staff member, and told to smile for the camera. The purchase was optional. The product would be ready by the time the event was winding down. It would be 20 dollars. Needless to say from the evidence above this paragraph, we chose to buy the product.

This map of Paradise Cove was mounted on a signboard just past the photography area.

We continued on into the Cove grounds, looking left. We saw a shop to the left, a bar across from it, and a long stretch of hard-packed sand in between that led to the water. A buffet room was just past the shop, and there were kiosks here and there all around the perimeter and by the water. More musicians were playing right in front of us, but we could see all this past them.

The seating area. The flowered tablecloths were for the luʻau package that we had signed up for.

Looking in the opposite direction from the stage, we could see another bar. This one was for the most expensive lu'au package, the one that include wait staff service and a bar. The bar that we saw near the shop was on the opposite side of this building. My mother and father found seats and brought their punch to the table, and then she and I went back around the other side of the center building for Mai Tai drinks.

    We had been told that we could have a couple of alcoholic drinks with our package, so my mother and I went around the other side of the central building to get them. We thought (well, it seemed logical!) that we would just get all three drinks and walk back to my father with them, but the people behind the counter said that that was not allowed. We would have to either make my father limp over to get his own (forget it!) or make a separate trip back for the third drink. We made a separate trip back. That was not impressive.

    Once we all had our drinks – a Mai Tai for me and for my mother, and a Blue Hawaiian for my father – I took just a couple of sips before exploring with my camera. I wanted to know what was on the right as we entered the Cove grounds. It was another performance area, and the pig-roasting pit was right in front of it. A huge semi-circle of bleachers arced around it. The tables were to eat at looked at the back of this stage, which had a separate area to its side with a small roof for the musicians.

The musicians' stand by the stage and pig-roasting pit.

Nothing was happening at the pig-roasting stage just yet, so I went back to my parents. My mother and I both wanted to go see the shop, kiosks, and whatever else there was to see near the bar where we had gotten our drinks. My father stayed at the table. He would have stayed there even if his hip were in perfect shape; he isn't interested in browsing.

These musicians were quietly playing lu'au tunes and singing softly as they faced the water and kiosks.

Here is the area with the kiosks on the perimeter. The shore of the cove is to the right, behind a group of people.

Here is the view of the cove shore.

The bar is to the left.

My mother and I walked all over the shopping area, looking at everything. We had each been given a shell lei to wear on the way in, and we still had the beautiful orchid ones that we were presented with at the airport, so we weren't about to buy any more.

We started with the shop. It was full of shirts – rack after rack – and some sarongs. We debated yet again whether or not to buy one for my father, and decided he wouldn't want another Hawaiian shirt. He was already saying he wouldn't wear the one he had in Connecticut. There were tee shirts, but we didn't see one we wanted, not for him or for David. We looked at other things: dolls, night-lights, candy, hair clips, and so on. I bought a night-light and a floral clip.

We got our dinner at this buffet area after dark. The pig was still roasting at this point.

This is the lavender-hued hibiscus hair clip I bought at Paradise Cove. It doesn't hold one's hair. None of these clips seems strong enough to do that. It just decorates it, but it's fun to wear. The clip is clear plastic with no grip.

    We wandered around past the buffet building, looking at the wares offered by each kiosk. My mother looked at necklaces in a variety of styles, but didn't buy any. I found some souvenirs that seemed worth buying, though: little sea turtles made of carved, charcoal-gray stone with shells of pink, white, or green stone (jade?). I bought 3: dark pink, pale pink, and green. Two would be gifts, for my aunt and for a friend's 16-year-old daughter.

    After that, we walked toward the water because we saw several brightly colored tropical birds on a stand near the shore. There was a pair of macaws, and a pair of large parrots. One parrot was red-and-blue, a color combination I had never seen before – beautiful. But the man at the stand wanted to charge people for photographs of them, and only if the customer allowed the bird to sit on her/his shoulder. I didn't want that – just some images of the birds.

This kiosk faced the dining area. I walked around the back to see the parrots.

The green parrot; the red-and-blue one. The pair of macaws sat calmly on their perch, observing the visitors.

There wasn't much else to see after that, so we returned to our table.

Here are the Mai Tai drinks and our ticket, telling us where to sit.

As we got settled into our seats, a couple sat down on the other side. They were from Las Vegas, Nevada, and were staying in the Waikiki area. They had ridden the Paradise Cove bus to get here, and attended a leaf-weaving lesson elsewhere on the grounds. Both husband and wife wore a headband made out of braided palm leaves, and the wife had a flower in hers. I took their photographs, and promised to e-mail them to the wife when we got home. They were fun to chat with, and we enjoyed sitting with them.

The wife told us that she worked in a call center doing sales and customer service, and that the pay was very good, but less with the economic downturn. She was very cheerful, a good conversationalist, and conveniently seated across from my mother and me. My father was on my other side, across from the husband, who was a security guard at a casino in Las Vegas. He was a large, powerfully-built guy with a gold tooth. I suppose he would have looked intimidating and forbidding at work in his uniform, but he was smiling and having a wonderful time at the lu'au. They each had a college-age daughter from previous relationships, but all four of them were a happy family together, and both girls were studying at local schools.

That was our experience of meeting and visiting with strangers. We couldn't hear the performance very well, and we didn't realize right away that it was starting. That was because it was happening not on the stage near our table but across the grounds, where the pig-roasting pit was. I rushed off abruptly so as not to miss out on taking pictures of it.

There was a grand entrance of the actors and dancers, who were decked out in traditional Hawaiian ali'i costumes, followed by hula dancing (one act), and the removal of the pig from the roasting pit. It was carried around the semi-circle for the audience to look at, but it was quick, and it was dark when that happened.

The cast of the ali'i retinue were dressed in red and yellow, which meant that they were not portraying Kamehameha and Ka'ahumanu (the highest ranking ali'i would wear all yellow). They must have been portraying the governor and governess of O'ahu. They were attended by ali'i with long wooden spears and kahili. This was not explained; I knew it from studying Hawaiian history and culture on my own. However, I doubt that it mattered to the audience.

The cast arrived and stood at attention while the hula dancers performed.

The hula dancers performed in front of the pig-roasting pit.

The pig-roasting pit, seen immediately after the pig was removed.

The pig is carried around for the audience to see.

All three of the musicians now performed together, with the dancers to their left.

When the performance was over, I went back to my table. It was now time to go to the buffet area and get our dinner. It was very crowded. We followed the throng around the central building and over to the buffet hall to get our food. We had to take a plate, napkins, cutlery, and food. The plates were basic round ones, and the food was…bland and fatty. There was shredded pork – the pig that had just been lifted out of the pit. There was also chicken, mahi mahi fish, and pasta salad with shredded carrots and a lot of mayonnaise. And little purple rolls, presumably made of purple sweet potatoes. Those looked interesting, but they tasted like any other rolls.

The actors posed with lu'au guests for photographs after the performance.

I looked for the lomi lomi salmon and poi. I had been excited to try that, but where was it? I asked for help, and a staff member explained and led me back, telling me to just cut through because I had already waited. The poi was a cold whitish paste, and it was to be ladled into a small plastic cup. I had mistaken the lomi lomi salmon for salsa; it had diced tomatoes and herbs and onions in it, and it was completely raw. I liked that a lot, but my parents didn't.

Dessert was coconut pudding squares and chocolate brownies.

We chatted with the couple from Las Vegas while a fast-paced fire dance was performed on the stage that overlooked the dining area. It looked exciting, but we didn't hear much about it and it was difficult to understand. What I had trouble with was a lack of a sense of an introduction, an explanation of the show's format, and not being able to hear it all.

Still, we had a good time, even though we didn't hear every detail of the performance, and didn't learn a lot. This experience turned out to be more about visiting with strangers and enjoying it than anything else. My father got tired after most of the performance, so we left. Before we did so, however, our new acquaintance from Las Vegas borrowed my camera and took a photograph of us enjoying the party. I'm glad she did.

Princess Kaʻiulani and Her Pet Peacock

Princess Victoria Kawekiu Lunalilo Kalaninuiahilapalapa Kaʻiulani Cleghorn was the niece of King David Kalakaua and of his sister and successor, Queen Liliʻuokalani. The princess was the heir to the Hawaiian throne. Kaʻiulani grew up preparing herself for her future role as queen of Hawaiʻi, but by the time she was an adult, the Big Five had stolen her country, and she was broken-hearted. Today, there is a statue of her with one of her pet peacocks where her estate once was, in Waikiki, three blocks south of the Ala Wai Canal.

Princess Kaʻiulani's mother was Kalakaua and Liliʻuokalani's sister, Princess Miriam Likelike, a vivacious beauty with a temper that overpowered her only daughter's until her death, when Kaʻiulani was eleven years old. Kaʻiulani was raised with servants, a nanny, and then governesses on her parents' estate at Waikiki, ʻAinahau.

Her mother had named it; ʻAinahau means "cool place" – a cool breeze from Manoa Valley to the north comes through it. Her aunt, the governess of the Big Island of Hawaiʻi, Princess Ruth Ke'elikolani, had made a gift of the land to her new niece when she was born.

Her father, Archibald Cleghorn, was a Scot who had come to the island with his dying father at age sixteen and stayed to make his fortune. He had three daughters (Rose, Helen, and Annie) with a Hawaiian woman, was widowed, and then married Princess Likelike after that. Cleghorn became a Hawaiian citizen the same year that he married the princess, and their daughter knew and visited often with her half-sisters.

The family lived on Queen Emma Street when Kaʻiulani was born on October 16, 1875. They attended St. Andrew's Episcopal Church, except when larger ceremonies involved their extended family of relatives. For those, they would go to Kawaiahaʻo Church, which is just a short walk away from ʻIolani Palace, in Honolulu. At that time, Kaʻiulani's parents were having a new home built on ʻAinahau, within sight of Waikiki Beach.

An ʻOhai-aliʻi plant in bloom at Foster Botanical Garden. This dragon-like blossom grew all over ʻAinahau when Princess Kaʻiulani lived there.

ʻAinahau was a paradise to the princess when she was a little girl. She had a fabulous banyan tree close to the house. When the famous writer and poet Robert Louis Stevenson – known as Tusitala to the Tahitians, or "teller of tales" – made the first of two visits to Hawaiʻi, he was staying across the street from ʻAinahau. Kaʻiulani was allowed to go and visited him there, and he visited her under her tree. Stevenson wrote her a poem about it when their weeks together were ending. She was going to school in Britain, and she would leave the Islands before he did.

But before that, she enjoyed about ten years on her estate, swimming the waters off Waikiki Beach, riding her pony, and enjoying the breezes under date palms and the cinnamon, teak, and cypress trees that grew there, and eating mangos on other trees at 'Ainahau. She spent her free time admiring hibiscus blossoms, and inhaling the scent of her favorite flower, jasmine, which grew everywhere she looked.

Peacocks always walked on the grounds. They were Ka'iulani's pets, she loved to feed them.

Her father had built an artesian well just for the three lily ponds, and one of them was built in the shape of a shamrock. A traditional, one-room Hawaiian hale was left on the estate as a garden house, but with a modern wooden floor and furniture added. Everything was a mixture of Ka'iulani's two backgrounds, Hawaiian and Scottish.

She was home-schooled at the estate after being raised by a nurse, May Leleo. Her governesses were a Miss Barnes and then an American, a Miss Gardinier, who left her post to get married. It was Miss Gardinier who did Ka'iulani a great favor: she insisted upon obedience and politeness. Princess Likelike realized this was the right thing to do, as it would teach her daughter to be a good leader later in life.

Whenever she went out in her family's carriage, Ka'iulani was taught to smile and wave, not to just ride comfortably and lapse into her own thoughts. She had to put on a public face of greeting to her people, who were happy at the chance to catch sight of her.

When Ka'iulani was eleven years old, she lost her mother.

Princess Miriam Likelike died a mysterious death. Native Hawaiians believed that she had been prayed to death by a kahuna priest. No doubt, there is a scientific explanation, but she appeared to lose her will to live and she stopped eating. Nothing helped, and she declined gradually over the course of a year and three months.

Traditional Hawaiian beliefs were invoked for the princess's illness again as the end drew near. The volcano Mauna Loa was erupting on the Big Island of Hawai'i, and a school of red akule fish had been seen in the waters offshore there. These had always been omens that an ali'i would die soon.

Just before she died, she told her daughter that she could see her future: she would go away for a long time, never marry, and never be queen. Ka'iulani ran from her mother's room to talk to Miss Gardinier, very upset.

Princess Ka'iulani left Hawai'i as a teenager to attend school in England before her uncle was forced to sign away most of his political powers. She walked up the gangplank of the ship that was take her as far as San Francisco on May 10, 1889, wearing a farewell lei from her former governess, who had come to see her off. The Royal Hawaiian Band played her uncle Papa Moi's *Hawai'i Pono'i* in her honor.

Her country went through many changes while she was away, and by the time she came home in 1897, she was no longer heir to the throne, only a princess without the purpose that she had studied for. She returned to her home by way of New York City and Washington, D.C. after pleading her country's case with the U.S. president and the press, to no avail.

When she got home, her father showed her what he had done at 'Ainahau in anticipation of her reign as Hawaii's queen, which was a sad tour knowing that now Ka'iulani would be simply an ali'i lady who cordially received visitors.

Archibald Cleghorn had worked very hard to surprise his daughter with a whole new Victorian-style mansion, complete with a suite of rooms upstairs for her to sleep and write in, and a kahili-coronet motif on the high ceiling. A huge drawing room below befitted an heiress to a throne that she would not occupy, and a wide lanai wrapped around the outside of the new house.

The princess went to visit her aunt, Mama Moi, the widowed Queen Kapi'olani, who had made her cousins, the princes David Kawananakoa and Kuhio her hanai sons.

They lived with her. The drawing room had an enormous, fabulous feather kahili in the center.

After making the rounds of greeting her family, an endless series of receptions ensued for callers and well-wishers who trouped through her drawing room at 'Ainahau, followed by social event after social event. Ka'iulani smiled graciously through it all, not saying a word about politics or her situation.

Portrait of Princess Kaiulani, taken by an unknown photographer. Kahili Room, Bernice Pauahi Bishop Museum.

The only political statement she made was done without words, along with her aunt, the deposed Queen Lili'uokalani, and her cousins Kuhio and Koa. They boycotted the annexation ceremony in Honolulu, staying away from it all at Washington Place.

In 1898, her cousin, Prince David Kawananakoa, announced their engagement.

But Ka'iulani never got over the loss of her country, and her grief wasn't about the loss of a throne. To her, the throne was a means for looking after the welfare of the Hawaiian people, so its loss meant that she could not do that anymore. After being raised and educated with that expectation in mind, she found it devastating.

Depressed, and with her immune system compromised by a change in climate – by moving home from years away in Britain – she had difficulty adjusting. She visited the Big Island and went horseback riding in Kona, where her godmother, the six-foot-tall Princess Ruth, had served as governor. The Big Island of Hawai'i has thirteen microclimates, and the mountains of Kona have frequent rainfalls. It had been years since Ka'iulani had been there, years since she and her mother had visited her aunt. Both women were dead, and Ka'iulani was twenty-three years old. She got caught in a rain that was more mist than rain.

Soon she was soaked, and Ka'iulani wore the fashions of late Victorian times. It was 1899, which meant that she wore several petticoats, a corset, and a bodice with an overskirt and underskirt on top of all that. The weight of women's attire in the late nineteenth century tended toward eighty pounds. She had not worn the raincoat that had been provided for her. The princess went back to her hosts' home, and was soon ill.

Her father came to get her. He brought her back to 'Ainahau, where she lay sick in her room for a month and a half. Ka'iulani lived in her room, visited constantly by her father, waited on by the household staff, while reports on her condition were published in local papers. She died at 2 a.m. in her room at 'Ainahau at the age of twenty-three on March 6, 1899.

Her flock of pet peacocks all screamed at once at that moment.

Today 'Ainahau is part of Honolulu, which has sprawled to encompass and incorporate 'Ainahau as it expanded from the area that surrounded 'Iolani Palace in the late nineteenth century to a much larger municipality.

This bronze statue of the princess was created by sculptor Jan Gordon Fisher, and unveiled on her 124th birthday, October 16, 1999.

On Kalakaua Avenue, which runs along the coast of the former estate, including Hermes of Paris, Bulgari, a large Apple computer store, hotels, and restaurants. The Ala

Wai Canal runs parallel to Kalakaua Avenue to its northeast. In between them is a neighborhood of streets and avenues named for the members of her family – cousins, parents, aunts, uncles, and so on. Small apartment buildings, low-rise, low-budget hotels, and parking areas now occupy the land that her childhood estate once occupied.

In the midst of all that sits a small triangular park with benches, palm trees, plumeria trees, grass, trash cans, and recycle bins. The park is bordered by Kuhio Avenue, Kanakepolei Street, and Kaiulani Avenue. Traffic consisting of cars, buses, and taxis rush noisily past and around it. Little notice to this park, or to what is in it, is paid by the occupants of those vehicles.

In that park is a tall, black statue of Princess Ka'iulani with one of her pet peacocks.

However, the princess is visited as she stands there, frozen in the act of feeding her pet. When I got there, it was a Sunday afternoon. The statue was draped with lei made of orange ilima flowers and pink-and-white orchids, and of long green leaves artfully woven together. Hawaiians have not forgotten her, and they still appreciate her.

Her house is gone, torn down in 1955, and replaced by a hotel: the Sheraton Princess Ka'iulani. It was built by the Matson Navigation Company, and it is a huge, sprawling, commercial property with all of the things that the Big Five would approve of: a swimming pool, an exercise room, conference rooms, and so on. South of that, across Kalakaua Avenue, with its back to Waikiki Beach, is the Moana Hotel, which was completed at the end of Ka'iulani's life. It is a large, symmetrical, Victorian structure, painted white. It opened in 1901; the website is http://www.moana-surfrider.com/propertyoverview/hotelhistory/

There was no sign of Princess Ka'iulani's favorite banyan tree, and I found that depressing, but not at all surprising. She has no direct descendants, and her half-sisters wanted the money from the sale of her property, so the estate was doomed to become an overdeveloped, commercial area with asphalt and high-rises. I stared up at the statue and wished it wasn't.

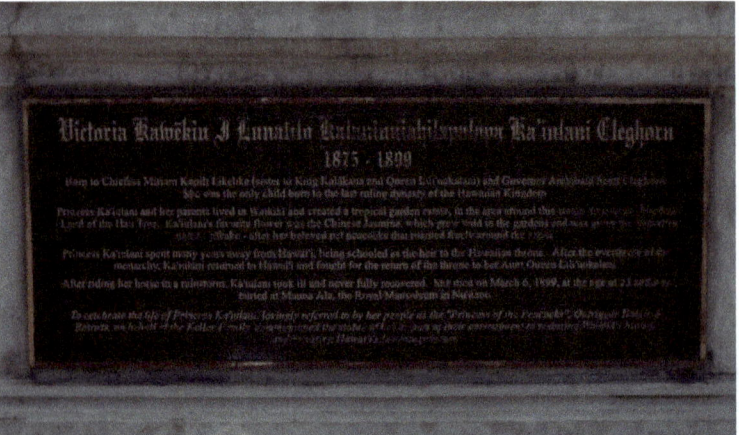

This is the pedestal below the statue, detailing the background on it and on the princess.

Before I went to Hawai'i, I read a few references to her in her aunt's autobiography (see *Hawai'i's Story by Hawai'i's Queen*), and watched a 2009 movie called *Princess Ka'iulani* starring Q'orianka Kilcher. I was intrigued, and caught up in the story of a princess who was unhappy, who loved her home and her people, and who did everything she could to hang on to it, to get it back, and finally to protect her people's interests before resigning herself to the loss of her nation and potential political powers.

As a result, I wanted to see the statue, and I asked my father if we could go there so that I could take some photographs of it. I wondered if he would be willing to do that, because it was out of the pattern of movement that he had imagined for our last full day on Oʻahu, and because we had been very close to that spot on the days that we went on the submarine tour and to ʻIolani Palace. But he was willing, and my mother hopped out of the car to see the statue with me.

It was beautiful, and I was glad to have had a chance to get so close to it. The fact that it was covered with lei made it even better, because it showed that the sad princess was still on the minds of her people, not forgotten to them.

But I wasn't satisfied with what I knew about her.

At ʻIolani Palace, I had bought a biography of her. I would read it when I got home, and I was looking forward to it. That was part of the fun of going on this trip: the enjoyment would continue even after the adventure was over with.

Na Kahili and a Petition:
The Bernice Pauahi Bishop Museum

The Bernice Pauahi Bishop Museum is named for the great-granddaughter of Kamehameha the Great, Princess Bernice Pauahi. She chose to live her life in the haole way so as to learn as much as she could about the foreign influences that would shape her country. Of course, her decision to marry a haole may have had something to do with that decision as well.

There is something that may provide a measure of excitement about the place: it has appeared on the popular television show *Hawaii Five-O* (the new version). The cops had a case involving an ancient Hawaiian weapon; to learn about it, they visited one of the museum's curators, Detective Danny Williams' girlfriend.

It was built in the late 19th century, and founded in 1889. Her widower, Charles Reed Bishop, Hawai'i's first banker, founded it. It opened in 1892 with just one elegant building, but Bishop kept going, and in 1894, the Polynesian Hall was ready for use. The Hawaiian Hall was completed and opened in 1905. The purpose of the museum was to house the family heirlooms that his wife had. Charles and Princess Bernice had no children. She had predeceased him, so this was the best idea for sharing them with future generations. Their ashes are buried inside the museum's original building.

Here they are together: Charles Reed Bishop and Princess Bernice Pauahi, with a maile lei over their picture.

Here is the contact information for the museum:

The Bernice Pauahi Bishop Museum
1525 Bernice Street
Honolulu, Hawai'i 96817
Phone: (808) 847-3511
Website: http://www.bishopmuseum.org/

The museum is open every day but Tuesday and Christmas Day.

When I visited, the price of admission was $17.95, but it has gone up since then by 2 dollars.

Parking is free, and the lot has plenty of room.

I went through the whole thing on my own. After my father took us to the Princess Ka'iulani statue in Waikiki, he dropped me off at the Bernice Pauahi Bishop Museum, which is northwest of most of Honolulu.

He drove us through a residential area with lots of small, private homes. One of them had a view of the front yard of the museum's original building, and its entire yard was full of Hallowe'en decorations. I had almost forgotten about Hallowe'en on this trip because I am used to cooler weather when that holiday is near.

This is the entrance to the museum grounds. The original building, the one that houses the museum collections, is in a courtyard past this one. Up these steps is the museum shop. To the right, through the shop, is the exit to the courtyard, with the ticket booth on the left just as one goes outside.

This is the view to the right as one approaches the entrance. The planetarium doesn't have an astronomy show – it's set up with a round, dark room full of environmental and ecological exhibits. The building past it is for meetings and lectures. I think one was going on while I toured the museum.

I went inside and glanced around the shop quickly. It had two large sections: books on the left and clothing and tote bags on the right. It looked really enticing…but I forced myself to turn right, not browse, and go straight to the ticket counter. It was after one o'clock, and the place would close at four, so there was no time to waste. I could shop after I had seen everything else.

This is the room on the left in the shop, with the books. The cash register was all the way to the left, near the door. This is the room on the right in the shop. Curving around to the right is the way out to the ticket booth. There were a couple of steps up immediately to the right with another small section that had shirts and tablecloths.

As I walked through the right side of the shop, it was full of distracting items that almost made me pause to browse, but I forced myself to keep going.

This is the view of the shop looking back from the door to the ticket booth.

Enough dawdling, I told myself. Time to get a ticket, whatever it cost, and see the museum. The girl in the booth was very nice, and assured me that I had plenty of time to see the whole thing, which was a relief. I paid cash for the ticket and went into the planetarium. The rest rooms were in its basement, down a winding staircase, and then down a short hallway. As I rushed past the exhibits in there, I saw the theme, but didn't pause to read the displays.

The ticket booth.

    The courtyard was yet another sunny paradise. I could see the main building across the yard to the right, and white tents set up here and there for outdoor events. I slowed down and took a few photographs, both of the museum itself and of the view from it.

Out in the courtyard, walking toward the original museum building.

Looking back the way I had come at the ticket area. It's on the right; the steps on the left go up to the planetarium.

There was downtown Honolulu in the distance, through the white tents.

I almost didn't want to go inside after seeing how nice it was outside, but I did.

The front entrance of the museum, with its original sign in the stone gable. The staircase in the front hall had a another plaque. This one was made of white marble.

History of the museum with floor plan. Floor plan of the museum.

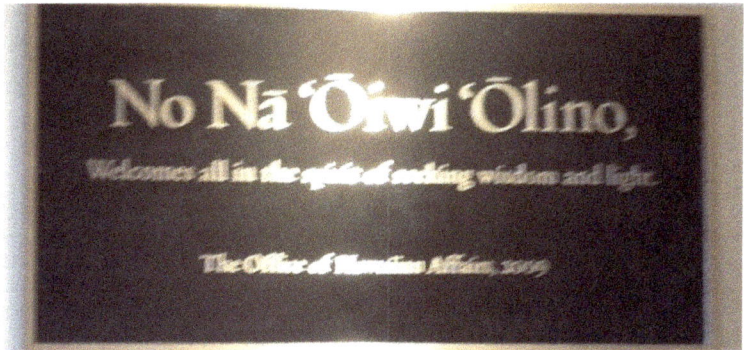

Welcome plaque in the front hall of the museum.

Welcome sign with a chant in Hawaiian.

The fun thing about visiting a museum that was built in the Victorian Era is the decorative detail: wood inlays, wood carvings and wainscoting, and beauty everywhere, not just in the exhibits.

After I had scrutinized, photographed, and otherwise studied the welcome signs, maps, plaques, dedications and history of the museum that hung in the foyer, I decided to go into the Kahili Room first, which was to the left, and then go back to the right for to see the J.M. Long Gallery and the Hawaiian Room. The Polynesian Hall was in the back, and it was closed. The Kahili Room was just one place on the left, and a dead end. It just made sense to see that first.

Kahili are feather standards, made in pairs, for individual aliʻi. Each pair is unique.

The room I visited contained a collection of these, called na kahili (don't add "s" in Hawaiian to make a noun plural; instead, put the word "na" in front of it). There is a line called a kahako that goes over the "a" in kahili to make it plural, but e-readers just turn a letter with one of those over it into a rectangular box. The collection covered the kahili of the Kamehameha, Lunalilo, and Kalakaua monarchies. There was even a display that explained how to make a kahili. It also contained studio portrait photographs of many of the Hawaiian royals.

The door to the Kahili Room.

This sign explained how the kahili are carried. Note the kahako over the word "kahili" in this sign, making the word plural. The e-reader can't ruin/obscure this example!

Kahili are used to salute the ali'i, and the bearers hold them straight up as standards just behind and to either side of the ali'i they are for. Kahili are also waved as fan over an ali'i who is sitting for a long period of time, such as at a dinner or ceremony.

Here is the display that shows how kahili are made.

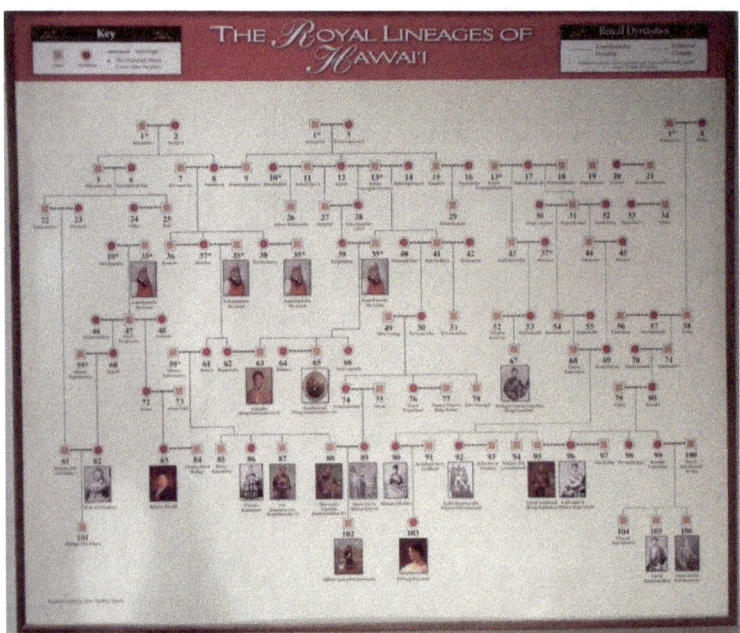

This family tree showed that Kamehameha appeared in four places, and that the tree doesn't branch in earlier times. This is why the Hawaiian royal family gene pools weren't healthy, and having children became impossible for many of them in the latter half of the nineteenth century. But it wasn't their fault; their predecessors didn't know the science that would have helped them with this.

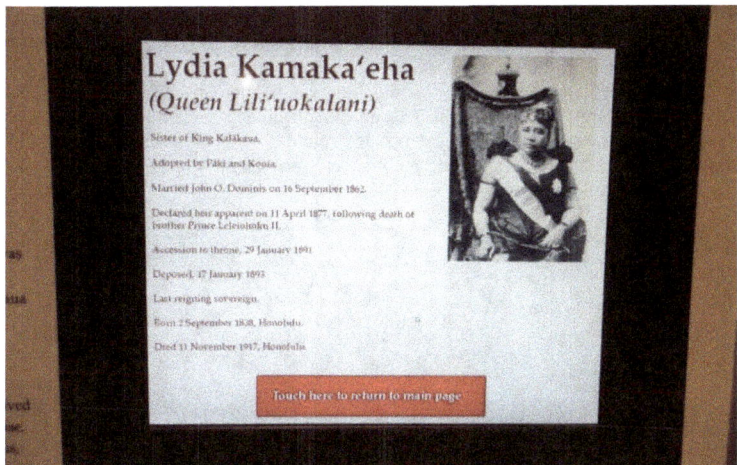

There was a touch screen in the Kahili Room that showed the photograph and biography of any member of the Hawaiian royal family that a visitor wanted to know about.

Princess Miriam Likelike, the mother of Princess Ka'iulani, and younger sister of Queen Lili'uokalani; Queen Kapi'olani with one of her hanai (adopted) nephews, Prince David Kawananakoa, Princess Ka'iulani's fiancé.

When I was through looking at the displays in the Kahili Room, I went back out into the foyer and headed across it to the J.M. Long Gallery. That room is full of colored poster boards – all in blue or purple – that detail the culture, geography, and artifacts of the Polynesian peoples. It was fun to see the real names of the different groups of islands in the South Pacific rather than just the names that Europeans had pinned onto them.

New Zealand is really called Aotearoa. I did know that Easter Island is really called Rapa Nui before arriving at this room, but at least they weren't all renamed. The exhibits in this room covered a triangular area, and the other island groups described were:

Samoa, Fiji, the Marquesas, the Society Islands, the Cook Islands, the Austral Islands, Tonga, and of course the Hawaiian Islands. The people from each group of islands had all traveled from what are known today as Indonesia and Micronesia.

It was after I came home and was watching yet another episode of *Hawaii Five-0* that I saw McGarrett and Danny in here, meeting with the curator to learn about an ancient Hawaiian weapon: a wooden paddle with the teeth of enemies (or a shark, depending upon what a warrior could get his hands on) set into the edge. It may sound silly, but I was having fun with that.

Here is one of the poster boards. Showing the one for Hawai'i first seemed like the right thing to do here. A tapa bark cloth with leaf prints.

Necklaces from Aotearoa, Samoa, Tonga, the Society Islands, and the last 2 on the right from Hawai'i.

This room had everything: cloth made of bark and decorated with patterns, necklaces made of sharks' teeth and wood, wooden carvings of gods, paddles, staffs with feathers, tattoo tools and a mask with a tattoo pattern as an example, wooden bowls and taro pounding pestles, and so on. I didn't rush through this room, even though I knew that the next one was huge.

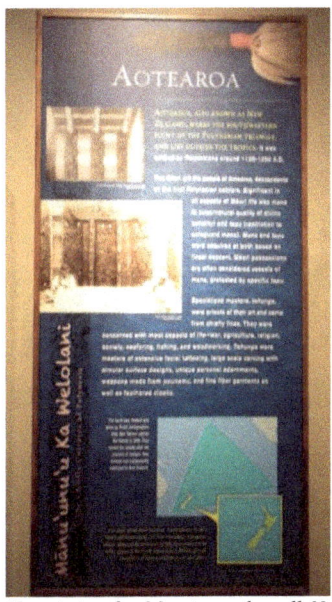 

Here it is: the Maori people call New Zealand Aotearoa. Carved artifacts from the Aotearoa Islands.

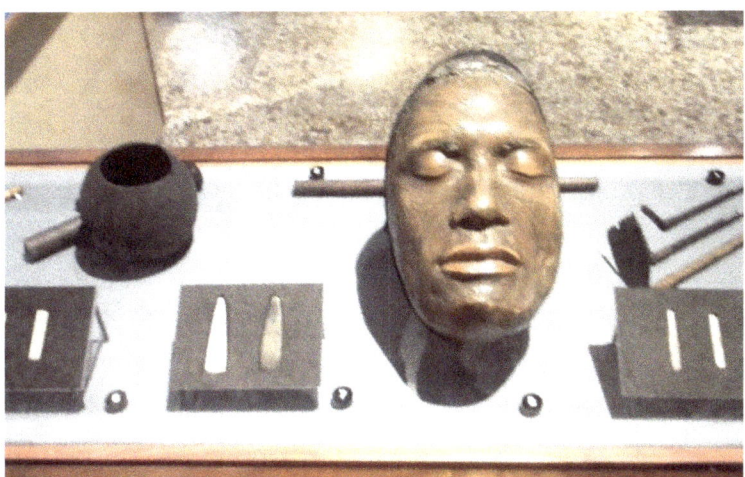

Tattooing tools from Fiji and Hawai'i.

The J.M. Long Gallery is not a large room. Its ceiling is a bit higher than that of a typical suburban American house, and the length and width is like a large living or dining room…with artifacts from all over the South Pacific island groups.

The Hawaiian Hall, with a miniature heiau, a couple of kiʻi statues, and a hale.

When I had looked at everything, I was ready for the Hawaiian Hall. The Hawaiian Hall is entered through a door at the back of the J.M. Long Gallery. It is a huge room with several displays across its floor, plus many more behind glass around the perimeter. That set-up is repeated all around the second and third floors, which overlook the ground floor from balconies. In addition, a Hawaiian canoe is suspended from the ceiling on one side, and a huge fake whale is suspended on the other, with one side of it cut away to show its skeleton.

The most frustrating part of this museum was the prohibition on using a camera flash, but no museum should allow that anyway. The problem with that was that in order to get decent images, I had to hold my breath so that I would hold the camera steady while it took a long time for each exposure. It was hit or miss, but after a lot of effort, I had some good photographs. Some other museum patrons saw what I was doing and smiled sympathetically as I tried and tried to get sufficiently clear results.

There was a miniature recreation of the Waha'ula Heiau. It was a heiau luakini – a sacrificial temple - built in the 13th century in Puna on the Big Island, and it was the first one. It stood until lava from Pu'u 'O'o erupted over it on August 11, 1997.

This is a hale pili – a one-room grass house, built just for the museum. It is a hale moe – a sleeping room. Here is some more data on the hale pili.

Once I had seen everything on the center floor of the Hawaiian Hall, I turned my attention to the perimeter. I started to the right of the hale pili. There was a great display of miniature ships that illustrated the craft that the Hawaiian people arrived in millennia ago. A story board behind it showed the path that they took to get from Indonesia and Micronesia to the Hawaiian Islands and all of the other groups of South Pacific islands.

The display of the trajectory of the Polynesian ships, and models of them.

Next, moving to the right, came a display case with feather capes that had been worn by Hawaiian kings and governors. All were red and yellow or red or yellow. The more yellow, the higher the rank of the owner. There were capes with swirls, stripes, and dots. The feathers came from the red, nectar-sucking i'iwi bird, and yellow 'o'o bird, the latter of which is now extinct.

The capes of the Hawaiian ali'i – all for men. The sign that gave details on the capes had a Hawaiian poem on the left.

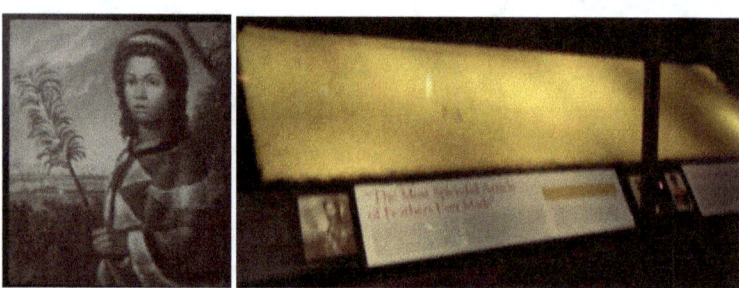

On the third floor, I found something really neat: a feather cape for the daughter of Kamehameha the Great, the Princess Nahi'ena'ena. It was the only one ever made for a woman. This is her portrait, and here is the fabulous yellow feather 'o'o pa'u of Princess Nahi'ena'ena. Forget jewelry with gold and precious stones – Hawaiians treasured feathers. That was the most precious commodity that they could ever hope to own, so this was the decorative accessory for Hawaiian royalty to have.

On and on through the displays I went, looking at: fish hooks carved out of oyster shells, koa wood spears that were so tall they were more than twice my five-foot-five height, taro pounding tools, carved wooden images of goddesses and gods, a huge piece of soft kapa cloth with red and blue patterns printed onto it, an oyster shell with a miniature painting in it by Princess Bernice Pauahi herself, cases devoted to each member of the royal families that were filled with their personal possessions, a Hawaiian flag from the late 19th century, a ukulele or two, hula gourds, and a detailed explanation of the anti-annexation petitions.

The scene painted inside this oyster shell is likely of the house that Princess Bernice Pauahi lived in with her husband, Charles Reed Bishop, before his career as Hawai'i's first banker took off and they moved to a mansion.

This image, despite repeated attempts to get a clear, sharp one that actually showed something, was the best I could do. It is included here because of its historical significance. The Anti-Annexation Petition display serves as a reminder that Hawai'i is a stolen paradise, taken over the expressly stated objections of the Hawaiian people. They

made sure to make themselves heard, and their queen organized this effort to stop the theft.

I was having a terrible time getting decent images as I went around the upper balconies of the Hawaiian Hall, but this was important. The petitions were here with original Hawaiian flags, but I won't reproduce the darkened images here. Suffice it say that this was a crucial action in Hawaiian history. Sovereignty was not surrendered without objection, not surrendered quietly, and the Hawaiian people have the documents to prove it. Every effort – legal, diplomatic, and the taking up of arms – was employed in the effort, and the rest of the world should know about it.

Native Sovereignty

INSPIRED BY AMERICAN INDIAN AND ALASKA NATIVE CLAIMS for sovereignty and reparations, and fueled by the evictions and the dire socioeconomic status of Native Hawaiians within their own homeland, Native Hawaiians began pursuing their cause in public and legal forums. Organizations such as A.L.O.H.A. (Aboriginal Lands of Hawaiian Ancestry) sought reparations to address the wrongs committed against the Hawaiian people by the United States. Today, sovereignty groups represent a wide range of perspectives, from nation to nation status akin to those of American Indian tribes to full independence. Despite differences, when threats to the Hawaiian community arise, tens of thousands gather in unity and solidarity.

A.L.O.H.A.: Aboriginal Lands of Hawaiian Ancestry. Sovereignty groups exist to this day, intent on protecting and regaining Native Hawaiian rights – rights of several kinds – and reparations.

When I saw this sign and read it, I thought about how it must feel to be a citizen of a culture and a nation that has been absorbed by a larger, stronger one – an empire. To try to understand it, I thought about how it feels to be a citizen of an empire. To be completely honest about that, it feels…good. It feels reassuring and safe.

It feels as though my country's government can be counted upon to maintain control of its territory, and thus counted upon to successfully protect me at all times (an idealistic feeling, but an illusion that many U.S. citizens feel much of the time). To be a citizen of an absorbed nation must feel just the opposite. Although this was not the first time that I had thought about this, it felt bad just to know that because I can feel good, others end up feeling bad.

After that pause of reflection, I went down the staircase to the ground floor, out through the J.M. Long Gallery to the foyer, and up the staircase that led to the Picture Gallery. When I got to the top of the stairs, however, I didn't go in right away. There were several interesting things to see there, including a beautiful metal hinge, a portrait on either side of the stairwell of Charles Reed Bishop and Princess Bernice Pauahi, some bas-relief profiles of non-royal Hawaiian people, and an interesting bench.

The stairwell landing outside the Picture Gallery. Above the wainscoting were bas-relief sculptures of Hawaiian citizens/subjects.

This bench was up on the balcony over the stairs, just outside the Picture Gallery. It looked too unique and fascinating not to photograph, so here it is.

That was all, so I went into the very dimly lit Picture Gallery. It had some beautiful paintings of lava eruptions, Hawaiian landscapes, and portraits of Hawaiian royalty on its walls. It also had a case full of ukulele, a stereoscopic postcard viewer (part of it didn't work, and part of it did), and some benches to sit on in the middle of the room.

The Picture Gallery, seen from the door to the stairwell.

The ukulele case, and a beautiful portrait of Queen Emma Rooke.

That was everything. I checked; there were other rooms in the museum, but they were not open, so I had definitely seen it all. I went back down the staircase and out into the yard. It was almost time to meet my parents, but not quite yet. I had enough time to visit the rest rooms and shop, plus take a few more photographs.

Time to enjoy the shop! I had done my homework, so I could let myself have fun now. (No one was making me see the museum on these terms but me – I won't enjoy a reward without working for it.) I was in book heaven, and I found two small paperback books, one on Hawaiian birds and the other on Hawaiian flowers. Next, I found a little paperback dictionary...and then another. I settled on the smaller of the two, as the first one was too heavy to carry. Finally, I found a biography of Princess Kaʻiulani and bought that, too. I had seen it for sale elsewhere earlier on our trip, but now I decided to go ahead and buy it.

The Hawaiian teenager who rang up my purchases was friendly. He had a friend who was there hanging out with him. I showed them the two dictionaries, and they agreed with my decision to get the smaller one. I asked if many people from the neighborhood visited the museum. They laughed and said no. I said that I would visit often if I lived near it, and I would.

The café counter, decorated for Hallowe'en, and the café seating area. The staff was closing up for the day.

The lawn by the parking area with white birds on it. My parents arrived, and my mother insisted upon buying me a gift: a pretty tote bag with the museum logo on it and a bird-of-paradise.

We could see the Punchbowl Crater from the museum grounds as we drove off.

Honolulu International Airport

The Monday after we arrived in Honolulu, we returned to the airport there to leave.

We would be flying on Hawaiian Airlines, which I thought would be a fun experience, and it was. The logo was a famous one, brightly colored with a Hawaiian woman in profile and a hibiscus blossom tucked behind her ear. It does go to the contiguous United States, and I had seen the cops of *Hawaii Five-0* and the agents of *NCIS: Los Angeles* take a flight on it once when they worked a case together. I looked forward to it.

The pretty logo for Hawaiian Airlines.

This flight would take a mere 44 minutes. The inter-island journey would be a lot easier and more comfortable than it was when Mark Twain visited and made the same trek in the 1860s. By reading his series of articles (that he sent to his employer, *The Sacramento Union*), I was able to discern that he was in Hawai'i in 1866, because he listed the members of the government and their positions, and mentioned the funeral of Princess Victoria Kamamalu, the kuhina nui.

Back then, Mark Twain had to take a steamer boat named the *Boomerang*. He said that it was as wide as a trolley car and as long as two of them, and that he could stand on its upper deck, reach over the side, and touch the water. He traveled with five other men and stayed in a tiny cabin with coffin-like bunk beds (his impression, which I shall not dispute). Native Hawaiian people, not royalty, who had paid much less, slept on the floor of a larger, flea-ridden area.

As he slept, Twain smelled rancid bilge water and felt a rat run across him. He tried sleeping on the floor, but cockroaches as large as peach leaves took up a position in his hair, so he got up. Sleep was difficult anyway, due to a rooster that wouldn't shut up. The journey took three days and two nights, with a Saturday departure from Honolulu and a Monday arrival in Kailua-Kona, which was where we were headed.

Yes, we were going to have it a lot easier.

My father dropped us off with all of the luggage except for his all-important camera bag and drove off to dispose of the rental car. We paced around, used the rest room, and tried to figure out where to go and when. After our journal from Connecticut, we had no intention of attempting to check ourselves in without a human being. The airport computer kiosks would just refuse to recognize our flight numbers, as they keep changing. I'm sure Mark Twain would have had a few choice words of disparagement about that.

The baggage check-in area at Honolulu International Airport.

After observing signs, people, and asking some questions, we identified the correct counter and waited for help with our AAA e-tickets. The people on duty were very nice; they didn't tell us to go use the computer kiosks, but instead checked us in and confirmed that the flight number had indeed been changed since the tickets were bought. We didn't even need my father to show up; we had his passport, so they just issued our boarding passes, put long white sticker tapes on the baggage that we wanted to check, and told us where to hand it over.

The ticket counter with Hawaiian Airlines agents. They were serious but pleasant and efficient.

My father soon appeared, and we did so, pausing at the rest rooms again.

The rest room signs were fun; they said "Women" in English, Hawaiian, and Braille. The left side looked like traditional Hawaiian bark cloth – kapa – with hand-printed designs on it.

While we waited for my father to catch up with us, I took a photograph of the map of the airport. It has two levels, with the gates all on the upper one. Baggage claim and the exits to rental cars and other transportation are downstairs. Shops, restaurants, and gates are upstairs.

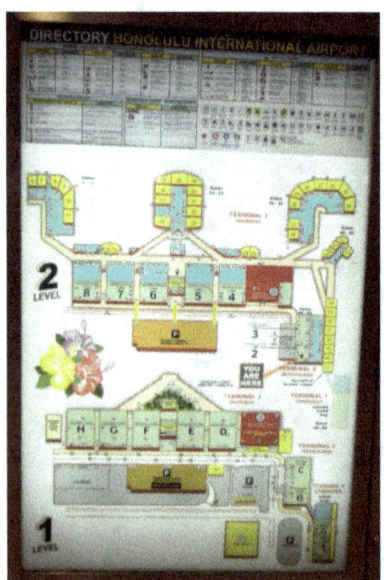

We left from the Terminal 2 area at the right, which handles Inter-Island flights.

Once my father had joined us, we decided to find our gate and get seats there before doing any exploring. This was an afternoon flight and a short one, so we weren't going to eat here. We found it, got settled, and looked around. It was pretty, which is more than one can say for a lot of airports. Most seem purely functional, neither ugly nor pretty, but this one had beautiful paintings of tropical flowers at either end of the waiting area.

The waiting area at the gate. There were paintings of orchids, anthuriums, and heliconias to admire.

One of the nation's many ubiquitous Starbucks coffee shops obscured our view of the gate's waiting area, but I quickly figured that out and led my parents around it. Once settled, my father wanted a cookie or a scone or something from there – just a small snack. I shared one with him, and got water for my mother.

After that, I sat down to read, determined to finish a Hawaiian history book that I had bought and downloaded to my Nook Color reader before leaving home. It was by a political science and Hawaiian language professor from the University of Hawai'i at Manoa. The book had first been published in print, and then digitized, which had messed up the display of any letter with a kahako over it ("a" and "u"). All of them showed up as little rectangles, which was very distracting. It slowed me down as I made educated guesses as to which letter was obscured.

A ukulele bought by a tourist. It is a Portuguese instrument, adapted by sugar plantation workers after they arrived in Hawai'i and had spent some time learning about Hawaiian music.

I wasn't concentrating very well. Announcements made it hard to focus, plus the surroundings were interesting. A woman sitting across from us had a small instrument case, so I asked her if it contained a ukulele. She smiled and said that it did. She had bought one on her trip, she told us, and was determined to learn how to play it. She took it out and let me photograph it.

After that, rather than put my camera away, I walked around, getting some images of the Hawaiian Airlines planes and baggage loading equipment, and of a hangar bay with mechanics in the distance.

One plane, with the pretty logo on it.

Honolulu International Airport is the sort that has every amenity, multiple restaurants offering a variety of cuisines, and plenty of shops. However, since we were only flying to another Hawaiian island, not leaving them, we did not see the L'Occitane shop or very many other ones – just a few seemingly ordinary souvenir shops.

A close-up of the hanger bay with a cart passing it on the tarmac.

We looked around in them, but we had enough recreational reading material. I did find a kiosk in the hall that had some fun souvenirs, though, and bought a small, soft-sculpture doll. She would be easy to pack and carry and not get damaged in transit. The dolls were all dressed in Hawaiian garb with lei in their hair and around their necks. Some had black hair and purple clothes, and others had brown hair and pink outfits. There were only a couple of choices.

It was after I got home and looked at the tag that I realized that the doll I had bought was named for President Obama's older daughter, Malia. Cool! It's a pretty doll.

Island Friends is the brand name of the doll, and her name is Malia – it shows on the tag.

As expected, our inter-island flight was quick and painless. The stewardesses had pretty uniforms (again), with more tropical flower patterns to admire, and they were very nice.

I had hope to see the four islands in between, but I was sitting on the wrong side of the plane to see Mauʻi very well. The plane banked away from it after I got a brief glimpse of Puʻu Kukui, the extinct volcano on the northwestern section of the island, and so it was impossible to see Haleakala, the other one to its southeast. Oh well…

Soon we were landing in Kona, and we could all see that landscape.

Aloha to Kona

The landscape on the Big Island of Hawai'i varies dramatically.

It can look as old as that of O'ahu, with green grass and lots of trees, flowers, bushes, and other plants growing profusely over its fertile volcanic soil, or it can have almost no vegetation due to a recent eruption, or it can be something in between those extremes. We would be seeing all of them over the next five days.

As the plane came in for a landing, we saw what looked like churned up soil, very dark, chunky, and somewhat rocky. The rocks were small, though, and looked more like soil that one could knock apart if one chose to stomp on it. As the plane taxied into the gate, however, it became clear that that was not what we were seeing.

The soil in Kona, which is on the west coast of the Big Island, was obviously volcanic, but it had not been there long enough to be completely covered with grass. What we were seeing was swathes of volcanic soil that swirled through grass and then stretched out to the shore. It looked as though a volcano had erupted over grassland, and then enough time had passed that the hardened magma had broken up enough to almost be fertile soil, but not quite.

We were fascinated. My parents had another emotion to add to that: mild trepidation.

I wasn't afraid of this landscape, however, because I had looked up all five of the volcanoes on this island before choosing where we would stay, and based the decision on which ones were reliably dormant. My parents had not done that, and now they were...worried.

I hastened to explain my research to them again.

The closest volcano to us was Hualalai, and it was active but dormant, a seeming oxymoron. It last erupted in 1801. That explained the landscape. Apparently, the people of the Kona district were living dangerously, because Hualalai might erupt again sometime, but it was far enough from the plume that was responsible for the formation of the Hawaiian Islands that I had decided to go for it and have us stay in Kona. We were going to drive all over this island anyway, so this was hardly the most unstable spot on our itinerary. Kona was built up all around the western coast that abutted Hualalai.

To the northernmost point of the Big Island was Kohala, the island's only reliably extinct volcano. Kamehameha the Great was born there. If I had really wanted to have us stay at the most unlikely-to-erupt spot on this island, I could have chosen the Kohala district, but my research had shown that it just wasn't that exciting to tourists, and we wanted to be near a fun shopping area, which Kona offered.

To the northeast on this island was Mauna Kea, the world's tallest mountain at 13,803 feet above sea level. But that statistic should be qualified: it is only the tallest if one measures it from its oceanic base, which is 33,500 feet from base to peak, and thus taller than Mount Everest. This volcano is dormant also, but not active. It is somewhat north of Hualalai, which may explain that. One of the world's most important observatories is based atop Mauna Kea, and I hoped to visit it. Astronomers with Ph.D.s had access to the cluster of observatories all the way at the top, while the public had access to a visitors' center lower down. Either way, I was intrigued to think that there was snow atop Mauna Kea, on a tropical island.

As for the other volcanoes on this island, I wouldn't even consider staying near them.

There were residents who did so, and I wondered about that.

Native Hawaiians first settled this island 1,500 years ago.

They didn't know that this place wasn't safe, but people know it now. I wondered about insurance rates, or even availability on the southern side of the island. I also looked forward to finding out more about human efforts to coexist with these volcanoes. Patterns of settlement and relocation as volcanoes erupted where humans lived promised to be a topic of interest.

Mauna Loa was the closest one to the south of Hualalai, and it was active. It is a shield volcano, and its eruptions tend not to be explosive ones; the lava just runs down. It is also the world's largest single mountain mass. The landscape around it is rather desolate.

I found a map at the airport and grabbed it (it was free). Orchid farms were just east of Kilauea, the world's most continuously erupting volcano. It has been active since 1820, with minor pauses of only a couple of decades a century ago. Mark Twain walked among its streams of magma, and almost sank into them a couple of times as he hiked in the darkness with only a lantern to guide him and a friend.

Southwest of Mauna Loa, all along the coast, were homes, churches, stores, and historic sites. The place where Captain Cook was killed, Kealakekua Bay, was directly west of Mauna Loa, and there was a monument to him there.

Kilauea fascinated me. I wanted to get near it and learn about it.

One of my husband's friends had mailed me some books to borrow before I came to the Big Island. The one that I found most intriguing was by a volcanologist who had lived here for three years, from 1969-1972, working with the Hawaiian Volcano Observatory. He and his new wife and their cat and dog had stayed near the place. He had a wonderful time walking up very close to fiery eruptions from Kilauea with colleagues, experiencing earthquakes as magma flowed, and learning the history of the eruptions here.

Back to our arrival...

We debarked, walking out of the plane onto the tarmac in the bright sunlight. Kona International Airport was a lot smaller than Honolulu International Airport. We walked around through the outdoor gate and into the baggage claim area. It was midafternoon, so I got a clear but fleeting look at the place: its décor was dark brown wood with little courtyard. Shapes of turtles and humans with paddles adorned to upper edge of the courtyard walls. (I would later learn that these were petroglyph motifs.)

We got our bags and went out to the main driveway of the airport to board a shuttle, which would take us to the Hertz rental car station. This one was far away from the main building, so no one was expected to walk across the driveway to get to it, unlike in Honolulu.

The rental car building was a tiny one surrounded by driveways, parking lot, and chain-link fences. Some benches were just outside under an overhang. My father went directly inside to wait in line. My mother and I arranged our bags by one of the benches, then I followed him to give him the sheet of paper with the necessary reservation data and bar codes on it.

When I came back, my mother told me to stay with the bags and joined him.

As I waited, two older couples arrived. The men wore beautiful Hawaiian shirts, and one of them sat down near me to wait. He chatted about the purpose of our respective visits. Theirs was to visit friends who lived on the Big Island.

After about twenty minutes, my mother reappeared and said that my father was getting the car. We waited another couple of minutes, and he appeared with a charcoal gray Nissan Altima sedan. It was the exact hue of cooled magma, I couldn't help thinking.

The car came complete with a GPS device mounted onto the dashboard. Just as on Oahu, we deactivated it every time we got into the car, not interested in paying for its use. We had maps and a sense of direction, and would learn a lot more by using those. It was more fun that way!

We loaded our stuff into the car, I took the front seat, opened the map, and off we went.

Aston Kona by the Sea

We turned right, which was southwest, out of the airport onto Queen Kaʻahumanu Highway, which was also known as Route 19. It was nice to see that the literacy queen had a long stretch of a well-traveled highway named after her. Soon the flat, desolate volcanic landscape gave way to grassy areas and a mountain view. The mountain was heavily settled, and its top was cloud-covered, despite the bright sunshine.

I scanned the map, and told my father that we would be turning right onto Palani Road, which would curve around to the left and south to become Aliʻi Drive. This was more than he wanted to know at first, but announcing it seemed necessary because we came to a major intersection in less than ten minutes, and there was Palani Road.

Queen Kaʻahumanu Highway meets Route 190 to the east and Palani Road to the west at a traffic light set-up with separate lanes for turning in every direction plus lanes for continuing straight, so one needs to be watching for the turn-off.

Up the sloping Route 190 were lots of strip malls with familiar franchises for tenants, plus other stores that were native to Hawaiʻi. I looked forward to exploring the area later. For now, my father turned right, and we went down the very short stretch that was Palani Road until it curved around and became Aliʻi Drive. At the curve, I noticed a large hotel on the right, with sprawling, manicured grounds that overlooked Kailua Bay. It was the Courtyard Marriott King Kamehameha's Kona Beach Hotel.

The car continued south, and we saw lots of colorful buildings with upper-story lanai that overlooked the water from the other side of the street. They were restaurants and boutique shops. A small house that was clearly a museum appeared as the car fully rounded the curve and Alii Drive straightened out for a stretch. Next was a red-roofed shopping complex, followed by hotel after hotel. One of the hotels we passed had a fabulous humpback whale decoration mounted on its façade, surrounding by musical notes as it dove toward volcanic cliffs.

Shortly after that, I saw the entrance to the Aston Kona by the Sea, our hotel, and we pulled into it. It had a pair of rocky signs on either side of the driveway, and the signage had a pretty, swirling font.

This palm tree had a thicker trunk than most, and a bushier, much larger set of fronds, too. It was by the right entrance sign.

The hotel was actually two large buildings joined in the center by an outdoor lobby under an awning. Parking was underneath each building, with a few additional spaces out front, under multiple species of palm trees. Mynah birds flew about, landing on the lawn to peck about.

The driveway of Aston Kona by the Sea forked toward its two buildings. We stayed in the one on the right.

My mother and I got out to check in while my father sat in the car. I noticed a solitary bird-of-paradise blossom sticking up in the garden as we went up to the desk. A small bookcase stood next to the window. It was full of books, both hardcover and paperback. These were apparently for the guests to read. The swimming pool area was through the lanai and out back.

The front desk was on the left, and the swimming pool, hot tub, and beach beyond it.

I could see this fan palm from my window. The garage entrance is at the lower left. Here is the fan palm from inside my bedroom window.

We got our key cards and quickly parked the car in the garage. My father made short work of acquiring a cart for all of our luggage, and we loaded it up. The stairs were at either end of the building, but the elevator (just one) was at the opposite end to our unit. Our unit faced Alii Drive, while the elevator shaft was next to the back staircase, so we trundled on down to it and got in. A huge, framed print of a red, blue and yellow macaw hung inside the elevator.

Up on our floor, which was on the third level, my father pulled the cart out onto the balcony and we all walked slowly around to the other end, admiring the plumeria and palm trees as we did so. We also noticed that each and every unit had its own sign with some variation of: "Mahalo for removing your shoes." No two signs were alike.

This was the prettiest of the signs. They all depicted flip-flop shoes.

We let ourselves into our unit and saw a short, ugly hallway that turned left at the end.

Looking back, I checked that the door was closed and locked, then followed my mother in. After that left turn, I saw my room on the left and the rest of the unit on the right, starting with the kitchen. It looked nice enough, but I suddenly realized that we wouldn't be cooking our dinners in it because of the schedule we were on. This island was just too big to count on getting back here for dinner every night, plus we had all stared out the car windows with enthusiasm at the array of restaurants on Aliʻi Drive.

This kitchen had a tiny coffee machine, a dishwasher, and a refrigerator that caught our attention. We never used the oven or stove.

Continuing on into the living room, we saw the eating area. There was a small table right next to the pass-through from the kitchen, with the unit's telephone by a window right next to it. the laundry closet was right across from it, with the dryer piled on top of washer.

The living room took up the rest of the large open space, with sliding glass doors that opened onto a small lanai overlooking the pool. Actually, the pool was off to the extreme right, but we could see it easily.

My parents' suite didn't have a door – just a sliding pair of slatted wooden panels to close it off, with a pretty bedroom and a pass-through to the sink area. The toilet and shower were closed off, though, with a door that closed on them. They had no bathtub, but they didn't care.

We ate breakfast at this table. My room is down the hall at left. In the mirror one can see the window, and me, taking the picture. A little bookcase with some books left by past guests is on the right. The modem for cable television and wi-fi access is under the chair at left.

The coffee machine only held four cups, which forced us to make coffee twice each morning in order for there to be enough for everyone. My mother asked me to show her how to use it the first morning; David and I had had a four-cup machine in Kuwait, so this wasn't difficult for me.

The living room was comfortable, with pretty, palm-patterned throw pillows on the sofa. The television was just to the right of my mother, on a table. It was a large flat-screened one.

We got settled as quickly as we could, because we wanted to go out and get groceries before dinner. The point of that was to have breakfast things for the next morning, prior to heading for Hilo.

I looked around, photographing everything before we could disturb any of it as at our previous hotel-condominium. The maid had literally just left when we arrived; she had been pulling her supply cart away as we trundled in with our luggage cart.

My parents' room.

The bathroom sink and pass-through. It was pretty, but even with those white-painted panels shut, the noise of one's roommate washing up would be a distraction, I thought. The rest of my parents' bathroom. It had been reconfigured and remodeled at some point.

My bathroom sink. There I am in the mirror, with the flash going off as I take the photograph. A tub! I was happy.

My room. I slept by the window. Mynah birds lived all around the Aston Kona by the Sea.

My only complaints about this hotel were: 1. The wi-fi signal was appallingly weak; and 2. The hotel cleaning staff ate lunch in the stairwell right behind my bedroom wall one afternoon as I attempted to relax and read, holding a loud conversation that made that activity impossible.

I attempted to rectify each situation by phone, but the wi-fi signal was hopeless. After much aggravation, complete with David calling me on the hotel phone to figure out why it was taking me so long to log onto my Nook Color and find out what my e-mail said, I was able to talk him through the steps of loading an anti-virus program onto his laptop computer.

As for the loud talkers, by the time the manager walked over to disperse them, they had left. There was a window in my room with a heavy curtain that looked out onto the balcony and stairwell, which I kept closed. All that window could do, I thought, was eradicate any semblance of privacy in my room. However, it also allowed me to glare out at the maids, who just stared back and stayed put. I realize that they wanted some fun in their workday, but this was ridiculous. Quiet enjoyment should be a standard and reasonable expectation in a hotel.

The pool was very nice, and we used it three or four times. We also met some nice people there, and had a good time chatting with them about their stay on the Big Island. They didn't tour around at all; they just stayed in and read.

The pool area was accessed by walking out the back from either the stairwell or the elevator area, then around the side and into first one gate and then another. The hotel key card was required for entry. Once inside, there were lots of chaise longue chairs, regular chairs, umbrellas, and a little round hot tub that was up a few steps at the opposite end.

The pool, seen from the hot tub area. Our unit was off to the right, on the third level. My father enjoyed the hot tub, and one afternoon, I wished I had brought my camera back here, because I saw two geckos by the ivory-hued, stucco wall at left. One was trying to match the pattern of the beige tiles, while the other stayed bright green with a few orange and turquoise spots and streaks on its back, trying to look like a leaf.

We could see the beach and a large gas grill over the stone wall, with more chairs and umbrellas, but we never went out there. The surf looked too strong. My father had had enough of swimming, so he enjoyed the hot tub and pool.

There was also a saltwater pool, but that wasn't part of Aston Kona by the Sea. It belonged to the place next door, adjacent to our building. It was closed, with signs hung indicating that it could be dangerous in bad weather. It was perched precariously close to the ocean wall.

Aston Kona by the Sea was an adequate and comfortable enough place to stay; it was not fabulous. Our AAA travel agent had not seen it, but we were, for the most part, satisfied with her recommendation. The fun of it was the feeling of being in a small resort of condominiums and getting a feel for the climate, and for the flora and fauna all around us. I made good use of the opportunity, and enjoyed it.

A Ride Between 2 Volcanoes but Not Over Another

The next morning, as planned, we took off for Hilo, which is on the opposite side of the Big Island of Hawai'i. We had a reservation with Blue Hawaiian Helicopters tour for a 2 p.m. flight over Kilauea. Check-in time was 1:15 p.m. Accordingly, we left just after nine o'clock after a rather purposefully eaten breakfast with great Kona coffee, bought the previous evening at a local grocery store.

It was time to use the lovely map that I had found at the airport again. This really was a great map; it focused exclusively on the Big Island, providing a cartoon-style series of insets that zoomed in on Kailua-Kona, Kohala Coast, and Hilo. The entire island was the large part, of course; it had little insets that depicted points of interest, complete with volcano names and points of interest.

Off onto Ali'i Drive we went, heading north. The map informed me that we would be going up Route 190, which picked up across the street from and continuing Palani Road. From there, its name would also be first Mamalahoa Highway and later the Hawai'i Belt Road. We would continue on Route 190 until it forked, then turn right, sharply southeast. It was quite a sharp turn; it reminded me of the top of an isosceles triangle when I looked at the map.

The map that we relied upon for the duration of our stay on the Big Island. Definitely get one when you land on it! I spread the map out in the back seat to look at where we were going – right through the middle of the Big Island, that's where. We went northeast, then sharply southeast, then east between Mauna Kea and Mauna Loa.

Our trip up Route 190 took approximately 45 minutes, and I stared out the windows at the landscape, curious to see things that I would not be seeing again. I was hoping to visit the observatory atop Mauna Kea at this point in our trek. We had brought warm clothes with us, in preparation for the cold weather and high altitude.

The landscape was grassy with patches of dark brown volcanic soil, as the car climbed upwards somewhat. I was on the lookout for horse ranches, because I knew that this was where the Paniolos lived. Paniolos are Mexican-Hawaiian cowboys. The first ones moved to the Big Island in the mid-nineteenth century to help the Hawaiians manage horses, and married Hawaiians. They are still in the ranch business to this day.

Here we are on Route 190, which goes northeast, and connects with Saddle Road.

Paniolo country. Paniolos are Mexican-Hawaiian cowboys. We were passing horse ranches.

It was a lovely sunny day, at least on the western side of the Big Island. I fully expected it to be different once we got closer to Hilo. The landscape went from pale, sun-scorched grasses to bright green grasses as we passed first Hualalai and then the smaller dome just north of it, called Puʻuwaʻawaʻa, or Furrowed Hill. We were in Paniolo country now. Horses walked and grazed in the hills all around us.

Still in Paniolo country, but we were getting closer to the mini domes that surround Mauna Kea.

Not only did we see horses, but we also started to see mini domes, some with rounded tops, others with tops that had blown off eons ago, and grown carpets of green grass over them.

Another mini dome near Mauna Kea, which is not active.

When we turned sharply southeast, we were on Saddle Road, also known as Route 200.

This road was a very long one.

The landscape abruptly changed to one of rocky, reddish brown soil with very little vegetation growing out of it. We saw Mauna Loa off in the distance to the right (south) before we saw Mauna Kea, but we saw lots of Mauna Keas mini domes all along Saddle Road.

Mauna Loa is off in the distance, sloping upwards, but it's quite far off. The road took us a lot closer to Mauna Kea than to Mauna Loa, but that was just fine, because Mauna Loa is still active.

As my father drove on Saddle Road between the two volcanoes, he said that it felt like a wiggly ride. It made him nervous because it seemed like the road curved down vertically, making it impossible to actually see the pavement. It's always reassuring to be able to see the road on which the vehicle that one is operating moves, but here there was none of that. He said he would never forget it.

Despite my repeated attempts to explain the states of activity of the volcanoes, my parents were tense for this entire stretch of road. This is what a volcanic landscape looks like – a cooled one, I kept telling them!

A U.S. Army base was the only sign of human habitation for most of this trek, on the south side of Saddle Road. The barracks were set far back from the road, behind barbed wire, and compared to Schofield Barracks on Oʻahu, it looked doubtful that families lived on this base – only military personnel. Maybe it was the forbidding landscape; maybe I was wrong, but that was the impression I got as I stared into the distance as the sparsely populated military area. I checked the AAA map later; it was the Pohakuloa Training Area Military Reservation.

Halfway between the ends of Saddle Road – between civilization and civilization – is a barbed wire fence that surrounds a U.S. Army base. Note the red soil and plants growing here and there on it. If plants were growing, I saw no reason to get anxious.

The U.S. Army base is off in the distance behind the fence, on the south side of Saddle Road, but well away from Mauna Loa.

After we had passed the military reservation, I went back to staring at the sights up close to the car: rocky volcanic soil with pinkish and red areas, red flowering shrubs, and green leafy plants growing up here and there from the soil.

My parents commented from time to time that they found the landscape eerie. They were very quiet as they looked out at it. This was highly uncharacteristic behavior for them. They usually chat and comment about topics unrelated to the drive, and my mother usually reads.

This was the rocky landscape that spooked my mother, but it could be that since it was only our first full day on the Big Island, she was just getting used to it.

Red flowering plants growing sparsely on the volcanic soil along Saddle Road.

We had been driving for well over an hour when I finally saw the entrance to access road that goes up Mauna Kea to the observatory, imaginatively named Mauna Kea Road. I just barely managed to get a photograph of it as the car went by. As soon as I saw it, I realized that we would not be coming back this way. My parents were too unnerved by the landscape, and we now knew that it would take longer to traverse Saddle Road than we were willing to drive.

At last, we saw it: the access road that goes up Mauna Kea. The little sign to the left indicates which road it was, although it was the only one that branched off Saddle Road. I shot this image as the car moved past, with my father less and less willing to come back this way with every mile that passed.

The ride went on and on, with more volcanic soil, until finally, abruptly, we entered a lush green area. The sky was overcast, and a misty rain was falling. The contrast that we had just experienced reminded me of Lucy's journey from the Spare Oom, into the wardrobe, through the fur coats that turned to fir trees as she walked and out into the snow-covered woods of Narnia in C.S. Lewis's *The Lion, the Witch, and the Wardrobe*.

We had come out of the rough, rocky terrain at last, and our thoughts (at least, mine and my mother's) were now taken up almost completely by a desire to find a rest room. Clearly, the state department of tourism had anticipated this, because we noticed a little beige-painted cement-block building on the right through the greenery. My father stopped and my mother and I availed ourselves of it. He chose to wait in the car.

We were very glad to see the first houses out of Saddle Road after driving on it for nearly two hours.

Back in the car, we settled in happily to stare at the private homes and neighborhood that surrounded Hilo. I looked up at the overcast sky and began to worry about our helicopter tour. My mother voiced that thought, saying not to be too disappointed if we couldn't go, but I made no promises about that emotion.

We saw this beautiful banyan tree in the front yard of a school on the outskirts of Hilo.

We drove down the Bayfront Highway, which ran into Kamehameha Highway. It passed some great park grounds, where we saw a small statue of Kamehameha the Great. It was a smaller version of the one we had seen in Honolulu.

This public park was rain-soaked and deserted, but in the spring, near Easter, an annual hula festival is held here. It's called the Merrie Monarch Festival, for King Kalakaua.

Hilo means "to twist" in Hawaiian. Kamehameha the Great named it for a rope that moored his canoe here, and his son, Liholiho and later Kamehameha II, was born here. The city has a tsunami museum. It is the leading distributer of macadamia nuts in the world. The nuts are grown close to the city, and shipped out from it.

Hilo is the least expensive place to live in Hawai'i. No wonder; the weather leaves a lot to be desired. It doesn't feel like fun there. In fact, the general feel of the place is like many a depressed area in rural New England in the summertime.

The first order of business was to find the airport and do some reconnaissance so that we would be exactly on time for our expensive booked activity later on. After that, we could go get something to eat. We drove directly through Hilo to the airport, which was on the eastern side of the city, and entered it on Airport Access Road. It was a long road, 2.2 miles, thick with tall, leafy trees on either side, and nicely paved.

The sky continued to look gray and the rain continued to sprinkle.

Airport Access Road, which leads to Hilo International Airport.

Another view of Airport Access Road.

The parking area at Hilo International Airport, facing the terminals.

The map of the Big Island depicts this airport as having five small buildings in a row along one of the legs of the x-shaped tarmac. We had to go through a ticket-spewing, arm-lifting mechanism and later pay to get out of there – twice – but it was worth it to find out what we should expect.

We approached the terminal and knew we were in the right place immediately when we saw the Blue Hawaiian Helicopters van parked out front.

The volcano tour that we were booked for was called "Circle of Fire and Waterfalls". We had been booked in advance, so my mother had already been charged for the experience. Each ticket cost two hundred dollars, and we were to be charged yet another fee of $39.50 (a fuel surcharge) just before takeoff. I was ready with our ticket voucher and confirmation number.

Our plan was to check in and find out what we had to do when, plus see if the pilots were going to cancel the whole thing due to the weather. I hoped not…

The back of the Blue Hawaiian Helicopters van.

A small crowd of people was gathered in front of the Blue Hawaiian Helicopters desk, and no one was smiling. This was not a good omen. It turned out that these people were supposed to go out on a morning tour. The pilots had flown over the volcano to check for visibility, seen that it was terrible, and reported this. That flight was cancelled.

These people did not go on their flight over Kilauea.

As for us, we were told that our flight wasn't cancelled yet, but that unless the clouds cleared up by two o'clock, it would be. My mother wondered if she could just have her money back now, but the answer was no, because no decision had yet been made. She was less than thrilled, but I was somewhat relieved. Disappointment was not yet assured.

Regardless of whether or not we were actually going out on the flight, it was almost noon and we were hungry. We were advised to go into Hilo and try the food at Ken's House of Pancakes, so we left the airport and did just that.

Ken's House of Pancakes in Hilo.

The inside of the diner was decorated for Hallowe'en.

We found seats that overlooked the parking lot and gave us a view of the whole diner. I deliberately turned my thoughts to enjoying some macadamia nut pancakes, a thing that I had not yet done on this trip but intended to do. My parents got sandwiches. The pancakes came with three kinds of syrup: coconut, mango, and guava. All were delicious. I also had pineapple juice.

When the meal was over, we went back to the airport.

There was still some time left before we were expected back at the Blue Hawaiian Helicopters desk, so my father pulled up to the post office that was on the left just inside Airport Access Road. He asked me to go in and try to buy some Hawaiian stamps. I took the money he handed me and went in, feeling skeptical. Hawai'i was a state, not its own nation. Why would it have different stamps? Sure enough, after a long wait, I was told that it didn't. I went back outside and gave him his money back. He wasn't upset; it was just a nice idea he had suddenly thought of for a philatelist friend in Connecticut. We drove back to the airport parking lot.

Back at Blue Hawaiian Helicopters, the situation hadn't changed.

The men who worked behind the counter tried to suggest that perhaps I could go see Kilauea erupting another time. I fixed a stony gaze on them and informed them of what could not have come as a surprise: I was a tourist who could not expect to come back to Hawaii any time soon. I was lucky to be here once, let alone able to just come back whenever I felt like it. If we couldn't go today, that was it; the opportunity was lost. They stopped the nonsense. Why do people bother with such nonsense, I wondered silently?!

But my mother still could not have her money back. We had to wait until exactly 2 o'clock on the off chance that the pilot would actually agree to go out on the flight. I took this information in with enthusiasm, but it was concealed from my mother. The reason for the enthusiasm was that after driving all this way and waiting, I would at least have time to look around and learn something before rushing off to the next event.

I walked around the desk to the shop that the men indicated. Inside were plaques for each of the three helicopter pilot, attesting to their safety records. At least there was nothing to be anxious about besides whether or not one actually got to go on the flight.

There were also hats, tee shirts, videos, and matted color photographs of Kilauea erupting. I bought one of those, and a video, figuring that if we couldn't go on the helicopter ride, at least we could watch this later.

A pilot safety award. They were hanging on the wall above the sales desk inside the shop.

This was the most dramatic of the matted color photographs for sale.

There was a door to the left of the sales desk in the shop. It opened into a room with seats along the walls benches here and there in the middle of the room. We saw parachutes in a cabinet just inside the door, and a large television screen in the far corner. Another door, inside to the right, led out the back of the building.

It was past 1:15 p.m., the check-in time. A crowd of people assembled. The man who had tried to suggest that I would go out on a flight some other time invited us all in to sit in that room. He passed out parachutes and told us that we needed to watch a safety and orientation video and demonstration. I was actually pleased, even though all illusions of actually going on the flight were now gone. The sky wasn't any clearer.

The video explained things that I had not known about riding in a helicopter, things that made perfect sense but were scary to think about: one must approach the aircraft from the front, and walk away from it the same way, because of the propeller at the back. Otherwise, one could get sliced like a carrot in a food processor without the container.

This sea turtle metal sculpture was out in the drizzling rain, and it seemed to be the only artwork at the airport.

There was more about safety, advice about hats and sunglasses, keeping one's raincoats tucked in safely, weight limits for each passenger, and so on. I saw one woman who was in a wheelchair and wondered how the company would proceed to cater to her needs, but of course that would only happen if we were actually going on the flight, so I never found out.

There was a couple with two little boys, perhaps eight and ten years old. I sat at the back of the room, up against the wall with my parents, watching the whole proceeding and video, waiting for it to be two o'clock. It was obvious that the disappointment wouldn't be confirmed until them. When it was, there was a collective sigh of disgust, and a particularly sad sound from the little boys.

At last the company was willing to refund the cost of the ticket reservation to my mother – in full. At least I had learned something as opposed to absolutely nothing. I could adjust to the disappointment on those terms, plus I was relieved that my mother's money had been promptly returned to her.

I told my parents that as long as we were here and had driven all this way, I wanted to walk up and down the airport and take a short look at the whole place. They agreed. I brought out my camera and walked around. It didn't take very long, but it was worth it.

There were places for shops, but only one was open: a lei stand. I went right over to it and asked if I could take some pictures. The two women vendors said yes, so I had fun photographing the many different kinds of lei that were for sale. The materials used included shells, beads, some painted plain black and others painted black with small flowers on each one, leaves, and flowers – plumeria blossoms and orchids.

My mother wandered over to look at the lei display and talk to the vendors. One of them told us that she drove across a bridge that led to Route 19 north every day. We rode on it later, and it was concrete with one lane each way, and old. We thought of her doing that every day so that she could sit here with very few customers to talk to all day. The airport was nearly deserted.

Lei made of orchids, and mostly orchids with some leaves. Combination lei with beads, leaves, and plumeria blossoms.

After looking at all of the lei displays and complimenting them, we thanked the woman and left. We drove north, following the coast for most of the return trip, taking it easy as we enjoyed the scenic route back.

Leaf lei – with variegated leaves and leaves of varying colors.

A Ride Back via Kohala

We returned to Kailua-Kona via the road that traversed the north side of Mauna Kea, known as Route 19 and the Hawai'i Belt Road, which then ran into Mamalahoa Highway, also Route 19. When we came to a right turn that led into Kohala, the district that forms the northern tip of the Big Island and is named for the extinct volcano there, my father took it. This was our detour, which took up the remainder of the afternoon.

Route 19 first took us out of Hilo and over the old but sturdy bridge. From there, it was a lovely drive along the coast for a while, or so the map led me to expect. Actually, we were sufficiently inland that we did not see much of the coast. Instead, we saw lovely forested land rising up on either side of a road that went uphill for most of the way.

A view out the front of the car along Route 19 north, leaving Hilo.

We went past the Hawaii Tropical Botanical Garden, a place that we planned to visit later in the week, and then past some falls and gardens that were not on our list of planned activities. I would have liked to see them, but hiking was involved, so I didn't waste time thinking about that. We passed town after town, with long stretches of beautiful forest in between.

When we got to the Kohala district, we saw mountain formed by the extinct volcano, all covered with a carpet of grass. The sun was out wherever we went on the northern part of the island. In fact, all we had to do was leave Hilo to get back to sunshine. We saw some more horse ranches, towns with schools, homes, and businesses. This was not a touristy area; it was what regular everyday life looked like for Hawaiian residents. There were farms with sheep here and there, which surprised me, and some cows, which did not.

The right turn that my father took brought us into Waimea. From there, the highway formed a loop on the map that stretched into Kohala and back out, with connections back to Waimea or south into Kona. The route numbers on that loop were all different: a right on the loop was Route 250, which led up to the tip of the island, where it became Route

270 until it connected with Route 19. But Route 19 went either back east along that loop as Kawaihae Road into Waimea, or it forked south as Queen Ka'ahumanu Highway. The number assignment for the routes was not logical. I wondered what my father, the planner, thought of it.

We saw this truck with people sitting in the back, and it surprised and alarmed us. In Connecticut, the police would stop the driver and object to this unsafe arrangement, we thought.

A view from Route 19, looking northwest to Kohala.

The mountains in Kohala were bright green up close, and sloped upwards to smooth domes.

A pasture along the way to Kohala.

My mother and I wanted to see some shops and slow down after the rigidly scheduled pace of the morning and early afternoon. Since we were almost back across the island, my father agreed that there was no reason to rush. He stopped in a small town full of boutique shops that had a cute café, and we all got out to walk around and browse for a while.

We were in Hawi, on the Akoni Pule Highway. We spent about an hour walking around. It was nearly four o'clock. The shops were all still open. We found a shop full of vintage and specialty clothing with a nice rest room in the back, and availed ourselves of it. Next door to that was the café, so we got cups of Kona coffee. My father and I shared a cookie, and he sat down outside to wait while my mother and I walked in and out of the small group of shops.

The boutique with the clothes was in this building. We parked to the left of it.

The Kohala Coffee Mill, with ice cream and cookies. My father is seated on the right, finishing his coffee.

The Kava Café was around the corner and set back from the road.

    The Kohala Inn appeared to be shut up tight, but I found plenty to amuse me. There was a pretty jewelry and crafts store right across the street from the café, left of the Kohala Inn. It was called Elements Jewelry & Fine Crafts. I walked all around it. Inside was a motif that I had seen before: an outline of a sea turtle, with a line drawn across its shell, from head to tail. I wanted to know more about it. It looked like ancient Hawaiian art, commercialized. It probably was, too.

After I had seen that shop and its contents, I walked up the street past the Kohala Inn and found another interesting shop. It was full of carved and varnished pieces of smooth koa wood. There were bowls and a large, finely executed shape of a sea turtle, among other things. A man with glasses, white hair, and a long white beard sat reading behind the desk. He was the proprietor and the carver.

I stepped closer to speak to him, then stopped in pleased surprise; he had a cat curled up in his lap, and it was asleep. He smiled and said that he had four cats, and that I could see them all close by. Sure enough, another one was walking around the shop, yet another was sitting under the counter looking up at me, and there was a shy black one out back, down the stairs, in the yard. The man told me that he avoided strangers. All seemed like nice pets, though.

It was nice in there with the koa wood art. The man got to chatting with me about my e-books, which I showed him on my Nook Color e-reader. He liked the cover art for my dystopian science fiction novel, *Nae-Née*. He got a kick out of hearing that while I was writing it, I had come across the fact that there is a Hawaiian goose called a nene. Its name is pronounced the same way as the title nanite birth control device, so I included a trip to Hawai'i in the novel just to talk about the nene goose. Why not? Environmental issues are a big part of the story.

The Kohala Inn.

We were chatting about this when my mother appeared, looking for me. She smiled at the cats, glanced around at the koa wood art when I pointed it out to her, then she told me it was time to go, so I said good-bye and left my business card with the artist.

Elements Jewelry & Fine Crafts.

We got back into the car and my father headed as far as he could go into Pololu Valley, which was a dead end road along a curving road that went through lush gorges and then up along a stretch with a beautiful ocean vista.

The view of Pololu Valley.

As we drove up the sweeping curves of this road, a police cruiser rushed past us, and then another one appeared and did the same. We let them go, and my father pulled over when we came to the beautiful vista so that I could take photographs. I wasn't the only person out there doing that.

While I was at it, a local woman with a dog on a leash came along and introduced me to her pet, who had a Hawaiian name. I don't remember what it was; I was about to try writing it down when a police officer appeared on foot, walking out from the end of the road. We couldn't see the end from where we were. He informed the lot of us that something was going on at the end of the road, and asked us all to leave the area.

I put my camera away and went back to the car, wondering what sort of CSI-like scene was unfolding just out of sight. Was it a dead body? Was there an emergency that wasn't over with yet? No tell-tale sounds emanated from that direction. Just as well...I rode away with my parents, noticing a couple of horses grazing in the brush behind a fence just before I got back in.

My next idea was to try to see the statue of Kamehameha the Great that was in Kohala. It had been lost at sea briefly, then recovered. It was identical to the one in Honolulu, but we couldn't find the right turn-off for it and gave up on seeing it.

We headed south, down Route 270. My father noticed a fork in the road that went north and turned up it, curious. It was a short dead end, and the only thing of interest here was a chain-link fence with shipping containers lined up behind it. Ordinarily, I would have found this to be the dullest, most mundane sight and paid no attention, but for the logo: Matson.

This was the corporation that had once maintained luxury passenger liners that ferried people between San Francisco and Hawai'i, until World War II. That was when the U.S. Navy had taken over those ships, painted them all gray, and used and abused them until the war was over, at which point they were returned to this Big Five corporation. The ships were fixed up at great expense, and used for a few more years until the standards means of travel became airplanes.

A Matson shipping yard full of empty cargo containers with the company logo on them.

My parents waited again while I pressed myself and the camera up against the chain link fence to take a few photographs. This was what was left of Matson: cargo containers for ferrying goods around the Hawaiian Islands. I hoped for a chance to get some better photographs of them before this trip was over; thus far, I had seen these things from the highways, but always while moving too fast for a decent shot. These containers were not in use at the moment. I wanted an image or two that showed them delivering goods.

That was it; I got back into the car and my father drove the short distance to Queen Ka'ahumanu Highway. He turned south, down the Kohala coast to Kona. We saw more mini domes in the distance, past pretty, green, grass-covered fields.

Along Queen Ka'ahumanu Highway we saw a series of entrances to several resort hotels. These hotels were luxury spa five-star ones, much like the Ko Olina resort, but possibly even more expensive. We had booked a dinner reservation for the next evening at the Fairmont Orchid Hotel, but only because when I was looking for a lu'au to attend on the Big Island, I had found a great one that put on its performance here.

It was after dark at this point in the drive.

My father pulled up to the porte-cochère of the Fairmont Orchid Hotel so that I could look around and find out about the restaurant. The place was beautiful, which was no surprise, but the restaurant was so expensive, with prices that seemed silly for gourmet food that could be had for less elsewhere, that we changed our minds.

It was just as well that the lu'au production company was performing elsewhere, because the other location turned out to be of historic significance. This was just a fancy setting without the benefit of history, but more on that later.

The benefit of my having even considered eating here was unexpected: as we rode down the long driveway in the darkness, I saw signs made of dark brown volcanic rock with white letters on them. The letters listed each part of the complex that included the Fairmont Orchid Hotel.

One part jumped out at me: Puako Petroglyphs.

I wanted to come back in daylight and see them!

My parents agreed to it; we would do this on Friday, on our way to the Tropical Botanical Garden, back the way we had come this afternoon.

That was it – that was how we spent our first full day on the Big Island of Hawai'i.

Another mini dome, seen from Kohala as we drove back to Kona.

Downtown Kailua-Kona on Ali'i Drive

On Wednesday, we decided to explore downtown Kailua-Kona rather than go on another marathon car ride. We would resume that activity later, but for now, we wanted to see the shops, the parks, the character of the place, and get a sense of the layout of it.

It was nice not to have to get up early or on a rigid mental schedule set by my father's guesstimate of how much time it would take to go somewhere, see the attraction, and return from it. This was a lazy day of wandering and meandering on foot, with no rush.

We enjoyed our breakfast of cereal, orange juice, and Kona coffee, and would go out for more groceries later. *Note to travelers*: the cost of orange juice in Hawai'i – real orange juice, not from-concentrate rubbish – is several dollars higher than on the continent. This was the one grocery-shopping disappointment on the trip. We found Shaw's grocery stores, which had those high prices. Later, when we didn't need to buy anything, we discovered that the quality of the food at Foodland grocery stores was higher and the prices a bit lower, but it was a moot point.

After we ate, we all got into the car and rode up Ali'i Drive to the see what there was to see.

Kona Inn Shopping Village on Ali'i Drive in Kailua-Kona.

The first place we wanted to visit was the Kona Inn Shopping Village. It has a red roof, and sprawls over the west side of the street, with a walkway between a variety of shops, plus more facing the street. The southern end of it is the Inn, but we paid no attention to that. The shops were fun. We found jewelry shops, art galleries, dress shops, coffee bars, surf gear and fishing shops, hair accessories for sale, and a luggage store.

This last was on our list: we had planned on buying one more small suitcase, and now was the time to do that. We wanted one on wheels (easy, that seems to be the only kind available now) with a collapsible handle. We also thought it would be fun to get one that had a Hawaiian pattern on it. It didn't take us long to find a place that sold them, and the bags were on sale.

Kona Inn, with is connected to the Kona Inn Shopping Village.

    The bag was the same size as the other ones that we had checked, but not big enough to make us worry about it being over the weight limit once packed. It had hibiscus flowers and, best of all, green turtles swimming and spewing air bubbles, with that lovely petroglyph stripe down their backs. It was perfect. It also took care of our space problem on the way home – we had enough room in our luggage for everything with this third bag.

Hawaii Spirit luggage with a sea turtle/petroglyph and hibiscus motif. We got this in the Kona Inn Shopping Village.

We came out of the luggage shop with me rolling the bag around and headed for the next one. (When we saw my father, we could give him the bag, but for now we had to keep it, looking like we hadn't checked into a hotel yet.) The next place we went into was a store with jewelry and carved wood art. I found some silver dangly earrings for my Aunt Joan Fox in the sea turtle petroglyph motif, and took a business card. (I saved the earrings for her Christmas gift.)

Next up, several dress shops and jewelry shops. The jewelry was very expensive, and we didn't need anything, so we just admired it. The recurring motifs that we saw included: orchids, hibiscus, plumeria, anthuriums, dolphins, sea turtles, and waves. The dresses had beautiful floral patterns and colors, but none fit me quite right, and most lacked pockets, which is a deal-breaker for me. I tried some on; my mother enjoyed looking with me, but I didn't buy one.

Finally, we came across a shop with a huge array of floral hair clips. These were much better than any I had seen thus far. The clips were made of metal and had a good grip to them, and were invisible under the carefully attached silk blossoms. There were many colors and species of silk flowers to choose from, but I am a sucker for pink, so I got one with four pink orchids on it.

A hairclip with pink orchids.

We sampled some Kona coffee and chocolate-covered coffee beans in a shop inside the Village, then came out to the street to look for my father. He was sitting on the low stone wall across the street, which bordered the paid parking lot, where he had found a nice shady spot. He saw us and got up to lead me to the car with the suitcase. I put it in the trunk and went back across the street.

The next thing to do was see other shops and other sites. The other stores in the immediate area were across the street in buildings that either had restaurants with lanai views of Kailua Bay above them, or else they were private homes. Most buildings had restaurants on top, though. We saw more than one ABC Store full of tee shirts, caps, candy, nuts, mugs, key chains, and a plethora of other touristy stuff. There was also a Na Hoku store, an Atlantis Submarines place, and several more art galleries.

One that is worthy of mention here is the Sloan Galleries. Although Sloan isn't the only artist whose work is displayed and sold there, it is the most memorable. He does volcanic landscapes set against starlit night skies, humpback whales swimming off the Hawaiian coasts, sea turtles, and historic Hawaiian scenes. This is the gallery's website: www.clintsloan.com

We walked out of the Kona Inn Shopping Village, looked north, and realized that we were next to a museum. I went to see which one it was: Hulihe'e Palace. I didn't know at the time what the history and significance of this place was, but I was determined to fit in a visit to it before we left the Big Island.

Just north of that was an open area that looked out onto Kailua Bay, and in the bay was a huge cruise ship. We asked around as we browsed in the shops and found out this Kailua-Kona is a popular stop for cruise ships. The ships drop passengers off for several hours on many of the Hawaiian Islands, they go shopping and eat lunch, then get back on board.

Celebrity Cruises ship. Note the sail-shaped sign: it's one of many that describe historic points of interest.

On our last day in Hawai'i, I was walking around the town again and met a guy from Brazil who was anxious about getting back to the ship on time, even though he had just gotten off! He was trying to plan his afternoon. He asked me where to eat lunch, and how close the best shops were, so I told him what I thought. On another occasion, we met a woman from Washington State, and one from Vancouver.

The drop-off spot for the cruise ships was not obvious. I had to be told that the spot next to Hulihe'e Palace was it. It was just a pretty, shady little park with benches, palm fronds, a big flowering tree, and a stone wall.

The Fish Hopper restaurant. We didn't try it. I took this photograph to show the Historic Kailua-Kona flags that were posted all over town, on the lampposts.

Looking up and down the east side of Ali'i Drive was like a restaurant row. All of the places offered seafood, and all were decorated prettily. We saw flags adorning the balcony over one building, with several signs depicting whales or large finfish at others.

A souvenir shop at the corner of Likana Lane and Ali'i Drive. This restaurant over shops had a great array of flags hanging out, so I shot the image from the car as we drove by.

Restaurants weren't the only businesses with attractive exteriors. There were buildings with ocean-blue hues with murals of sea life leaping across the walls. We looked at them, then wandered in and out of the shops to see what was offered.

My mother found a boutique that intrigued her, and I wandered off toward the water again.

Looking north at Kailua Bay, I could see the Courtyard Marriott Kamehameha the Great with its beach and lawns in the distance. It wasn't until Saturday, after we had attended a lu'au there, that I realized that I was staring across at a historic site: Kamakahonu. It is a Hawaiian hale, a one-room sleeping house, and a recreation of the original.

Look for the straw hale in the upper right – it's Kamakahonu, the building on the cover of this travelogue.

South of the Kona Inn Shopping Village, on the east side of the street and inside the same stone wall that enclosed the paid parking lot, was a covered market. We wandered around that market twice; once on Wednesday, and again on Saturday, our last day in Hawai'i. The market sold fresh fruit – lychee, dragonfruit, papaya, mango, pineapple, starfruit, and guava – and lots and lots of other things.

We found knockoffs of the same luggage we had just bought, Hawaii Spirit brand, but on closer inspection, my mother found that it wasn't the same, and of lower quality, so she had no regrets. There were necklaces with floral charms in white or colored enamel, or carved wooden turtles, or fishhooks made of carved oyster shells. There were dresses and shirts. There were magnets. Also, the heat was oppressive under the tents and tarpaulins that covered the entire market. I couldn't stay under there for long, but my mother had a great time looking at it all.

This sign was posted in the parking lot of a covered market in downtown Kailua-Kona. Fresh starfruit – on the right. I couldn't ask the vendors about the other fruits... it was just so hot, they were busy, so I went back out into the fresh air. The fruits in the bin to the right of the starfruit are mangos.

Fresh red and yellow dragonfruits.   *Fresh lychee fruits.*

Fresh pineapples.   *Fresh papayas.*

    After we had seen enough of the shopping areas (enough for the day, not the entire trip) in downtown Kailua-Kona, we went to find another grocery store. We had already seen one that was around the corner on Palani Road on Monday evening, called KTA Super Stores. It was small, and now we wanted to know what other grocery stores were in this area.

My father drove across Queen Ka'ahumanu Highway, up Route 190, and turned right after a couple of blocks. We were on a hill with a great view of the bay and the town below, when we saw a Shaw's grocery store on the right as we rode downhill. He pulled into its parking lot. My mother and I got out to buy groceries. We got some lunch foods so that we could pack food for the next long car ride, plus more breakfast items. Forget dinner; we had definitely decided not to cook in our unit, or plan our days around getting back early enough to do that.

We weren't in a hurry, so before I got back into the car, I walked out to the edge of the lot, on the left side of the front of the store. Then I looked out over the adjacent lot, which was a flat area about twenty feet lower than this one. Several Matson cargo containers sat off to the side of the lot, propped up on metal stilts, empty of goods and waiting to be hauled away. At last I could get a really good shot of some of these, with no fence or car window in the image.

Matson trucks in the parking lot of the Kona strip malls up the hill from Palani Road. I shot this image while we were grocery shopping, facing down the hill to the shore at the time.

This is how the hillside of Kona usually looked, even on a sunny day: hazy, like a cloud was over it, which it was. There were houses all the way up that hill, too.

As we drove back to our hotel with the food, we looked south on Palani Road, and noticed a store that we had been on the lookout for: Hilo Hattie. We were looking at the back of it, but the sign with its red hibiscus flower was unmistakable. It was named for the hula dancer who performed and traveled with the Royal Hawaiian Band, and she had worn a hat. Later that evening, we went back there and shopped.

The place was one huge box of a store with nice people working in it. We couldn't get enough of it, just as had been promised by other travelers who had told us about it. There were household goods: placemats, napkins, table runners, mugs, potholders, and oven mitts, all in pretty, tropical florals. There was a huge area with Hawaiian shirts, and another with dresses. I found one with pockets. There were key chains, candies, nuts, and calendars. The staff gave away a shell lei with each purchase. When we got back into the car, we found out that my father had gone in and bought three different wall calendars.

A bag from the Hilo Hattie store, named for the famous hula dancer.

On the way back, we went back around Palani Road, curving to Ali'i Drive. My mother asked for a stop just before it straightened out and went south. She wanted to see if the boutique on Likana Lane was still open. It was, so my father stopped and waited up the street. I got out too, to walk around. That was when my mother and I noticed that there were several silent dogs on leashes, resting on a shop's front steps in the darkness.

These dogs were tied up at night outside this shop on Likana Lane in Kailua-Kona. Each one was on a leash, and there was a huge metal mixing bowl full of water for them. They were on guard, and very well-behaved.

There were seven of them – six on the right and one all by itself on the left corner shop. They looked right at us, but didn't lift their heads. They looked well-trained, and bored. Clearly, they were under control and not about to bark and bother every passerby that they saw, but they were there to guard the property. They had a huge metal mixing bowl of water and blankets. But when a tiger-striped cat flitted past, they suddenly stood up and started barking at it! That was when a man appeared and told them to be quiet. It worked; they laid back down and resumed their watchful state of repose.

This dog was one of the group, but tied up on the shop to the left, by itself.

On Thursday evening, after attending a great lu'au, we looked around this area some more, and bought candy and souvenirs to give to our relatives. I was saving mine for Christmas: I found a deal that offered a price for 3 men's caps, and got my cousin and uncles each a hat. There was one that said "Kahuna" and depicted a huge wooden ki'i carving, another with a Hawaiian fish that had a very lengthy name, and another with a petroglyph (my cousin the artist got that one). As for my mother, she got candy for my grandmother.

Hale Halawai Park on Ali'i Drive in Kailua-Kona: This was the town information and public rest room building, with a beautiful sea life mural outside.

Saturday afternoon, we decided to kill a few hours in the town again. There were still a few more things to see, or to take a closer look at. We shopped in the covered market, and I found some necklaces with hibiscus charms to give as Christmas gifts to my cousin's fiancée, my aunt, my grandmother, and some writer friends in Connecticut. But it was terribly hot in there, and I had to get out again, so I crossed the street and walked south a bit, into Hale Halawai Park.

Hale Halawai Park: All over the island, this was the shape of any tourist sign: a sail.

Hale Halawai Park is just a little lawn with a sign about marine life and a small public building with rest rooms, but I was glad it was there. A beautiful plumeria tree grew by the road, and blossoms were falling to the grass. Across the street was another fabulous species of palm.

This palm tree was on Aliʻi Drive, and it was so round and beautiful that I had to take a photograph of it. Plumeria blossoms that had just fallen from the tree on Aliʻi Drive. They were white with yellow near the center on the upper side, and edged with dark pink on the underside.

I lined up three fallen plumeria blossoms, photographed them on the grass, and took them with me because they smelled so good. My mother accepted one when we met up later and agreed; it had a pretty, sweet scent.

Next, I turned south and walked into Waterfront Row, a tall, blue-roofed building with balconies and lots of glass walls. From a distance, it resembled an amusement park ride. It was full of shops and a Bubba Gump Shrimp restaurant.

Waterfront Row: This building has shops in it; the tallest part with the rounded top on the left is the entrance.

There wasn't much else within walking distance, so I went back up to the covered market to see what my parents were up to. They were ready to get back into the car and explore down the road. We drove south, almost back to the Aston Kona by the Sea, and my father parked outside a craft fair. Tents were set up in a large circle on a grassy plot of land next to the blacktop and flowering trees.

We found different things in this comfortable market. No overheated, dark, oppressive tarp covered the wares. Each vendor had her or his own tent, with cool air circulating throughout it. There were tee shirts, dresses, more Hawaiian shirts, magnets, painted trinkets, carved wooden bowls and other crafts, and food. Some people even had pet dogs and cats in their stalls for company.

This craft fair was south of downtown Kailua-Kona. This Madagascar gecko kept us company while we sat here. A Madagascar gecko. This species was carelessly introduced by visiting graduate students, a woman resident told me. It preys on native Hawaiian geckos, which are smaller, nocturnal, and can camouflage themselves. Fortunately, the

Madagascar gecko is diurnal, so they only meet at twilight and dawn, giving the native Hawaiian gecko a fighting chance. I saw some native Hawaiian ones by the pool at our hotel.

After we had looked at all of it, we decided to get a cool treat. A middle-aged Portuguese couple on the far left had a stand that offered shaved ice with colored fruit syrups poured over it. The ice came in large, plastic, colored cones with short, colored plastic straws. I chose tigerfruit, which was a bright but dark hue of red. The woman opened her freezer and took out a huge cylinder of ice with a hole down the center. She placed it in a machine that looked like a trepanning device and brought the serrated metal cone down on it. It pulverized the ice in a few minutes, she poured the tigerfruit juice over it, stuck three straws into it, and passed it to me. Another food adventure! I could have chosen a more mundane and familiar flavor, but that seemed silly. This was delicious. My parents thought so, too.

We sat at a table enjoying the tigerfruit treat until it was all gone. As we did so, I noticed a little gecko on the umbrella pole and took out my camera. I had asked a woman in a shop about these creatures the day that we drove all the way to Volcano National Park to see Kilauea's cooled magma, so it was fun to have a chance to shoot lots of images of one.

Before we left, we talked to a man with a tent that was devoted to koa wood carvings. My father had fun discussing what it was like to work with that kind of wood. He has lots of experience making furniture out of cherry, oak, maple, birch, mahogany, and walnut, but this was new to him.

The man gave us his business card. It said "Sawmill Direct Hawaii: From the Forest to the Finish[sic] Product!" He told us that he worked with pieces of wood that he cut himself, but that people couldn't just cut down koa wood without rules. I forget what the rules are, though. He did explain them, and they sounded like a good conservation system for a finite and special resource.

Palm trees waving in the Pacific breeze in Kailua-Kona.

We had a wonderful time exploring Kailua-Kona on the Big Island of Hawai'i.

Kona Mountain Thunder Coffee Plantation

After we had seen downtown Kailua-Kona, and had a taste of Kona blends at a gourmet coffee bar, it was time to follow through on another plan: a visit to the Kona Mountain Thunder Coffee plantation. Trying authentic Kona coffee was one my fantasies even before I started researching ways to have fun in Hawai'i.

I loved good coffee, and this was a great way to learn what makes it great. Little did I know that in order to understand what makes coffee delicious, one must also hear about what makes it taste awful, but that was fine with me. It answered some questions I had long left unanswered but still on my mind every time I found myself with a cup of burnt, dark, bitter-tasting coffee.

Accordingly, I had looked it up on the Internet, and found this company. Kona Mountain Thunder Coffee is a business, a plantation, and a roaster that wins an award from a group in San Francisco every year for its products. It is on Facebook, plus it has its own website. Here is the contact information:

Mountain Thunder Coffee Plantation
75-1027 Henry Street #143
Kailua Kona, Hawai'i 96740
U.S.A.
Toll Free 888-414-KONA (5662)
http://mountainthunder.com/

There was a map with directions from Kailua-Kona. It showed that there were actually 2 places to visit. It was just as well that we chose the one to the north, because when we got there, our guide told us that the other one didn't host tours. We drove past it the next day, and there it was, just a small sign in the brush on Route 11.

It only took us 15 minutes to drive up the hill from sunny downtown Kailua into a rainy, misty cloud on the top of the mountain. It was weird to realize that the whole time we were up there atop that mountain, in which it was alternately misty, drizzly, or rainy, and completely overcast, the sun was shining on Ali'i Drive, but it was.

Up Palani Road we went, across Queen Kaahumanu Highway, up Route 190, past Route 180, and shortly there it was: Hao Street. After that, it got confusing, so I was glad

I could show the map that I had copy-pasted from the Internet to my father. The map showed a sort of figure-eight of a road with a fork of dead ends on the eastern end of it. One of those lines is Hao Street, and the other is Kaloko Drive. The end of the southern fork was our destination.

Looking north up Hao Street – it's misty up in the Kona Mountains and looking south on Hao Street, back the way we came.

We had entered the criss-cross on Hao Street, and followed it until we turned right on Kaloko Drive, which was the easiest way to get there. We were going to the Kaloko Cloud Forest Estate. We found it, and saw that it was a misty, well-paved street that we could park on the side of. Lots of other cars were there. It was so misty that, even though the road ended up ahead, we couldn't see the end.

We all got out and went in the gate. The pavement did not continue inside, but the soil was packed hard enough that we had no trouble walking around in the dampness. A sign assured us that we were in the right place; pale green painted buildings stood on either side. Straight ahead were some red picnic tables, most under an awning, but one out in the rain. My mother turned right immediately, so I looked that way and saw a small shop with two open doorways.

The tasting and video bar is straight ahead, under the awning. My mother was facing the shop.

The shop was filled with people who were listening to a woman talk. She was really lecturing, doing a rehearsed performance that was filled with information, and they were all listening with interest. The shop had lots of things for sale besides coffee, but I didn't go in. Shopping seemed like the thing to do last, not first.

Just inside the visitors' entrance on the right is the shop. This is the left side of the shop, with bags, tee shirts, hats, and the cash register. This is the right side, with the coffee ready for sale.

    My mother went right in, so I left her to it and headed farther into the grounds. Under the awning, a video was playing on two large flatscreen televisions. A small coffee tasting area was set up. In between the shop building and that area one could look straight into the plantation: there were the coffee plants, just a few paces away. I wasn't about to go over and touch any, though. I could wait for an explanation of it all.

    I turned right again, my attention distracted by a beautiful rooster that was pacing around the corner from the shop. I followed him, and saw that the shop building had a small wing with more picnic tables, and a little bench under the overhang. The rooster avoided me, but not before I took his photograph a couple of times. Then, better than a rooster, I found a beautiful, big, tiger-striped cat sleeping on a burlap coffee sack on the bench. His name was Huey.

Going in past the shop was a rain-soaked set of picnic tables. This beautiful rooster was pacing around the yard when we walked in. A little room was around the corner, with a coffee roasting machine in it.

    Just then, a man in blue jeans with a rain jacket, cap, and glasses appeared, smiling and greeting me. He was the owner's father-in-law, he told me. He and his wife were always invited when it was time to harvest coffee or when some special event was going on. One such event was playing on the video: the star of the *Dirty Jobs* show, Mike

Rowe, had visited the plantation and participated in the production and harvest of some coffee.

Here is Huey the cat, napping on a box and a bag. Here is the room with the roasting machine, which was not in use, and the owner's father-in-law, who smiled and held up a coffee sack when he heard that I was doing a travelogue.

I thanked the father-in-law and turned to see the place where the video was playing.

Across from the shop is the tasting bar and video viewing area. The tasting bar is around to the left of the seating area, with yet another video screen, and some Kona Mountain Thunder umbrellas in a bucket. Those are for tours, not for sale.

After a few minutes, I sat down long enough to get a sense of how things worked on the plantation: growing, picking, drying, shelling, roasting, and so on. My mother took the camera away from me long enough to shoot some images of me watching the video. As I watched, I noticed that there were two young women sitting there with us, and realized that they would be going on the next tour with us. After the tour began, a few more people appeared.

The tasting bar included a choice of sugars, milk, and three different urns of Kona Mountain Thunder coffee. The coffee urns were lined up on either side of the viewscreen. Here are some ripe coffee beans, just picked, on the screen. The guy from the *Dirty Jobs* show, Mike Rowe, was in the video, helping with the harvest and explaining the process.

My parents and I gathered around the coffee tasting area, tried each kind, and took seats under the awning to watch the video. I must admit that I was so busy photographing everything and meeting the three other cats who lived at the plantation that I only watched part of it, but I was having a really good time. So were they!

Here are my parents in the tasting area, watching the video. Of course, we each tried every kind of coffee while we were in there.

Bobo the cat joined us during the video viewing, and settled onto a barrel just behind and between my parents to stare at us.

My mother photographed me watching the video too – evidence that I was there, not just concealed behind the camera lens, I suppose.

The other cats who lived there were Bobo, Diablo the kitten, and Pumpkin. All were very quiet, and willing photographic subjects. Diablo took up a position in front of the laminated, waterproof tour papers. There were four of them, so I made records of them with my camera.

Diablo the kitten settled into a tray of brochures – with the rain dropping onto her fur – in front of the sugar and cups. Behind her was the entrance to the coffee roasting barn. Laid out on the table in front of Diablo the kitten were 4 different laminated papers. Each described a different tour. The first one was free.

Pumpkin joined him. On the other picnic table were two dishes of coffee beans – berries and shelled ones – to show the phases of readiness that the product goes through.

Off to the left of the coffee tasting area was an open barn with noise emanating from it. This was where the coffee was taken after harvesting to be dried and put through the rest of its pre-packaging processing.

The woman who had been lecturing in the shop appeared at this point and invited us to try all of the coffee blends at the counter if we hadn't yet done so. She also informed us that in a few more minutes, she would be leading us on the free tour of the plantation, which would take us briefly across the street, then inside that barn, and finally to the shop.

When it was time to go on the tour, the woman in charge told us each to take an umbrella and follow her out the front gate.

After we had tasted some more of that delicious coffee, it was time to find out what made it so great. By the time our hostess and guide was through with us, I no longer wondered what made a great cup of coffee and what made a bad one. I took plenty of photographs, and listened to her explain each thing on the tour, so here they are:

Here are some beans on the vines, red and green, in varying stages of ripeness. Several geese waddled past as we listened to the tour guide, who soon led us back inside.

It was misty and still quite rainy as our guide led us across the street, and it stayed that way, but it was easy to take photographs from under that huge umbrella. She explained how the coffee trees grow and the cherries ripen, and that they are in the gardenia family, which was a neat thing to learn. She also told us that the Big Island of Hawaii had thirteen different micro-climates on it, which was very easy to believe as we stood listening to her in a cloud.

The tour guide took up a position right across the street and talked about coffee plants and how they grow. Bobo came with us, and wound himself all around her. Coffee plants are in the gardenia family, the tour guide informed us. Here is one with a blossom on it.

As we went back in, I noticed these kahili ginger plants growing just outside the gate, and thought of the feather standards that the Hawaiian aliʻi all had. The gaggle of geese had plenty of time to exit and reenter before we were back inside. Their job is to leave droppings under all of the coffee plants, as fertilizer. What an easy job, just to go to the bathroom!

I had heard the word "cherry" before in reference to coffee. Our guide told us that when coffee is on the vine, it is a cherry with a bean inside. The cherry is picked, dried, and then split open to get to the coffee bean inside it. Then the bean is dried some more.

She pointed out the resident gaggle of geese that fertilized the coffee plants. We all went back across the street with them, and into the entrance. The barn was next. I tried to listen to the guide, who did raise her voice over the din, but understanding her was difficult.

The next part of the tour was in this barn. The first room we saw was the drying area, which is the first thing that happens to picked coffee beans.

We all went inside, and my father joined us at this point. We had started off with just me, my mother, and the two women who watched the video with us, but now we were accompanied by him and two families with teenage children. It was a decent-sized crowd at this point, with few enough people that no one had to stand in the back.

The guide showed us everything, leading us through two very loud rooms in the barn, each with enormous processing and bagging machines that she turned on while explaining the functions of. It was a bit dark in there, with large, rectangular fluorescent lights high overhead.

We saw coffee cherries drying on a low rack, coffee beans cracked open in a huge, tall, roaring, crackling machine, coffee beans separated out – perfectly formed keepers versus shriveled rejects – and poured into huge burlap bags.

 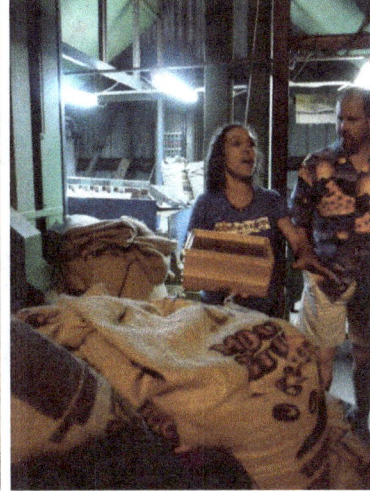

The beans don't just sit on a rack. They also go through one of these machines, which dries them out even further. The tour guide kept explaining the process over the roar of the machines. I think she was talking about how they get the beans out of their shells at this point.

Our guide explained something important at that point: the shriveled rejects went into Starbucks and Maxwell House and other inexpensive, canned, and low-end coffee brands. Huh...no wonder they didn't taste good! I add extra milk to such coffee when I can't avoid it.

This was the machine that best explained why Kona Mountain Thunder Coffee Plantations win awards every year. It is a separator. It separates the perfectly formed beans from the twisted, shriveled mutated ones. Good ones go up to the left, sub-standard ones fall down to the right. The tour guide held up some coffee beans to make her point: on the left are the high-quality, perfectly-formed beans, and on the right are some shriveled disappointments.

Some coffee beans do not split, she told us. Those are called peaberries, and they taste sweeter than the ones that do split. The plantation sells a blend of peaberry coffee, and when we tried it, I thought it was the most delicious of all of them.

This is the huge part of the separator machine that the beans go through before landing in that long tray and falling into sacks on either side. From there, we walked through this room, where the coffee is packaged up prettily, to get to the roasting room.

When that was over, she led us through a side door that brought us abruptly into a much quieter, lighter environment. It was time to see the final touches being put on the coffee beans themselves, which included roasting to a medium level of darkness, and then packaging.

The roasting room. It had two machines in it. She turned the roaster on, and it began to heat up. Note the digital control – white plastic on a short metal pole – at right, against the wall. When it was medium roasted, the tour guide poured the beans out into the tray. Steam rose up.

The guide told us that the Mountain Thunder Coffee Plantation roasts its beans to a medium level of dark rather than all the way to the top of the scale, which is dark. This brings out the taste and aroma without hiding anything, because when the best beans are the only ones in the blend, there is nothing to hide. It's those shriveled ones that get roasted to full dark, to hide the fact that they don't taste good!

The freshly roasted Kona coffee looked and smelled wonderful. To check her work, the tour guide pulled a little shovel out of the front of the roasting machine. It held just a small scoop of beans, spread out in a small layer. She explained some more about the stopping point of the roast.

Finally, the guide had a point to make about packaging: if bags with little round, clear plastic air holes aren't used, and the coffee is vacuum-packed instead, the quality isn't as high. Those vents are what keeps the beans fresh. Sure enough, all of the bags had those air vents. Also, the coffee is sold only in the form of beans – NOT ground. Grinding decreases the shelf life of coffee, so that step is left to the consumer.

We went into the shop, where we saw a fabulous array of prettily package Kona coffee. There was Vienna Roast, French Roast, Peaberry, and regular bean coffee, and coffee from each estate of the plantation: Cloud Forest and Holualoa. Vienna Roast is lighter than French Roast, the guide added.

In the shop, we saw Peaberry coffee, bagged and ready for sale, and Cloud Forest Estate coffee, bagged and ready for sale on the shelves.

There were also macadamia nuts for sale. They came in three flavors, including plain, and were packaged in small cylindrical containers. I had promised my husband that I would buy him some macadamia nuts on this trip, but when I saw the price of the little containers, and remembered my promise to also buy Kona coffee, I decided to just get one plain jar of nuts.

The coffee smelled wonderful, and it continued to smell wonderful when I took it back to our hotel and packed the six bags and one tin of macadamia nuts in the new suitcase. I ended up zipping that bag shut just to stop thinking about how much I was looking forward to grinding and brewing some of that coffee!

Here are the types of coffee I bought – 2 bags of each, one for me, and one for my husband.

New Landscapes
– Volcanoes National Park

There is something that occurs when a volcano is spewing smoke: vog. Vog is volcanic fog. It contains sulfuric acid and sulfates, a reaction of volcanic gases meeting oxygen, moisture, and sunlight. It is dangerous to breathe and dangerous to navigate in. It is not smog; smog is from burning fossil fuels, and that causes problems too, but different ones.

There are times when Hawai'i is inundated with vog in places, and Kilauea, the southernmost volcano on the Big Island, is the source of it. It has been continuously erupting since 1983. Kilauea has three other spots that exude vog: the huge Halema'uma'u Crater, the vent of Pu'u 'O'o, and the East Rift zone where the lava falls into the Pacific Ocean.

At this point, I should confess that we did not encounter any vog on our trip.

I'm not sure that I regret that.

If I had seen and experienced it, mostly likely that would have meant no visit to Volcano National Park. It also would have presented a health and safety risk. But, not having seen vog means that I can't describe it in this travelogue.

On Thursday morning, we set out for Hawai'i Volcanoes National Park, driving first down the west coast on Route 11, then east as it curved north of the huge caldera to the park's entrance. The landscape stayed oddly lush and green for the whole drive, even into the park.

The drive took us 3 hours, plus one rest room and refueling stop.

That's not counting the time spent inside the park, which was at least two and a half hours.

We left after breakfast, and got back just after five o'clock.

This was the first indication that we were almost at our destination: a nene goose.

When we were getting close to the park, I commented that I was really, really hoping to see a nene goose, the state bird of Hawai'i. Nene geese are the same size and build as Canada geese, but they have different markings, are native only to Hawai'i, and are a protected species.

They have recently been reintroduced to the Big Island after a successful conservationist program of captive breeding managed to raise enough of them to set them loose to live on their own in the wild. Unfortunately, there are mongoose on the Big Island, so the nene population is not self-sustaining.

Nene geese live near volcanoes, and subsist on nuts and berries. Feeding them is illegal.

Nene geese have black heads with beige necks that appeared to have swirling stripes, but that is just folds in the feathers on their necks. The rest of the feathers on their bodies have brown-and-beige barring. Like Canada geese, the females and males look the same.

We were almost at the park when my father suddenly said, "There's one!" and did a U-turn onto the opposite side of the road. The nene was close to the brush and greenery, and came waddling out from there across the dusty gray clay.

It was friendly, and it was alone. Bobbing its head and looking from side to side as it approached, it came all the way up to the car. I opened my window and readied my camera. The nene continued to approach, looking directly up at me.

My mother began to worry out loud that it would leap up at me and chomp me in the face, but I wasn't concerned at all. For one thing, I had a camera in front of my face. For another, I wasn't holding out any food to it.

Meanwhile, the nene kept coming, and I shot image after image of it, and thanked it.

It is my opinion that humans interact more successfully with creatures when we announce our intentions and ask politely for what we want than not…unless we are hunting them, which I wasn't. All I wanted was a series of photographs.

By the time this close encounter with a nene was over, I had six great images.

That was enough. We certainly weren't going to feed the nene. I knew it was illegal, and I knew why: if the geese get too much at ease around humans, they will get hurt. We are dangerous. Nene could get hit by cars, or abused by those of us humans who are just selfish. It is important to know the reason behind a law; enough said about that.

I put my window up and my father resumed the drive. Soon we were at the last stretch of road before the park entrance. What intrigued me at this point was just how much greenery there was: grass, tall, leafy trees, other plants. But then, volcanoes don't choke off all life just because they spew lava and hot gases. The stuff goes in a random, meandering pattern, down the low points on a terrain, sort of like the lines on a topographical map. Whatever the eruptions don't touch stays pristine and pretty.

The last stretch of road before the gate to Volcano National Park.

The gate to Hawai'i Volcanoes National Park.

When we got to the gate of the park, there was an admission fee for each of us. My parents got a senior rate; I got the adult rate. Admission came with a great map of the park, which I eagerly photographed, opened, and studied.

This is the map, closed, looking at the front cover.

And this is the back cover of the closed map, with lava spewing from the huge caldera.

Here is the inside of the map; the circled area is the caldera. A road goes down to the east of it to the ocean.

We rode into the park and soon found the Kilauea Visitor Center. The building includes all-important rest rooms to the left, a gift shop, a theater, a desk with park rangers to talk to, and a large museum room that explains how the Hawaiian Islands were formed and how things came to grow and live on them.

Kilauea Visitor Center.

Outside the Visitor Center, to the right, were three permanent displays that explained the history of Hawai'i Volcanoes National Park and the Hawaiian Volcano Observatory (HVO). The grounds of the Observatory, with its laboratories and geologists' housing, are north of the caldera, and southeast of Mauna Loa. The Hawaiian Volcano Observatory began its operations in 1912, so it had been in existence for a century when we visited the park.

This plaque commemorated the first Scientist-in-Charge of the HVO, Thomas A. Jaggar, whose tenure was 1912-1940.

The Hawai'i Volcanoes National Park is a World Heritage Site, this plaque informs.

One of Franklin Delano Roosevelt's Works Progress Administration programs was the Tree Army at this park. It provided jobs to men who were then able to send money home. They landscaped, built roads and stone walls, and did many other things to make the park a comfortable and convenient place to visit.

    My father pulled into a space in front of the Visitor Center and we all got out. After a quick stop in the rest rooms, we scoped out the place, noting the shop, museum room, theater, and displays outside under the overhang. We lingered under that outdoor overhang for a short while, listening to the park ranger explain the dangers of Kilauea and reading the environmental posters. This was important, because we didn't want to go where noxious fumes could hurt us.

Here it was: confirmation that nene are not to be fed by humans.

A volcano can also exude dangerous carbon dioxide fumes that give off no smell on a windless day, too. Hikers can suddenly find that they can't breathe and die. This has happened to Hawaiian people in the past; others came upon whole families at the top of a crater and found them lying on the ground as if asleep, but they were dead. This has also happened to volcanologists, but they knew what was going on and ran for breathable air.

This park ranger told us where to go and what to see...and where not to go and what not to do.

It turned out that the caldera was closed to hikers, not that we had planned to do any hiking. But we were glad to know this; we didn't want to go driving where we could get into trouble. The caldera was in fact spewing noxious, sulfuric fumes, so that left Chain of Craters Road.

Chain of Craters Road meanders down to the Pacific Ocean. It has site after site along the way to stop and look at. Each site is a cooled vent of Kilauea. Kilauea has no dome; it keeps on erupting, with hot lava bursting through spots in the ground, straight up, like geysers. After a while, a vent stops spewing and the whole mess cools into a crater of dark magma in swirls of black, charcoal gray, brown, red, and even pink. Small plants start to grow up through the cracks after it cools, too.

Chain of Craters Road used to go all the way around the southern coast of the Big Island. But in 1983, Kilauea spewed hot magma all over a stretch of it, right into the Pacific Ocean. It didn't just cover up a paved road; it got a lot of the ancient Pu'u Loa petroglyphs, and later, in 1997, the ancient Waha'ula Heiau (temple) that dated back to the thirteenth century.

This to-scale model of the Big Island of Hawai'i gives visitors a sense of where they are going in the park.

Visitors tend to focus their attention on this segment of the model, to understand the scope of Kilauea.

This wall poster elaborated on the routes that hikers and motor vehicles can take inside the park.

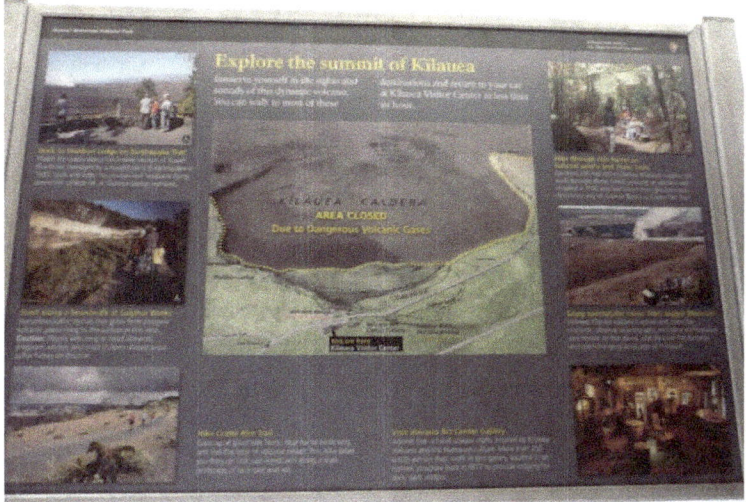

Another poster, this one with a close-up of the Kilauea caldera.

And another poster with more data on the caldera, plus the immediate area around it.

The gift shop had DVDs, books, posters, tee shirts, caps, and more.

This painting of the volcano goddess, Pele, hung inside Kilauea Visitor Center.

The Goddess Pele
by Arthur Johnsen

Pele is the revered goddess of Hawai'i's volcanoes whose mana (spiritual power) is still felt today throughout the Hawaiian chain. In this painting, she moves downslope, toward the sea, burning the forest as she recreates the land.

Atop her 'ō'ō (digging stick), named Paoa, is a ki'i (carved image) of her uncle Lonomakua, who taught Pele the wise use of fire's sacred power. The goddess also carries an egg bearing her youngest sister, Hi'iakaikapoliopele, whose regenerative power restores life to the land.

This placard explained Pele's importance in Hawaiian culture.

"Pele, the sacred living deity of Hawai'i's volcanoes, controls the limitless power of creation through her perseverance, molten strength, and unearthly beauty. Her passion emanates from her ancient existence. Revered and honored is the fire goddess. She is my spiritual guardian and forever the heartbeat of my soul, continuously giving life to her land and its people."

Pele Hanoa
August 8, 2004 (her 81st birthday)

This one had an ode to Pele by a Hawaiian woman.

Museum room displays about the flora and fauna found on the Hawaiian Islands.

A detailed display that described the rare and protected i'iwi bird, a nectar sucker with a long, curved beak.

Waves and wind carried some plant life to the Hawaiian Islands.

Birds brought more seeds to the Islands, and then decided to stay on permanently.

This poster board about Kilauea and artwork was outside, under the overhang in front.

The last important piece of information we noticed before getting into the car again was notice that required visitors to leave no trace of their time in the park. No food wrappers or containers, rubbish, nothing was to be left behind; humans are expected to clean up after themselves and put their garbage in trash cans. I have seen places where this hasn't happened – everyone has – but it didn't happen here. The park was very clean everywhere we went.

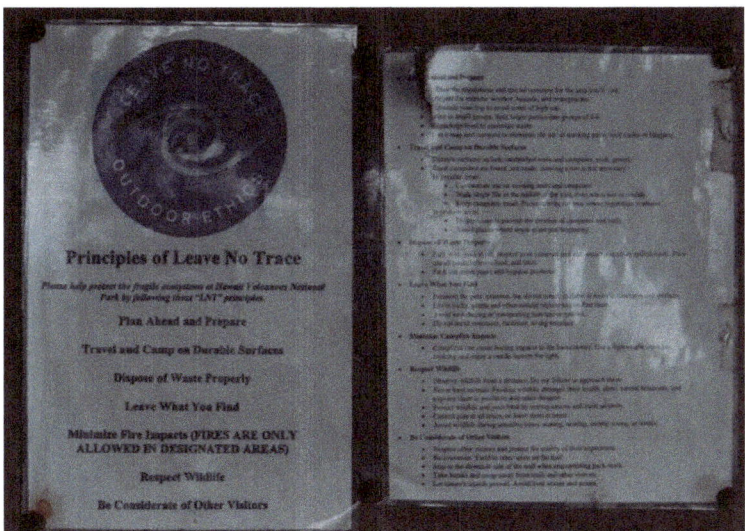

The Leave No Trace notices.

We got back into the car and set out to see the craters. There was one last view of forest before it began to open out into areas with huge gray craters inside patches of forest, and then soon it was open plains of charcoal gray.

The view of the beginning of Chain of Craters Road, just out of Kilauea Visitor Center.

My father handed me his camera and told me to take the photographs. I got it ready, and a pattern of getting out of the car and shooting image after image while my parents sat in the vehicle commenced. It continued throughout the park.

The first crater we saw was on the right (west) side of the road. It wasn't very big. I could image it as a small pond set low into a forest clearing, but instead of water with fish, tadpoles, and ducks, it had a solid, swirled, more-or-less flat filling of cooled, gray magma. This was the Lua Manu Crater.

1st Crater – the Lua Manu Crater.

The second crater, on the left (east) side of the road, was vast by comparison. This was the Puhimau Crater. Off to the east, in the distance behind this, is the extinguished vent of Mauna Ulu, which erupted in 1969.

2nd Crater – the Puhimau Crater, an extinct vent of Kilauea.

There was a lookout point on the left, so I walked up to it and shot the above image.

2nd Crater lookout point.

2nd Crater – Mahalo for not polluting or tromping all over the vegetation.

My mother did not get out of the car to look at this amazing sight. I got back in and my father stepped on the gas, taking us to the third stop. This one was the Pauahi Crater. There wasn't much to see in the way of a crater. The land was high up, very flat, and the soil looked recently churned up and cooled, with few plants. The only ones that we saw here were tiny green shoots.

At this point, we were about halfway to the Pacific Ocean, and I saw a sign at the lookout point that informed visitors of this. We weren't going to be anywhere near the active vents of Kilauea, not the East Rift, and not Pu'u 'O'o. The sights, sounds, and smells of those sites were left to the trained professionals – volcanologists who know how not to get killed while visiting them. We were well west of those areas.

3rd stop – smooth pavement and flat, black-lava landscape.

3rd stop – swirls of lava looked like a marble cake of charcoal gray... a literal marble cake, not a culinary one!

Lookout point at the 3rd stop.

Keauhou Trail sign at the 3rd stop.

I got back into the car, studying the map, and wondered what we would see at the next stop. Every time my father saw another parked car and a lookout point, he pulled over. The next stop was labelled Mauna Ulu, though I didn't realize it until I had walked out to the lookout point and read the signs. There were metal signs and a poster board sign.

The metal sign for Mauna Ulu was covered with etchings – the graffiti of visitors past.

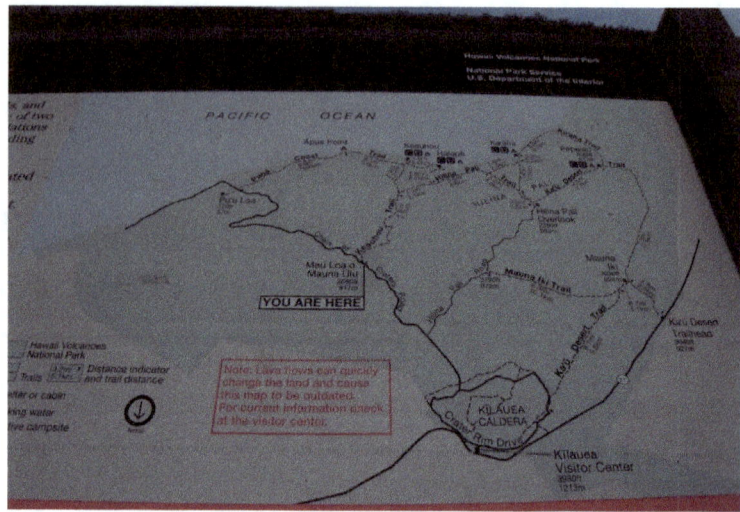

Map at Keauhou – showed that we were halfway to the Pacific Ocean and the end of the line.

The land was quite new here, and it showed. Very little vegetation was growing around the cooled magma, and not much of it had the feel of dirt under my feet. It felt more like I was walking over rock. It was the kind of rough rock that made traction easy enough as long as I paid attention to where I put my feet, because the rock wasn't breaking apart. For all that it looked broken, it was actually petrified in the twisty shapes that I stared at.

4th stop – pink and charcoal grey swirls of cooled lava.

This was the cooled flow of Mauna Ulu, a vent that erupted in 1969. Plumes of hot, orange magma shot upwards like a geyser of fire, minus the clockwork regularity. It was odd to know that I was the same age as the landscape that I was seeing. I saw every possible color of cooled magma here. It was pretty, strange as that may seem. This particular spot was not close to Mauna Ulu; it was actually called Mau Loa a Mauna Ulu. That explained why I didn't see a crater here.

4th stop – Mauna Ulu. This is an extinct mini-crater. Kilauea has lots of these. It's the main spewer, with little eruptions spurting out here and there between its main caldera and the shore.

Mau Loa o Mauna Ulu was another high, flat area. The metal sign had a landscape map drawn under the name of the extinguished vent. I paused to study it. As I stood there, I realized that it wouldn't be until later, when I was at home in front of the computer writing this chapter, that I would be able to make better sense of what I was seeing. At that point, I could compare the map, photographs from the visit, and my memories of walking around in the park and understand what was where.

5th stop – seismic sensor.

The fifth stop brought us to a spot that overlooked the Pacific Ocean from a distance, and it had a lot of green plants growing up around it. This was Kealakomo. It was situated between gray oozes of cooled magma. It was like stopping between the places where two giant fingers had pressed into the earth, with shadow for the fingers and grassy areas with a lookout point in the empty space where they had not touched the ground.

5th stop – lookout point where some people stopped to eat picnic lunches.

I walked out to the lookout point of Kealakomo and saw people taking out boxed lunches on the picnic tables there. Two men were speaking French, so I said "Bonjour" to them, and they smiled and said it back to me. After taking some photographs, I went back to the car again.

5th stop – the view of the Pacific Ocean from the lookout point.

We had started to turn east when we got to Kealakomo. Now we went southeast down a long hill, turned sharply back west and drove almost all of the way back until we were south of Kealakomo, and paused when we were almost at the curve that turned south down it. There was a place to pull over on the right side of the road, which gave an unimpeded view of the ocean.

But that was not the attraction here; it was the way that the hillside above us looked. It was marbled in light and dark gray. The ooze had flowed down this hill, leaving pretty patterns with green grass growing on either side. I couldn't get close enough for a good panorama shot, so I contented myself with three: left, middle, right.

6th stop – left side of the downward cooled lava flow.

My parents stared up at this from the car and seemed both awed and alarmed by the sight. As usual, I was unconcerned and kept taking photographs. This lava flow was long over with. Seismic sensors around us were registering no activity, we were feeling no rumbling underground, and the color had long cooled out of this magma flow. It was fine here.

6th stop – middle of the downward cooled lava flow.

6th stop – right side of the downward cooled lava flow.

After I shot the makeshift panorama series of images, I pointed the camera straight up this marbled hillside and took a shot of its horizon. There were some small trees growing up from the areas that the magma flow had missed.

6th stop – looking up at the cooled downward lava flow.

One more shot – I wanted an image of the place where we had parked, and the curve in the road. The sky was blue under some clouds. I supposed that Hilo was overcast today; the clouds got thicker toward that direction.

6th stop – lookout point. We just got out of our cars to look out – no platform here.

Back in the car, down the hill, and almost to the Pacific Ocean was another stop. This one had a sign on the left (east) side that faced a long, low, flat area that appeared to be nothing but another cooled magma flow. But it wasn't just that; it led to the Puʻu Loa petroglyphs, many of which had been lost under at least two magma flows.

There was a sign that explained this, and that explained what petroglyphs are. This was the place that was described in the Hawaiian Hall of the Bernice Pauahi Bishop Museum in Honolulu. This was the place where a heiau had been obliterated in the 1990s, a heiau that was recreated in that hall, and had dated back to the thirteenth century. It was both intriguing and disappointing to contemplate what the volcano had done. Nothing that we humans make can last forever, because the Earth will shift and change and eventually obliterate it.

7th stop – there used to be petroglyphs here, but Kilauea erupted all over most of them.

When I saw that it would take me forty minutes to walk out to the remaining petroglyphs, see them, and return, I decided to just get back into the car. I couldn't go that far for everything. There was still the end of the line to see, and that felt like the main event. Besides, there were a lot more petroglyphs – intact ones – to see in Kohala.

Pu'u Loa is yet another little eruption point of Kilauea. It's the place where the petroglyphs were obliterated. Some few remain, but to walk out there would take up too much time.

Also somewhere out that way are the footprints of a party of warriors. They would have fought against Kamehameha the Great on behalf of Keoua, but Kilauea erupted over them and killed them in transit. That was in 1790, and it helped Kamehameha the Great to rise to power.

Down the last stretch we rolled until the car could only go east, parallel to the coast.

It was a pretty view, and we opened our windows to smell the breeze.

I imagined Hawaiian people living in this area two centuries ago, before the haole arrivals. They built homes, fished, and farmed here, even though they knew that a volcano spewed fire quite close to them. I would have wanted very much to move!

8th stop – the Pacific Ocean. And here we stopped driving – it was the end of the line. I got out of the car and walked at this point, while my parents sat in the car.

At the end of the line were some portable toilets and a few National Park buildings – the institutional sort with dark wood and information on posters behind glass. The buildings were open on the sides, and contained lots of useful information on the dangers of volcanoes, the environment, responsible visitor behavior, and some data on the volcanic activity taking place even now under the surface of the Pacific Ocean, just off this coast.

When I got out, I saw a couple of port-o-potties and three little open National Parks buildings with glass-covered posters about volcanoes.

It was at this point that I got out, quickly perused the signs, and stared down the stretch of road that was closed to motor vehicles. People were walking at a fast pace into the distance and back. I realized that down that stretch of pavement was more cooled lava, and that it would be an amazing sight, one worth seeing and photographing. I had to go there.

No driving beyond this point: Pu'u 'O'o erupted north of here, and still does, oozing lava down over the coast.

So, without another word, I started to walk. I can walk very fast. How long could it possibly take?! I didn't see any signs offering a guesstimate. Ten minutes out, I began to worry – how much more time? A Dutch couple appeared in hiking clothes and I asked them. Another ten minutes and I would see the lava, they told me, but part of the fun was to walk over it and look around. And the lava was high to climb over. No, I thought, I wouldn't spend any more time doing that. I just wanted to get there and see that much! I thanked them and resumed my brisk pace. No way was I going to fly all the way from Connecticut to this island and not do this.

"CAUTION: Avoid the steam plume – it is hazardous to your health and may be life threatening." This sign greeted me as I started walking briskly into the distance, but all I saw was clear blue skies and all I felt was the hot sun beating down, mitigated by the cool Pacific breeze.

As I walked to the end of Chain of Craters Road, I kept looking to the right at the Pacific Ocean and taking photographs of the beautiful dark blue waters under the clear pastel blue sky. Plants grew along here, and there was colored sign after colored sign to identify each one. A botanist would have been very happy with this; as it was, I was happy to see and document them.

'Akia growing along the coast.

'Ākia sign, describing the plant. There were lots of these all the way down the road to the hard, blackened, cooled lava at the end of the pavement.

There were at least ten, if not more, small colored signs with the plants that grew along what I thought of as a walkway of lava. I shot images of 6 pairs of sign and plant, but decided not to show them all here. I mention them to point out the fun that a botany tourist could have here.

A cluster of palm trees by the water caught my attention at one point, and I asked some people who were passing by if there was anything there, but they said no – just the trees. It is funny how a sight such as that can excite one's imagination and trick it into creating a human-made structure and a story that could have taken place there.

A cluster of palm trees close to the Pacific Ocean.

People walking out to the shore from the end of Chain of Craters Road.

This large mound of cooled, black magma looked like a little volcanic dome, but it wasn't.

At last I reached the end of the pavement and saw it: a short wall of blackened magma, arrested by cooling contact with the Pacific breeze as it had crawled over the stretch of road that had once hugged the coast. This happened in 1983.

This was the most amazing sight of all, and worth the hurried, brisk walk in the hot sunshine.

I turned north to look at the landscape, fascinated to see the contrast.

The view north of the very end of the pavement on Chain of Craters Road.

There in the distance was the mountainscape with the marbled, cooled, chalky-and-charcoal gray flows that had run down them. Yellowish grasses grew up in between dark brown soil. Right in front me was blackened and hardened fingers of magma. It really did look like fingers.

I fired away with the camera, and suddenly a man with thick white hair and a beard in a Hawaiian shirt, shorts, and sneakers appeared, calling out to me. He informed me that his wife had seen me with the camera and ordered him to take photographs of me on the lava with it, so I let him do that.

He was a professional photographer, so he needed no time to familiarize himself with my camera. What great luck! I ended up with a series of photos of myself sitting on that crawling, hardened hand of blackness, like a glove that reached out and made a seat before it rose higher and became something to climb and hike across.

The man on the right walked up to me and introduced himself as a wedding photographer from Chicago.

When the photographer was satisfied with his efforts, he handed the camera back to me and introduced me to his wife and the couple that they were traveling with. They let me take their picture on a picnic table that sat near the black magma fingers.

Then it was time to walk all the way back, which took twenty minutes. By now, I was convinced that my parents would be worried about time, and walked even faster than before, but the cool breeze made it bearable. I also had people to chat with, as the group from Chicago went back with me. The photographer's friend told me that he worked as an inspector for outsourced sweatshops, which meant traveling to India, Thailand, the Philippines, and other Southeast Asian nations. Sometimes he was barred from entering, and couldn't do his job. We knew what that meant: conditions were anything but up to health and safety standards in those factories.

One more shot of me on the blackened fingers of lava.

Sure enough, as I reached the end of the walkway of lava, my mother appeared. She said that my father was worried about the time it would take for the return drive, because we were booked for a lu'au that evening in Kona. All it really meant was that we would have to attend the event without stopping at our hotel, showering, and getting dressed up, but that was okay.

We walked the rest of the way back, pausing to look at an amazing geoscience poster board that explained how the next Hawaiian Island and volcano, Lo'ihi, was forming underwater.

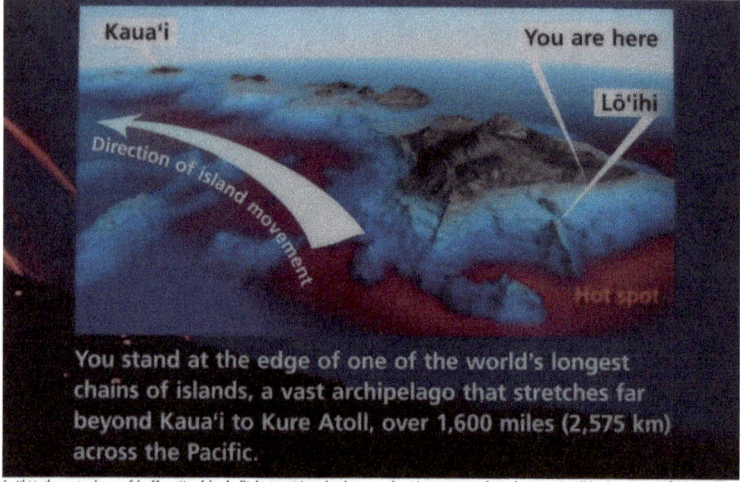

Lo'ihi is the next volcano of the Hawaiian Islands. Right now, it's under the ocean, but it's growing, and in a few eons, it will be the next and 9th Island. Of course, it could happen sooner than that...

The Loʻihi explanation was actually just a small inset of this larger poster board.

Back in the car, my father took off with a purpose for the Kilauea Visitor Center, retracing the path that had taken us to the end of Chain of Craters Road. With difficulty, he was persuaded to stop at the Thurston Lava Tube so that I could take photographs.

Would I be able to see hot magma down there, I wondered? I couldn't take the time to look.

But I did photograph the area around it, Japanese and American tourists, guides, and all.

People on a guided tour heading from their bus to the walkway that goes down to the Thurston Lava Tube.

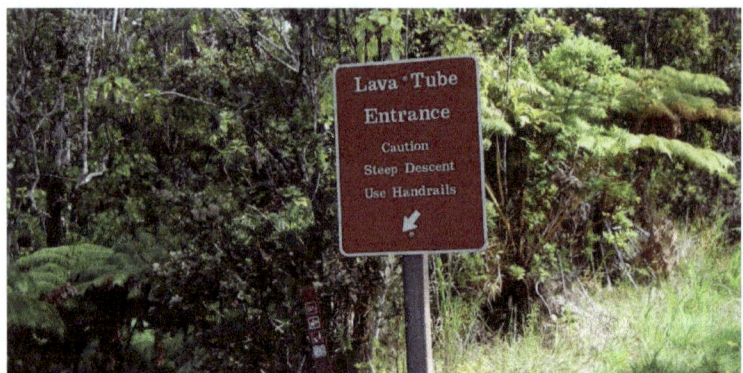

There is a steep descent into the Thurston Lava Tube, with a path and railings, but I just peered down into it. All I could see were trees and fronds and brush, and people walking through it all.

This hiking path led southeast of the Thurston Lava Tube, also known as Nahuku.

A sign over the Thurston Lava Tube about the birds that live in the area.

Tourists being led down to the Thurston Lava Tube by their guide. Without them in the image, it would not have shown that there is a path leading down there.

The parking area is to the left, the path down to the lava tube to the right, and hiking trails lead away in the other directions.

We stopped back at the Kilauea Visitor Center next because we wanted to use the rest rooms again, shop, and rest briefly before our trek back to Kona. My mother bought a bottle of dragonfruit juice, and we all shared it. It was delicious. I wish I could find it at home!

Hawaiians holding a ceremony to honor Pele, the volcano goddess. A chant on a placard honoring the goddess Pele.

In the shop, I found a couple of DVDs about the volcanoes, and asked the staff which ones they thought were the best before deciding. There were a lot of great books, too. Petroglyphs were something that I wanted to learn more about, so I bought a short one about them, complete with maps throughout showing where on the Big Island each collection of them was, plus detailed descriptions and interpretations of them.

The Visitor Center had some images about ceremonies to placate the Volcano Goddess, Pele, so I looked at those. Not all Hawaiian people have been willing to convert to Christianity; some still worship the deities of their own culture. This has included a governorness (female governor – that's the title she had when she was in office) of the Big Island, Princess Ruth Ke'elikolani.

At home, after processing (labeling, rotating, resizing) over 2,600 photographs, I took a break to go over back newspaper issues and recorded television shows. But during that whole time, I kept reviewing the trip in my mind, remembering little details and considering how best to write them up.

One of the things in the back issue of the newspaper (*The Hartford Courant*, which is the oldest one in the United States, and is itself older than the United States) was…the horoscope section. I am not superstitious; I read it for laughs. If a particular day's entry doesn't relate to my life and that of my family, I take it with a grain of salt.

Still, as I read through and saw what it had to say for each of the days of our time in Hawai'i, I decided to recall what we did on each day, and consider whether or not the entry fit with that.

Well…it fit for the day that we went to Volcano National Park!

It was hilarious; it summed up my parent's comments and worries perfectly.

My father's: "You could waste time plotting and scheming when all the facts are not within your grasp."

My mother's and mine: "Secret fears and an overactive imagination can make things look worse than they really are."

Hmm…he did obsess over time constraints that turned out not to be exceeded.

And…she did freak out when we met that friendly nene goose, and remark repeatedly that the lava landscape was very scary.

And…my imagination was running away with thoughts of an irate father waiting in the car as I walked down the last stretch of Chain of Craters Road with his camera.

But, as I had said to him before going, we hadn't come all that way to not do things.

Later, my mother was asking me about my thoughts as I chose to walk all the way to the lava flow and back, despite the concern about time. I explained that if I let any negative thought about going there hold me back from getting the shots of that amazing sight and experiencing it firsthand after she had spent so much money to bring us to it, I would always regret it, and I didn't want to be that person.

She approved.

Of course, it helped that we were enjoying a luʻau at that moment, that it was as awesome an educational and cultural experience as I had promised, and that we had arrived just in time for it. Yes, that walk was definitely worth it.

A Lu'au at Historic Kamakahonu

The lu'au was to start at five o'clock; we got there a few minutes after that. As it turned out, we hadn't missed anything because people were still arriving. Check that worry off the list...

My parents had complained the evening before that they hadn't like the lu'au at Paradise Cove, and asked me to try and cancel this one. I really didn't want to do that, because this one promised to be so different – educational – and I had put a lot of effort into researching it.

But, I tried to cancel it. I contacted AAA and was told that cancelling that close to the time of an event isn't possible. I thought, "Well, good!" and calmly told my parents the verdict. They resigned themselves to attending.

A few minutes into the performance, I looked at them and found them both smiling, impressed by the presentation and enjoying themselves. I pointed this out to them and they laughed and admitted to it. Problem over; another worry off the list.

We looked fine for the lu'au in our Hawaiian tee shirts and the orchid clip in my hair.

When we arrived, my father drove around the back of the hotel grounds and into the parking lot. We found a spot, got out, and headed into the back door, which looked as attractive as the front door. A sign advertised the hotel restaurant, which was named for the sea turtle in Hawaiian – Honu. Tall thin palm trees and a few plumeria ones graced the lawn.

The back entrance to the King Kamehameha's Kona Beach Hotel. The king's main residence had been on this property, it turned out, so his name was on the hotel.

In the back door, down the hall to the left, and around to the left again we went. We presented the voucher at the desk that was to the right of the main lobby check-in area, and were told that we were all set. We turned around and faced the length of the lobby. It was beautiful. I noticed that one of Clint Sloan's fabulous and fanciful night scenes of Kilauea was hanging on a nearby wall. At the opposite end of the room was a huge painting by another artist, a historical scene of King Kamehameha the Great at his court, greeting some visitors.

The lobby of the Courtyard Marriott King Kamehameha's Kona Beach Hotel, with the king's court painting.

An example of Clint Sloan's work – Kilauea erupting on a starry, moonlit night. A photograph of Clint Sloan, wearing a maile lei, hung in a plaque next to the painting, called Pele's Masterpiece.

My mother and I stopped to look at this board game as in the beach side of the hotel. The ancient Hawaiians, with no contact with other humans, created a game that looks a lot like those of other cultures. Humans are the same everywhere, it seems.

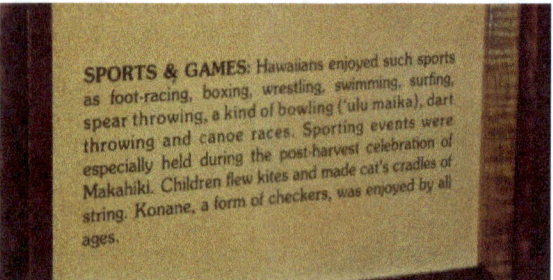

This sign by the board game described the kinds of recreation enjoyed by Hawaiians before other people arrived.

The Mahoe – koa wood canoe.

It was after the luʻau was over that my mother and I went into the back lobby of the hotel to see more exhibits. The detour was entirely worthwhile; we saw a huge racing canoe made of koa wood called The Mahoe, and a terrific painting of the literacy queen, Kaʻahumanu.

She was the favorite wife of Kamehameha the Great. He demanded that she not take any other husbands than himself because she was so important to him. Ancient Hawaiians (not really so ancient – this is only 2 centuries ago!) practiced polyandry as well as polygamy.

Very few drawings of Queen Kaʻahumanu were made when she was alive. One shows her sitting at court, outside on the ground with her kahili in hand and another pair of kahili being waved over her head by attendants, with her hair down long. She is wearing a long paʻu made of soft, beaten kapa cloth. She is a very tall, large, imposing woman, and it shows even as she sits staring fixedly at a spot on the ground, lost in thought.

There was another painting of her in ʻIolani Palace, dressed like a haole. It is hung next to one of Kamehameha the Great as an old man, and he too is dressed like a haole. After learning all about them, and how they grew up and lived as ruling adults before the haole arrivals, they look bizarre to me in those portraits. But she was one of the main instigators in ending the kapu system that held Hawaiian woman back from enjoying life as they wished. I like her!

The portrait of Queen Kaʻahumanu, the literacy queen. The sign next to her 21st century portrait mentioned her role in Hawaiian literacy, and the example she set by also learning to read and write.

But back to the moments just before the luʻau, as my parents and I arrived.

We exited onto the beach side of the hotel, and saw the Honu restaurant to our right, and an infinity pool. There was a historic site sign that explained the significance of this spot, and told us that it was called Kamakahonu. This was when I realized that the Hawaiian royal court had been on this site when Kamehameha the Great was king. My reading had not told me so.

We looked out at the beach and realized that this was going to be great!

There was Kailua Bay, with a little human-made cove of a private beach that curved right up to the sand outside the hotel. There was a small hut off to the left with surfing gear, a yellow-painted waʻa canoe to the right, and a stretch of lawn that extended away to the right. That was the entrance to the luʻau grounds.

Best of all, straight across the little cove, was a traditional Hawaiian hale. It had to have been hand-made, I thought to myself. This is Kamakahonu, a name from the words "ka maka honu" – "the turtle eye" in Hawaiian. There used to be a large rock to the left of it that resembled a turtle.

I followed my parents to the right, where a small crowd of people was entering the luʻau grounds, ushered in by attendants.

The gate with wooden paddles standing on either side that led to downtown Kailua. The little surfing supply building on the hotel's beach.

The yellow canoes with Kamakahonu in the background.

My parents went up the path while I lagged behind with the camera. My mother is in the distance, with the ushers.

Here it is: the image that I knew would be the cover art for this travelogue the moment I shot it: Kamakahonu.

This plaque states that Kamakahonu became a protected National Historic Landmark in 1964.

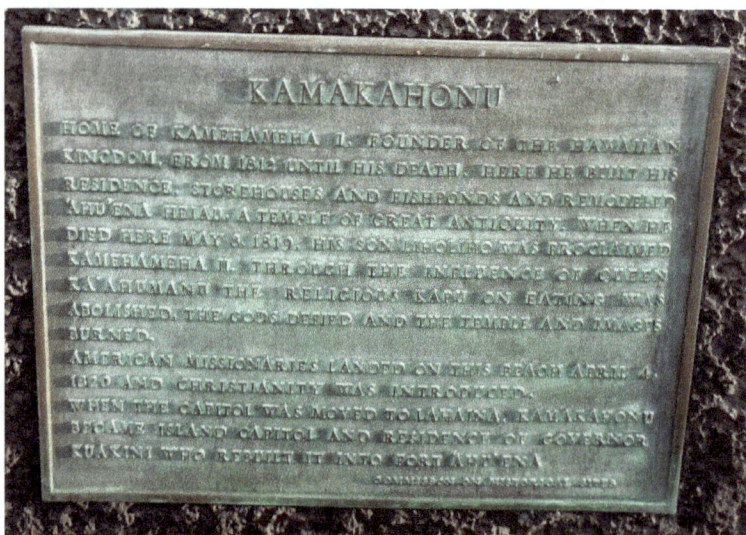

The hotel sign and historic Kailua notice notwithstanding, this more permanent plaque explains it.

My mother shot two images of me near Kamakahonu. This one was the close-up near the "Keep Out" sign. We went around to the other side to get this shot because of the hale that appeared to be under construction.

This sign stood to my right as I posed for the second image: "KAPU – DO NOT ENTER!" Kapu means taboo and sacred in Hawaiian. Keep out and don't touch or otherwise disturb sacred sites, because to do so is taboo.

This was absolutely perfect! A lu'au at historic Kamakahonu, complete with a performance that would explain and demonstrate the history, language, culture, dance, and music of Hawaii was exactly what I went looking for when I researched the company that puts this on:

Island Breeze Lu'au
http://www.islandbreezeluau.com/
Island Breeze Productions: (808) 326-4969

The Lu'au Schedule:
• 5:00pm - Shell lei greeting, photo taking, hosted seating, arts & crafts, Imu ceremony
• 5:30pm - Open Bar
• 6:00pm - Torch-lighting, Royal Court Arrival
• 6:30pm - Lu'au dinner buffet
• 7:15pm - Island Breeze Polynesian Revue
• 7:30pm - Open Bar Close
• 8:30pm - Lu'au ends

We went up to the first check-point, were let in, and passed a lei vendor. Her offerings were beautifully and brightly colored, but we didn't buy any. She had pink plumeria lei for woman and black bead lei for men. Next, we met girls who were handing out a shell lei to each guest. They were dressed in Hawaiian clothing, with lei on their necks and crowning their hair, and they were smiling and enjoying their jobs. They looked to be in their late teens; this was probably their first job. The shell lei were included in the luʻau package, so we accepted these.

The lei vendor, with one of the lei givers in the background. Here is one of the two girls with the shell lei.

As we continued up the path, we noticed the area where the pig was roasting to our right. This was very different from the previous luʻau we had attended in that guests did not have to detour in order to see the pig roasting pit; seeing it was unavoidable as one entered the place.

The ukulele stand.

The Mai Tai punch bowls table was just a few paces away from the pig roasting pit. The Mai Tai punch table. It was good spiked punch!

Next up was the expected, obligatory photo-op with Kamakahonu behind us.

The last thing we saw before we reached the entrance to the dining area and stage was a ukulele stand. They were attractively situated on a small table to the left, complete with a selection of CDs of Hawaiian music.

This is the entrance to the dining area, with hot drinks available on the left.

The dining area had a view of downtown Kailua-Kona, with cruise ships in the distance. The tables farther away from the stage had red tablecloths, while those closer had a pattern.

There was a stand for the musicians off to the left of the stage, and this enormous drum stood in the middle. The amplifiers and more Hawaiian percussion instruments stood to the right on the musicians' stand. This beautifully decorated drum stood alone on the stage until the performance got underway.

As before, I had not signed us up for the most expensive lu'au package. It was the same food and the same show either way, I had reasoned. We were seated at a table with a red tablecloth, a bit far from the stage. But now I had some regrets about the previous one: I had not been able to photograph the buffet and desserts before taking some, and I had forgotten to get images of the food on the koa wood dishes.

I went across the dining area to talk to a blond woman in a Hawaiian shirt (the staff uniform of people who were not performing). She was very nice; she had worked for Island Breeze Productions for over twenty years, she told me. I explained that I was writing a travelogue that would become an e-book for Nook and Kindle, and hopefully be in print after that, and of course this event was going to be a part of it.

She was very pleased to hear this, which came as no surprise. Everywhere I went in Hawai'i, it seemed that people were eager to assist me with this travelogue. The blond woman chatted with me at length, promising to tell me when the lids were first removed from the buffet so that I could photograph everything immediately, and led me over to the tables for pictures of everything as it was before it was touched.

Next, she surprised me by following me back to my table and moving me and my parents to one of the tables that was much closer to the musicians, off to the left of the stage. We now had a much better, closer view of the stage! It was a small table, with room for eight people.

The only other people who joined us were two friendly Japanese woman who spoke very little English. I greeted them with a smile, saying "Konichiwa" to them, and they said it back, but we soon realized that conversation would be impossible. That was just as well; it meant that my attention was on the performance. I listened to it carefully and learned a lot.

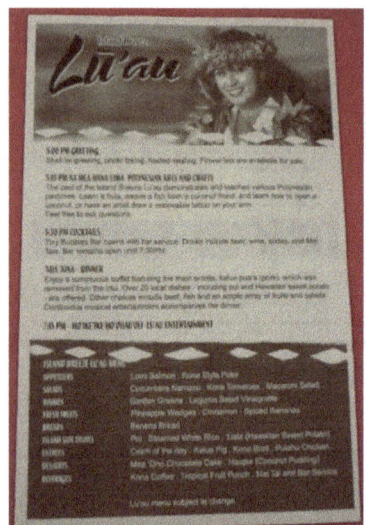
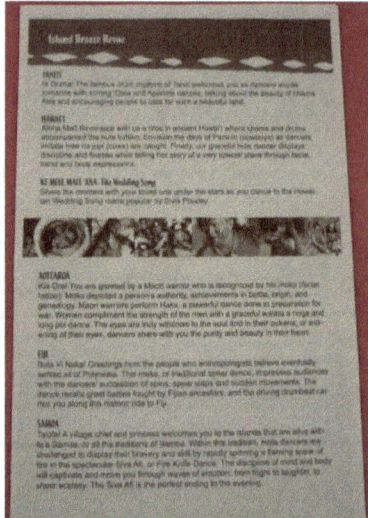

This was the handout that each guest was given upon arrival, outlining the evening's agenda and menu. The back of the handout detailed the different Polynesian cultures that would be described during the performance.

The koa wood plates were all stacked and ready for the guests to descend upon them. The buffet table as it was before dinner, with the wooden boxes all closed.

The dessert table, with haupia (pineapple upside-down cake), and coconut squares, called 'mea ono. Banana bread.

Palm-weaving supply line.

This guy was funny. He taught a palm-weaving class in just a few minutes, and kept the audience laughing and on its toes as he joked about how and how not to make palm-braids and what to do with them.

Tattoo artists worked for cash on the lawn at the same time as the palm-weaving lesson. It turned out that the tattoo artists and the palm-weaver were also performers in the show that we were about to see.

There were two pairs of tattoo artists, women and men. The men are shown here.

This actor was the other character of the performance. Here he is making the Hawaiian shaka sign that means "hang loose; everything is okay – great, even!"

A close-up of the pig roasting pit before the pig was lifted out.

My parents, enjoying the luʻau...and this was before we were moved to better seats! They had Mai Tai drinks...

The Hawaiian man in the waʻa going to get the cast of the show.

As I walked back over to my parents, I noticed something that was silently happening: a long Hawaiian man was rowing a waʻa – a huge double canoe – out of the cove and into Kailua Bay. He was obviously going to get the performers, so I told them what was going on. My father didn't want to get up and watch, so my mother and I went back to the front path alone to watch the whole thing. Soon the canoe was back, with the cast.

The cast of Island Breeze portraying the arrival of Kamehameha the Great and Queen Kaʻahumanu. The king and queen were met on the shore, bowed to, and escorted with great solemnity, pomp, and kahili to the luʻau grounds.

A grand arrival ceremony was enacted and explained as the venerable Hawaiian royal couple, Kamehameha the Great and Queen Kaʻahumanu, arrived and strode proudly ashore. The king wore a long yellow cape and a warrior's helmet, and the queen was decked out in a long yellow paʻu with a yellow lei crowning her head and another around her next. Attendants carried tall yellow kahili beside them.

The procession made its way slowly and with great dignity toward Kamakahonu.

The procession paused while the achievements of the king were extolled; he united the Hawaiian Islands in peace.

This attendant carried a tall spear and a shell. He was portraying an ali'i, one of the aristocrats of the royal court. The ali'i in his warrior's costume blew into the shell he carried, sounding a loud blare of a note.

Standing next to the actors was a man in a black outfit with a white shell necklace. He was announcing and explaining everything that took place. He turned out to be the emcee for the performance of several Polynesian dances after dinner. He also provided Hawaiian language lessons during each costume change. He told us that he was Hawaiian, and that he had been married to a Samoan woman for over twenty years.

Our emcee and Hawaiian language instructor.

The entrance ceremony quickly moved on to a rapid hula dance by the women of the court. They moved very fast and close, so the photographs didn't come out great, but that was okay. The best part had been the arrival, and a lot more dancing was to come.

Next, the pig was lifted out of the pit.

The pig being lifted from the roasting pit. People gathered closely around it. Getting this image was difficult; I had to plead with them to let me in close enough to do this.

Dinner was announced as soon as the pig was carried away, so we all proceeded to help ourselves. The nice blond woman in the Hawaiian shirt reappeared and escorted me to the buffet table quickly, keeping her promise to let me photograph all of the food before it was touched.

Shredded roast pig. *Sliced roast pig.*

Roasted purple sweet potatoes. *Sliced roasted chicken.*

Poi with lomi lomi salmon – 2 kinds, large-cut and diced small. Sliced mahi mahi fish.

Lomi lomi salmon – finely diced. I love sushi, so I thought this was delicious! Large-cut lomi lomi salmon. This was delicious, too.

Sticky rice.   *Pineapple and spiced banana.*

Lu'au dinner on a koa plate, with some of everything. Lu'au dessert: German chocolate cake, haupia (pineapple upside-down cake), and coconut squares, called 'mea ono.

The performance was suspended while the guests all got up, filled their plates at the buffet, and had an opportunity to buy their photographs with Kamakahonu in the background. I bought ours, and was pleased with the result.

Our group photograph with Kailua-Kona and Kamakahonu behind us.

With that, the show resumed…loudly and with enthusiasm. It started with a coconut-cutting demonstration by the guy who had posed giving the shaka sign. He was funny. He started off with the tale of a haole guy who had bought a coconut and tried to open it. The guy was staying on the fourth floor of the Kona Marriott, so he dropped it off his balcony. "That didn't work," the coconut lecturer told us. The haole guy tried backing his rental car over it. "That didn't work either," he said.

Finally, he got down to business. He explained that the first step is the get a strong stick and drive it into the ground. Next, find the "face" on one end of the coconut, formed by three dark, round spots. Position it away from you, and drive the coconut onto the stake. After that, take a huge, long scimitar of a knife with a short handle and a long, wide, curved blade, and hack the coconut's outer layer off in thirds. From there, you can cut the center in half and drink the coconut water, and slice out the coconut meat.

After that, we heard Hawaiian and Polynesian music and watched the dances of Hawai'i, Fiji, New Zealand, Samoa, Tahiti, and New Guinea, and learned more Hawaiian words than we could remember in such a short time. I solved that by taking the travel plan I had made out of my handbag and writing them down on the back, with definitions.

The musicians performing for the dance show.

Show – Fiji segment, with female and male dancers.

Show – Fiji segment dance.

Entr'acte language lessons were provided by the Emcee.

Among the Hawaiian words that we were taught by the emcee were "ohana" (family), "ono" (delicious), and the phrase "ke amau mana nui" (be endowed with more power, spiritual strength, and authority). We already knew "aloha" and "mahalo" – he didn't belabor those points.

The language lessons were both fun for the audience and necessary for the performers. Getting ready for the next act wasn't just a simple matter of changing one's costume; they often came out with elaborate facial tattoos, which obviously had to be washed off and redone in each interval. The emcee was stalling so that they would have enough time for all that.

Sometimes, the performers would teach us things to say in other languages. During the Samoan segment, the funny guy who had taught palm-weaving coached us in saying a word that sounded different from "Toyota" until he twisted the pronunciation and teased us. Then he tried again, the audience loudly said the word to his satisfaction, and he said, "Very good. You can come back tomorrow."

Show – Maori dance.

Show – Tahitian dance.

Show – New Guinea dance.

Show – Samoan dance.

Show – Samoan segment. This was the funny guy, and he led the audience in a Samoan language lesson.

Show – Samoan dance.

The last big hurrah of the show before the Hawaiian hula dance encore of a finale, was a fire dance. The young cheerful guy, the one who had shown me the Hawaiian shaka sign, performed this. He lit two long, thin sticks and set fire to both ends of them, and twirled them in circles at high speeds. I'm not sure, but I think it was some sort of fake fire. (I would love to know how that is accomplished!)

He even ran out into the audience with his flaming batons, spinning and waving them over the heads of the people at the tables in the center of the dining area. I was glad to be off to the left at that point! It was impressive just to realize that he does this three or four nights a week, and thrills the audience with his adept, death-defying act every time.

Fire Dance.

The fire dancer went out into the audience for a couple of minutes.

After the fire dance, there was one more act: another energetic, happy Hawaiian hula dance with the entire cast. I thought back to my reading about this, and recalled that it is possible to major in hula dancing in at least one college or university in Hawai'i.

When it was over, the fire dancer reappeared, sans his flaming batons, and the emcee stood in the center of the back row, grinning from ear to ear while a young alii warrior stood to the right. The beautiful hula dancers, male and female, stood in a back row and knelt in the front row. Several of them were giving the shaka sign. The audience was clapping with enthusiasm, hyped up and in a great mood.

Hawaiian hula dance.

Hawaiian segment – the emcee reviews the language lessons.

Finale and bows with the full cast.

A good time had been had by all. The whole performance had been a happy celebration.

The cast members posed for photographs with guests, and I posed for one.

Posing with a dancer who made the shaka sign.

Petroglyphs

After persuading my father that it would not take too long to see the Puako petroglyphs in Kohala, which were, after all, on the way to our planned activity on the other side of the Big Island, he agreed to make a short detour back there.

Petroglyphs are part of Hawaiian archaeology. They are carvings in flat-sided stones made by ancient Hawaiians that depict various aspects of their life and culture. There are warriors, animals, sea creatures, men waving canoe paddles, women and children, women giving birth, dancers, and other images.

We had seen the area in the darkness a few nights earlier. Darkness comes on fast near the Equator in the Pacific Ocean. It had been a brief excursion on the way back from a day-long drive of sightseeing. My mother and I were curious to see the place in more detail.

By "the place," we meant the Fairmont Orchid Hotel as well as the petroglyphs, which were to the right (north) of the hotel. We wanted to see the lobby, the shops, and whatever else non-guests were allowed to peruse as business invitees.

Accordingly, we rode up Route 19 – Queen Ka'ahumanu Highway – and down the very long driveway that led to the hotel, the beach, the gated community of condominiums next to the hotel, the small upscale shopping area, and the petroglyphs. All of this was down the same long paved entrance, set well back from the highway. The whole thing gave the impression of being a gated community, but it was really just an upscale development. Anyone could go in to visit.

We drove in there and turned right. The petroglyph park was all the way down on the right, which meant going west down a long driveway with nothing but open, flat, untouched land on either side until we were in the development, then right. As we drove to the right, we saw the huge gated community of condominiums that we had not noticed in the dark.

Finally, we saw the lava-rock sign that told us we had arrived, and my father pulled in.

All of the signs in the development looked like this one, font and all.

We found ourselves between the walkway to the petroglyphs to our right and a landscaped and manicured clearing with a circle driveway to our left. Palm trees were on the lawn of the circle, and to the left was a rest room. We would look at that later; for now, I headed straight for the petroglyph area, camera ready.

The petroglyphs were through the trees in the background at left.

Before I went down the path to see the actual petroglyphs, I paused to read the signs.

This sign explained what petroglyphs are, at least as best the archaeologist can interpret.

This sign outlined the rules for visiting the petroglyphs.

According to the first sign I looked at, we had come at the ideal time of day: late morning. That is when the sunlight is perfect, because the sun is low in the sky. Great...I looked east, down the path that led to the ancient carvings. The sign also said that the petroglyphs were carved between 1000 and 1800 C.E./A.D.

The path looked like it had been recently landscaped, no doubt to alert visitors that they were close to the petroglyphs.

Without further delay, I started walking down the path, looking on either side, puzzling over where the petroglyphs might be. I didn't see any as I walked down it. They must be at the end, I mused, and glanced up to the right.

That gave me a view of the gated community of condominiums, so I shot a photograph of them. It's possible that I was looking at a wing of the Fairmont Orchid Hotel, and that the condominiums were off to the left, but it was difficult to be certain of that.

The buildings of the hotel and/or community next door showed over the wall and through the trees.

I kept going, looking back at the churned up volcanic rocks and soil on either side of the path. Had the ground looked like this for millennia, and the paved path been the only addition since the petroglyphs were made? Obviously, the hotel construction crew would have done the path, as this archaeological site was an attraction for visitors and a protected site. But I wondered just how much dressing up of this spot had been permitted, or done.

At this point, my mother appeared behind me. I hadn't expected her to follow me in here, but I was glad she had. It's a lot more fun to look at something with a companion than without. She was curious to see the petroglyphs.

We walked the rest of the way down the path and came to a little round area, a circle of paved pathway that had petroglyphs in the middle, and more around the perimeter. Off to the left was a continuation of that path, and it led into a shady area that came to a dead end, with a sign saying that we couldn't go any farther.

The volcanic soil was fascinating up close. Previously, I had seen this from the car, or on the south side of the Big Island, in Volcanoes National Park.

With that, I starting looking at the petroglyphs and taking photographs of them. My mother had fun; she pointed out the more elaborate of them and asked questions. I had started flipping through the short paperback book on petroglyphs that I had bought the day before, so I had some answers for her, which made it even more fun.

This one looked like Hawaiian people walking and sitting, and maybe dancing.

Adult and child dancers...a guess. A woman – wahine in Hawaiian.

My mother and I were having a great time looking at every last one of the petroglyphs. Each rock was a different size and shape, but the carvings themselves were similar in scale. The largest was perhaps a foot tall and almost as wide.

A kahuna priest... maybe. It seems a bit silly to say "maybe" after most of these, but I have little choice. I'm not an expert archaeologist, and I don't believe in writing with authority rather than admitting that I am guessing. This other petroglyph looks like a man and boy, but I don't know why the boy is in the air upside down. It could be a warrior tossing a foe over a cliff, as Kamehameha the Great and his warriors did to conquer other Hawaiian Islands, but that's another guess.

A warrior or a dancer. This profile petroglyph is definitely of a warrior wearing a helmet.

A man with a paddle. This image is one of the ones in the collage on the cover of this book.

This kane – man – is holding a long spear high over his head. A battalion of ali'i warriors.

It was only later, when I had had the time to read the book on the petroglyphs, that I found out that these were all replicas for people who wish to make rubbings. The actual petroglyphs are through the trees. I looked for them on Google Maps, and was looking straight down at a forest of trees – no carvings could be seen from above. This is what happens when you travel: you find things that seem exciting, and they turn out later to be something else. Still, this last one looked more convincing than the others. I hope it was authentic.

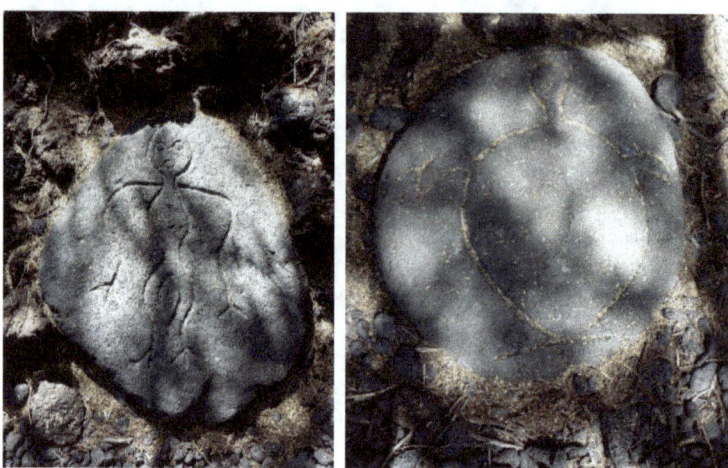

I wasn't guessing about this one – it's a woman giving birth. The book I had bought said so! This was the one I had most looked forward to seeing: a honu – a turtle. I was a little disappointed that it didn't have a line through its shell from head to tail, but at least I was seeing a honu petroglyph.

When we had seen them all, my mother and I reversed course and went out to the beach.

This was the path straight across from the petroglyph path, with the circular driveway and palm trees behind us.

This map showed us the layout of Holoholokai Beach Park.

Looking straight west on the beach, with my mother walking out toward the water.

Looking north on the beach.

Looking south. It was very rocky; if we had tried to walk barefoot, it would have been uncomfortable.

We quickly decided that we had seen it all at the beach. It was pretty, but we had no plans to hand around for a long period of time, so we used the rest rooms in the little building to the south of the palm tree circle and got back into the car.

Next stop: the Fairmont Orchid Hotel.

Out of the Petroglyph Park and to the next turnoff in the long and winding driveway we drove, and we were there. Time to wander around what we guessed was a five-star hotel. There were some shops in it, and of course many orchids.

This was the porte-cochère, complete with a waterfall and an orchid motif on the columns.

This is the waterfall out front, seen from under the porte-cochère.

The sign on one of the front columns. A close-up of the pretty copper orchid motifs on the columns.

This fabulous floral arrangement stood on a beautiful table in the front lobby, across from the desk. It had pink ginger, anthuriums, heliconias, palm fronds and, of course, orchids.

Straight through the lobby, looking out onto the Pacific Ocean off Kohala's beaches, was an outdoor restaurant. It was open for lunch, and some guests were already eating there, even though it wasn't yet noon.

Hallowe'en skeleton couple in the shop.

Around to the left was the shopping area. I led my mother over to the window with the Hallowe'en display of a skeleton couple all dressed up. We had forgotten about that holiday, which felt odd. I love Hallowe'en, but I was so caught up in experiencing Hawai'i that it had slipped my mind. Now I was thinking about what it must be like to celebrate it in the tropics.

We went in and saw high-end everything: bathing suits, sarongs, designer handbags, lotions, soaps, golf shirts (there was a golf course just outside), dresses, blouses, skirts, shoes, you name it. A smiling older woman, the shopkeeper, approached and asked if she could help us. I said that we were just looking, that we had seen the petroglyphs and then wanted to see what was in here as long as we were so close to the hotel. She nodded and smiled, and then chatted pleasantly about our trip with me for a few minutes.

We looked over some orchids on this balcony, down at a beautiful stairwell, and over into a palm garden. Here is the balcony with cultivated orchids growing on it, in several colors and varieties.

After we had wandered all around this shop – and it had several rooms to it, laid out in a haphazard maze of fun to browse in – we came out and looked at the lobby. The lobby wrapped all around the hotel, part indoors and part outdoors. The hotel had several wings to it, so the orchids and koi ponds were all over the place.

We looked down another orchid-topped balcony into this koi pond.

More orchids. All were grown in pretty gray oval pebbles, out of a small bit of brown tree bark. One more orchid display; after we saw this one, we were ready to go.

After we had seen what seemed to be every cultivated orchid in the south wing of the hotel, my mother and I decided that we had seen enough and went back out to my father, who was calmly waiting for us in the car. He knew perfectly well what we had been doing. After all, who runs in and out of a five-star hotel without looking around?!

We got in the car, and he drove off toward the northeastern side of the Big Island, to the Hawaii Tropical Botanical Garden. It was a lovely, sunny ride all the way.

Hawaii Tropical Botanical Garden

After our almost-visit to the Puako petroglyphs, we took off for the northeastern side of the Big Island, to proceed with the main event on our agenda for the day: a visit to the Hawaii Tropical Botanical Garden. I had researched this garden on the Internet before leaving, and was looking forward to seeing the place with both of my parents. I also hoped to see a mongoose.

There is a short road off Route 19 called the 4 Mile Scenic Route, and the garden is on it.

The 4 Mile Scenic Route lives up to its name, and it connects on both ends to Route 19, bowing away from it to the east. My father found it with precision, approaching it from the north. We drove over a one-car bridge when we were almost there.

It was a thickly forested tropical area with beautiful, bright sunshine coming through the leaves and palm fronds; another perfect day in Hawai'i. Suddenly, there it was, with the sign for the visitor center on the right, and the entrance to the garden on the left.

The sign for the garden was topped off by a Hawaiian warrior – not Kamehameha the Great. Notice that this warrior's cape has a lot of red in it! This one would have been a governor of the Big Island.

We parked on the far side of the parking lot, right next to a thickly forested upward slope. The moment my mother got out of the car, she saw the backside of a mongoose. It was rapidly vanishing into the brush, spooked by the sudden movement of humans. I had heard it, but I hadn't seen it, so I held out hope of getting a photograph of one inside the garden.

The website for the garden had led me to believe that for a small fee ($5), we could rent a golf cart. Thus, I arrived with the impression that it would be easy for my father to come with us and see the whole garden. I was wrong…and not pleased. I wanted him to have fun, not sit and wait for us every time we went in somewhere, like when we went shopping. This wasn't a thing that he didn't care about, after all; it was a special site!

It turned out that the golf cart was only driven by an employee, and that the ride would only take people to the bottom of the sharply downward sloping trail. After that, everyone had to get out and walk. My father didn't seem that upset, but I said I was. My mother and I ended up going through the garden while he waited. However, the garden was definitely a great place to visit.

Hawaii Tropical Botanical Garden

Hawaii Tropical Botanical Garden

27-717 Old Mamalahoa Highway
P.O. Box 80
Papaikou, HI 96781
Phone: 808-964-5233
Fax: 808-964-1338
Website: http://htbg.com/

Admission is $15 per adult. The site says that children under 6 enter for free, but it doesn't explain the cost of admission for those over 6. I noticed that there is no okina in the garden's name, which surprised me.

This is the visitor center, seen from the spot where we parked.

Here is the golf cart, just outside the entrance to the visitor center. It was a comfortable place, with a shop, a museum room, and rest rooms, which are near the golf cart. My father sat outside the visitor center, on this bench in front of it, to wait for us while we saw the garden.

The first thing we did was not to go into the garden – instead, we decided to eat lunch. This put off the discovery about the golf cart problem for a few minutes. We had a lunch in the trunk – grocery store food. It was good, and light, and we were shortly ready for another adventure.

The next thing we did was to scope out the visitor center so that we could plan our time out. There was a nice clean rest room, and a shop on the right, which was the front of the building. The shop was where the tickets were sold, so we got ours without further delay. The tickets came with a map of the garden, which was stapled to the tickets' receipt.

I walked around the shop quickly, trying to plan what would be worth spending more time on later: it was one large room with a cash register just inside the door on the right. The shop sold hats, tee shirts, glass bowls and dishes, carved koa wood figurines, books, knick-knacks, magnets, and bulbs and seeds, which were on a rotating rack outside. There were also some coconut palm plants in clear plastic bags against the wall near that rack.

The shop, with the art and books for sale. Straight back is a large portrait photograph of the garden's founders. The other side of the shop, with the tee shirts and knick-knacks.

The garden's founders: Dan and Pauline Lutkenhouse.

There is a door on the left inside the shop that leads to a museum room. The room is actually two rooms, and full of glass cases. It houses the collection amassed by the garden's founders after traveling in Asia. One cabinet is made of black-and-gold-painted wood, and open at the top.

This cabinet is the first thing that visitors see when they enter the museum room. This is the view of the museum rooms to the right. We looked at this after walking through the garden.

After assessing the place, we were ready to go into the Hawaii Tropical Botanical Garden to see it all. The entrance was across the street. Almost no cars drove between the parking area and the entrance. It was quite safe and easy to cross. We saw the golf cart taking its time to go back and forth. A man sat at a table just inside the gate, under an awning, checking tickets.

The path went down to the right, then curved and dropped sharply. We couldn't see much beyond that point, which added to the mystery and excitement of the visit. Without further delay, we went across the street with our map and tickets.

This is something worth considering. We were fine, having just finished lunch, and glad not to carry water.

The general pattern of movement inside the garden is as follows: Walk down the sharply dropping path, left into the Jungle Trail and Onomea Waterfalls, then double back and go left on the Heliconia Trail to see the Banyan Canyon and statue of Ku. Come up from there and turn left, see guava trees, continue left to the Orchid Garden, the Founders Birdhouse, Anthurium Corner, and Lily Lake. Double back toward the birdhouse and turn left and left again to get to Onomea Bay.

Go all the way out to see Blowhole Cove and Onomea Bay with the Twin Rocks. Double back; we tried to go along the coast to see what was there (Turtle Cove, Rock Island, etc.), but that area was fenced off. We turned around and came back at that point, opting not to see the path that goes to the south, with three different trails. Coming up the steep path back out, we noticed plants that we hadn't looked at carefully on the way down, such as ginger and ferns.

The entrance to Hawaii Tropical Botanical Garden is guarded by an attractive metal fence...

...and this man. He was very serious, until I turned back to take his picture, and then he smiled.

 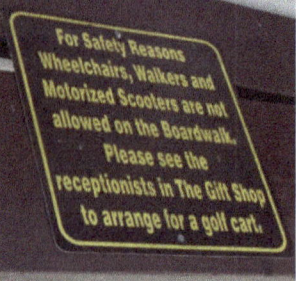

No wonder he was so serious; he is the enforcer of paid admission. Golf carts only in the park... and then walk.

Dan J. Lutkenhouse – Founder.

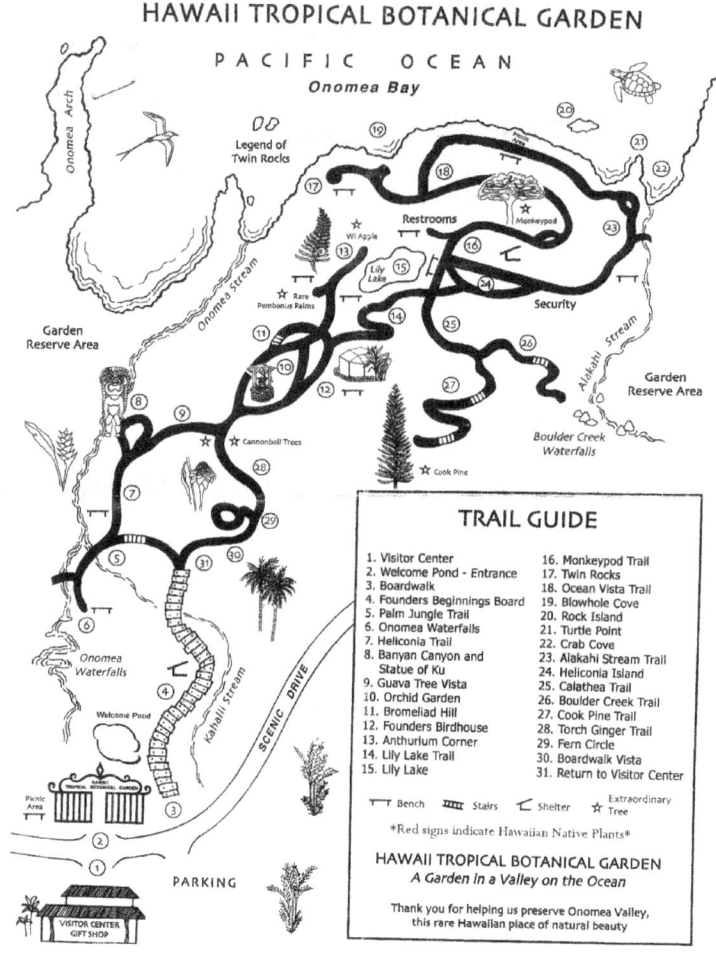

The map of the Hawaii Tropical Botanical Garden. We referred to it constantly.

The view from across the street and just inside gives visitors little indication of just how much lower the elevation of the bulk of the Hawaii Tropical Botanical Garden is. It starts out with a nice plaque to the founder, and a paved path with beautiful flowering trees and ferns, then it curves down to the left.

We saw the golf cart go down ahead of us, though. That was our first clue. We would be comfortable going down and walking throughout the garden. What would be real exercise would come at the end, as we came back up the path. We realized this as we began to walk down it. So much for planning ahead and knowing exactly what to expect, which is how I like to operate!

The golf cart disappearing down around the curve into the garden. This bell and plaque were on the outside curve of the corner. The bell is from the original visitor center, which burned down and was replaced.

This bell stood on the outside curve of the corner before the path sloped downward. Dan and Pauline made this gift in 1984.

Down the path my mother and I went, staring up and down and all around. Everywhere we looked, there was something to see. We were moving a bit faster than we did on the way back, which is just as well, because we noticed things that we had not looked at and appreciated on the way down. I had my father's professional camera again, and shot hundreds of images. I hoped that he would be pleased with my efforts later, when he got it back and clicked through them.

Down the path into another micro-climate.

It did not surprise us to see that this garden also had a cannonball tree.

There were some things in this garden that thrilled me more intensely than others simply because I had long been curious to see them growing in nature rather than always on television or in cultivated situations, such as hothouses and pots. Others excited me because I had never expected to see them at all unless I looked them up on the Internet, like cacao beans. Those I had seen on the Internet, but it wasn't long after walking into this garden that we saw them up on a tree. They were in an early phase of growth; ripe cacao pods are bigger, rounder, and browner.

Palm fronds with cattails.

Another view straight up through the heavy tree coverage.

To get to the Onomea Waterfalls, we walked through a dark forest. There were banyan and palm roots wherever we looked, and a wooden footbridge to walk over. We crossed it and came out into a hard-packed dirt path that led to a place that overlooked the falls to the left over yet another footbridge, and the stream to the right. Down the stream, a woman had taken off her shoes and was walking in the shallow water, but she was gone when we walked back.

Walkway to Onomea Waterfall. Onomea Waterfall.

Next was Heliconia Trail. These were intriguing plants; they grew in red pairs of claws, looking like a multi-legged insect hanging down by its tail.

Some heliconias hung down high overhead, twisting as they stretched away from their stems. We were on Heliconia Trail at this point, and there were lots of these, including lobster claw heliconia.

After we had seen the heliconias, we saw a sunny spot that sloped down in a circle. A koa wood statue of the god Ku stood down there by a bench of the same wood, overlooking the stream from Onomea Falls. A huge bamboo tree loomed with its many stalks up on the right.

Banyan Canyon – my mother went down it first. I was still taking pictures.

Ku Tiki ki'i statue and sign. An explanation of Ku the Hawaiian god and Ku the Tiki, which is a carved representation of him.

The next attractions were the Orchid Garden and the Founders Birdhouse, which were close together. These were the most colorful sights in the garden.

The Orchid Garden had a long row of the flowers with another row of tree stumps that hosted the flowering plants up a slope next to it, and a circular path with a wishing well and more orchids around and in it.

This wishing well is in the Orchid Garden. The wishing well bucket contained nothing but orchids.

    The orchids came in several varieties and colors, with petals that were curved and pointed, and edges that were either crinkled or smooth. Some petals were solid colored, while others were speckled. We saw white ones, purple ones, yellows, pinks, and even dark red.
    The Founders Birdhouse was a huge, oval cage. It had a peaked roof, and warnings to stay back from it. As for just how far back one should stay, there was a border of greenery and a railing for a suggestion. The macaws seemed very happy in there. They had a little stream, trapezes to swing on, a water bowl that was set into the far side of the cage, and plenty of food.

The Founders Birdhouse is just south of the Orchid Garden, and full of macaws.

    There were at least three birds living in the cage: two were red-blue-and-yellow, and a blue-and-yellow one. We watched the macaws for a few minutes. One went over to the water dish, which was how we noticed it. The others, the other red and the blue one, climbed high atop a branch and perched there, as if to avoid visitors' prying eyes.
    The whole place was well shaded, overlooked by a lovely jungle of ferns and palm fronds.
    We wandered around the area, taking our time to see it all and photograph it.

My mother took the camera from me at this point, determined to have me in at least one of the photographs.

After seeing the orchids and macaws, it was time to get moving again. We headed for Lily Lake, a water lily pond full of orange koi fish. It had some lily pads, but not so many as to block out the surface and hide the koi.

On the way up the path to it, we found something intriguing that I had seen in the garden book that I bought in the shop at the Foster Botanical Garden: a bat flower. It was black with round, dangling parts that looked like eyes, and many long whisker-like appendages that hung down on either side of the blossom. They contrasted nicely against a backdrop of the plant's huge green leaves.

The black bat flower grows wild in China, I found out when I looked it up. The Hawaii Botanical Garden is actually a plant collector's project. The Lutkenhouse couple traveled to Brazil and many other places, bought plants, and brought them home to grow in this garden. I wondered how they got permission to do this when I thought of the agricultural declaration form that all visitors to Hawai'i must fill out.

Bat flower – I saw one in a book sold in the other garden we toured...and there it was, a real one.

    Next to the black bat flower was a huge jackfruit. Both grew in front of a large tree. Huge variegated elephant ears stood next to them, in front of and around that tree. I had seen elephant ears every summer growing in the gardens around the Harriet Beecher Stowe House in Hartford, Connecticut, but here I saw them in several varieties: black, variegated (green with white stripes), and solid green.

Jackfruit and bat-flower – with variegated elephant ears.

An Indonesian red ginger plant.

Lily Lake Pond on the Lily Lake Trail, with koi swimming in it.

After we had seen Lily Lake and its koi, we headed for Onomea Bay. We didn't know what to expect there. As we came out to the coast, we saw that we were on an overlooking area with heavy brush hemming us in and fences to keep us safely back. Just before we got to the view of the water, we noticed some gravestones with no labels. This property was a sugar plantation a century earlier, and although the identities of the people in the graves are unknown, they were likely Portuguese plantation workers.

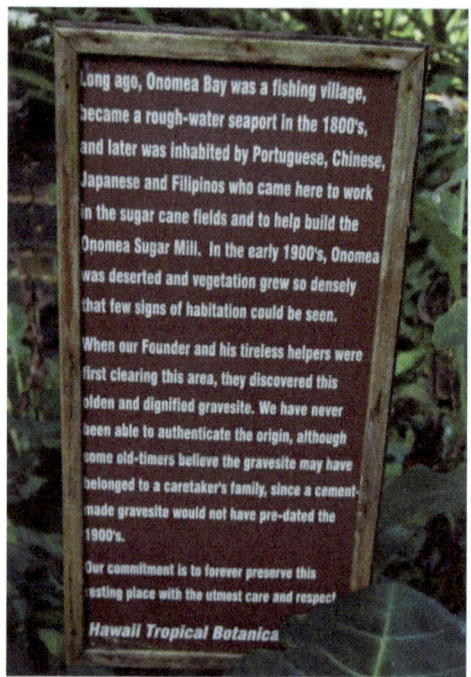

Onomea Bay was a fishing village for most of Hawaii's human history. Then it was a sugar plantation. Some of the workers lived and died at this place, and were buried there after that. Later, it became an abandoned, overgrown place. The Lutkenhouse couple bought it and grew this garden on the site.

Graves of sugar plantation workers. The stones don't say who they are.

We continued past the graves and saw that out in Onomea Bay was a pair of jagged rocks with waves crashing around them. The rocks served to make the bay difficult for a boat to navigate, particularly a large one. They are called Twin Rocks, and there was a romantic legend about them. It is that the rocks were once a pair of lovers who sacrificed themselves to protect Kahaliʻi, the Hawaiian village that once stood to our left, farther inside the bay.

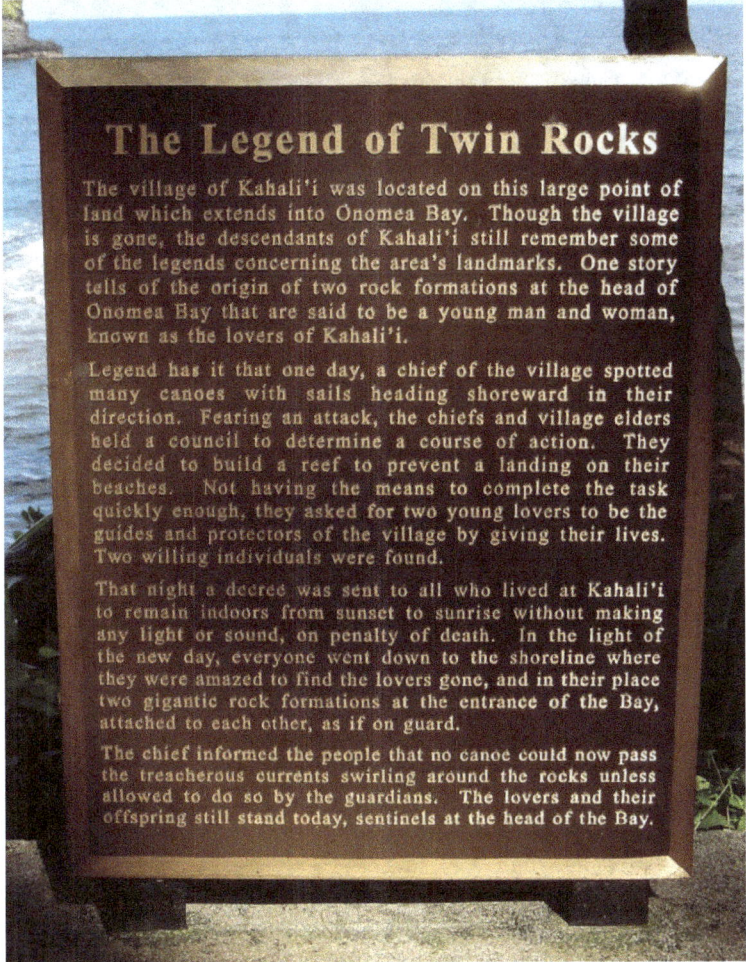

This sign explained the legend of the Twin Rocks in detail. It's both a lovely and a sad story.

Directly below the lookout point where we admired the Twin Rocks was a place called Blowhole Cove. As we watched, the waves crashed into the bay behind the rocks that formed this cove, pushing a gush of water and spray through a small hole.

Twin Rocks in Onomea Bay.

Blowhole Cove – water whooshing out.

When we had seen all of that, and I had shot many photographs of the Twin Rocks, we turned right and walked toward Turtle Cove to the south. But when we were almost there, we could not go in. A chain-link fence blocked our way, and a sign said that work was being done there. It was just as well; we didn't want to leave my father waiting all afternoon, and he would certainly have to wait for at least an hour or the visit would be a waste.

As we headed back the way we had come, I suddenly noticed something exciting: orchids growing wild, not planted on trees stumps, not potted, and not cultivated in a garden. They were subsisting on the dew and mist and whatever water they could get from raindrops, high over our heads. They clung to the bark of palm trees, and they were more beautiful that way than in pots.

Orchids living on dew and mist, growing on the sides of palm trees.

Farther up the path, under such thick tree cover as to make the path rather dark, we saw a mongoose! It was near the brush on the edge, nosing around at the fallen leaves.

We saw this mongoose on the darkened trail as we walked back.

After seeing the mongoose and shooting nine photographs of it, we decided to go back up the path. We noticed another path to our left, but we had seen enough, so we skipped it. I kept shooting photographs of everything else that we saw along the way, however. The opportunities to view more interesting plants never ceased.

Parrot's beak flowers.

Persian shield with dark pink flowering plants.

Elephant ear vines on a palm tree in the sunshine.

Pink bromeliads with blue flowers. This pretty plant is also known as a pink quill.

Sign: "Removal of plant material is strictly prohibited."

Walking up the path. It was humid in the garden, and we were really feeling it on the way back up.

Huggo's on the Rocks…and Other Eateries

For our first evening in Kailua-Kona, we had no clear plan for dinner. Instead, we simply intended to read menus on Aliʻi Drive and try whatever offered fish and seemed okay. We did exactly that, and rather quickly, reading only a couple of menus on the street before deciding to eat in a loft restaurant that overlooked the street and Kailua Bay.

We had asked the hotel staff for suggestions, which was what led us to LuLu's Kona Big Island restaurant. The place was up a steep wooden staircase, and seating was on an open lanai. We chose a spot by the balcony and looked around just before the menus were brought over. Dollar bills were stapled to the walls and pillars from floor to ceiling, and some were written on in pen and black magic marker.

Here is the logo for the restaurant:

I could not get the menu to appear online, only this logo, which appeared with two others, because LuLu's has branches on other islands.

The food was okay. I won't say great, because it wasn't, but it was decent, and it filled us up. We had beer – local Hawaiian brews – and fried fish and chips. There was spicy cocktail sauce and tartar sauce served with it.

When it was over, my parents announced that they didn't love the place and did not wish to return. I had no objection. Fried fish is fun, but we did not need to eat like this every night. It isn't healthy, and the flavor isn't that exciting. There are just a lot more flavors in fresh fruits and vegetables. We didn't eat dessert, either. We just went back to the hotel.

The next evening, as we were riding around in Kohala, my mother ripped a short ad out of a magazine and passed it back to me. It had a small photograph of a beautiful fish dinner at the bottom. The fish fillet appeared to have been sautéed, and it was carefully placed over some purple mashed potatoes. A coconut sauce with light green sauce drizzled into it surrounded the pile of food on the plate.

Wow…

If we could eat there, I definitely wanted one of those, I thought to myself. THAT was a food adventure, and one that looked nutritious. It was colorful, another indication of nutrition and great taste.

The place was called Huggo's, and it was on Aliʻi Drive, so we figured that finding it would be simple enough. Well, easier said than done, but we were determined to figure it out. We found something called Huggo's on the Rocks at a small fork in the road, parked across from the entrance under a leafy tree with branches that stretched down nearly touching the car, and got out. I walked over to the Huggo's on the Rocks, looking around, feeling slightly confused.

It was a cocktail bar and lounge.
A wooden sign with a hole in the hula figure's face stood to the left of the entrance.

    I found a table for my parents to sit at while I continued walking around and asking questions. Since there wasn't someone available instantly, I took out my camera and took some photographs of it. It was a pleasant place, and it had some interesting features, including a nautical artifact that evoked memories of the 1990s *Titanic* movie. It was a speed control mechanism.

The evening's entertainment was about to get underway as we found a table: a hula dancer with a singer-guitar player. She smiled and began to dance, and I took some pictures.

At last I found a staff member behind the snack counter and showed him the ad from the magazine, and asked about the restaurant. It was next door, he told me, and explained how to find the entrance. Out the door, turn right, and look on the right until we see the entrance. It was close by; I could tell by looking up from the table where my parents were. People were sitting at tables above us, and waitresses were coming and going from each one.

Huggo's on the Rocks was just a small outdoor place, with a sandy floor. It was hard-packed soil and sand behind a well-built retaining wall above the bay, hence the name. The wall was made of dark rocks, and the hula dancer was up on a platform of rock.

I told my parents we had to go next door. They got up and followed me out.

It wasn't much of a walk to Huggo's the restaurant. We saw a pretty, flowering tree up ahead with lights and the yellow-lettered sign, and to the right was the building with the entrance. We went inside and knew we were in the right place:

huggo's *"Island Style Dining at the Water's Edge"*

75-5828 Kahakai Road
Kailua-Kona, Hawai'i 96740
Phone: (808) 329-1493
Website: www.huggos.com

This tree and sign were just across from the restaurant. The entrance to Huggo's restaurant.

The foyer was nice. The light fixtures had pretty artwork that depicted backlit dancers, and a beautiful tropical bouquet was on the hostess desk. Business cards and matches were on it.

My mother seated in the cocktail lounge, where we sat until they called us to our table. A hula dancer silhouette on a light fixture in the lounge.

The hostess took our name, told us it would be about fifteen to twenty minutes, and suggested that we wait in the cocktail lounge, so we did that. We each ordered a beer. I sipped mine slowly, planning to make it last with a large glass of water through dinner. Too much beer, I told myself...must switch to red wine soon! But, this was a vacation. I promised myself to eat and drink more responsibly (read: healthfully) after this trip was over.

It didn't seem like much time had passed before we were shown to a great table that overlooked Kailua Bay. My mother took the camera away from me and shot a photograph of me looking out at the water. Out on the water were at least four yachts in a row, anchored for the night. After this meal, we looked out at the bay every night, and saw those yachts each time. They were all different. The cruise ships were gone, out to see for the night, probably on their way to the next port on their routes.

The rocks below Huggo's, which show that the place is aptly named.

The next fun thing that happened was the arrival of our waiter. His name was Island Johnny. He was a tennis player, or a golfer, or maybe both (I don't remember, but the point was, he worked as a waiter to support a life of fun). Island Johnny is just the moniker he goes by at work, but that is enough of an identifier.

Island Johnny – everyone's favorite waiter at Huggo's.

Island Johnny was exuberantly cheerful and friendly. He was full of useful information about the Big Island, and knew ALL about each and every gourmet dish that Huggo's offered. I told him about the magazine ad that had lured us here, and he pointed out the item on the menu. Great! I signed up for it.

Monchong – large-sickle pomfrette – over purple mashed potatoes with coconut sauce, lime juice, and black sesame seeds. It looked just like the advertisement, and was delectable.

Bread was served while we waited. It was both plain and with a bit of cheese on it. We drank our beers and waited, enjoying the view of the water some more. After about twenty minutes, which seemed just right, the food arrived.

Dinner was absolutely delicious, and lived up to our expectations. My mother surprised me by not ordering an entrée; instead, she said she wasn't hungry enough for one and got a great salad. She gave me a bit of it, and I insisted that she try some of my fish and the purple potatoes. My father got something that he could have had at home…again. Where was the food adventure?

Dessert was a little more adventurous; we each got the same thing.

Banana and macadamia nut crisp with ice cream.

Wednesday evening, we decided to return to trolling the possibilities along Aliʻi Drive.

Before leaving, we read through a little booklet at the Aston Kona by the Sea. It showed sample menus from just about every restaurant on Aliʻi Drive. At last, we settled on one called Tante's Island Cuisine, which was a Portuguese place with Hawaiian themes to its food. Off we went, parked, and walked up the steps and into the place. The door was on the left, and it overlooked the street and the bay. Tante means "aunt" in Portuguese, but that was all we knew.

Tante's Island Cuisine – another Portuguese restaurant, but a far cry from Huggo's. The ukulele player-singer is in the front corner.

Seafood lu'au dinner: spiced shellfish in coconut sauce, rice, and carrots. Fried shellfish with mashed potatoes and sauces. My mother got this; my father had the same thing with a baked potato.

The place was brightly lit, and we glanced around at the clientele. It had the feel of a diner, but it was more of a family-style restaurant. Older couples and groups of single women filled up about half of the tables, leaving the rest empty. The waitress was nice. A woman with a ukulele and a tropical flower clip in her hair sat in the corner, playing.

Ukulele player singer in the corner. She was a nice, friendly lady to talk to.

My food was spicy, with the kick to it mitigated by coconut sauce. My parents had fried food, and said it wasn't that great. It was good food, nothing harmful, but not really healthy. If we ate like this all of the time, we would get terribly fat, I could see from the menu.

After nearly two weeks in Hawai'i, I was catching on to the fact that Hawaiian cuisine tends to both emphasize fried food, roasted pork, and taro or sweet potatoes and be less than healthful. To be fair, that is inexpensive food everywhere. When it is a bit more upscale – gourmet – it is healthier, IF the customer wants it that way. The ingredients are fresh and varied, and raw foods are part of the selection. One can either eat cheap and greasy, and suffer weight gain and ill health, or pay a bit more, and have lighter and healthier fare.

When dinner was almost over, I decided to get up and chat with the musician. She seemed like a nice lady, and she was. I asked her about the tsunami that had hit eastern

Honshu in Japan the previous spring, and whether the debris that it had washed away from there had come to the Big Island yet, as news reports had started to say. It had, she said, but it was cleaned up fast. I saw no trace of it on our trip, but imagined refrigerators, cars, and smaller personal effects washing up to Kona.

As we walked out of the restaurant, I glanced into the little garden area by the stairs and immediately took my camera back out. Bananas were growing there! Lots and lots of ripe bananas grew upwards in four rows in the front, and more around to the right side. My mother was fascinated, too.

This banana tree was growing in the garden just outside Tante's restaurant.

We had just two more evenings of dinners in Kona.
Thursday was the luʻau at Kamakahonu, so that was decided.
Friday was open. My father said he wanted to go back to Huggo's, so we did. Why not? It was great! We decided to get dressed up for the occasion.

Here we are, dressed up again in our Hawaiian clothes.

The only downside to it was that we couldn't have Island Johnny for our waiter, but he came over and visited with us for a few minutes, gave the shaka sign, and smiled. He was waiting on a large wedding party that marched past our table (another great one on the lanai with a view of the yachts), down into the lower patio, and to the tables there.

Shrimp with garlic and butter. My mother ordered it. She could have gotten this dish at home! Steak over mashed potatoes with green beans. My father ordered this. No food adventure here…

Seared ahi tuna with sesame seeds over black rice and mango salad. It's key lime pie… in the Pacific! Pandering…er, catering to the tourists. Huggo's is ready for anyone.

    I met the manager, and asked him about the name of the restaurant. He said that it was owned by a Portuguese man named Hugo, but an extra "g" was added because local Hawaiians had been unable to pronounce it properly, and it came out like the word "hug" every time. Interesting.

    My parents did not go on a food adventure, and I did, repeating our earlier pattern. At least my mother ordered a filling shrimp dish, though. I had seared ahi tuna, and my father got another steak. We ended the feast with dessert again.

    Once again, everything was absolutely delicious. We definitely recommend this place.

Hulihe'e Palace

All week, I had looked at the stucco-covered house with the palm trees behind the lava rock wall as our car went past it on Ali'i Drive. It had a great view of both Kailua Bay and Kamakahonu, and was obviously a museum. I was determined to visit it. On Saturday afternoon, I had my chance. My mother wanted to shop some more, and I didn't. We both wanted to spend our last afternoon before going to the airport in the same area.

Admission was $6 dollars. Shoes must be left outside in the front steps, and photography is not allowed inside. I took lots of photographs outside, and then stuffed the small camera case into my pocket. I had left my heavy handbag with my father in the car, so I was ready to enjoy the visit and relax.

The Daughters of Hawai'i turned this place into a museum in 1927, and have maintained it since then. It was placed on the U.S. Register of National Historic Places in 1973. The building, despite the name Hulihe'e Palace, is actually a six-room house. It was a vacation residence for Hawaiian royalty throughout the nineteenth century and into the early twentieth.

Hulihe'e Palace, seen from Ali'i Drive, with a historic interpreter greeting visitors on the front steps.

Like the wall that surrounds the property, Hulihe'e Palace is built out of lava rock.

Hulihe'e Palace was built in the early nineteenth century for an ally of Kamehameha the Great, John Adams Kuakini. He was the Governor of the Island of Hawai'i, and one of the first to take up western haole ways, hence the style of the house. The house did not have a stucco veneer then; the lava rocks were left exposed on the exterior.

This plaque, set into the wall next to the front gate, briefly outlines the history of Hulihe'e Palace.

When Governor Kuakini died in 1844, he left the place to his hanai (adopted) son, William Pitt Leleiohoku I, who only lived in it for four years, then died of the measles in 1848. Leleiohoku I was married to Princess Ruth Ke'elikolani, and they had a son, John William Pitt Kinau, so the son inherited it. But Kinau died at the age of 16, in 1859, and his mother inherited it next, adding to her vast land holdings.

Princess Ruth Ke'elikolani was a very wealthy woman who knew haole ways and the English language, but chose to adopt very few of them. Instead, she preferred to speak Hawaiian, live in a traditional Hawaiian hale next to Hulihe'e Palace on what is now its north lawn, and to worship Hawaiian gods and goddesses. She did not have a happy life.

Princess Ruth was a granddaughter of Kamehameha the Great, and she served as Governess of the Island of Hawai'i from 1855 to 1874, when King Kalakaua came to power and the office went to another alii from his family. She was vastly wealthy in her own right, with over 353,000 acres of land to her name. She gave 10 acres in Waikiki to her goddaughter, the Princess Ka'iulani, which is how her parents ended up building the estate of 'Ainahau there. Ka'iulani wrote her many affectionate letters, calling her "Mama Nui," which means "Great Mother."

Like her land holdings, Princess Ruth was a vast woman: she was 6 feet one inch tall and came to weigh over 400 pounds. This was the ideal of traditional aristocratic Hawaiian beauty. She had a booming voice, and loved children, but unfortunately, the historic interpreters in Hulihe'e Palace told me, with the exception of Princess Ka'iulani, they tended to be afraid of her.

Princess Ruth got married again in 1856, but her second husband, Isaac Young Davis, was nasty. They had fights, and he broke her nose. Three years later, her son by her first husband died. She had a son with Davis, Keolaukalani Davis, in 1862, and had him adopted according to tradition as the hanai son of her cousin, Princess Bernice

Pauahi Bishop. This was against his father's wishes. The boy died at the age of a year and a half in August of 1863.

The front gate, with its ornate posts.   *A kahili motif on the hinge area of the post.*

Princess Ruth and Isaac Young David divorced in 1868.

She adopted a hanai son, the younger brother of King David Kalakaua, Queen Lili'uokalani, and Princess Miriam Likelike, but he died at age 23. His name was Prince William Pitt Leleiohoku (Ruth named him for her first husband), and like his siblings, he wrote music.

A Hawaiian crown that looks like taro leaves graces the top of the hinge post.

The royal Hawaiian crest tops each of the gate doors.

When Princess Ruth died in 1883, it was at her hale at Hulihe'e Palace. She willed it to Princess Bernice Pauahi, along with her vast land holdings and a new Victorian mansion in Honolulu (no longer standing), the size of which outstripped 'Iolani Palace. Her estate formed the endowment for the Kamehameha Schools, which continue in operation today.

Princess Bernice Pauahi Bishop lived on O'ahu with her husband Charles Reed Bishop, the banker. She was not going to live in Kona, so she sold the place to King David Kalakaua, who used it as a vacation residence, and his wife, Queen Kapi'olani. At that point, some renovations were undertaken, and Hulihe'e Palace acquired its stucco veneer.

When King Kalakaua died in 1891, his widow, Queen Kapi'olani, inherited the palace.

Queen Kapi'olani died in 1899, having spent her time living on O'ahu. She left Hulihe'e Palace to her hanai nephews, the Princes Kuhio and David Kawananakoa. The princes spent some time there, but they were away a lot. Kuhio was elected to the U.S. Congress as the Representative from the Territory of Hawai'i, so he spent much of his remaining years in Washington, D.C. Kawananakoa spent more time there, with his wife, Princess Abigail Wahi'ika'ahu'ula, and the upstairs south bedroom is set up as it was for them. He died in 1908.

My visit to Hulihe'e Palace was great fun. I left my sandals outside, paid the six dollars, and was delighted to find out that I could ask as many questions as I wished. There was no tour. A historic interpreter sat at the desk just inside the front door on the right, and another stood in the room on the south side of the building (left). She was a tall, smiling Hawaiian woman with a pretty silk flower in her hair, she wore a floral-patterned muumuu.

The front hall contained several beautiful pieces of furniture made of koa wood, and portraits and photographs of all past residents and owners of the palace hung in it. A desk that was owned and used by King Kalakaua faced the one for the historic interpreter, with its back to the back door, which opened out onto a lanai. The back of the building had an upstairs lanai as well.

Hulihe'e Palace has Queen Emma lilies growing next to its wall, and a historic sign depicting a Hawaiian Island governor in traditional Hawaiian attire over the plants.

A museum room full of beautiful handmade koa wood cabinets with glass doors had all sorts of great artifacts. I went inside and found a young Hawaiian man standing in there, taking questions. He told me about kapa cloth and the tools for making and printing patterns on it when I peered into the case just inside the door. Knives and fishhooks were in another case.

'O'o feathers were explained on the back wall, with a beautiful framed color drawing of one of those birds on the wall above the case there. The interpreter told me that the 'o'o had gone extinct, which was sad to hear. I wondered how that happened; all that was taken from it were a few yellow feathers, not the entire coating of them.

The other room on the ground floor was the dining room. It was filled with lovely koa wood furniture, porcelain dinnerware, and the best of the usual sorts of things that one expects to see in a dining room. I could see out the back windows; the view of Kailua Bay was idyllic. Visitors were not allowed out that way, though, so I went back into the hall.

This group of musicians arrived and settled in as I walked up to the palace.

It was time to go upstairs and see what was there, so I went out past Kalakaua's desk and over to the left side of the hall, and looked up. The stairwell went halfway up, then turned right and went the rest of the way up. The staircase was made of wood. On the landing halfway up was a set of long koa spears.

The historic interpreter appeared in the hall and shared more fascinating facts with me: these belonged to Kamehameha the Great, so they were fourteen feet long, which was twice his height! They also had the dried blood of his enemies on them. While he was on the subject, the guide added that Queen Ka'ahumanu was six feet seven inches tall, and that Hawaiian ali'i were typically huge, tall individuals who put on weight as they aged, growing more massive. So it was during my visit to Hulihe'e Palace that I learned this detail.

With that, I went upstairs. The upper hallway doesn't really exist; the stairs simply end in a huge, high-ceilinged sitting room with pretty Victorian-style furniture. A low, poufy sofa sits back from the windows, with plenty of ornate tables and knick-knacks surrounding them.

The north bedroom is set up with two beds. One is a haole-style bed. The other is Princess Ruth Ke'elikolani's original, traditional Hawaiian bed. It looks like a large, long, low cot. It is made of bamboo with a strong, tight cloth stretched across its frame, and kapa cloth was laid over it. I tried to imagine the enormous woman who had been described to me downstairs resting on it night after night. She must have been comfortable, though, because she wanted traditional Hawaiian things, and she had them.

The last room I saw was the south bedroom, made up as if for Prince Kawananakoa and his wife, Princess Abigail. It contained a huge canopy bed of carved wood, some other accompanying pieces, and a fabulous carved armoire of koa wood. When I saw that, I wished that photography were allowed in there. The armoire won an award at the 1893 Chicago World's Fair, I was told. Five Hawaiian figurines, all a part of the same piece of wood that formed the top of the armoire, graced it. One was a hula dancer; I don't remember what the others were.

That was all, so I went downstairs and thanked the historic interpreters, and left.

This wide open gate leads to the side yard of Hulihe'e Palace.

Outside, I wandered around the grounds, listening to a troupe of musicians who had settled in to play on the lawn just inside the front gate for a few minutes. There were ukulele players, violinists, flutists, and other instruments. It looked like a group of talented volunteers, but I wasn't about to interrupt them to ask for more information.

This is the north side of the palace grounds. The earthquake that hit in 2006 caused cracks in the upper right of the side of the building, but it has been completely restored.

The lava rock wall surrounding the palace.

This coconut tree is on the right as one walks up to the front door. The sign reads: "Watch for falling coconuts."

In all, I spent another half hour with my camera, enjoying the yard. The coconut tree on the lawn was just so beautiful that I had to get some photographs of it, and I got some postcard-quality shots. I was very glad I spent my afternoon visiting this place.

I walked over to the north side of the building, using the sidewalk outside the wall to get there, and went into the gate. This had to be where Prince Kawananakoa and Princess Abigail had driven their car when they lived here, I guessed. And before that, from a photograph that I saw later on, somewhere on these grounds stood Princess Ruth's hale. Where, though? The photograph shows a church steeple behind it. Maybe the lava rock wall went up after her time here, and perhaps Aliʻi Drive was different in her time.

Kona International Airport

Kona International Airport is a small, attractive airport with petroglyph motifs on the upper moldings of its inner courtyard, and a beautiful copper statue of three hula dancers in motion in the center. A plaque describes the work, with credit to the artist, Lady Grey Dimond-Cates.

Hula dancers in motion, a statue in copper.

The plaque about Hula Kahiko, the art on display in the airport's courtyard.

This concludes my compliments about Kona International Airport.

There will be no litany of them, because: 1. The place is too small for much of a list; and 2. It is lacking in many basic amenities. The airport is not a comfortable one to wait in. Once one's rental car is turned in, one is trapped with few options for food and almost none for relaxation.

We made a mistake. We didn't eat lunch or do anything about dinner in the late afternoon. We foolishly assumed that we could just get something to eat at the airport, and that it would be okay. This was our idea, with a flight that left 9:21 p.m. at night.

My father dropped us off at four-thirty, bags and all, and drove off to surrender the rental car. Then he took the airport shuttle back to meet us. Once that was done, we were stuck.

We looked into checking our bags in, but found out that the ticket counter was closed until at least six o'clock. There was another option off to the front of the building, but there was a fee for that, and it seemed complicated.

We settled in to wait with other early arrivals on a low stone wall in the sunshine, just outside the open-air, covered ticket area. The baggage inspection area with its security personnel waited in chairs next to those machines, with hours of down time.

I looked behind me at the grass and saw lots of finches pecking at the ground. Some were gray-and-brown; some were bright yellow.

A mother and her teenage daughter waited with some red luggage at the far end of the low wall to our right. They were reading. A couple to our left investigated the luggage situation and availed themselves of the check-in with a fee. A family with a grandmother in a wheelchair settled in close to where we were sitting. There was an adult daughter in charge, with her husband and grown son. We chatted with the grandmother and found out that they were from Canada, in Ontario.

When six o'clock finally came, we were getting hungry. We lined up to check our bags in and get the tickets squared away. The line snaked around through the ropes, and we watched as people with large bags weighed them to make sure that they were under the limit. Some people had to do a lot of last-minute repacking to meet the requirements. We didn't, thanks to our smaller luggage. Soon we were putting the accepted and tagged bags through security, and they were taken away.

Next came a very long, slow line that led to the security check-in for passengers.

When that was over, we found ourselves admitted to the inner sanctum of the airport, the courtyard with the hula statue. A quick tour of the perimeter revealed a shop with souvenirs, a newsstand, a vending machine or two, and a single restaurant that was closed.

Closed?! But there were lots of people here!

We sat down on some benches with the Canadian family next to us again.

We were all talked out, and getting hungry and a bit cranky.

We had an all-night and all-day air travel schedule on our minds, and there were reports of a huge storm brewing in the northeastern contiguous United States.

It did not make for a happy state of mind.

At last, after over an hour, lights came on in the restaurant, and the door was unlocked.

I went to check it out the Laniakea Café.

Alas, it was a greasy, unappetizing, grill.

A nice blond woman with glasses and a ponytail took charge of the grill.

Off to the left of the grill was a refrigerator with yogurts, sodas, and fruit drinks. I found a really good drink in there, a mildly filling, thick one – strawberry banana. There were some fruit cups in there too, full of questionable-looking cut-melon mixtures. I didn't take one. My father got drinks for himself and my mother that were thinner – sugary fruit juices, I think.

Then it was back to the problem of what to eat: breakfast foods seemed appealing, but the woman behind the grill informed me that she was only making dinner. The most I could hope for was a toasted plain bagel with plain cream cheese. Oh yeah, I thought, calorie-laden, empty carbohydrates. I ordered one. The smell of frying burgers and crinkled French fries cooked in beef oil bothered me.

The awful, only eatery in Kona International Airport, with its grill in the back to the right. The cash register inside the café had some stools in front of it, and a few customers pulled up to it right away.

The woman behind the grill smiled and told me that I should have realized by now that Hawaiians don't care about eating healthy or having healthy food choices.

I replied that they should think about the wishes of the tourists who pay to visit.

She was a blond woman, not a native Hawaiian, so I felt okay saying what I really thought. But would native Hawaiians really be so upset by criticism as to be unable to hear the truth about an unhealthy cuisine and a sense of being trapped with no other options? I doubt it; every last native Hawaiian person that I met on this trip was a lovely, nice person to interact with, and seemed to be a logical, reasonable thinker.

My parents didn't eat any of the greasy food, either. The Canadian family ate some of it all, but didn't finish their fries. They offered us some; we ate a few, but they weren't good. They tasted like grease more than anything else.

We cleaned up our food wrappers, tossed them into the trash, and returned to the courtyard to wait until we were called to our gate. We knew where it was, but passengers weren't being admitted to that area just yet.

My mother and I went into the airport shop and looked around while my father sat on the uncomfortable wall in the courtyard with our carry-on luggage.

It was a disorganized mix of wares: hats, tee shirts, perfumes, lotions, and so on.

I found a little spray bottle of plumeria perfume. After recalling how much I enjoy it when my parents go to Florida and bring me those little bottles of orange blossom perfume, and thinking of how much I had come to love the scent of plumeria blossoms, I bought it.

Soon after that, we were admitted to the boarding gate.

Rows and rows of chairs lined the area.

We could go out to use the rest rooms if we needed to after coming in here, which was good to know. We got settled among lots of families and other travelers and settled in to wait in the darkness and bright lights. We would be boarding the plane by walking across the tarmac and up a staircase that was rolled to the door of the plane.

Somehow, my father and the grandmother from Canada managed it.

The Return Trip...an Unwanted Adventure

All week, as we enjoyed and explored the Big Island of Hawai'i, I noticed that my parents were alternately focused on weather reports for the northeastern continental United States. They look at the weather reports a lot at home, too, so at first I didn't really notice the reason why...until I heard that a superstorm was coming, and that the meteorologists had named it.

It's always an ominous sign when they name a storm. This one was Superstorm Sandy.

Here it was in October, the same time as the storm of the previous year that had left us shivering by the light of battery-powered lanterns at night with no heat or hot water for eight days. What was this year's storm going to do to us, I wondered in disgust?

The previous year's storm had done a lot of damage, and restoring utilities had taken an inordinate amount of time due to something else: corporate restructuring. That in turn had motivated me to write *The Book of Thieves*, a fairy-tale retelling of the economic meltdown that is still in progress. What creative result would come from this year's storm?

I really wasn't looking forward to the inconvenience of it, not that anyone does. Not even if I got another book idea out of it did I want to deal with a superstorm! I was concentrating on my travelogue, which was still unfolding and would continue to do so until we got home and greeted our cat.

But...nature could care less. The Earth will do whatever it is going to do, regardless of our wishes, or perhaps because of them. Climate change drives these superstorms, intensifying them, and making them come at times of the year that we are not used to, as we humans drive climate change by overuse of fossil fuels and other resources.

I had to put aside such thoughts and focus on the Hawai'i work and fun, though.

It seemed silly to fail to fully enjoy Hawai'i because trouble was looming for the return trip.

So, I toured and loved the rest of the trip, but by the morning of our departure, I woke up after an anxious, fitful sleep. No amount of positive thinking could change the fact that our itinerary was this: get up on Saturday morning, check out of the hotel, tour all day, go to Kona International Airport, fly overnight to San Francisco, wait, fly to Chicago, wait again, and then fly to Connecticut, arriving at almost ten o'clock at night on Sunday.

No sleep...I'm not good at relaxing into a deep sleep on a plane. It's not a stopping point, so sleep seems silly. Time to think of ginger gum and sickly sweet fruit drinks with no food again...

Added to that was the thought that we might get stuck along the way in a crowded airport with lots of other stranded travelers and be expected to sleep there. It nagged at me, ruining my sleep that last night in Hawai'i.

By the time we got stranded, it seemed likely that we would be overtired and desperate for a hotel room, I worried. My father would be utterly miserable with his hip, and difficult to deal with. My mother would cope, but it wouldn't be good for her. Some ending to a vacation! One is supposed to return from one feeling relaxed, not exhausted and physically traumatized.

I would be miserable during the return trip under such circumstances, but I could sleep it off at home when we finally got there...if the utilities weren't off for the next week. And what if our home was somehow ruined? I told myself to stop that. We live in north-central Connecticut, slightly up a hill. It wasn't going to get washed or blown away, and the one tree that could have fallen on the building had been removed a few years ago.

No, we were going to see news reports of abject misery elsewhere.

Sometimes it is depressing rather than satisfying to be right.

Once again, when we were strapped into the United Airlines plane and in the air, the ad for the company's huge new 787 plane came on. These monster planes had funky-looking engines with serrated back edges and looked like the latest and greatest in flight technology.

But it turned out that they didn't work thanks to problems with their lithium-ion batteries. Yet we saw the ad extolling the virtues of this aircraft on every flight. Where was the safety video? I just don't remember seeing it; perhaps the memory of that routine item was overshadowed by the 787 one.

It wasn't until later that the battery problems grounded the new aircraft, and I got curious enough to look at all of the airports we had visited on Google Maps. Directly above Chicago's O'Hare Airport, the view focused on the planes at the gates, and some of them looked like giants compared to the others.

Those were the new United Airlines 787s, all grounded. There are 50 of them, according to a report in *The New York Times*. I wondered how many planes the airline owns in total; it seems to have so many as to be almost an anti-trust issue, dominating the passenger flight market, and controlling prices.

We took off from Kona in the dark, so there was no staring out my window at the landscape to study the shape and contours of the Big Island, even though I had a window seat this time. I chewed the ginger gum and made an effort to doze. So did my parents. It was a five-hour and 4-minute flight to San Francisco International Airport. We landed when it was nearly half past five in the morning. It was still dark out there.

We debarked and entered the now-familiar terminal, and ate breakfast in a restaurant there. It felt like a relief to eat a big meal after the inadequate café in the Kona airport, and we happily downed fresh-squeezed orange juice, coffee, crab cakes, eggs, and bacon. By the time we were out of the restaurant and walking around, looking for the next departure gate, the sun was up and there seemed to be more people about than when we arrived.

At the departure gate, I made an unpleasant discovery: not only would we be seated far apart all over the aircraft rather than together, but our flight to Connecticut from Chicago was in fact cancelled! The woman at the ticket counter went on to say that United Airlines was moving all of its aircraft out of the area that were in the trajectory that Superstorm Sandy was expected to take.

To add anxiety to the announcement, she said that she doubted that we would be able to get a hotel room in Chicago, because all hotels in the city were booked for conventions and conferences.

Well…all of my worries were confirmed. At least I wouldn't have to feel stupid for worrying about any it, because it was really happening, exactly as I had obsessed about it all!

I went back to where my parents were sitting and told them the bad news.

They were not thrilled.

My mother said not to worry about the hotel until we got there, but I worried.

Next, she said that we ought to go browse the shops and see if we could find David or my father any good tee shirts. She was just trying to keep me distracted, but I got up and went with her, back to the same circular area of shops that we had trolled two weeks earlier. We didn't buy anything in them.

We went back to my father, who said he didn't want a San Francisco tee shirt anyway.

I don't think David wanted one, either.

I did find a hippie-era peace key chain for my activist politician friend from Iran, though.

After that, I took out Michael Crichton's *Micro*, a science fiction novel about nanobotic technology that takes place on Oahu and started to read it. It was the book that my mother had just finished, the one that she bought in Connecticut's Bradley

International Airport before we left. At least it took my mind off things until we were called to board.

We were called in groups, first my parents, then me. An airport employee realized that we were together and moved me with them for the boarding process, but I was still many, many row back from my parents, who were seated on different sides of the aisle. I don't think my father got an aisle seat, either, which meant he had to keep his bad leg scrunched in uncomfortably.

I couldn't help them with their carry-on bags by heaving them into the overhead compartments – another thing to be displeased about. They were tired and my father's leg no doubt hurt and I couldn't do any heavy lifting for them. More unhappy, negative thoughts…

…but what else nagged at me? Something…I struggled to figure it out.

All by myself…well, I could talk to strangers, IF they were friendly. No…ginger gum! That was it! My mother was too far away to ask her for it. This flight had all male stewards on it. They seemed nice, and I managed to flag one down.

He came over, smiling, and I told him that my mother was way up the aisle, and that she had the motion-sickness ginger gum I needed in her handbag. I showed him her photograph (I keep a collection in my handbag). Could he please go and get that from her for me? He did it right away. I thanked him, put a piece in my mouth, and chewed with a slightly desperate feeling.

At half past ten on Sunday morning, the plane took off for Chicago. There were few movie screens; just one every few rows, so there was no choice of what to watch. At least one of my favorite shows was playing, *The Big Bang Theory*. The steward told me he loved that show, too. Five hours later, in mid-afternoon Chicago time, we landed at O'Hare Airport.

Now what?!

We could sense some semblance of disruption at that point; stranded people were all over the place, sitting and standing around. Many were using their iPhones, Droids, laptops, and whatever other electronic devices to explore their options. Seats were nearly filled everywhere we looked.

We used the rest rooms, then decided to go get our checked bags when we were told that regardless, the bags would sit unattended somewhere for the duration of the superstorm if we didn't. Now we had a rented cart and a lot of stuff to push around. My father did it.

A United Airlines employee who worked full-time at the airport gave us a voucher and told us it would entitle us to a discount at whatever hotel we could get.

I didn't believe that we would be able to get a room.

My father had doubts about it, too. It showed; he was getting autocratic about my every move. If I veered off so much as a couple of paces on my own, just considering checking out an unvoiced idea, he would tell me to come back. That just made the experience worse.

My mother decided to go to a counter and ask about hotels. A woman on a bench near the line that we stood in was using her laptop (or notebook – it was small) told me that for seven bucks, I could get online with my Nook device and search for a hotel. I looked up the link she suggested, then decided to wait. What if we did get a hotel room? Wi-fi would be free.

Amazingly, my mother managed to get a room at a Hilton Gardens Inn by the airport! She was given a stranded travelers rate. Every day, she had to call the AAA reservation line at 7 a.m. to get a new room reservation. Fortunately, they let us keep the same room each day.

The catch was that it was by the airport, not in the city; those were hotels that were full, with conference goers. That suited us just fine. Any hotel in a storm would do. My mother got her confirmation number, and we went downstairs in a huge elevator to get on the shuttle.

We were starting to really feel tired at that point.

We had been up for a day and a half, so that made sense.

We had put on our fall clothing again, with socks and fleecy jackets, but my father still wore his cargo shorts. Great for the Windy City in late October…pun intended. He was cold!

Down the elevator, out of it, across the hall, and out the sliding doors we went, with my mother telling me to walk on ahead and try to spot the shuttle or at least the best spot to catch it. My father brought up the rear with the cart, increasingly displeased that I was so far ahead yet still in sight. He hadn't noticed what my mother told me to do…

What fun! Overtired, stranded, pushing our stuff around…I told myself that it could be a lot worse. We could be without hope of a hotel room. Rest was at least on the horizon. And none of our luggage was missing! I could read later…we could cope.

We joined a small throng of people waiting across the front drop-off driveway of the airport terminal, walking under a bridge across two divided lanes of traffic to the front of another building that looked like a wall of glass.

Shuttle after shuttle crowded in front of the wide sidewalk, all with different hotel names. It took a while to spot the one we were supposed to take, but at last we saw it. It was just as well, because the delay gave my father ample time to catch up with the luggage cart.

Once we were in the shuttle, the driver, who had a heavy Chic*aaa*go accent, greeted us all and chatted in a friendly monologue about where he was taking us. We didn't have much sense of where we were going; we were just happy to be going there!

It was on a divided highway not too far from the airport.

He pulled up to it, let us out, and gave us our bags.

This large painting was straight ahead as we entered the building, and the front desk to the right. My father can be seen by the large plant, pushing the luggage cart toward it.

We looked at the front door for about five seconds, then went right in.

We were glad to see the place, whatever it was like.

It was a nice, new, clean, modern building. The lobby was attractively and succinctly laid out, with a table a few paces inside the front doors. On it were cookies and a water cooler with cut strawberries in it, which looked enticing. This would be nice just because of the strawberries, I found myself thinking. I started to relax a bit.

My father got a hold of a luggage cart without delay and we heaved everything onto it.

My mother headed for the desk to check us in. Rest was getting closer…

The strawberry water cooler that I liked so much when we walked in the door; it was right next to a long dining table that stretched all the way to the wood-floored aisle. This living-room style seating area was to the right of the front doors.

The dining area and sports bar was to the left. It was all wide open and compact.

    We were checked in fairly quickly. My mother handed me a plastic key card, and we followed my father into the elevator, helping him maneuver the cart. The hallway was around to the right, and the elevators were on the right partway down it. After the elevators, there was another hallway that went around the corner to the right. The swimming pool and hot tub were there, but we didn't care just yet.
    We saw other stranded people checking in with all of their things in large plastic shopping bags, and wondered absently what had happened to them and their luggage. Into the elevator we went, determined to feel lucky and get comfortable.
    When I was cleaned up and better rested, I intended to call friends and relatives and explain what had happened. That evening, I called my Aunt Joan, and Beth, my best friend from college, and asked them to e-mail David about where I was and why. I left other calls for later.

The lobby of the Hilton Garden Inn of Chicago.

My parents shoving the luggage cart into the elevator. I caught up and helped after I took this photograph.

We got out of the elevator on the third floor, turned right and then left, and went down the hall about fifty feet until we found our door on the left. Good – our room faced the front of the building. My father shoved the cart into a parking spot by the one luggage rack and said to leave it there until we left the hotel. He didn't want to have trouble getting one again.

We left it there for three days.

I looked out; it was just a street that gave me no sense of where we were. I lost interest and turned back to the room. Two double beds with three pillows laid out diagonally on each one, lamps, a table and chair by the window, a lounge chair there also, a bureau, a large flat-screen television, a coffee machine, a fridge, a closet, and a good, clean bathroom. Heaven.

Okay, not heaven, but definitely a haven until we could go home to our cat and unpack.

We got cleaned up and went down to the dining room for dinner.

The menu reflected the pattern of immigration in Chicago, with Italian, German, Polish, and not many other options. My mother and I found something good, though: penne pasta with pear and hazelnut cream sauce. I don't remember what my father ate, only that he commented on the reflections in the menu.

The room...a great spot to read and watch television and wait.

Other travelers sat nearby, constantly thumbing and double-thumbing their hand-held electronic devices, no doubt plotting their escapes. We did see some people whose plans had not been affected by Superstorm Sandy, too; their trips had taken them from the west coast to Chicago, and they would go back that way later, away from the chaos of the storm.

We ate, went upstairs and cleaned up, and tried to fall asleep as we watched storm reports.

The next morning, we ate at the buffet downstairs. It was like eating dinner, except that it was self-service and carry-over to the dining room tables. The food was good, and the hotel staff was very nice.

Thus began a three-day and three-night stay. I spent my time using the Nook Color device in the lobby and making cell phone calls to see how my friends and relatives were doing. Oddly, the storm did not hit my aunt in Rhode Island or my friend in eastern Massachusetts (she lives directly east of my aunt, so that came as no surprise).

We contacted our next-door neighbor and found out that the power never went out, a welcome change from the previous year's storm. My uncle continued to go over there and feed our cat, who never emerged while he was there...but each time, he could see that the food had been eaten.

I read the book on petroglyphs in a day, sitting in the hotel room. My mother was surprised at how fast I read, so I showed her that it was full of pictures, maps, and photographs.

We all used the swimming pool and hot tub, and discovered that it was just what my father needed to make his hip hurt less. (When we got home, he was signed up to go to the one at a local health club.)

My mother and I watched David Letterman do his show with an empty theater. Denzel Washington came in wearing a black outfit with a bright yellow rain jacket, which he proceeded to shake out when he arrived, and huff and puff in mock exhaustion as though he had fought his way with great difficulty through high winds in order to reach the Ed Sullivan Theater.

The breakfast buffet area. The dining room is to the left.

JFK and La Guardia Airports were flooded with rainwater.

Lower Manhattan was without power from 23rd Street on south.

My cousin, who lived on West 20th Street, went with her roommate, cat, and roommate's Yorkie to stay with a nice friend in northern Manhattan who took them all in.

People who lived on Staten Island had their homes wiped out by the storm – gone.

We had it so easy, missing the whole thing in Chicago and watching it on television! We even ordered in on the third evening there, rather than eat in the hotel restaurant. It was Indian food, and the place had great tikka masala and curry.

After three days of me checking the United Airlines website and contacting our AAA agent, we were cleared to return home. We packed everything up and returned to the airport. It was Hallowe'en, and we expected to be home by early evening.

When we tried to check in, we couldn't.

There was some problem…the AAA agent (not ours, someone else!) had reserved our spaces on the flight but failed to actually book it. What next?!

It took over an hour of negotiation by my mother, but a manager came over and eventually succeeded in getting us on the evening flight to Bradley Airport. We were going home. My mother is good at this sort of thing; I am not. My father went across the huge room and sat on a chair in a row of them to wait.

Every which way we looked, people were dressed for Hallowe'en, including the guy who checked us in. He looked like a chainsaw murderer without his mask, wearing a dark blue janitorial jumpsuit. I didn't realize that he was supposed to wear a shirt and tie until he told me so, and then he showed me his scary rubber mask. I don't know many horror movies, so I have already forgotten what character he had dressed up as, but it was a fun moment.

Finally, we were waved through and went to the security check-in.

It felt strange to be happy to see the TSA people.

After that, we found our gate and settled in to wait all afternoon and into the early evening.

We saw a woman dressed as a red devil, another as a cat, and someone else as a leopard.

We were experiencing what little of Hallowe'en we could at an airport, and we enjoyed it.

For dinner, I walked down the concourse, found some wrap sandwiches, chips, water, and chocolate, and brought it back to my parents. We were hungry, and my mother didn't want to move or find food. She had brought bananas from the hotel breakfast buffet, but we ate those early in the afternoon.

I took out *Micro* and resumed the tale of shrunken terror in the tropical mountains of Ko'olau on O'ahu. It was fun to fully understand the landscape involved, and the story went along fast. Micro kept me happily distracted until it was almost finished, when my father commented, "I see another problem looming."

I looked up. What could possibly go wrong now? The storm was over! We were going home! I didn't want anything else to worry about. "What?!" I asked.

"You're running out of book," he replied.

I rolled my eyes and got back to it. It was great.

Then it was time to think about the plane ride. This time, we had seats near each other. We were close enough that we could pass things to each other. My mother was behind my father and they were both across from me. I was by a window with, oddly, an empty seat between me and a woman who wanted to hear all about my e-books. So did another woman in front of us. I gave them each one of my business cards.

We landed in Connecticut at half past nine, got our luggage, and walked out to the parking garage together. I stopped us once to unload the cart, which my mother was pushing this time. The heavier bags had wound up on top, and kept falling off. I reloaded it, handed my father his carry-on with the handle extended, and it fit.

Soon we were in my car after two and a half weeks of travel, and driving home in the darkness. We called my grandmother and uncle to tell them so.

When we got home, all was well, except that the cat was mad at us. He saw us, mewed, and bolted for parts unknown. My father found him under some stuff in the cellar, after we had been home for about an hour. I went down there and talked to him until he decided to come out and rub himself up against me. All was well at last.

Now I had something else to look forward to, and I was VERY happy about it: reading every book I had acquired on this trip, watching every DVD, listening to the CDs, poring over every photograph taken, and organizing the material into a travelogue.

Best of all, the cat would keep me company throughout the project.

Glossary of Hawaiian Words

Hawaiian was solely an oral language for approximately a millennia and a half, from 300 C.E., when they first arrived at the eight islands in their long na wa'a (canoes) to 1800 C.E. The Hawaiian people kept records of their cultural history, their individual histories, and their way of life by memorizing it all and writing beautiful lyrics to describe it, singing it at births, significant life events, deaths, and whatever else. They have had a long tradition of creating unique songs that are specifically for one person. Such a song is sung when someone is born, and again when they die. Hawaiians measured time in generations, and referred to nights, not days.

Then, in the early 19th century, some Christian missionaries from the United States – New England – took it upon themselves to travel to Hawai'i and teach their religion and culture to the people there. The fact that the Hawaiians were perfectly happy and had a rich and complex culture of their own was utterly irrelevant to the newcomers.

The New Englanders were Calvinists who, like many Christian Caucasians before them, were absolutely convinced that their way of life was better than that of the people whose country they were visiting. Determined to teach the Hawai'ians Christianity, along with their own attitude that work would bring one closer to divinity and that sex for any reason other than procreation was a bad thing, they set to work.

The first thing that the missionaries realized they would have to do was to learn the Hawaiian language. Without doing that, they would not be able to communicate any of their own allegedly better ideas about life to the people they sought to indoctrinate. This meant writing down what they heard and learned phonetically using the letter system that they were used to.

The result of this is that when Hawaiians began to write their language, they were using a European-based character system.

The Hawaiian language is more about vowels than about consonants.

There are 5 vowels, just as there are in English, French, and many languages of European origin:

A, E, I, O, U

They are pronounced the same way that French vowels are pronounced:

A, as when a doctor asks a patient to open her/his mouth and say "aah" – like "watch".

E, as in the word "cake".

I, as in "feet".

O, as in "boat".

U, as in "boot".

There are 8 consonants, but one of them is not a letter:

H, K, L, M, N, P, W, and the *okina*.

The okina looks like an upside down apostrophe, and is a glottal stop in word pronunciation.

It looks like this: ʻ

There is also something called a *kahako*.

The kahako is a horizontal line that goes over vowels – over the A and the U.

Any letter with a kahako over it gets a double-length pronunciation.

Unfortunately, many electronic readers don't support software that includes this symbol, and this book was written for electronic media first, so it won't appear here. It is better to have the correct letter be visible to the reader than to see only a portrait-oriented, rectangular box where a letter with a kahako should be. At least with the letter showing, the reader won't be as confused or forced to guess whether the box represents an "a" or a "u" with a kahako.

Here is a list of words that I encountered both as I studied for my trip to Hawaiʻi and as I traveled in the country/state:

aliʻi = aristocrat, chiefly caste.

aliʻi nui = high chief or king.

Aloha = Hello, Good-bye, may the breath of Heaven be with you.

hale = house.

haole = foreigner. This can often mean white person, but a white person who lives in Hawaiʻi is not a haole. The word is pronounced "how-lay".

hoku = star.

honu = turtle.

kahili = feather standard carried in pairs by aliʻi attendants, and also waved over them as fans.

kahuna = learned advisor, guru. When combined with another word, it is more specific, denoting the discipline that the advisor has studied and practiced, such as priest, doctor, politician, professor in whatever field, etc.

kanaka = native Hawaiʻian person.

kane = man.

kapu = taboo, forbidden, sanctified.

kauhale = royal compound of houses and related buildings.

kuhina nui = queen regent.

lahui = people.

lanai = veranda, balcony.

luʻau = feast.

mahalo = thank you.

moʻi = king or queen; first used by Kamehameha III.

na = peaceful. With a kahako over the vowel, it is plural for "the".

ohana = family.

ono = delicious.

pono = kosher, okay.

wahine = woman.

And here are some place names and a sentence:

Honolulu = Sheltered Bay.

Puʻuloa = Pearl Harbor.

Ke amau mana nui. = Be endowed with more power, spiritual strength, and authority.

Bibliography of San Francisco Research

This bibliography is purely about fun – infotainment. The purpose of our trip was to explore Hawai'i in depth, with a brief pause in San Francisco to rest on the way there while having a good time, so this list reflects that.

Book

Assia Rabinowitz, Raphaelle Vinon, and Stephanie Wells. SAN FRANCISCO: THE CITY IN SECTION-BY-SECTION MAPS. New York, New York: Alfred A. Knopf, Publisher. 2011.

Restaurants

Alioto's Italian Seafood on San Francisco's Fisherman's Wharf

#8 Fisherman's Wharf
San Francisco, California
Reservations: (415) 673-0183
E-Mail: Info@Aliotos.com
Open Daily 11 a.m. to 11 p.m.
http://www.aliotos.com/

Yank Sing – Traditional and Contemporary Dim Sum

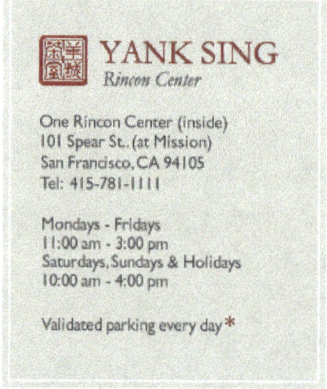

http://www.yanksing.com/home.php

Greens Restaurant
http://www.greensrestaurant.com/
Fort Mason, Building A
Marina Boulevard (Buchanan)
San Francisco, California
Phone: (415) 771-6222

This is a famous gourmet vegetarian restaurant in the former Fort Mason. I found it when we were in our hotel in the map guide of the city, and suddenly remembered that I have a copy of *The Greens Cookbook*.

Chef Annie Somerville

Lunch
Tues - Fri 11:45 am - 2:30 pm
Brunch
Sat 11:00am - 2:30pm
Sun 10:30 am - 2:00 pm
Cafe Dinner
Sun - Fri 5:30 pm - 9:00 pm
Prix Fixe Dinner
Saturday 5:30 pm - 9:00 pm
Greens to Go
Mon - Thurs 8:30 am - varies seasonally
Fri - Sat 8:30 am - varies seasonally
Sunday 9:00 am - 4:00 pm

Chocolate

Recchiuti
www.recchiuti.com

Photo by: Tom Seawell/Courtesy of Recchiuti Confections

This store sells delicious lime-soaked slices of pear coated with dark chocolate, truffles, cardamom chocolate, and lots of other delectable treats.

One Ferry Building, Shop #30
San Francisco, California 94111
Phone: (415) 834-9494
Store Hours:
Monday-Friday 10 a.m. – 7 p.m.
Saturday 8 a.m. – 6 p.m.
Sunday 10 a.m. – 5 p.m.

Ghirardelli
http://www.ghirardelli.com/

The headquarters of this company is in San Francisco. It is in its own square, as described below in an online quote. The square is slated for some upscale residential and commercial development in the near future. Ghirardelli chocolates are for sale in grocery stores all over the United States, and San Francisco Airport had stores both inside and outside of the boarding gates.

Ghirardelli Square is located at 900 North Point Street at the corner of Beach and Larkin Streets. It is on the West side of Fisherman's Wharf, two blocks east of Van Ness Avenue and one block west of the Cable Car turnaround at Beach and Hyde Streets.
http://www.ghirardellisq.com/visitor-info/directions

Shopping

WILLIAMS-SONOMA
340 Post Street
San Francisco, California 94108
Phone: (415) 362-9450
www.williams-sonoma.com

This is Williams-Sonoma's west coast flagship store on San Francisco's Union Square. The store has five stories and balconies on each upper storey overlooking the ground floor. The test kitchen is on the top floor. There were two chefs working there who said that Chuck Williams himself still appears there once a week, at the age of 97. He would be bored if he didn't keep cooking and baking, they added.

Ferry Building Marketplace
http://www.ferrybuildingmarketplace.com/
Ferry Building Marketplace
One Ferry Building
San Francisco, California 94111
Phone: (415) 983-8030

This is a fun place, full of gourmet food shops of all kinds: chocolate, honey, wine, fish and shellfish, cheese, bread, pastry and other desserts, tea and coffee. It also offers clothing, books, and other gifts.

Viewing Deck

Top of the Mark
http://www.intercontinentalmarkhopkins.com/top_of_the_mark/

This is a great bar and viewing deck with views in every direction of the entire city. We saw the Transamerica Tower, the Golden Gate Bridge, Grace Cathedral, and the famous Nob Hill, which was directly below us. It is at the top of…

The Mark Hopkins Hotel
http://www.intercontinentalmarkhopkins.com/
One Nob Hill
San Francisco, California 94108
Phone: 415) 392-3434

Bibliography of Hawai'i Research

Some of these sources were printed copies, but most were e-books downloaded to a Nook Color device. Many of the items from the 19th and early 20th centuries were scanned as they were into a computer, skewing the images somewhat. Other texts included Hawai'ian language punctuation and character markings that came through on the electronic reader as boxes, which made it difficult to learn the words as they should appear.

Humor

1. Mark Twain/Samuel Langhorne Clemens. MARK TWAIN IN HAWAI'I: ROUGHING IT IN THE SANDWICH ISLANDS – HAWAI'I IN THE 1860'S. Foreword by A. Grove Day. Honolulu, Hawai'i: Mutual Publishing. 1990.

Fiction

2. Jack London. THE HOUSE OF PRIDE. Barnes & Noble edition published by B&R Samizdat Express. 1912.

3. Robert Louis Stevenson. THE BOTTLE IMP. Barnes & Noble edition published by B & R Samizdat Express. 1891.

4. Alan Brennert. HONOLULU. New York, New York: St. Martin's Griffin. 2009.

5. Michael Crichton and Richard Preston. MICRO. New York, New York: Harper. 2011.

Poetry

6. John Dominis Holt. HANAI: A POEM FOR QUEEN LILI'UOKALANI. Honolulu, Hawai'i: Hawai'i: Topgallant Publishing Co., Ltd. 1986.

Music

7. King David Kalakaua, Queen Lili'uokalani, Princess Likelike, and Prince Leleiohoku II. NA LANI 'EHA. Selected songs written by the four royal siblings featuring Ku'uipo Kumukahi and The Hawai'ian Music Hall of Fame Serenaders. Honolulu, Hawai'i: The Hawaiian Music Hall of Fame. 2007.

8. Scott C.S. Stone and bandmaster Aaron David Mahi. THE ROYAL HAWAIIAN BAND: ITS LEGACY. CD Recording: Leon Siu, Producer – Haku Mele Hawai'i; Dale P. Madden – Island Heritage. Honolulu, Hawai'i: Island Heritage Publishing. 2004.

Autobiographical, Biographical, Social, Political, and Cultural History

9. Manley Hopkins. HAWAI'I: THE PAST, PRESENT, AND FUTURE OF ITS ISLAND-KINGDOM. AN HISTORICAL ACCOUNT OF THE SANDWICH ISLANDS (POLYNESIA). London, England: Longmans, Green, and Co. 1866.

10. Lydia Liliu Loloku Walania Wewehi Kamakaeha Liliʻuokalani. HAWAIʻI'S STORY BY HAWAIʻI'S QUEEN [Illustrated]. Boston, Massachusetts: Lothrop, Lee & Shepard. 1897.

11. Professor William De Witt Alexander. HISTORY OF LATER YEARS OF THE HAWAIʻIAN MONARCHY…AND THE REVOLUTION OF 1893. Hawaiʻian Copyright by W. D. Alexander. October 16th, 1897.

12. David Malo, translated by Nathaniel B. Emerson. HAWAIIAN ANTIQUITIES, MOʻOLELO HAWAIʻI. Honolulu, Hawaiʻi: Bernice Pauahi Bishop Museum. 1898.

13. Elizabeth Kekaaniauokalani Kalaninuiohilaukapu Pratt, Great-great-granddaughter of Keoua. HISTORY OF KEOWA KALANIKUPUAPA-I-KALANI-NUI, FATHER OF HAWAIʻI KINGS, AND HIS DESCENDANTS, WITH NOTES ON KAMEHAMEHA I, FIRST KING OF ALL HAWAIʻI. Honolulu, Territory of Hawaiʻi. 1920.

14. Alexander MacDonald. REVOLT IN PARADISE – THE SOCIAL REVOLUTION IN HAWAIʻI AFTER PEARL HARBOR. New York, N.Y.: Steven Daye, Inc. 1944.

15. Richard A. Wisniewski. THE RISE AND FALL OF THE HAWAIʻIAN KINGDOM: A PICTORIAL HISTORY. Honolulu, Hawaiʻi: Pacific Basin Enterprises. 1979.

16. Allan Beekman. THE NIʻIHAU INCIDENT. *The true story of the Japanese fighter pilot who, after the Pearl Harbor attack, crash-landed on the Hawaiʻian Island of Niʻihau and terrorized the residents.* Honolulu, Hawaiʻi: Heritage Press of Pacific. 1982.

17. Richard Zeigler and Patrick M. Patterson. RED SUN: THE INVASION OF HAWAIʻI AFTER PEARL HARBOR – A FICTIONAL HISTORY. Honolulu, Hawaiʻi: The Bess Press. 2001.

18. Noenoe K. Silva. ALOHA BETRAYED: NATIVE HAWAIʻIAN RESISTANCE TO AMERICAN COLONIALISM. Durham, South Carolina & London, England: Duke University Press. 2004.

19. Scott C.S. Stone, photographs by Mazeppa King Costa. THE ROYAL HAWAIIAN BAND: ITS LEGACY. Honolulu, Hawaiʻi: Island Heritage Publishing. 2004.

20. David Stannard. HONOR KILLING: RACE, RAPE, AND CLARENCE DARROW'S SPECTACULAR LAST CASE. New York, N.Y.: Penguin Books. 2005.

21. Allan Seiden. THE HAWAIIAN MONARCHY. Honolulu, Hawaiʻi: Mutual Publishing. 2005.

22. Alton Pryor. LITTLE KNOWN TALES IN HAWAIIAN HISTORY. Roseville, California: Stagecoach Publishing at Smashwords. 2011.

23. Nancy Webb and Jean Francis Webb. KAʻIULANI: CROWN PRINCESS OF HAWAIʻI. 4th Edition. Honolulu, Hawaiʻi: Mutual Publishing. 2011.

24. Allan Seiden. PEARL HARBOR – FROM FISHPONDS TO WARSHIPS: A COMPLETE ILLUSTRATED HISTORY. 18th printing, softcover. Honolulu, Hawaiʻi: Mutual Publishing. 2012.

News Articles

25. Associated Press and United Press. "War! Oahu Bombed by Japanese Planes – Six Known Dead, 21 Injured, at Emergency Hospital." *Honolulu Star-Bulletin 1st Extra*. Sunday, December 7, 1941. Evening Bulletin, Est. 1882, No. 11287. Hawaiian Star, Vol. XLVIII' No. 15359.

26. "Movement for Sovereignty is Growing in Hawaii," *The New York Times*, 5 June 1994, http://www.nytimes.com/1994/06/05/us/movement-for-sovereignty-is-growing-in-hawaii.html

27. "Native Hawaiians Seek Redress for U.S. Role in Ousting Queen," *The New York Times*, 11 December 1999, http://www.nytimes.com/1999/12/11/us/native-hawaiians-seek-redress-for-us-role-in-ousting-queen.html

28. Carolyn Said, "Macy's Owner Buying Liberty House," *San Francisco Chronicle*, 22 June 2001, online at http://www.sfgate.com/business/article/Macy-s-owner-buying-Liberty-House-2907331.php

29. Mike Gordon, "The Massie Case," *The Honolulu Advertiser*, 2 July 2006, online at http://the.honoluluadvertiser.com/150/sesq2massiecase

30. Associated Press, "Hawai'i Governor, Police Chief to Review Law Enforcement Response to Palace Takeover," *The Hartford Courant*, 17 August 2008, http://www.courant.com/news/nationworld/nation/wire/sns-ap-palace-takeover,0,307537.story

31. Jennifer Koons, "Supreme Court Backs Hawaii in Land Dispute," *Greenwire* in *The New York Times*, 31 March 2009, http://www.nytimes.com/gwire/2009/03/31/31greenwire-supreme-court-backs-hawaii-in-land-dispute-10366.html

32. "Climate Change Threatens Endangered Honeycreeper Birds of Hawai'i," *Science Daily*, 27 May 2009, online at http://www.sciencedaily.com/releases/2009/05/090526140840.htm

33. "In Hawai'i, Birds' Friday Night Flights Turn Out the Lights on Prep Games," *Associated Press* in *The New York Times*, 24 October 2010, page SP10, online at http://www.nytimes.com/2010/10/24/sports/24birds.html?hpw

34. Jesse McKinley, "As the Mainland Shivers, Hawai'i Basks in Tourism's Glow," *The New York Times*, 16 February 2011, online at http://www.nytimes.com/2011/02/17/us/17hawaii.html?_r=1&hp

35. Adam Nagourney, "For Honolulu's Homeless, an Eviction Notice, *The New York Times*, 14 March 2011, page A22, online at http://www.nytimes.com/2011/03/15/us/15homeless.html?_r=1&hpw

36. Gustave Axelson, "The U.S. Issue: An Eden for Rare Birds in Hawai'i," *The New York Times*, 15 May 2011, page TR5, online at http://travel.nytimes.com/2011/05/15/travel/treks-through-kauai-exotic-and-bittersweet.html?ref=travel&pagewanted=all

37. Lawrence Downes, "My Kailua," *The New York Times*, 4 September 2011, page TR4, online at http://travel.nytimes.com/2011/09/04/travel/return-to-kailua-hawaii.html?pagewanted=all

38. David Venditta, "Pearl Harbor Radar Men are Reunited at Allentown," *The Morning Call*, 3 December 2011, online at http://articles.mcall.com/2011-12-03/news/mc-pearl-harbor-radar-vets-reunited-20111203_1_radar-unit-pearl-harbor-joseph-lockard

39. Associated Press, "Hawai'i lawmaker: Oracle CEO Ellison plans no major upheaval on Lana'i after big land buy," *The Washington Post*, 23 June 2012, online at http://www.washingtonpost.com/national/biographer-flashy-oracle-founder-likely-to-go-epic-with-next-big-buy-_-a-hawaiian-island/2012/06/21/gJQAfVkNtV_story.html

40. Reuters, "Oracle CEO Ellison Buys Hawai'i's Lana'i Island – No Price Revealed But Pegged at Over $500 Million," *The Chicago Tribune*, 23 June 2012, online at http://articles.chicagotribune.com/2012-06-21/business/chi-oracle-ceo-larry-ellison-buys-hawaiis-lanai-island-20120621_1_pineapple-fields-hawaii-s-lanai-sixth-largest-island

Legal and Legislative History

41. Kamehameha III and His Government. LAWS OF HIS MAJESTY KAMEHAMEHA III, KING OF THE HAWAI'IAN ISLANDS, PASSED BY THE NOBLES AND REPRESENTATIVES AT THEIR SESSION, 1853. Honolulu, Hawaii: Printed by Order of the Government. 1856.

42. Thomas H. Ball. AGAINST THE ANNEXATION OF HAWAI'I: SPEECH OF THE HON. THOS. H. BALL OF TEXAS, IN THE HOUSE OF REPRESENTATIVES. Wednesday, June 15th, 1898.

43. E.A. Mott-Smith, Secretary of Hawai'i. ELECTION LAWS OF HAWAI'I. Honolulu, Territory of Hawaii: Hawaiian Gazette, Co., Ltd. July 15th, 1910.

44. LAWS OF THE REPUBLIC OF HAWAI'I, PASSED BY THE LEGISLATIVE ASSEMBLY, SPECIAL SESSION. Honolulu, Territory of Hawai'i: Robert Grieve, Steam Book and Job Printer. 1895.

45. Henry E. Chambers. CONSTITUTIONAL HISTORY OF HAWAI'I. Herbert B. Adams, Editor. Baltimore, Maryland: The Johns Hopkins Press. 1896.

46. Kalakaua Rex and Government. LAWS OF THE HAWAI'IAN ISLANDS RELATING TO AGRICULTURE AND FORESTRY. Honolulu, Hawai'i: The Hawaiian Gazette Company. 1898.

47. Chief Justices Alexander George Morison Robertson and James Leslie Coke, and Associate Justices Ralph Petty Quarles, James Leslie Coke, Samuel Barnet Kemp, and William Seabrook Edings. HAWAI'I REPORTS, VOLUME 24: CASES DECIDED IN THE SUPREME COURT OF THE TERRITORY OF HAWAI'I – AUGUST 1, 1917 TO JUNE 23, 1919. Honolulu, Territory of Hawai'i: Honolulu Star-Bulletin, Ltd. 1919.

48. Hawaiian People [Hawai'ian Language Edition]. UNIVERSAL DECLARATION OF HUMAN RIGHTS. Honolulu, Hawai'i: Hawai'i Institute for Human Rights. 1948.

Travelogues

49. Isabella Bird. THE HAWAI'IAN ARCHIPELAGO: SIX MONTHS AMONG THE PALM GROVES, CORAL REEFS, VOLCANOES OF THE SANDWICH ISLANDS. Illustrated. Barnes & Noble E-Book: Girlebooks. 1875.

50. Brian Lawrenson. HAWAI'I ALOHA. *U.S.A. Canada Series*. Smashwords Edition. 2011.

Travel Guides

51. Jeannette Foster. HAWAI'I DAY BY DAY. Frommer's 1ST Edition. Hoboken, New Jersey: Wiley's Publishing, Inc. 2010.

52. Rita Ariyoshi. HAWAI'I. Washington, D.C.: National Geographic Traveler. 2009.

53. United States Army Service Forces, Special Service Division. POCKET GUIDE TO HAWAI'I. August 7, 1945.

Hawaiian Language Guides

54. Kahikahealani Wight, Illustrated by Robin Yoko Racoma. ILLUSTRATED HAWAI'IAN DICTIONARY – POCKET EDITION. 3rd Printing. Honolulu, Hawai'i: Bess Press. 2009.

55. BOOK FOR TRAVELERS. Filiquarian Publishing Language Books. Hawai'i: Barnes & Noble HAWAI'IAN PHRASE E-Book. 2011.

Archaeology

56. Van James. ANCIENT SITES OF HAWAI'I: ARCHAEOLOGICAL PLACES OF INTEREST ON THE BIG ISLAND. 5th Edition. Honolulu, Hawai'i: Mutual Publishing. 2005.

Nature Guides and Natural Histories

57. William Tufts Brigham. MEMOIRS OF THE BERNICE PAUAHI BISHOP MUSEUM OF POLYNESIAN HISTORY AND ETHNOLOGY, VOLUME II: THE VOLCANOES OF KILAUEA AND MAUNA LOA ON THE ISLAND OF HAWAI'I, THEIR VARIOUSLY RECORDED HISTORY TO THE PRESENT TIME. Honolulu, Hawai'i: Bernice Pauahi Bishop Museum Press. 1906-1909.

58. Leland Miyano and Douglas Peebles [Photographs]. A POCKET GUIDE TO HAWAI'I'S FLOWERS. Honolulu, Hawai'i: Mutual Publishing. 1997.

59. Clayton and Michele Oslund. HAWAIIAN GARDENS ARE TO GO TO: A TREASURY OF TROPICAL PLANTS AND GARDENS. Duluth, Minnesota: Plant Pics. 1998.

60. H. Douglas Pratt [Text]. Jack Jeffrey and H. Douglas Pratt [Photographs]. A POCKET GUIDE TO HAWAI'I'S BIRDS. Honolulu, Hawai'i: Mutual Publishing. 2002.

61. H. Douglas Pratt [Text and Photographs]. A POCKET GUIDE TO HAWAI'I'S TREES AND SHRUBS. Honolulu, Hawai'i: Mutual Publishing. 2004.

62. Hawai'i Audubon Society. HAWAI'I'S BIRDS. Honolulu, Hawai'i: Island Heritage Publishing. 2005.

News Videos

63. Avi Lewis. INSIDE USA – THE OTHER HAWAI'I – SEPT 26 – PART 1. *AlJazeeraEnglish* – YouTube Video. September 26, 2008. Online at http://www.youtube.com/watch?v=gIq8x9vnLf4&feature=relmfu

64. Avi Lewis. INSIDE USA – THE OTHER HAWAI'I – SEPT 26 – PART 2. *AlJazeeraEnglish* – YouTube Video. September 26, 2008. Online at http://www.youtube.com/watch?v=1QqOJGSKGWQ&feature=relmfu

Movies and Documentaries

65. Vivian Ducat. HAWAI'I'S LAST QUEEN: THE EMBATTLED REIGN OF QUEEN LILI'UOKALANI. Narrated by David McCullough II and Anna Deveare Smith. PBS: American Experience. 1997.

66. Marc Forby. PRINCESS KA'IULANI. Starring Q'orianka Kilcher, Barry Pepper, and Will Patton. Produced by Matador Pictures, Island Film Group, and Trailblazer Films. 2009.

67. Mick Kalber. VOLCANOSCAPES V: HAWAI'I VOLCANOES NATIONAL PARK – AN HISTORICAL PERSPECTIVE. Narrated by Dunbar Wakayama. Produced and edited by G.B. Hajim and Mick Kalber. Hilo, Hawai'i: Tropical Visions, Inc. 1996.

68. Atlantis Submarines Hawai'i. ATLANTIS SUBMARINES: WAIKIKI – MAUI – KONA. EXPERIENCE OUR HAWAI'I. Atlantis Submarines, YNR Marketing. 2010.

69. Blue Hawai'ian Helicopters. VISIONS OF HAWAI'I: BIG ISLAND – MAU'I – MOLOKA'I – LANA'I – KAUA'I – O'AHU. Featuring the music of Keali'i Reichel and Amy Hanaiali'i. Narrated by Pulama Collier. Produced and directed by David J. Chevalier. 2012.

Acknowledgements

I would like to thank my parents for taking me on this wonderful trip. My father drove us everywhere we wanted to go in record time despite having never been there before and not knowing, as he prefers, every groove in every roadway. My mother thought of the idea of going on a trip and financed it all.

My mother also edited this entire book, patiently taking each printed chapter on long car rides with a red pen, or sitting in the kitchen or living room with the manuscript on her days off.

David D. Haines, Ph.D. encouraged me in my writing career at every turn. He took questions about my every idea and offers great advice. He was wonderfully accommodating about saving copies of everything for me as a backup, and then reading through each chapter to offer his assessment of it. For this book, he had the fun of identifying a relative of his on the wall of the USS *Arizona* Memorial.

Doug Lubic lent me four of his own books about Hawaiian volcanology and flora and fauna.

Mary D'Esopo, our travel agent at AAA in Avon, Connecticut, shared her knowledge of Hawai'i with us and fielded question after question, no matter how seemingly trivial. We would not have enjoyed this trip without her help. She saved us a great deal of stress, and made it all about having a good time.

Brianna, a Hawaiian girl at my local bookstore, was very enthusiastic and encouraging about this project. She chatted with me about Hawaiian culture and history, and shared details about hand gestures.

Finally, I would like to thank all of the great people that we met in Hawai'i. They were consistently friendly and welcoming, happy to answer questions and pose for photographs, and enjoyable to talk to.

About the Author

Stephanie C. Fox, J.D. is a historian, writer, and editor. She is a graduate of William Smith College and the University of Connecticut School of Law. She lives in Connecticut.

She runs an editing and publishing service called *QueenBeeEdit*, found at www.queenbeeedit.com, which caters to politicians, scientists, and others. Her imprint is *QueenBeeBooks*.

Ms. Fox has written several books on a variety of topics, including the effects of human overpopulation on the environment, Asperger's, cats, and travel to Kuwait.

Her areas of interest include – but are not limited to – history, biographies, women's studies, science fiction, human overpopulation, ecosystems collapse, law, international relations, Asperger's, and cats.

www.ingramcontent.com/pod-product-compliance
Lightning Source LLC
Chambersburg PA
CBHW071134300426
44113CB00009B/970